WHAT'S GOING ON AMONG THE LUTHERANS?

A Comparison of Beliefs

Patsy A. Leppien
J. Kincaid Smith

NORTHWESTERN PUBLISHING HOUSE
Milwaukee, Wisconsin

Library of Congress Card 92-80393
Northwestern Publishing House
1250 N. 113th St., Milwaukee, WI 53226-3284
© 1992 by Northwestern Publishing House.
Published 1992
Printed in the United States of America
ISBN 0-8100-0427-5
15 N 0544

DEDICATION

This book is dedicated to all those stalwart souls throughout past generations who have, by God's grace, held fast to the truth of his Word despite seemingly overwhelming odds.

And to our children and grandchildren, and future generations, who will be called to continue to fight "the good fight" and "contend for the faith" until the day of our Lord (2 Timothy 4:7; Jude 3).

CONTENTS

Preface 7

Acknowledgments 9

SECTION I

The Historic Lutheran Faith or the New Thinking? 13

1. What's Going Wrong Among the Lutherans? 15

2. Resources.. 26

3. The Controversy 30

4. Inspiration and Inerrancy 53

5. Creation 61

6. Adam and Eve 65

7. The Old Testament — Moses as Author 70

8. The Old Testament — Prophecy and Authorship 74

9. The Words of Jesus 78

10. Miracles... 83

11. The Virgin Birth 88

12. The Deity of Christ 96

13. The Trinity 101

14. The Atonement 105

15. The Resurrection 113

16. The Immortality of the Soul 122

17. The New Morality 126

18. The Way to Heaven 159

19. Missions 170

20. The National Council of Churches and
    the World Council of Churches 189

SECTION II

The Great Strengths of Lutheranism 199

21. What It Means to be a Lutheran 201

22. Disunity and Division in the Church 210

23. The Roman Catholic Approach to Scripture 216

24. The Reformed Approach to Scripture 222

25. Pietism 250

SECTION III

American Lutheranism's Drift into the New Thinking 269

26. Lutherans in America 1634-1874 271

27. Unity and Realignment 1875-1988 301

28. Ecumenism Means Doctrinal Indifference 342

Appendix I   Questions for Discussion 381

Appendix II Ask Your Pastor 389

Bibliography 391

Addresses for Resources 401

Name Index 402

Topic Index 405

PREFACE

This is an unusual book. It is a reflection of the struggle of the layperson to understand, and of the pastor-theologian to explain, the great theological changes taking place in most of Christendom. It is also the book the authors searched for and could not find. While many books and articles have been written regarding these changes, they are intended for the theologically trained audience, not the average layperson, and are not easily accessible to either pastors or laity.

The struggle that led to this volume began in 1984 when a small group of lay people in an American Lutheran Church (ALC) congregation engaged in extensive research on the coming merger that would make their church body a part of the Evangelical Lutheran Church in America in 1988. When they became aware of the radical nature of the theological changes taking place in most Christian denominations, and how deeply these changes had infiltrated Lutheranism, they felt called to leave the ALC.

Convinced these changes could ultimately destroy their faith, as well as the faith of their children and grandchildren, they felt an obligation to share the results of their research with their brothers and sisters in Christ. Thus, in 1986, they joined with other concerned Lutherans and organized Lutherans Informed for Truth (L.I.F.T.). This book is the culmination of L.I.F.T.'s ongoing efforts to inform Lutherans in all synods of the real doctrinal differences dividing today's Lutherans.

The book is divided into three sections, with each chapter building upon those that precede it. Section I compares the historic Lutheran faith with the new thinking, identifies and explains the nature of the controversy, and thoroughly documents both positions. Section II points out the great strengths of historic Lutheranism and explains the fundamental differences between Roman Catholics, Lutherans, and other Protestants. This comparison illustrates how the great strengths of Lutheranism distinguish it from all other denominations. Section III describes American Lutheranism's drift into the new thinking through doctrinal compromise and indifference and explains the error of today's ecumenical movement. It concludes with a call to the straying shepherds and sheep to return to their confessional Lutheran heritage.

Just as this book came about in an unusual way, so also has the joint authorship. As the book developed, most of the research and writing became this author's responsibility, a responsibility that could not have been fulfilled without the guidance of the other. Without Pastor J. Kincaid Smith's teaching, special insights, and many contributions to the manuscript—both quoted material and many other additions blended into the text—my task would have been impossible.

The book contains extensive quotes, so that the reader can see from primary sources in their original context what the real issues are. We have carefully checked and double-checked the quotations for accuracy. There still remains the possibility of some small errors slipping through, but to the best of our knowledge the quotes are precise.

Out of difficult trials flow abundant blessings, for when the Lord calls his servants to a task he provides for every need.

> Now to him who is able to do immeasurable more than all we ask or imagine, according to his power that is at work within us, to him be glory in the church and in Christ Jesus throughout all generations, for ever and ever! Amen (Ephesians 3:20,21).

Patsy A. Leppien
Reformation Sunday, 1991

ACKNOWLEDGMENTS

There are different kinds of gifts, but the same Spirit. There are different kinds of service, but the same Lord. There are different kinds of working, but the same God works all of them in all men (1 Corinthians 12: 4-6).

This book could not have been written without the support, encouragement, and talents of many people. The authors and Lutherans Informed for Truth (L.I.F.T.) would like to express their appreciation to all who helped make this book possible through formal and informal contributions. In particular, we would like to thank the following:

Pastors David Jay Webber, Paul R. Harris, Carl Hoffmeyer, James P. Olsen, Roland Cap Ehlke, Gaylin R. Schmeling, John A. Moldstad, Jr., and the Doctrinal Board of the Evangelical Lutheran Synod for their critical reviews of the manuscript and many helpful suggestions; Pastor James Sherod for the synodical charts; Nancy Ryan, who not only served as an editor but also taught us much about writing books; Lynn Metzker, graphic designer; and Claudia Eisberg, whose art work inspired the page featuring the Castle Church doors at Wittenberg, Germany.

A special note of thanks must go to Dr. Gregory L. Jackson, who not only reviewed the manuscript but shared many insights and resources while writing his book *Liberalism: Its Cause and Cure.* He also contributed the "Questions for Discussion" and prepared the index and bibliography-resource list.

We also appreciate the interest and suppport of the staff at Northwestern Publishing House, especially Pastor Roland Cap Ehlke, editor; Pastor Gary P. Baumler, vice president of editorial services; and Mark C. Brunner, vice president of sales and marketing.

The authors gratefully acknowledge their spouses, Carolyn Smith and Richard Leppien. Carolyn spent many hours typing the manuscript and making the editorial changes, while both served as readers and a constant source of encouragement.

DEAR FRIENDS,
ALTHOUGH I WAS VERY EAGER TO WRITE TO YOU ABOUT THE SALVATION WE SHARE, I FELT I HAD TO WRITE AND URGE YOU TO CONTEND FOR THE FAITH THAT WAS ONCE FOR ALL ENTRUSTED TO THE SAINTS. FOR CERTAIN MEN . . . HAVE SECRETLY SLIPPED IN AMONG YOU. THEY DENY JESUS CHRIST OUR ONLY SOVEREIGN AND LORD.

JUDE 3,4 (NIV)

Section I

THE HISTORIC
LUTHERAN FAITH
OR THE NEW THINKING?

1.

WHAT'S GOING WRONG AMONG THE LUTHERANS?

Most Lutheran lay people today are aware that there are differences among the various groups of Lutherans. Many became aware, as the merger of the American Lutheran Church (ALC), Lutheran Church in America (LCA), and Association of Evangelical Lutheran Churches (AELC) drew closer, that these were very serious differences. Conservatives became the most alarmed, while moderates and liberals contended that the differences were minor and should not stand in the way of the merger.

The merger became a reality on January 1, 1988, when the Evangelical Lutheran Church in America (ELCA) was formed. The doctrinal differences remain, and every indicator points to an ongoing accelerated effort by the leadership of the ELCA to move the laity away from the teachings of the historic Lutheran faith (conservative) into a "new thinking" (liberal).

This book provides a comparison of the conservative Lutheran position, Position A, and the moderate or liberal Lutheran position, Position B. The conservative Position A identifies with the historic Lutheran teaching—Lutherans who believe the Bible is not only true but entirely free from error. The moderate or liberal Position B, on the other hand, identifies with the "new theology" or "new thinking" that has gradually come about over the past few decades.

The conservative Position A is that formerly held by all Lutherans, including the ALC (before the 1960s), and still held by the Wisconsin Evangelical Lutheran Synod (WELS); its sister synod, the Evangelical Lutheran Synod (ELS); the Church of the Lutheran Confession (CLC); and various smaller Lutheran groups. This is also the *official* position held by the Lutheran Church—Missouri Synod (LCMS).

The liberal Position B is the position taught in the seminaries of the former ALC, LCA, and AELC (now those of the ELCA), as well as in most mainline Protestant and Catholic seminaries. Although not all moderates endorse each liberal position listed, they do ask for tolerance of them all.

The following pages provide a comparison of the commonly held beliefs of the two groups. Position A represents what conservative pastors openly teach and proclaim, both publicly and privately. Position B represents the commonly held beliefs of most liberal and moderate pastors. However, what they teach and proclaim publicly is often much more subtle than what they teach and say privately, especially among the seminarians, college students, and other young people. This will be demonstrated in Section I, which documents the comparison column.

POSITIONS A AND B: A COMPARISON OF BELIEFS

1.1 The controversy

Position A

There is a real doctrinal struggle in which the very foundation of the Christian faith, the gospel itself, and every other basic Christian doctrine is endangered and finally destroyed because much of the Bible is "questioned" and denied.

Position B

The only real differences among Lutherans today are minor, "picky" points of doctrine that don't touch the heart of the Christian faith, which is the gospel. The real issues are more political and cultural than doctrinal.

1.2 Inspiration and inerrancy

Position A

All Scripture was inspired by God. The Holy Scriptures are absolutely true because God *gave the writers the very words* they wrote (verbal inspiration). The Holy Scriptures contain no errors or contradictions. Since God is the author of all Scripture, its teachings do not contradict one another. Only the canonical books of the Holy Scriptures are to be regarded as inspired.

Position B

All Scripture was "inspired" in the same sense that someone is inspired to write poetry, etc. The Holy Scriptures were written by well-intentioned men of God. They wrote what they *believed to be* from

God, but they were also affected by the cultural beliefs and influences of their times. The Holy Scriptures contain errors and contradictions. Since the Scriptures were written by many different men, their various teachings often contradict one another. The traditions of the church and the witness of Christians today may also be just as "inspired" as the Holy Scriptures.

1.3 Creation

Position A

God created all things, including man, within the six days of creation. It is contrary to Scripture to hold that man evolved from lower forms of life.

Position B

The story of creation in Genesis is a myth. We got here by a chance process of evolution that God directed or at least used.

1.4 Adam and Eve

Position A

Adam and Eve were two real historical individuals created by God. Noah, Jonah, and Job were also real people. The Bible contains no myths.

Position B

Adam and Eve are symbols of humanity and not real people. They never really existed. "Adam" just means "humankind." Their story is a myth containing important spiritual truth, just as the stories of Noah, Jonah, and Job are myths.

1.5 The Old Testament—Moses as author

Position A

Moses was the author of those sections of the Old Testament that are ascribed to him—the first five books, which are commonly referred to as the Pentateuch. Jesus Christ himself witnessed to this fact.

Position B

The first five books of the Bible were written centuries after Moses died and came from various sources commonly identified as J, E, D, and P.

1.6 The Old Testament—prophecy and authorship

Position A

The Old Testament prophets foretold the coming of Jesus Christ, God's Son, the Savior of the world. Whatever the New Testament teaches about the authorship of the books of the Old Testament is true. The books of Isaiah and Daniel were written by Isaiah and Daniel, respectively. Jesus Christ himself witnessed to this fact.

Position B

There are no prophecies in the Old Testament that actually refer to the man Jesus Christ. Whatever the New Testament says about the authorship of the books of the Old Testament is not necessarily true. Isaiah and Daniel were written, at least in part, by others. Our Lord either accommodated himself to error or he did not know better.

1.7 The words of Jesus

Position A

Jesus Christ really made all the statements attributed to him and recorded in the New Testament.

Position B

Many, if not all, of the statements attributed to Jesus Christ in the New Testament were not made by Jesus but were added by the early church.

1.8 Miracles

Position A

All miracles recorded in the Old and New Testaments actually and historically occurred.

Position B

"Miracles" found in the Bible must be understood as ways of conveying spiritual truths, not as actual historical events.

1.9 The Virgin Birth

Position A

We believe that the Virgin Birth is a biological miracle as taught in the Holy Scriptures. Jesus Christ did not have a human father.

Position B

Jesus Christ was not born of a virgin. We are not sure who his physical father was—perhaps Joseph or an itinerant Roman soldier. The early church honored Jesus by pretending his only father was God.

1.10 The deity of Christ

Position A

Jesus Christ is God. His true deity is clearly taught in Scripture.

Position B

The doctrine of the deity of Jesus Christ is not taught in the Bible but was developed by pious early Christians.

1.11 The Trinity

Position A

The doctrine of the Trinity is clearly taught in Scripture.

Position B

The doctrine of the Trinity is not taught in the Bible but was developed by pious early Christians and made a later addition by the church.

1.12 The Atonement

Position A

Jesus Christ died for the sins of the world. God took his anger for our sins out on his Son to save us and thus revealed a Father's heart toward us. He is not angry with us anymore; we are forgiven and reconciled to him because of Jesus. This action of God through Jesus is called substitutionary atonement or propitiation and is the heart and center of the Christian faith.

Position B

Jesus Christ "died for us" in the sense of a man dying for his friends, not in the sense of God punishing him for the sins of others. Such would portray an unjust God. God has always loved us. Jesus has shown us this.

1.13 The Resurrection

Position A

The resurrection of the body will occur on the last day of history. The souls of all who died in faith will be reunited with their glorified bodies to live forever in heaven with Jesus Christ. Jesus actually *physically* rose from the dead and *physically* showed himself to the disciples. The tomb was empty on Easter morning.

Position B

It is doubtful what the "body" is. The corpse that is buried is not the body. Therefore, "resurrection" concerns some kind of "spiritual body," not our earthly remains. The tomb was not empty on the first Easter morning. Jesus Christ did not "physically" rise from the dead. Perhaps we may speak of some "spiritual" resurrection.

1.14 The immortality of the soul

Position A

We believe, as the Bible teaches, that man has a soul that survives temporal death. At death the soul of the Christian believer goes to heaven, while the unbeliever's soul goes to hell.

Position B

We should not speak of the soul, because the Bible does not teach that we have an immortal soul. We really cannot speak of what may be beyond death. Perhaps in some sense we may "be with Jesus."

1.15 The New Morality

Position A

Moral absolutes are clearly taught in Scripture. Moral teaching in the Bible is clear and does not allow for exceptions dependent upon the situation. Extramarital and premarital sexual relations are sins clearly condemned in the Holy Scriptures. Homosexuality, both the act and the thoughts (lust), are sin and are condemned in Scripture. As with any sin, the repentant fornicator, adulterer, and homosexual have forgiveness and the grace that can change their lives.

Position B

Many questions of moral behavior must responsibly take all circumstances in a given situation into account. Narrow, rigid application of moral values would be legalistic and inconsistent with the precept of love in the gospel. Extramarital and premarital sexual relations are not always sinful but must be judged by the situation and the precept of love. Homosexuality in the life of a responsible loving Christian should be acknowledged as a valid lifestyle. Even if viewed as sin, homosexuality is no worse than any other sin.

1.16 The way to heaven

Position A

Jesus Christ is the only way to heaven. Those who die without faith in him are lost in hell.

Position B

Jesus Christ is not the only way to heaven. Sincere followers of non-Christian religions may also get to heaven. We must allow for the possibility of Universalism.

1.17 Missions

Position A

The primary mission of the church is the proclamation of the saving gospel of Jesus Christ. Genuine Christian love, of course, will always result in ministering to the earthly needs of people as well.

Position B

Once the shift in our thinking takes place and we see behind the mythical notions of the divinity of the man Jesus Christ, primitive ideas of spreading a message about a spiritual, other-worldly redemption from sin can be seen as missing the authentic message of the man Jesus. Jesus must be seen as the man for others, especially the poor and downtrodden. His chief concern was the elimination of poverty and oppression.

Christians should not seek to "convert" sincere followers of other religions that also teach love and concern for mankind. Instead, we should join our efforts with theirs in the true spirit of Jesus. Other religions sincerely followed as equally valid as Christianity.

1.18 The National Council of Churches and the World Council of Churches

Position A

Lutherans should not join the National Council of Churches or the World Council of Churches. Not only are these organizations not Lutheran, but their primary emphasis is political and social and leans heavily on Marxism.

Position B

Lutherans should join the National Council of Churches and the World Council of Churches.

1.19 The Ecumenical Movement

Position A

All doctrines of the Bible are important and provide foundation and support for the chief doctrine, the gospel. While God's Word commands our fellowship in the body of Christ, that fellowship is to be the outward expression of unity in faith and doctrine. Therefore, Lutherans should join in fellowship with those bodies that subscribe to the Lutheran Confessions and whose teaching and practice is consistent with their confession.

Position B

Joining with non-Lutherans, both in worship and eventually even merging with them, is desirable as long as we agree with them, in a sense, that "Jesus Christ is Lord." Our differences can be worked out through dialogue and compromise.

* * *

The doctrinal differences described in the preceding comparison columns are the differences directly responsible for the absence of altar and pulpit fellowship among the larger Lutheran synods and various smaller Lutheran groups.

Within ELCA, Position A describes the beliefs held by the majority of the laity, whereas Position B is held by the vast majority of theologians and pastors. While the pastors and leadership of all Lutheran bodies know of these differences, most lay people are completely unaware of them.

OTHER COMPARISON COLUMNS

At this point we should note that Lutherans Informed For Truth (L.I.F.T.) is not the first concerned group of Lutherans to write such a comparison of beliefs in an attempt to reach others with the truth. This comparison column is a composite of three other comparison columns written over a period of 24 years. The sources of these comparisons will be of interest to the reader.

1. *Lutherans Alert—National* (LAN), sponsor of Faith Evangelical Lutheran Seminary and the congregations of the World Confessional Lutheran Association (WCLA), Tacoma, Washington. LAN was formed in 1965 by a small number of conservative ALC pastors and congregations. Their comparison of beliefs was written as a part of an ongoing effort to halt the ever-increasing apostasy (a deliberate turning away from the faith) in the former ALC and LCA after the mergers of the 1960s and now of the ELCA.

2. "What Is Going On? Going Into Exile," Herman Otten.[1] It was written by conservatives at the time of the split that occurred in 1974 in the LCMS with the organized walkout at Concordia Seminary, St. Louis, Missouri, of most of the professors and more than 400 students. Those who walked out formed Christ Seminary-Seminex and later joined with sympathetic LCMS congregations to form the AELC. Otten is a

---

[1]Herman Otten, "What Is Going On? Going Into Exile," *Christian New Encyclopedia*, 4 vols., ed. Herman Otten (Washington: Missourian Publishing Co., 1983), 1:632. We highly recommend these volumes as an unparalleled source of information about American Christianity.

conservative Lutheran pastor serving an LCMS congregation. As editor of the *Christian News,* he has been documenting both sides of the controversy since 1962.

3. "Twenty Questions," Roger Kovaciny. Kovaciny is a conservative Lutheran pastor of WELS. The occasion for his comparison was the 500th birthday of Martin Luther. Following are a few remarks from the introduction:

If Luther were here for his own 500th birthday party, I am sure that one game he would insist on playing with all the preachers would be Twenty Questions. Luther's Twenty Questions would surely be about theology. And while I can't claim that the following twenty are the twenty he would pick, surely he would want them answered. Because there is a great theme that runs through the Scriptures and is reflected in Luther's writings. That theme is the fact that all through history, there have been true and false churches running parallel to each other . . . the major heresy of the day is religious liberalism. Luther would want to know which a pastor is [conservative or liberal]. And this little chart will help you play Twenty Questions with your own pastor.[2]

LIBERALISM IN OTHER DENOMINATIONS

The doctrinal differences noted in the preceding comparison column are not unique to the Lutheran church. In fact, L.I.F.T. research reveals that the departure from historic Christian doctrine began in virtually all of the old mainline denominations[3] in America at the turn of the century. Lutheranism in America did not begin to capitulate to the onslaught of the liberal theologians until the late 1930s, the problem worsening after World War II. Many books have been written on the subject of the mainline denominations departing from the faith, and many mainline denominations have conservative groups within their ranks that publish materials similar to L.I.F.T.'s. A few of these books are listed in the Bibliography.

One such book is *Baal or God.* In the preface to the second edition, the author (Otten) tells us:

---

[2]Roger Kovaciny, "Twenty Questions," *Christian News Encyclopedia,* 4:2636.

[3]The most prominent mainline denominations today are the United Methodists, the United Church of Christ, the Presbyterian Church (USA), the Episcopalians, and the American Baptists.

The author wrote *Baal or God* in 1965 to show Christians in all denominations what was happening within Christendom and how far major denominations and modern liberal theologians had departed from historic Christianity. . . . *The Christian News Encyclopedia* shows that since the first printing of *Baal or God* there is considerably more evidence to show that theological liberalism has thoroughly infiltrated most major denominations. The National Council of Churches at a special anniversary convention used the evolutionary confession of a Roman Catholic theologian together with the non-Trinitarian Statement of Faith mentioned in *Baal or God*'s chapter on the Trinity. A year after *Baal or God* was published, the NCC admitted into full membership the Church of the New Jerusalem, a Swedenborgian cult which has a unitarian theology [they deny the doctrine of the Trinity]. A survey taken by the NCC at one of its conventions revealed that only about one fourth of the delegates at the NCC convention believed in such miracles as the virgin birth of Christ. The leaders of the World Council of Churches at their last assembly in 1983 repeatedly made it clear that they did not believe that Jesus Christ is the only way to heaven. Spokesmen from various non-Christian religions, who addressed the assembly, were greeted as fellow believers in the true God.[4]

In the introduction to his book, Otten describes the nature of the controversy and makes some interesting and accurate observations:

Baal or God shows there are basically two different religions within external Christendom. The difference between these two religions is the difference between God and Baal. Informed Christians ought to recognize that the real difference within external Christendom does not lie along traditional denominational lines but within the major denominations. On the one hand there are those within these denominations who accept the fundamental truths of historic Christianity; on the other hand there are the modern liberals within these same denominations who reject historic Christianity. The situation in Christendom is like that in American politics. There are conservatives and liberals in American politics. There are conservatives and liberals in each major political

---

[4]Otten, *Baal or God* (Washington: Missourian Publishing Co., 1988), p. ii.

party. So there are believers in historic Christianity and modern liberals in the major denominations.

One honest clergyman, who admits: "I identify myself as a liberal," claims that most liberal protestant clergymen "simply do not realize that they have already rejected basic, historic Christianity." He correctly observes, "Should the majority of liberal Protestant ministers ever decide to be intellectually honest with their congregations, the Lutheran Reformation would seem altogether mild by comparison. Protestant parishioners would, I am convinced, leave their churches wholesale."[5]

The remaining pages of this book will be devoted to documenting the truth of the claims made in the comparison column as they apply to the Lutheran church. It should be noted, however, that liberal theologians all speak the same language. While the quotations are from the lips and pens of Lutherans, they are representative of the manner in which all liberal theologians speak and teach, regardless of their denominational affiliation.

----

[5]Ibid., p. iii.

2.

RESOURCES

The preceding comparison columns have no doubt raised some questions in the reader's mind. Before proceeding with the documentation, we will clarify a few points concerning the resources and methods used in preparing this book, particularly regarding Section I.

Position A

The tendency of most lay people is to gradually forget the specific doctrines of the Christian-Lutheran faith they learned as children or adults. In order to recognize error, it is necessary to know the truth. Position A carefully documents the historic Lutheran faith from the Bible, the Lutheran Confessions, Martin Luther, and conservative Lutheran theologians. Not only will this documentation enable the reader to recognize the error in Position B, but it can strengthen his or her faith. All Scripture is from the New International Version (NIV) of the Holy Bible except where noted.

Position B

The documentation in Position B is taken, with few exceptions, from books, articles, and educational materials written by influential theologians and professors of the Evangelical Lutheran Church in America (ELCA). The majority of these materials were published by Augsburg Publishing House, American Lutheran Church (ALC); Fortress Press, Lutheran Church in America (LCA); and the new publishing house of the ELCA, Augsburg-Fortress.

The quotations have been selected not only to show what the leading theologians and professors believe, but to allow these scholars to speak for themselves on the doctrinal position of the ELCA. These quotations have been carefully selected in an effort to illustrate the diversity of theological opinions held by the liberal scholars. Some of the quotations are very obvious denials of historic Christianity, whereas others are more subtle. The quotations range from the outright denial of basic doctrines of the Christian faith to the simple casting of doubt. Taken as a whole, the documentation clearly illustrates the false teaching within the ELCA and the subtle manner used to promote it among the unsuspecting laity.

The documentation is by no means exhaustive. The ELCA has published so many attacks on the faith that this book can only list a limited sample.

Each individual quotation is preceded by information concerning the source, the author, the author's influence in the ELCA, and other important facts. *Any emphasis added to the individual quotations is our own unless otherwise noted.*

The chapters concerning "inerrancy" and "homosexuality" (Chapters 4 and 17, respectively) are of special interest because they illustrate much more than the chapter titles indicate.

SUGGESTIONS FOR USING THIS BOOK

This book can be used in a variety of ways and situations. Some readers may want to share the entire book with others. Other readers may want to share individual chapters with a particular person or group or to those who are not likely to read more than a few pages at a time. Pastors may wish to teach a class on the subject or use sections or chapters when teaching Bible classes or as a resource when writing papers.

LITERARY STYLE AND FOOTNOTES

With all of the above possibilities in mind, we have developed each chapter as a stand-alone unit. Thus, we have taken certain liberties with the customary rules of writing, particularly in the areas of footnoting and repetition. We have left some material that would normally appear in footnotes in the main text to emphasize the value of the quotations. There is also repetition of full footnotes and a few short statements in the text used to identify the quotations. These departures from the usual rules of writing are predominately found in the documentation of Position B. Where the author's identity was not essential to illustrating the importance of the quotations, or for continuity when one author was quoted several times, the name appears in the footnote.

This book can also be used in a classroom situation or as a resource book. Therefore, we have designed the material for easy scanning and quick reference. We have included subtitles and, beginning with Chapter 4 ("Inspiration and Inerrancy"), numbered all documentation. In addition, we have included a section entitled "Questions for Discussion" at the conclusion of the book for those who would like to do additional study.

While this material is intended for use by both pastors and lay people, we have prepared it with the needs of the laity in mind. Much has already been written on the subject, but the vast majority of it has been written for theologians, professors, and pastors and makes use of technical language and theology that is much too difficult for the untrained lay person. We have deliberately avoided the excessive use of technical terms and lengthy theological explanations.

TWO IMPORTANT RESOURCES

The information provided with each quotation adequately identifies the source with the exception of two resources, *Christian Dogmatics* and *Search Weekly Bible Studies*. These two resources are primary teaching tools in ELCA seminaries and congregations and are thus of added importance. For this reason, we will examine these two sources in more detail.

1) *Christian Dogmatics,* Braaten/Jenson, the primary theology textbook used in all ELCA seminaries for training future pastors.[1]

When *Christian Dogmatics* was published in 1984, the six contributing authors were teaching systematic theology at various LCA and ALC seminaries. The editors, Dr. Carl E. Braaten and Dr. Robert W. Jenson, were named among "the finest" of the LCA theologians, and *Christian Dogmatics* is described as "a massive work of scholarship written by six American Lutherans that could compete with the major textbooks earlier produced in Europe and translated into English."[2]

The authors include the editors, Braaten and Jenson, as well as Gerhard O. Forde, Philip J. Hefner, Paul R. Sponheim, and Hans Schwarz, all leading theologians of the ELCA. As professors in ELCA seminaries the authors all teach, or have previously taught, systematic theology—the study of the fundamental doctrines of Christian faith and how they interrelate.

Christian Dogmatics, as its title indicates, makes a definite and authoritative statement concerning what the authors really believe about Scripture and Christian doctrine. In its role as a primary text-

---

[1]*Christian Dogmatics,* 2 vols., eds. Carl E. Braaten and Robert W. Jenson (Philadelphia: Fortress Press, 1984).

[2]Timothy F. Lull, "A Church Called Lutheran," *The Lutheran,* December 1987, p. 13.

book used to teach systematic theology in ELCA seminaries, it is shaping the theological thinking of future ELCA pastors and leaders; therefore, we cannot overstate its importance.

2) *Search Weekly Bible Studies,* a primary ELCA adult Bible-study program.

Search is a highly recommended five-year Bible study series for adults. Originating in the ALC and led by the laity, it is a program of major influence in terms of outreach and teaching. Within three years of its introduction in 1983, 85,000 people in 1,620 ALC congregations and an unspecified number in the LCA had used *Search.*[3] The series continues to be a major influence in the ELCA. It is clearly a deliberate attempt to introduce unsuspecting lay people to historical criticism (the "new thinking") and alter their way of thinking about the Bible.

Again, as the primary sources for teaching theology in ELCA seminaries and congregations, the importance of *Christian Dogmatics* and *Search* cannot be overestimated. For this reason, we will quote from both of these sources throughout Section I of the book. We will also include a few quotations from books that are recommended by *Search* as resources for additional study. The reader will notice that the authors of these books, not necessarily Lutherans, are more open about what they believe than are the authors of *Search,* and they express their beliefs in the same theological language that liberal Lutherans use.

---

[3]Michelle Sanden Johlas, "Search Program Remains Popular; Sparks Renewal," *The Lutheran Standard,* September 5, 1986, p. 34.

3.

THE CONTROVERSY

Position A

There is a real doctrinal struggle in which the very foundation of the Christian Faith, the gospel itself, and every other basic Christian doctrine is endangered and finally destroyed because much of the Bible is "questioned" and denied.

ROOTS OF CHANGE

Most people have seen the changes that have taken place in society in the last few decades, not only in this country but in Europe as well. However, few people have really understood the primary source of these changes. Church historians have traced the roots of the changes back to the mid-17th century in Europe. Up until that time, Martin Luther and the Reformation had brought about a clear preaching of the gospel and the spreading of a vast amount of biblical knowledge. Although not everyone was a Christian, the majority of the people generally accepted the absolutes of the Bible. This became a major factor in shaping their values, governments, and world view. The United States, as an extension of Northern Europe, also came under this influence.[1]

The mid-17th century saw a new movement of thought, the Enlightenment, begin to emerge. This movement reached its clearest form in 18th century Germany and was essentially an intellectual movement. The Enlightenment placed emphasis on the sufficiency of human reason; rejected the supernatural elements of the Christian religion; and made the happiness of man, in this life, of paramount importance. Additionally, the movement saw man as being basically good and overlooked the reality of sin.[2]

---

[1] Francis A. Schaeffer, *The Great Evangelical Disaster* (Westchester, IL: Crossway Books, 1984), p. 22.
[2] Ibid., p. 33.

Kurt E. Marquart, a conservative theologian and seminary professor in the Lutheran Church—Missouri Synod (LCMS), describes the rationalistic thinking of the Enlightenment and its emphasis on reason:

> This movement believed with a vengeance in the supremacy of human reason. Mankind had come of age, it was thought, and no longer needed primitive superstitions and religious authorities. Enlightened human intelligence itself could establish everything necessary to religion, namely the existence of God, the immortality of the soul, and morality or virtue as the way to heaven. All the mysteries beyond the grasp of human reason, such as the Trinity, the Incarnation, the Redemption, the Sacraments, and the like, were discarded as so much ancient nonsense and mumbo-jumbo.[3]

As the concept of the Enlightenment became more clearly defined, it, like the Reformation, began to exert great influence on the minds of men. The movement's emphasis on reason and rejection of the supernatural brought the Bible under attack from within the Christian church for the first time in history. Up until that time, Christians may have disagreed on the interpretation of God's Word, but no one disputed the fact that it was *God*'s Word and inerrant and true in all that it said. The "new thinking," built on the foundation of human reason and the rejection of the supernatural, changed the world view of those who accepted it. Many of these people were Christian scholars who were faced with the dilemma of holding on to a faith based on supernatural events while maintaining a world view that rejected the supernatural.

This dilemma gave rise to the *historical-critical method* of biblical interpretation. Those people who accept this method begin with the presupposition that the supernatural or miraculous events in the Bible are not possible. Therefore, an explanation must be found for these events that is compatible with reason and scientific knowledge.

Dr. Robert D. Preus, a noted LCMS theologian and historian and former president of Concordia Theological Seminary, Ft. Wayne, Indiana, identifies this method as a product of the Enlightenment and describes it as being comparatively new:

> . . . let me make an historical observation. The Historical-Critical Method is a comparatively new method of approaching Scripture, originating at the time of the Enlightenment

---

[3]Kurt E. Marquart, *Anatomy of an Explosion* (Grand Rapids: Baker Book House, 1978), p. 19.

and Rationalism in Europe. Luther was not a forerunner of this method, as Robert Smith implies, certainly not Jesus Himself, as Roy Harrisville implies. Hans Conzelmann, Ernst Kaesemann, [Rudolf] Bultmann, as well as those who have written and traced the history of the method all date the origin of the method to the period of the Enlightenment when scholars had generally abandoned the inspiration of the Bible, rejected the doctrine that Scripture presented divinely revealed doctrine and were convinced that historical criticism could be applied to the Scriptures with the same force and consistency as to any other writings. The method as it is now generally used could not have arisen before that time in history, at least within Christian circles.[4]

THE HISTORICAL-GRAMMATICAL METHOD

Before we go into any further description of the methods of the historical-critical scholars it will be helpful to examine the historical-*grammatical* method, also commonly referred to as the *grammatical*-historical method, which is the method of historic Lutheranism.

The historical-grammatical method begins with the presupposition that all things are possible with God. God is the ultimate author of the Bible—which was inspired by the Holy Spirit working through its human writers. As such, it is a book of special revelation different from all other books and the sole, infallible authority in all matters pertaining to God and man and the whole of creation. Because of the Bible's unique status as a sole authority, historic Lutheran doctrine has always insisted on Scripture's self-interpretation. Clear passages of Scripture are used to interpret less clear passages—Scripture interprets Scripture. Those who employ this method seek to find the most accurate Greek or Hebrew texts from which to translate and interpret. This method is a constructive and legitimate tool of conservative Lutheran scholars that is not to be confused with the historical-*critical* method.

The late Dr. Siegbert W. Becker, a noted conservative Lutheran scholar in the Wisconsin Evangelical Lutheran Synod (WELS), describes this method in greater detail:

> Luther and Melanchthon, as well as countless Bible students before and after their time, were convinced that the only method which yields sure and certain truth drawn from

---

[4]Robert D. Preus, "May the Lutheran Theologian Legitimately Use the Historical-Critical Method?" *Affirm,* Spring 1973, p. 31.

the Bible is what has usually been called the "historical-grammatical" method. It is sometimes also called the "literal method," and, confusingly enough, the "historical" method.

Basic to the historical-grammatical method is the acceptance of the Holy Scriptures as the verbally inspired and inerrant word of God. Up until the rise of the critical school, all Christian scholars, (even if they were not always agreed on what the words meant) accepted the words of the Bible as being the source of truth because they were the very words of God.

To understand what God was saying to us, according to the grammatical method, we need to study the meaning of the words in their ordinary and biblical usage. When we have discovered what the words mean, we know what God wants to say to us. What the words say is then accepted as God's truth. It is particularly this last point that we have in mind when we call it the *historical*-grammatical method. Above all else that term means that in the Bible we have true history, a true account of what was said and done. The historical-grammatical method assumes that the men who claim to have written the Bible really wrote it at the time they claim to have written it. It assumes that the people who are spoken of in Scripture really lived and really did the things described unless there is something in the context itself that compels the reader to think otherwise.[5]

Becker points out that this was also the view of Luther:

When Luther said that he read the Bible historically he meant that he believed that what was recorded in the Bible was real, true, accurate history, that people like Adam and Eve, Jonah and Abraham had really lived on this earth and that what the Bible tells us about them really happened.[6]

THE HISTORICAL-CRITICAL METHOD

In direct opposition to the historical-grammatical method is the historical-critical method of biblical interpretation—the "new think-

---

[5]Siegbert W. Becker, "The Historical-Critical Method of Bible Interpretation," *Wisconsin Lutheran Quarterly,* vol. 74, 1977, pp. 15, 16.

[6]Ibid., p. 17. Excellent resources in support of the historical-grammatical method are: Werner H. Franzmann, *Bible History Commentary,* and *The People's Bible,* a Bible commentary series written for laymen that includes the complete Bible text (NIV), (Milwaukee: Northwestern Publishing House).

ing." This is a destructive tool of liberal scholars and the source of the statements listed in Position B in the comparison column of Chapter 1. As previously stated, this method arose out of the need to reconcile two contradictory positions. Joe E. Schruhl, a conservative LCMS pastor, defines historical criticism as "an attempt to synthesize Scripture with science. It holds that the miraculous, that is, the direct intervention by God into human history, is unacceptable."[7] He also traces the historical criticism roots back to the mid-17th century:

> It is helpful in order to understand the Historical-Critical Method of Biblical Interpretation to know where it came from. . . . Its real emergence came in the age of rationalism and pietism. Man had "come of age" and it was time to put away primitive notions about God, Scripture, and the miraculous. The name to remember as the father of the present Historical-Critical Method of Biblical Interpretation is Johann Salamo Semler (1725-1791).

> The church and society of Semler's time seemed to be moving in opposite directions. Society was moving toward humanism, pietism, and rationalism, and this signaled for Semler the complete destruction of faith. The church, on the other hand, was striving for renewed orthodoxy and a blind and unquestioning faith, and to Semler this meant a complete destruction of reason. He sought some middle road between Orthodoxy and Rationalism.[8]

For Semler and his followers, the search for a middle road between orthodoxy and rationalism resulted in the formulation of many theories and conclusions concerning Scripture that are contradictory to the teaching of the historic Christian faith. The following is a brief comparison of these views, beginning with the doctrines of inspiration and inerrancy. A more detailed study and corresponding documentation will be provided in the chapters that follow.

A brief comparison

Historic Lutheranism teaches that as the creation accounts and the early history of God's people were transmitted through succeeding generations, God miraculously preserved truth and accuracy and caused the writers of the Bible to write what he wanted recorded— verbal inspiration. God is the author of the Holy Scriptures.

---

[7]Joe E. Schruhl, "Historical-Critical Method of Biblical Interpretation," *Christian News Encyclopedia*, 4, vols., ed. Herman Otten (Washington: Missourian Publishing Co., 1983), 1:237.

[8]Ibid.

While this early history (from Adam to Moses) may have been orally transmitted, it may also have been recorded on clay tablets. There is a general agreement among conservative scholars that Moses could very well have compiled this history from a library of clay tablets produced by Adam, Noah, Abraham, etc., in much the same manner as the history of their Near Eastern neighbors was preserved. Archaeological evidence of the past 100 years supports this as being a very likely possibility.[9]

In contrast, *the liberal scholars believe* that there was some kind of transmission from God to man (or simply from man alone) that was then orally transmitted over thousands of years. This supposedly resulted in many substantial errors, changes, omissions, and additions. The liberals also claim that the Bible has many unknown authors who were influenced by the time and culture in which they lived; therefore, their writings must reflect their own opinions and understanding.

The liberal scholars believe that other non-biblical materials (commonly referred to as source materials, strands, or layers) were added after they were edited or modified to make them more acceptable as biblical literature. This editing was supposed to have been carried out by additional unknown writers through the processes of form criticism, redaction criticism, etc. The liberals identify this material and the writers in the Old Testament as J, E, D, and P, and in the New Testament as Q, ML, M, and L.

The historical-critical scholars approach the Bible as if it were just another man-made document, not as a book of special revelation, different from all other books. It is assumed that the Bible, like many ancient documents from the past, contains legends, myths, stories, fables, and folklore that must be studied and sorted out using the best "scientific" tools available. These scholars reason that there is no way to be sure of what is actual history and what is merely "tradition." Tradition is defined as the handing down of stories, opinions, beliefs, and customs from parents to children over succeeding generations. Things considered "tradition" were seen as originating from man.

Miracles, the "new thinkers" reason, are merely added by the writers of Scripture to add "emphasis" and to impress primitive readers with the authority and validity of their message. The *historical-critical* scholars explain this reasoning by citing examples of literature from pagan cultures that have stories about miraculous events, such as floods and earthquakes, which are similar to the events

---

[9]Uuras Saarnivaara, *Can The Bible Be Trusted?* (Minneapolis: Osterhus Publishing House, 1983), pp. 95-97.

recorded in the Bible. They fail to take into account the fact that since all men descended from Adam and Eve, all have heard the real history of mankind. Therefore, some elements of the truth appear in their writings as well.

Those who use the historical-critical method conclude that the biblical writers saw the world in very primitive and unscientific terms and merely recorded what they believed was happening or what they heard from someone else. Thus, the scholars suggest that Jesus did not walk on the water, but along the water's edge. It only appeared to the disciples that he was on the water—after all, was there not a storm that interfered with their ability to see? It follows, then, that when Peter slipped from the boat and almost drowned he merely slipped on the wet "stepping stones," and Jesus' admonition only meant that he should not have looked down or been distracted by the wind and waves.[10]

The historical-critical scholar who accepts these theories believes he has the ability to "get behind the text." That is, he can strip away the "legend and myth" and search for the true meaning—subject, of course, to his own private opinion.[11]

Users of the historical-critical method present their method as being very scholarly and scientific. They imply that anyone who holds to the historic Lutheran view of Scripture is hopelessly out of date. In reality this is not the case. Modern scientific thought supports the historic Lutheran view of Scripture in that it allows for the possibility of the miraculous or supernatural. In the last 15 years, every major university has established a parapsychology department. Parapsychologists are investigating the supernatural realm of the occult, but they think they are investigating some "new dimension of reality." The very widespread interest in the occult and in Eastern religions in the West is evidence of this shift in the attitude of science.

The domino effect

Those who adhere to the historical-critical method insist that it is a neutral method. In reality it is not. Becker describes the destructive progression of this method:

> It must be emphatically stated that the method is not neutral. It clearly rejects the claim of Scripture to be a book which is different from every other book in the world. . . . [With this method] each individual account of an historical

---

[10]Schruhl, op. cit., pp. 237, 238.
[11]Ibid.

nature in the Bible is simply studied without any preconceived notion of whether it is right or wrong, factual or nonfactual. . . . We are told unendingly that the holy men who wrote the Bible were children of their time who were limited in their knowledge and understanding of science and history by the undeveloped state of the culture in which they did their work.

It is obvious from what has been said that the method certainly cannot be neutral on the question of biblical inerrancy. It is a foregone, fixed conclusion, presupposed in the practice of this kind of interpretation, that the Bible can be wrong at almost any point. The more conservative practitioners of the method try to safeguard what they call the theological side of Scripture, but even they hold that the Bible could be wrong on almost every point at which it treats either history or natural science.

Whenever men have given up the doctrine of biblical inerrancy they have eventually come to realize and admit that if that premise is once accepted, the doctrine of verbal inspiration simply cannot be maintained for long.

When the verbal inspiration and inerrancy of the Holy Scripture are denied, the doctrine that the Bible is the Word of God can no longer be maintained. If the words of the Bible are not given by God to the holy writers and if, as is universally asserted by those who hold to the historical-critical method, the statements of the Bible are in numerous places contrary to fact, then it must be clear that not all of this book, and perhaps none of this book, can really, in a literal way, be called God's Word.

Once the critic has disposed of the doctrines of verbal inspiration and inerrancy and has given up the identification of the Bible as the Word of God, the concept of biblical authority has also been undermined. If the words of the Bible are not the words of God and if those words are not true just because they are not the words of God, then obviously it is no longer possible to believe what the Bible says just because it is written in the Bible. "It is written" becomes not a final argument, as it is in the New Testament and on the lips of Jesus, but just the proposal of a human opinion which may or may not be true.[12]

---

[12]Becker, op.cit., pp. 133-148.

Truth becomes relative

With the abandonment of the absolute authority of Scripture, truth becomes relative and certainty becomes uncertainty. Marcus R. Braun, a conservative LCMS layman, suggests that the question "What is truth?" may be considered by future historians as the great issue of our age. He compares the conservative and liberal views of truth.

> Perhaps liberals and conservatives will be able to under-stand each other better if they clearly understand that each group is basing its argument on axiomatic assumptions which differ from the other. To demonstrate these differ-ences let us examine the liberal and the conservative answer to this basic question: What is the nature of truth? . . . Con-servatives consider truth to be absolute and immutable, as unchanging today as it was thousands of years ago. . . . [They believe that] the *Holy Scriptures* are absolute, im-mutable truth. Liberals by and large consider truth to be relative, changing with every age and moment. Liberals are inclined to scoff at concepts of absolute truth. . . . [They be-lieve that] the truth of Scripture is relative, changing from age to age, from year to year, from day to day, or from per-son to person. . . . The conservative says that two plus two has always equaled four and will always equal four. The lib-eral may say that two plus two is somewhere between three and ten, and then philosophically speculate as to what could be done if it actually did equal ten.[13]

Doubt and confusion

The historical-critical method certainly cannot be regarded as a neutral tool for interpreting Scripture. This method of biblical criti-cism puts man in judgment over Scripture rather than Scripture over man. Once it is left to the individual to decide for himself or herself the definition of truth, then it is no longer God's absolutes that rule, but man's notions. Doubt takes the place of certainty and, as Becker points out in the following quotation, "hopeless confusion" reigns among the scholars.

> The proponents of the historical-critical method admit that theirs is a method of doubt. We have heard one of the critics

---

[13]Marcus R. Braun, *What is the Nature of Truth?* (Kansas City: Marcus Braun, 1970), pp. 2, 3, 9. Originally presented as a paper before the Board of Control at Concordia Seminary, St. Louis, Missouri.

say that the goal of historical criticism is to decide what is more or less probable. A slogan that is commonly heard among theologians who follow this type of biblical interpretation is "Probability is the guide of life." Commenting on the subject of historical research Paul Tillich [a liberal scholar] says that "the historian can never reach certainty in this way, but he can reach a high degree of probability." The ideal of historical research, he says, is "to reach a high degree of probability," but, he admits, "in many cases this is impossible."[14]

The result of the employment of this method has been hopeless confusion among the scholars. What one scholar holds to be very probable another considers to be very unlikely. The very great diversity of their conclusions drawn from the same evidence demonstrates how unreliable the method must be. The better we understand the method, the clearer it will become that Luther was right when he said that only by the historical-*grammatical* method can we ever reach certainty in regard to the doctrines of the Bible.

This vacillation in scholarly opinion is accepted as normal. It is a common view among theologians today that the only thing we can be certain about is that nothing is certain. But if they are so sure that nothing is certain one is inclined to wonder how they can be so sure of this—nothing is certain.[15]

Schruhl lists just a few of the many liberal scholars who have followed in Semler's footsteps and illustrates the diversity of some of their theories and conclusions.

It is interesting that in spite of his rational approach to Scripture Semler still held to and defended the doctrine of divine creation.

In the last century, David Frederick Strauss produced his four volume work *The Life of Jesus*. For Strauss, Jesus is an historical myth; the full embodiment of the Jewish hope, a super-prototype of Moses, Jonah, et al. Strauss even goes to the trouble of listing the miracles and giving rational explanations.

Albert Schweitzer, the humanitarian, produced a compendium of essays entitled *The Quest for the Historical Jesus*.

---

[14]Becker, op. cit., p. 21. Author's endnote. Citation reads: Paul Tillich, *Systematic Thelogy*, 2 vols. (Chicago: University of Chicago Press, 1957), 2:104-107.
[15]Ibid., pp. 21-24.

Schweitzer traces the endeavors of Strauss and other theologians to strip away the "legend and myth" and "get behind" the Gospels and find the "real" Jesus. He concludes it is an impossible task.

Rudolph Bultmann, a theologian of recent fame, wrote in terms of "demythologizing" the Scripture. Yet Bultmann did not deny the existence of Jesus. He urged that Jesus lived, and, even though the miracles of Jesus were myth, we must stress the message and proclaim Jesus to all.

Karl Barth, also a recent theologian, seeing the direction of current theology because of critical scholarship, introduced us to a new term, "Neo-orthodoxy." This was an attempt to recover the Orthodoxy and faith of the past without sacrificing all of modern scholarship. His commentary on Romans published in 1919 caused quite a stir. He did not regard the Bible as a collection of pious stories and fanciful myths, rather, he maintained that the Bible contained the Word of God—though the Word of God is not limited to the Scriptures. He felt the dynamic of the Reformation is lost in dead orthodoxy but is freed in neo-orthodoxy to follow the leading of the Spirit. For Barth, the actual happenings of Scripture are not as important as their proclamation. (For Barthians it really doesn't matter if Jesus lived or not as long as he lives in the proclamation—*kerygma.*)

Following Bultmann's footsteps, and generally ignoring Barth's efforts, came Tillich, Cox, Altizer, Hamilton, et. al, and the "Death of God" (author's emphasis).[16]

Diversity and pluralism

The diversity of theological opinion demonstrated by Schruhl is no less in vogue today. In the preface to *Christian Dogmatics,* editors Dr. Carl E. Braaten and Dr. Robert W. Jenson substantiate Becker's claim that the great vacillation in scholarly opinion is accepted as the norm in the Evangelical Lutheran Church in America (ELCA).

The conception of this book took place in the late 1970's as the editors again remarked on the fact that almost all our usable dogmatics have been imported from Europe. In the decades since World War II we have used all or parts of the

---

[16]Schruhl, loc. cit.

imposing volumes of the continental theologians—Emil Brunner, Karl Barth, Gustaf Aulen, Regin Prenter, and Paul Tillich [all liberal theologians]. As teachers of dogmatic and systematic theology, we have had no textbooks that reflect the American context from the standpoint of the Lutheran tradition. . . . We hope our work will be a textbook in the theological instruction and a resource for those who practice the art of ministry. It lies in the nature of a work such as this to seek the widest possible churchly acceptance, since dogmatics speaks from the church to the church, by way of disciplined reflection on the sources of its faith and tradition. But theology at present is fragmented into an unusually large number of schools and movements. The fact of theological pluralism is inescapable. We have chosen to make a virtue out of a necessity by way of multiple authorship. A dogmatics by any one person would likely be received only as advocacy for the positions of that person's own school of thought, and thus fail to command the wide churchly use inherent in the notion of dogmatics. Hoping to avoid this fate, we offer this joint work of six authors.

Although all of us stand within the Lutheran tradition, the differences among us, and the consequent inconsistencies in the book, are considerable. Those who like to label theologians—"hope," "process," etc.—will by our calculations need seven or more labels for the six of us. . . . At some points the authors simply disagree, and this disagreement occasionally reaches the point of contradiction. We will leave it to the readers to discover the places where this occurs. Whether these differences and disagreements be taken as bane or blessing, they follow from the initial reason for multiple authorship.[17]

The inconsistencies and contradictions in *Christian Dogmatics*, a primary seminary textbook in the ELCA, are representative of the majority of the materials produced by historical-critical scholars. Their attacks on the miraculous events in the Bible range from simple casting of doubt to outright denial. Most authors list not only their own various theories and opinions, but those of other historical-critical scholars as well. The reader is left free to draw his or her own conclusions or perhaps come up with a new theory. This is, of course,

---

[17]*Christian Dogmatics,* 2 vols., eds. Carl E. Braaten and Robert W. Jenson (Philadelphia: Fortress Press, 1984), 1:xvii.

consistent with these scholars' theology, because they do not hold to any certain or absolute truths. While in many instances the historic Lutheran doctrines are included, they are generally presented as a way of thinking and believing that has been largely abandoned in the light of "modern scholarship." The reader is left with the impression that hardly anyone now holds with the "old" thinking.

Braaten and Jenson have pointed out that theological pluralism or diversity is inescapable. Becker addresses the issue of "whether these differences and disagreements be taken as bane or blessing."

> Those who adopted the historical-critical method are con-vinced that they have made spiritual progress. Like the persecutors of the apostles against whom the Savior warned His followers, they are convinced that by this adoption they have done God and their church a service. . . . Proponents of this methodology believe that the his-torical-critical method has made it possible for us to un-derstand the Bible better. . . . On the other hand, other Christian scholars are just as firmly convinced that the historical-critical method does not benefit the church. . . . The historical-critical method is a damnable heresy against which all Christians ought to be on their guard. . . . May God help us to see the dangers into which it plunges the church.[18]

A destructive heresy

Dr. J. Kincaid Smith is a conservative pastor in the Evangelical Lutheran Synod (ELS). What he writes in the following articles supports Becker's conclusion.

> In 1973 when I graduated from an LCA seminary in Ohio, I did not believe in the Virgin Birth nor, for that matter, in the bodily resurrection of Christ, and neither did any of my fellow graduates, and certainly none of our professors. We had been systematically led to reject any element in Scrip-ture which could not be explained by natural science. What an empty Christmas I knew in those days, what an empty faith! We did not realize, or could not face, that in letting go of all the miraculous things in the Scriptures, the very faith itself had slipped away.[19]

---

[18]Becker, op. cit., pp. 13-15.
[19]J. Kincaid Smith, "The Real Virgin Birth of Our Lord Jesus Christ," *The Lutheran Sentinel*, December 1987, p. 4.

As a former liberal who held and defended the Historical-Critical method (the non-inspired view of the Bible), I can tell you this: that the difference between historic Lutheranism and the "new thinking" is not some minor insignificant difference. They are 180 degrees apart—totally opposed. In the liberal position I lost my faith in Christ. The knowledge that the Bible is truth, as historic Lutheranism teaches, restored my faith and continues to support it. A real puzzle to me now is to understand, how back then, I actually considered myself a Christian.[20]

Position B

The only real differences among Lutherans today are minor, "picky" points of doctrine that don't touch the heart of Christian faith, which is the gospel. The real issues are more political and cultural than doctrinal.

LCA, ALC, AND AELC ACCEPT HISTORICAL CRITICISM

Articles in the official magazines of the former Lutheran Church in America (LCA) and American Lutheran Church (ALC) demonstrate that the historical-critical method of Bible study was accepted and promoted in the seminaries and congregations of the now-merged churches of the ELCA.

Dr. David W. Preus, bishop of the former ALC, writes in *The Lutheran Standard* that historical criticism is a "legitimate tool" to be used and promoted in ALC congregational Bible studies.

To help us understand the Word of God, the American Lutheran Church's Division for Theological Education and Ministry has issued an "occasional paper" called "The Doctrine of the Word in the Lutheran Church" (copies of the statement have been sent to congregations in the ALC's Unified Mailing). . . . These essays . . . help us to understand the use of the "historical-critical" method of biblical study. Properly understood, the method seeks only to bring all legitimate intellectual tools to work in the study of the biblical text.[21]

Dr. Todd W. Nichol, assistant professor of church history at Luther Northwestern Theological Seminary (ELCA), St. Paul, Minneso-

---

[20]"The 'Dismantling' of the Christian Faith or the Historical-Critical Method," *The Christian News*, April 29, 1985, p. 11.

[21]David W. Preus, "God's Word—Our Great Heritage," *The Lutheran Standard*, May 18, 1984, p. 29.

ta, is the author of an article entitled "How Will ELCA View the Bible?" This article appeared simultaneously in the official magazines of the LCA[22] and the the ALC[23] as one in a series of articles concerning the merger. We will quote extensively from this article because an ELCA historian and seminary professor is saying exactly what we are saying concerning the growth in the use of historical criticism in the Lutheran Church. However, his presentation differs from ours in that he views historical criticism as a benign method while we recognize that it is destructive of the Christian faith. The article also serves as an example of the subtle manner used by many liberal theologians to promote this method among unsuspecting laity. Nichol begins his article with a brief history concerning the historic Lutheran view of the Bible.

> The Bible is not an event but a book, and American Lutherans have not agreed always about what kind of book it is or how to use it. . . . The fate of more than one merger has hung on a decision about what kind of book the Bible is. . . . Before World War I, most American Lutherans were used to saying that the Bible was God's inspired and infallible word. . . . Lutherans thought God had inspired the writers of the Bible in their choice of words and that Scripture spoke literally where it did not use obviously figurative language. . . . "Scripture cannot be broken" was a favorite quotation from John's Gospel.[24]

Nichol then proceeds to identify historical criticism and describes its onset and effect on American Protestantism in the early 1900s.

> Lutherans in the United States were thankful for the ocean that separated them from Europe. They remembered that the churches of Europe were not in robust health. They knew, too, that new theologies in Europe had snipped and clipped at Christian confidence in the Bible. They had read about dramatic discoveries by Charles Darwin and other scientists that challenged old assumptions about the creation. Pastors and theologians also knew that European scholars had uncovered evidence that the Bible had been written over many centuries, that it included literature of many kinds

---

[22]Todd W. Nichol, "How Will ELCA View the Bible?" *The Lutheran,* October 15, 1986, p. 11.

[23]Nichol, "Pure Power," *The Lutheran Standard,* October 24, 1986, pp. 4-8.

[24]Nichol, "How Will ELCA View the Bible?" p. 11.

from a multitude of sources and that it had been put together by editors working in a variety of times and places. These
findings were the result of a scholarly method called historical criticism. The new method was debated hotly within and
outside the churches. Wherever anyone stood, almost everyone agreed that historical criticism was a challenge to the
authority of the Bible.

Wise heads knew that sooner or later historical criticism
would cross the Atlantic, and by the end of the Civil War it
had. Lutherans watched and shook their heads, but at first
they did not pay much attention to the hubbub. But by 1920
they were worried.

In the 1920's American protestantism cracked and split
down the middle. On one side were "Modernists," who believed they could fit the faith to the findings of the scientists
and the historical critics. On the other were "Fundamentalists," a loose coalition of Christians who had rallied to the
defense of the Bible. Most Lutherans in the United States
sympathized with the Fundamentalists. They liked their
emphasis on the Bible. They understood making the inspiration and "inerrancy" of Scripture a final line of defense
against the Modernists. "Inerrancy" was a new word for
Lutherans, but for many it summed up their confidence in
the authority of Scripture. By 1920 it had become an article
of faith for some American Lutherans.[25]

While Nichol does acknowledge that historical criticism was involved in the split in American Protestantism, he neglects to define it
as the destructive heresy that it is. In his book *The Great Evangelical
Disaster,* the late Dr. Francis Schaeffer, a conservative Presbyterian,
more clearly describes the role of historical criticism in the battle for
orthodoxy in the mainline denominations. He begins with a reference
to the ideas of the Enlightenment:

The central ideas of the Enlightenment stand in complete
antithesis to Christian truth. More than this, they are an
attack on God himself and his character.

In the late nineteenth century it was these ideas which began to radically transform Christianity in America. This
started especially with the acceptance of the "higher critical"

---

[25]Ibid., pp. 11, 12.

methods that had been developed in Germany. Using these methods, the new liberal theologians completely undercut the authority of Scripture. We can be thankful for those who argued strenuously against the new methods and in defense of the full inspiration and inerrancy of Scripture. One would remember especially the great Princeton theologians A. A. Hodge and B. B. Warfield, and later J. Gresham Machen. But in spite of the efforts of these men and scores of other Bible-believing Christian leaders, and in spite of the fact that the vast majority of lay Christians were truly Bible-believing, those holding the liberal ideas of the Enlightenment and the destructive methods of biblical criticism came into power and control in the denominations. By the 1930's liberalism had swept through most of the denominations and the battle was all but lost.[26]

As the mainline denominations succumbed to liberalism, the stage was set for the liberal infiltration of some segments of Lutheranism. Already doctrinally weakened by mergers of the past (see Section III, Chapters 26 and 27), the predecessor bodies of the ALC and the LCA were fertile soil for the seeds of historical criticism.

Nichol continues his historical reporting with accounts of the mergers that began in the 1920s. In each of these mergers, historical criticism caused a great deal of controversy. The issue of "inerrancy" became the focal point of the dissension. In most cases, a compromise was reached by altering the constitution to satisfy both parties and a new synod was formed. Nichol gives an example of one such compromise that resulted in the formation of the "old" ALC in 1930. He begins by stating that some of the involved parties wanted the word "inerrant" removed from the new constitution. He then continues:

An explosive controversy followed, but eventually a compromise was patched together. The Bible was called "infallible" in the doctrinal article of the new constitution and "inerrant" in an appendix. The scrap over Scripture was settled, and the American Lutheran Church—now remembered as the "old" ALC—came into existence in 1930.[27]

As the various mergers took place, the historical-critical method began to find its way into the seminaries and churches of the resulting new synods. The method brought with it additional controversy,

---

[26]Schaeffer, op. cit., pp. 33, 34.
[27]Nichol, "How Will ELCA View the Bible?" p. 12.

and in some instances it stood in the way of merger. Nichol traces its development and progress:

> By 1930 historical criticism was finding its way into the Lutheran churches of the United States. As they do today seminarians nodded off trying to keep straight the scholarly shorthand identifying the editors of the Old Testament: J . . . E . . . D . . . P. . . . Learning a new way of reading the Bible was painful for some and liberating for others. Members of seminary and college faculties often were at odds over these matters, and students sometimes wondered whether to believe their Sunday-school teachers or their theological professors.

> Historical criticism first was accepted widely in the United Lutheran Church in America, the largest of the bodies that eventually merged to become the Lutheran Church in America. In 1930, new faculty members brought the approach to the seminary of the Augustana Synod in Rock Island, Ill. But the advent of the new method opened a breach between these and other Lutheran bodies.

> When the LCA and the new ALC appeared on the scene in the early 1960's, many people wondered, "Why two churches instead of one?" One reason was a division of opinion over Scripture. The leaders of the churches that formed the ALC insisted on the position their predecessors had taken in 1919 and 1930, when they described the Bible as "the divinely inspired, revealed, and inerrant Word of God" in the constitution of the new ALC. The LCA constitution, on the other hand, shows the influence of the historical-critical approach: "The Holy Scriptures are the divinely inspired record of God's redemptive act in Christ, for which the Old Testament prepared the way and which the New Testament proclaims."

> In spite of the provisions of its constitution—and because of them—the new ALC was threatened by controversy over Scripture. A document incorporated into the Articles of Union for the ALC, the United Testimony on Faith and Life, was a lengthy statement framed by theologians of the American Lutheran Conference prior to the merger that brought together four of its churches. The United Testimony left the door open to the use of historical criticism. That made it possible for those uneasy with the notion of inerrancy to use the new method and enter the new church in good con-

science. But this was unsettling to advocates of inerrancy, who could point to the constitution of the new church for support of their position.

Even before the merger there had been signs of trouble over Scripture. But with the skillful leadership of Fred Schiotz, the first president of the new ALC, with retreats that brought the district presidents and theologians together, and with the publication of *The Bible: Book of Faith,* written by ALC theologians, the historical-critical approach was introduced and accepted widely, though not universally, in the ALC in the 1960's.[28]

Nichol also addresses the role of historical criticism in the 1974 split in the LCMS and the formation of the Association of Evangelical Lutheran Churches (AELC), the smallest of the three merging bodies of the ELCA.

Some years later the LCMS was convulsed by a quarrel over inspiration, inerrancy and historical criticism. Controversy swirled around the faculty of its Concordia Seminary in St. Louis. In 1974 most members of that faculty were charged with false doctrine. The chief complaint was that the teachers had embraced the historical-critical approach to the Bible. Eventually, most of the faculty left the seminary and established a new school. Later a number of congregations and clergy left the LCMS to form the Association of Evangelical Lutheran Churches, one of the partners forming the new Evangelical Lutheran Church in America.[29]

In the concluding paragraphs of his article, Nichol asks the question: "What will the ELCA say about the Bible?" He answers by quoting the proposed ELCA constitution, which he states allows for both views of Scripture—one which insists on inerrancy and one which opposes it.

The constitution proposed for the new church says: "The church accepts the canonical Scriptures of the Old and New Testaments as the inspired word of God and the authoritative source and norm of its proclamation, faith and life.". . . . The statement is strong in its insistence on biblical authority. It does not exclude those who say that the Scripture is in-

---

[28]Ibid., pp. 12, 13.
[29]Ibid., p. 13.

errant. It welcomes them and joins them in paying honor to the Scripture.[30]

As mentioned earlier, Nichol neglects to define the true nature of historical criticism in his article. Inerrancy appears to be the only doctrine called into question by this method. In view of the record of merger compromises, the reader is left with the impression that the issue is not all that important. Nichol's closing statements support the continued use of the historical-critical method in the ELCA.

> . . . the proposed statement also makes room for historical criticism. Lutherans who have studied the ALC's "Search" or the LCA's "Word and Witness" programs have learned that the authority of Scripture increases for them as they learn more about it and the worlds from which it came. They think that with help of scholarship and intellectual honesty the word can be understood and believed in today's world. They, too, honor the Bible as the source and norm for the faith and life of the church.[31]

Not only is there room for historical criticism in the ELCA, but Nichol makes it appear that the method is an essential aid to understanding the Bible and that through its use the authority of Scripture is actually increased. Nothing could be further from the truth—a fact that will be fully illustrated in the chapters that follow.

The general tone of Nichol's article could lead the reader to believe that historical criticism has been openly taught in the congregations that comprise the ELCA. Many would disagree with that assumption. In truth, the ALC's *Search* and the LCA's *Word and Witness* adult Bible-study programs are subtle attempts to lead an unsuspecting laity into the acceptance of historical criticism. This evaluation is supported by Craig Stanford, who attended two ELCA colleges and one ELCA seminary.[32] He relates his experiences with *Search* in his book, *The Death of the Lutheran Reformation.*

> The late Dr. Fred Schiotz, the first president of the ALC, and the late Dr. Warren Quanbeck, one of the ALC's most influential theologians, and others, tried to sell modern criticism to the lay people of the ALC during the 1960's and 70's through

---

[30]Ibid.
[31]Ibid.
[32]Carthage College, Kenosha, Wisconsin; Concordia College, Moorhead, Minnesota; and Luther Northwestern Theological Seminary, St. Paul, Minnesota.

a number of books intended for lay reading, but these books fell far short of their desired effect because very few lay people read them. So particular theories in historical criticism remained restricted to the college and seminary level.

In the 1980's, however, the landscape of the local parish is changing rapidly. This can be attributed to the renewed interest in Bible study, which was noticeably absent from the Church in prior decades. This fresh interest in the Bible has created a great opportunity for both liberals and biblically-minded evangelicals.

Comprehensive Bible studies have become very popular in churches of all theological stripes, but studies rooted in *historical criticism* are sweeping the market place. The Bethel Bible Series, in existence since 1961, is considered by many to be a conservative Bible study program. In its first edition it gave slight indications that it accepted historical criticism, but in 1981, a second edition was more bold in its historical assertions. While it is more subtle than studies produced by the publishing houses of the ELCA, it still plants the seeds of historical criticism in the minds of those who do not think critically about its contents.

The leadership of the ALC and LCA saw this renewed interest as a great opportunity to advance their agenda and introduce historical criticism into the local congregation. The *Search* Bible Studies Series would prove to be the real workhorse for this task and it has exceeded everyone's expectations. Disguised as the most comprehensive Bible study ever produced by Augsburg, it has been the ELCA's single most effective tool in altering the way Lutheran lay people think about the Bible. This five year program, with an estimated 90,000 participants, has turned tens of thousands of Lutheran lay people into higher critical thinkers without their knowing it.

One Augsburg official, speaking to a seminary class on Christian education, pointed out that the creators of *Search* understood the unique opportunity given them, regarding this as their chance to bring lay people up to speed in the area of historical criticism and the modern view of revelation. He admitted that Augsburg knew this would be controversial, and said after *Search* was first released they received thousands of letters from people who objected to the approach, but Augsburg decided that these letters were not to be taken seriously because they had come from "reactionary parts of the country." The official expressed surprise over the number of "fundamentalists" still in the Lutheran church. Because most of the ELCA's pastors accepting historical criticism, and because of the long silence of the Bible in the church, *Search*'s acceptance was virtually guaranteed. The period of silence created a hunger for biblical studies and *Search* provided a meal (though a poor one). *Search* has also given pastors the opportunity to come out of the historical-critical closet and opened the door for more liberal and radical pieces of curriculum. Perhaps for the first [time] in the history of the ALC and LCA (now ELCA) there is a theological agenda being systematically laid out and followed in an attempt to alter the way Lutheran lay people think about the Bible and theology.[33]

The LCA's *Word and Witness* program made its appearance in 1977. One of the authors, Dr. John Reumann, states in *Jesus In The Church's Gospels* that "we must use the historical approach in studying Scripture. This is necessary because the revelation came in history and is witnessed to in historical documents. This means use of the so-called historical-critical method of study."[34]

A review of *Word and Witness* reveals the influence of the historical-critical method. Listed among the recommended resources are Reumann's book and a few of the books listed by the authors of *Search*. These resources are much bolder concerning the conclusions of the historical-critical method of biblical interpretation than those contained in *Word and Witness* or *Search*. This is an important observation, because the laity most likely to study the recommended resource books are the leaders of Bible study classes. These people are often leaders in other areas of the church as well and can thus encourage other church members to accept the "new thinking."

FORMAL STRATEGY

Stanford refers to *Search* as having provided an opportunity for pastors to "come out of the historical-critical closet." This conclusion is supported by Dr. J. Kincaid Smith, author of an article entitled "The Confession of a Former Liberal LCA Pastor."

---

[33]Craig Stanford, *The Death of the Lutheran Reformation* (Ft. Wayne, IN: Stanford Publishing, 1988), pp. 271-274.

[34]John Reumann, *Jesus In The Church's Gospels* (Philadelphia: Fortress Press, 1968), p. xiii.

As liberals in the ALC-LCA seminaries we were trained to be careful how we talked around conservative lay people. We knew of pastors who were getting themselves into trouble because lay people were finding out what they really believed. . . . A very important part of our formal *strategy* coming out from the seminary was that bringing about this radical change would take time. We had to go slowly and carefully, change would come and would pick up momentum. Everything was on our side, not only in the church, but in the secular realm. . . . When I was a liberal we knew that it was especially the kids who would receive the new thinking. They were soft clay to be molded. . . . Pastors are more open about what they really believe in Jr. Confirmation Class.[35]

TRUTH OR HERESY?

The historical-critical method is a radical change in thinking. It is a change in thinking that, when carried to its extreme by theologians, leads to the denial of every basic doctrine of Christianity. Used in a lesser degree, it leads at best to a partial denial and the casting of doubt upon the remainder. It is important to remember that the tendency with this kind of thinking is not to remain at some point of moderation but to move into the extreme.

The documentation that will be presented in subsequent chapters will demonstrate the extremes to which this method has been carried within the ELCA. It will provide sufficient evidence to enable the reader to decide for himself or herself whether the historical-critical scholars have done God and their church a service, as proponents of this method claim, or if they are teaching a damnable heresy against which all Christians should be on their guard.[36]

---

[35]J. Kincaid Smith, "The Confession of a Former Liberal LCA Pastor," *Christian News Encyclopedia,* 4 vols., ed. Herman Otten (Washington: Missourian Publishing Co., 1988), 3:2165.

[36]Becker, op cit., p. 15.

4.

INSPIRATION AND INERRANCY

Position A

All Scripture is inspired by God. The Holy Scriptures are absolutely true because God gave the writers the very words they wrote (verbal inspiration). The Holy Scriptures contain no errors or contradictions. Since God is the author of all Scripture, its teachings do not contradict one another. Only the canonical books of the Holy Scriptures are regarded as inspired.

1) The Bible.

All Scripture is God-breathed (2 Timothy 3:16).

Sanctify them by the truth; your word is truth (John 17:17).

For prophecy never had its origin in the will of man, but men spoke from God as they were carried along by the Holy Spirit (2 Peter 1:21).

Jesus said, "Scripture cannot be broken" (John 10:35).

2) The Lutheran Confessions, *The Book of Concord* —Large Catechism.

My neighbor and I—in short, all men—may err and deceive, but God's Word cannot err.[1]

---

[1]*The Book of Concord,* trans. and ed. Theodore G. Tappert (Philadelphia: Fortress Press, 1959), *Large Catechism,* 57, p. 444.

3) Martin Luther.

> I confidently believe that not one of their authors erred. . . .
> For it is certain that the Scriptures do not lie. . . . Scripture
> agrees with itself everywhere.[2]

4) As with all doctrines of the historic Lutheran faith, the doctrines of inspiration and inerrancy are solely derived from the Scriptures. The following statement from *This We Believe,* published by
the Wisconsin Evangelical Lutheran Synod (WELS), clearly demonstrates this. In plain, clear language, it states the orthodox Lutheran
position.

> We believe that God has given the Holy Scriptures to pro-
> claim his grace in Christ to man. . . . We believe that God
> gave us the Scriptures through men whom he chose, using
> the language they knew and the style of writing they had.
> He used Moses and the prophets to write the Old Testament
> in Hebrew (some portions in Aramaic) and the evangelists
> and apostles to write the New Testament in Greek.

> We believe that in a miraculous way that goes beyond all hu-
> man investigation, God the Holy Spirit inspired these men to
> write his Word. These "men spoke from God as they were
> carried along by the Holy Spirit" (I Peter 1:21). What they
> said, was spoken "not in words taught us by human wisdom
> but in words taught by the Spirit" (I Cor. 2:13). Every
> thought they expressed, every word they used was given
> them by the Holy Spirit by inspiration. St. Paul wrote to
> Timothy: "All Scripture is God-breathed" (II Tim. 3:16). We
> therefore believe in the verbal inspiration of the Scriptures,
> that is, a word-for-word inspiration. This, however, is not to
> be equated with mechanical dictation.

> We believe that Scripture is a unified whole, true and with-
> out error in everything it says, for our Savior said: "The
> Scripture cannot be broken" (John 10:35). We believe that it
> therefore is the infallible authority and guide for everything
> we believe and do. We believe that it is fully sufficient, clear-
> ly teaching us all we need to know for salvation, making us
> "wise for salvation through faith in Christ Jesus" (II Tim.

---

[2]Martin Luther, *Wider Hans Worst,* quoted in C. F. W. Walther, *Die Evan-
gelish-Lutherische Kirche Auf Erden* (St. Louis: Concordia Publishing House,
1981), p. 131 ff.

3:15), equipping us for every good work (II Tim. 3:17). No other revelations are to be expected.

We believe and accept Scripture on its own terms, accepting as factual history what it presents as history, recognizing a metaphor where Scripture itself indicates one, and reading as poetry what is evident as such. We believe that Scripture must interpret Scripture, clear passages throwing light on those less easily understood. We believe that no authority, be it man's reason, science or scholarship, may stand in judgment over Scripture. Sound scholarship will faithfully search out the true meaning of Scripture without presuming to pass judgment on it.[3]

Position B

All Scripture is "inspired" in the same sense that someone is inspired to write poetry, etc. The Holy Scriptures were written by well-intentioned men of God. They wrote what they believed to be from God, but they were also affected by the cultural beliefs and influences of their times. The Holy Scriptures contain errors and contradictions. Since the Scriptures were written by many different men, their various teachings often contradict one another. The traditions of the church and the witness of Christians today may also be just as "inspired" as the Holy Scriptures.

1) *Christian Dogmatics,* Braaten/Jensen, the *primary* theology textbook used in all seminaries of the Evangelical Lutheran Church in America (ELCA).

Concerning God's inerrant word Braaten writes:

It is finally for the sake of Christ alone that the church continues to regard the Bible as a book without equal in the history of human literature. For this reason the churches that claim the heritage of Luther and the Reformation still affirm the Bible as the Word of God. This is not meant in the fundamentalistic sense that *everything* in the Bible stands directly as the Word of God. . . . This valuation of the Bible as the Word of God is asserted with greater awareness of the historical *problems* involved in Biblical interpretation. . . . The role of the Bible in constructive theology is radically qualified today by historical consciousness. Luther believed that the literal meaning of Scripture is identical with its historical con-

---

[3]*This We Believe* (Milwaukee: Northwestern Publishing House, 1980), pp. 4, 5.

tent; things happened *exactly* as they were written down. Today it is impossible to assume the literal historicity of all things recorded. What the biblical authors report is not accepted as a literal transcript of the factual course of events. Therefore, critical scholars inquire behind the text and attempt to *reconstruct* the *real* history that took place.[4]

A LETTER FROM THE BISHOP

2) The Bishop of the ELCA, Dr. Herbert W. Chilstrom.

The following documentation is taken from a letter written by Bishop Chilstrom to Dr. Robert T. Jensen of San Antonio, Texas (not to be confused with Robert W. Jenson), while Chilstrom was serving as bishop of the Minnesota Synod of the Lutheran Church in America (LCA). The events leading up to the writing of this letter are described as follows:

Jensen, a Lutheran layman, had carried on an extensive correspondence with Bishop Chilstrom. A portion of the correspondence concerned a minority report that had been filed with the LCA by a retired LCA seminary professor and former missionary to Africa, Dr. H. Daniel Friberg. Friberg's report had been filed by way of a letter written to the Synod on May 4, 1984. In his letter, Friberg, as a member of an LCA synod committee, voiced his objections to the committee's conclusions concerning the absolute authority of God's Word. He stated in his letter to the synod:

> I dissociate myself from all in the report which is inconsistent with holding the whole of Scripture to be God's statements and as such, free from errors as first written down by the inspired writers and ask that this dissociation be recorded as a minority report.[5]

This prompted Jensen to write to Bishop Chilstrom again and ask him the following two questions:

1. Do you feel that Lutherans who believe in the inerrancy of Scripture as defined by the International Council on Biblical Inerrancy or as expressed by Dr. H. Daniel Friberg should remain in or leave the churches now forming the new Lutheran church?

---

[4]Carl E. Braaten, *Christian Dogmatics,* 2 vols., eds. Carl E. Braaten and Robert W. Jenson (Philadelphia: Fortress Press, 1984) 1:76, 77.

[5]David R. Barnhart, *The Church's Desperate Need for Revival* (Eagan, MN: Abiding Word Publications, 1986), p. 85.

2. If the New Lutheran Church desires to be truly inclusive and encourage the inclusion of Lutherans who concur with the ICBI and/or Dr. Friberg's statement, would you advocate employment of at least a minority of Lutheran theologians who concur with this more conservative view of Scripture on the faculty of our Lutheran seminaries and colleges so that these alternative views may be presented to students?[6]

Bishop Chilstrom responded to Jensen's questions in a letter dated February 27, 1985. A portion of the letter follows:

In my opinion, people who believe in the inerrancy of Scripture should be welcome to remain within the new Lutheran church. Dan Friberg is a case in point. He has a right to his opinions regarding the inerrancy of Scripture. But it is clear from his own statement that he realizes that his conjectures about errors or lack of errors in the first writings are speculation. I do not argue with those who say that they hold that as an opinion, so long as they do not make their opinion a standard position for the new church.

It is for this reason that I would not support the employment of Lutheran theologians who hold a view similar to that of Friberg. It is well and good for our seminary students to be exposed to the fact that there are some who hold this opinion. But it is quite another thing to advocate this view in our seminaries. *It would be out of character with any of the churches which are identifying with the new Lutheran church.*

As for admission standards, I would welcome any students who come to our seminaries who meet the admissions standards. I'm sure there are many who now come to our seminaries who hold the view that the original writings of Scripture were inerrant and infallible. Let them test those views in an arena where they will be challenged. And where other possibilities for understanding the glory and power of Scripture can be set forward.

Bishop Chilstrom makes his position concerning inerrancy very clear. He also recommends that those students who hold to the historic Lutheran doctrine of inerrancy should enter the "arena where they will be challenged and where other possibilities for understanding the . . . Scriptures can be set forward." In the following quota-

---

[6]Ibid., p. 86.

tions, Dr. J. Kincaid Smith relates his experiences as a student who went off to the seminary and faced this challenge.

THE "NEW THINKING"

3) "The Confession of a Former Liberal LCA Pastor," Dr. J. Kincaid Smith.

Smith is now a conservative pastor in the Evangelical Lutheran Synod (ELS).

> I was trained in the "new thinking" at Hamma School of Theology, now merged with Capital and called Trinity. . . . Accepting the "New Thinking" was no easy matter. I went off to seminary a simple Christian. Like other lay-people, I was not aware of the radical changes that had been taking place in the theology of the Lutheran Church. I had always trusted and believed Lutheran pastors and after a very difficult first quarter with the shock of the New Theology (and morality), I settled in and decided I had better get my head on straight, grow up from my "naive Sunday-school faith," and come into the 20th century.
>
> I graduated in January 1973 and took a call in an LCA congregation. I had fully accepted this "new theology or thinking," having first gone through a traumatic time in which the Christian faith with which I had arrived there with was "challenged." The reason which is presented for this challenging was to bring us to really "think through our theology," to "stretch" our faith, "to move us to a deeper understanding of the faith." This was the rationale which was presented when more conservative members of the constituency in the synod would question us about what was going on when they would hear from outspoken students and vicars what was being "taught." This really was deceitful because the aim and intention, as I came to know later as a more sophisticated initiate, was not to "stretch our faith" but to move us from the historical faith into the "new thinking." We all knew this was a *great shift*, that's why it was so traumatic, but we presented it as representing only minor doctrinal differences. . . . When I graduated in 1973, to the best of my knowledge, none of my classmates, nor I, believed in any of the miraculous elements in the Bible, in anything super-natural. . . . In retrospect I have to say that when I graduated from seminary in 1973, I was not a

heretic, I was apostate, I had completely departed from the Christian faith.[7]

The next quotation illustrates that the "formal strategy" for bringing about radical change, referred to by Smith in an earlier quotation, has obviously had results. Notice how much more openly the "new thinking" is presented to seminary students in 1988 as compared to the more subtle approach experienced by Smith in 1969. Of special interest is the warning given to the students concerning the expected effects of this teaching on their faith.

LOSING FAITH

4) "On Spiritual Life and the Saving or Finding Thereof," Dr. Jay C. Rochelle.

Rochelle is associate professor of worship and dean of the chapel at the Lutheran School of Theology at Chicago (ELCA), Chicago, Illinois. This address is taken from a message he delivered to the incoming students and reprinted in *Lutheran Partners,* a bimonthly magazine for those in the ELCA public ministries. Rochelle begins his message:

> I want to talk to you today about the problem of *losing your faith* while you are at seminary. I am not even going to quibble about whether or not this will happen. I am going to *assume* that it will. There are a number of ways in which this will happen, and I don't want you to be afraid of them. Some of the ways you will lose your faith are actually necessary and helpful to the process of becoming more deeply rooted in Christianity. Here are a few of the ways that it will happen. 1) You will lose your faith because you have placed your faith in a text [Bible], and you are about to undergo a process in which the text will be dismantled critically before your eyes and ears. This may cause some of you great consternation. The process of seminary education involves a rigorous examination of the root teaching, images, and metaphors of the faith. The people who assist in this process are called exegetes. Their task is to help you to look at the text with all the machinery of critical apparatus, as if the text were on the *same level* as *any other* form of literature. For some of you who have not experienced such a method

---

[7]J. Kincaid Smith, "The Confession of a Former Liberal LCA Pastor," *Christian News Encyclopedia,* 4 vols., ed. Herman Otten (Washington: Missourian Publishing Co., 1988), 3:2165.

before, there will be grave difficulties. It will appear as if your faith is being ripped out from under you; the underpinnings of your faith will seem to disappear when you apply critical methods to texts you have long revered in a simple fashion. . . . But when the process works correctly—and there are many people in this place whose aim is to help you beyond the NO-saying. . . . You [will] have learned to move from the literal to the symbolic meaning. . . . 2) You may lose your faith because you have placed it in a particular belief form. . . . You may find that the form by which you believed is given back to you renewed, restored, and redeemed for a deeper life. You may not, of course, and then you will have to find your way through the tradition to a new point of view. . . . 3) You may find your faith shattered because you have been accustomed to a particular form of worship. At LSTC we have a crossroads between Lutheran traditions and innovative patterns of worship. There is a lot of consternation about worship in general these days, and we work with all of the hopes and broken dreams over the course of the year.[8]

Dismantling the Bible and treating it as if it were on the same level as any other form of literature results in the abandonment of the doctrine of inerrancy. Quoting once again from Smith, "Once the line of strict inerrancy is crossed, the progression is always toward the denial of more and more until the heart [of the faith] is gone."[9] This will be documented in the chapters that follow.

---

[8]Jay C. Rochelle, "On Spiritual Life and the Saving and Finding Thereof," delivered to incoming students, Lutheran School of Theology, Chicago, IL, n.d. *Lutheran Partners,* January/February 1988, p. 13.

[9]Smith, loc. cit.

5.

CREATION

Position A

God created all things, including man, within the six days of creation. It is contrary to Scripture to hold that man evolved from lower forms of life.

1) The Bible.

For in six days the Lord made the heavens and the earth, the sea, and all that is in them, but he rested on the seventh day . . . (Exodus 20:11).

So God created man in his own image, in the image of God he created him; male and female he created them (Genesis 1:27). Jesus said: Have ye not read, that He which made them at the beginning made them male and female? (Matthew 19:4 KJV)

Position B

The story of creation in Genesis is a myth. We got here by a chance process of evolution that God directed or at least used.

1) *Search. Unit 3. Genesis 1-17,* Leader's Guide, Dr. James Limburg.

Search is a primary adult Bible-study program in the Evangelical Lutheran Church in America (ELCA). Limburg is professor of Old Testament at Luther Northwestern Theological Seminary (ELCA), St. Paul, Minnesota. He instructs the leader on the subject of creation versus evolution should it come up in class discussion.

At this point, if the matter comes up you should point out that the biblical creation accounts can be harmonized with an evolutionary theory of the origin of the human species. It is possible to take the position of *theistic evolution* which holds that the Bible tells *who* created, and the evolutionary explanation attempts to clarify the matter of *how* things came into being.[1]

2) *Evangelical Catechism.*

This book is used for adult instruction in the ELCA congregations. It was written by liberal German theologians and was translated and adapted for an American readership by eight highly influential theologians and professors of the ELCA—Dr. Paul Jersild, Professor Wayne Stumme, Harold Ditmanson, Charles Lutz, Dr. Paul Martinson, Dr. Philip Quanbeck, Professor Mons Tieg, and Irene Getz. They allow for the possibility of evolution:

> Biologists talk about the evolution of life on earth. Isn't it possible that God could have directed such an evolution?[2]

3) *Dr. David W. Preus,* presiding bishop of the former American Lutheran Church (ALC).

In *ACTS,* Preus leaves the door wide open for the acceptance of "theistic evolution." This simply means that we can now believe that God created everything through the process of *evolution.* He summarizes his views as follows:

> Certainly youngsters need not feel Christian faith or biblical truth threatened if the eternal God used 10 million years instead of 10,000. God's creative providence is no less manifest if there has been evolutionary development as well as a "big bang" to start things off.[3]

4) *Word and Witness,* "Understanding the Bible I," Foster R. McCurley, Jr., and Dr. John Reumann.

Word and Witness is a primary ELCA adult Bible-study program.

> We have dealt with the issues of the picture of creation and the division into seven days. We know that the picture of creation is one we cannot accept in a starkly literal sense. We have concluded that the seven-day phenomenon is a literary device. What then is left for us of value in Genesis 1?[4]

---

[1]James Limburg, *Search. Unit 3. Genesis 1-17,* Leader's Guide (Minneapolis: Augsburg Publishing House, 1983), p. 34.

[2]*Evangelical Catechism* (American Edition), trans. Lawrence W. Denef (Minneapolis: Augsburg Publishing House, 1982) p. 93.

[3]David W. Preus, "From the Presiding Bishop—Creation and Evolution," *ACTS* (The American Lutheran Church), April 1987.

[4]Foster R. McCurley, Jr., and John Reumann, *Word and Witness* (Philadelphia: Fortress Press, 1977), pp. 186, 187.

It should be noted that not everyone in the scientific world agrees with the preceding authors. One approach that has gained a lot of attention is Creation Science. The Institute for Creation Research, El Cajon, California, is an organization that publishes many books by scientists with advanced degrees who reject evolution in part because it is unscientific. One of the best introductions to the creationists' point of view from a purely scientific perspective can be found in *What Is Creation Science?*[5] However, Lutherans should be wary of Reformed attempts to prove through human reason (see Chapter 24) that the Bible is true. Luther compared that to using our bare hands against deadly weapons. The Word of God, not human reason, is our weapon against falsehood. Today's science will be tomorrow's example of primitive thinking, but the Word of God remains forever.

In conclusion, Dr. J. Kincaid Smith, a former liberal who once defended the theory of evolution, writes of the essential incompatibility of the biblical account of creation with evolutionary theories.

> Theologians who accept the Bible as being God's verbally inspired word, consistently agree that attempts to merge biblical creationist views with theories of evolution inevitably result in the kind of hybrid fables which are acceptable neither to the true scientist nor to the faithful theologian.

> The real historicity of the biblical account of the six-day creation, including the account of Adam and Eve, is absolutely essential to the integrity of the theology and the world view which is presented throughout the rest of Scripture. If Adam and Eve were not two real historical people who were created sinless but fell into the temptation of the devil, then there would have been no original sin and consequently no need for Christianity's redeeming Savior. You simply can't have it both ways. When that one thread is pulled, the thread of biblical creation, the vital systematic relationship between all the other doctrines of the historic Christian faith unravels at the seams. Without the biblical doctrine of creation, all the underpinnings give way and the very fabric of the Christian faith quickly disintegrates.[6]

---

[5]Henry M. Morris and Gary E. Parker, *What Is Creation Science?* (El Cajon, CA: Master Books, rev. ed., 1987).

[6]J. Kincaid Smith, "A Progression of Error, The Unraveling of the Christian Faith," unpublished paper.

Smith's words anticipate the next chapter on Adam and Eve and underline the inter-linking progression of error that results when any part of the whole, the interwoven fabric of God's inerrant Word, is torn loose.

6.

ADAM AND EVE

Position A

Adam and Eve were two real historical individuals created by God. Noah, Jonah, and Job were also real people. The Bible contains no myths.

1) The Bible.

So God created man in his own image, in the image of God he created him; male and female he created them (Genesis 1:27).

As it was in the days of Noah, so it will be at the coming of the Son of Man (Matthew 24:37).

For as Jonah was three days and three nights in the belly of a huge fish, so the Son of Man will be three days and three nights in the heart of the earth. The men of Nineveh will stand up at the judgment with this generation and condemn it (Matthew 12:40, 41 KJV).

As you know, we consider blessed those who have persevered. You have heard of Job's perseverance and have seen what the Lord finally brought about. The Lord is full of compassion and mercy (James 5:11)

We did not follow cleverly invented stories when we told you about the power and coming of our Lord Jesus Christ, but we were eyewitnesses of his majesty (2 Peter 1:16).

In the book *The Foolishness of God, The Place of Reason in the Theology of Martin Luther*, the late Dr. Siegbert W. Becker illustrates the clear position that Martin Luther held on Scripture and thus on the historicity of Adam and Eve.

The place of logical processes in Luther's theological thought comes into sharp focus when we examine the basic principles which underlie his whole approach to the interpretation of Scripture. It is well known that when Luther began his exegetical lectures at Wittenberg, he quickly turned away from the allegorical method, by which he said that Origen and Jerome had made fools of themselves. Finally he abandoned the method almost entirely.

Today we see a disguised revival of the allegorical method in the tendency to reduce the Scriptural account to the level and status of mythology. But those who seek to claim Luther for neo-orthodoxy ought to keep in mind that Luther insisted on what he called the "historical literal meaning which is consistent with the text."

An approach to Scripture which insists on this cannot be called irrational. And this was Luther's consistent exegetical method. He demanded that, in the interpretation of Scripture, "the natural speech is the Kaiser's wife, and it is to be preferred to all subtle, sharp, and sophistic interpretations. One must not depart from it unless one is compelled to do so by a clear article of faith, or else not one letter of Scripture can be maintained against the spiritual jugglers."

In the introduction to his Genesis lectures, Luther indicates clearly what method he will follow. This world, of which Moses speaks, Luther holds, is no allegorical world. It is a real world, and these are real creatures, and (anticipating Darwin by three hundred years) the days of Genesis One are real days.

Of the creation of Eve, in this same commentary, he says that we should forget all the foolish glosses of the scholastic commentators. He announces his resolution to treat the account as true history. Again he makes special mention of the fact that he believes that Adam's rib was a real rib. Scholastic theology had always allegorized the account of the Fall, at least in its theological significance, just as neo-orthodoxy mythologizes it away. But Luther urged his students to believe that the serpent was a real serpent, that the woman was a real woman, and that the man was a real man. He says, "According to this interpretation the serpent remains a serpent, but possessed by Satan, the woman remains a woman, and Adam remains Adam."[1]

---

[1]Siegbert W. Becker, *The Foolishness of God, The Place of Reason in the Theology of Martin Luther* (Milwaukee: Northwestern Publishing House, 1982), pp. 82, 83.

Position B

Adam and Eve are symbols of humanity and not real people. They never really existed. "Adam" just means "humankind." Their story is a myth containing important spiritual truth, just as the stories of Noah, Jonah, and Job are myths.

1) *Search. Unit 3. Genesis 1-17,* Leader's Guide, Dr. James Limburg.

Search is a primary adult Bible-study program in the Evangelical Lutheran Church in America (ELCA). Limburg is professor of Old Testament at Luther Northwestern Theological Seminary (ELCA), St. Paul, Minnesota.

> If the story of Adam and Eve is really a story about all of humankind, the story about Cain and Abel is the same. We have said that, like other material in Gen. 1-11, these chapters are not concerned only with God's people, but with all people. And they are not historical reports but rather stories or narratives which say something about all of humankind.[2]

2) *The Evangelical Catechism.*

This book is used for adult instruction in the ELCA congregations.

> None of the biblical creation stories are historical reports. Instead they talk about the relationship between God, human beings, and the world, using the language of symbols and images.[3]

3) *Affirm Series. Old Testament,* Teacher's Guide, catechism materials for seventh- and eighth-grade children.

> Genesis 1-11 is not meant to be scientific history. There is no way that we can check the events to be sure things happened just as described. Rather, these stories were written to give answers to the religious questions the people had.[4]

4) "Women of Spirit," *Scope*—Bible-Study Resource Book, Margaret Wold.

Scope magazine was the official magazine for women in the former American Lutheran Church (ALC). Wold is the chairperson of the

---

[2]James Limburg, *Search. Unit 3. Genesis 1-17,* Leader's Guide (Minneapolis: Augsburg Publishing House, 1983), p. 49.

[3]*Evangelical Catechism,* American Edition, trans. Lawrence W. Denef (Minneapolis: Augsburg Publishing House, 1982), p. 83.

[4]Stephen Ringo, *Affirm Series, Old Testament,* Teacher's Guide, eds. Susan Niemi Tetlie and Lori L. J. Rosenkvist (Minneapolis: Augsburg Publishing House, 1984), p. 2.

board of directors at Pacific Lutheran Theological Seminary (ELCA), Berkeley, California, and a faculty member of the religion department at California Lutheran University, Thousand Oaks, California.

> We will simply have to take the biblical account as it stands and do our best to understand it, keeping in mind that it is not an historical account we are dealing with but a theological reflection in *story* form.[5]

5) *Invitation to Faith,* Dr. Paul Jersild.

Jersild is academic dean, director of admissions, and professor of ethics at Lutheran Theological Southern Seminary (ELCA), Columbia, South Carolina. He is also one of the translators of the *Evangelical Catechism,* which is used in the ELCA for adult instruction.

> In previous ages there was no problem in understanding Adam and Eve as historical figures and the fall as an historical event. . . . During the last couple of centuries, however, our understanding of the story of Adam and Eve has undergone a profound change. We recognize today in the story of the fall a particular literary genre, present in other sacred scriptures as well, which theologians generally call *myth.* . . . In theology a myth expresses a profound truth about the structures of human life and our relation to God by means of an imaginative story involving God in interaction with human beings. . . . This means that the story of Adam and Eve is not an account of a historical event occurring sometime in the primordial past. They are representative figures, standing for you and me.[6]

Most of the writers quoted under Position B state variously that the accounts in Genesis 1-11 are: "not historical reports" (Limburg and the writers of the *Evangelical Catechism*); "not meant to be scientific history" (Ringo); and "not an historical account" (Wold). Their implication is that the biblical writers *themselves* did not believe that they were writing real history of actual events, but that they were consciously writing mythological stories "to give answers to the religious questions the people had" (Ringo).

By this implication they would enlist the "writers" of Genesis (they do not accept Moses' authorship) to support their own historical-critical view.

Jersild, who wrote *Invitation to Faith* for a more initiated readership, equates the "mythologies" of Genesis with the mythologies of

---

[5]Margaret Wold, "Women of Spirit," *Scope,* August 1985, p. 7.
[6]Paul Jersild, *Invitation to Faith* (Minneapolis: Augsburg, 1978), pp. 63, 64.

other religions. He, too, apparently believes that the prophets wrote in the form of history what they knew not to be true.

The internal evidence of Scripture itself simply does not support such a conclusion. Nowhere in Scripture do any of the writers indicate or demonstrate the slightest awareness that what they write is anything less than real history. The writers of both the Old and New Testaments, the prophets and the evangelists, consistently quote and apply Scripture in ways wholly inconsistent with the assumptions of the critics.

The historic critics are forced to their conclusions because their assumption that the supernatural is not possible (a claim that can not be supported scientifically) leaves them two assumptions. Either the *writers of the Scriptures* consciously wrote what they knew was not real history, or the *originators of the oral tradition* consciously made up and passed along what they knew not to be history.

Both assumptions are, of course, false. If the critics really hold the latter view—that the originators of the oral tradition were the only ones conscious that they were making up their material—then to imply that the *original writers* intentionally wrote mythology "to answer the people's religious questions" is at best intellectually dishonest and at worst sophistry, the intentional manipulation of the less informed lay people.

What more powerful and persuasive argument could there be with lay people who look to the *authority* of Scripture than to argue that the writers of Scripture did not believe that the accounts they were writing were actual history?

In such a deception the writers of Scripture, the original *authorities,* are enlisted into the ranks of the detractors of God's Word. This is one more example of the seducing subtlety of those who intentionally seek to move unsuspecting lay people (who trust their Lutheran pastors) into the acceptance of the "new thinking." Here we see one more step on the path to the denial of the heart and center of the Christian faith.

7.

THE OLD TESTAMENT— MOSES AS AUTHOR

Position A

Moses was the author of these sections of the Old Testament that are ascribed to him—the first five books which are commonly referred to as the Pentateuch. Jesus Christ himself witnessed to this fact.

1) The Bible.

A. Jesus refers to Moses as the author of the Pentateuch:

Did not Moses give you the law? (John 7:19)

What did Moses command you? (Mark 10:4)

B. Jesus also addressed the Sadducees:

Have you not read in the book of Moses, how in the bush ...? (Mark 12:19-27. In reference to Exodus 3:2-6).

Position B

The first five books of the Bible were written centuries after Moses died and came from various sources commonly identified as J, E, D, and P.

1) *Search. Unit 3. Genesis 1-17,* Leader's Guide, Dr. James Limburg.

Search is a primary adult Bible-study program in the Evangelical Lutheran Church in America (ELCA). Limburg is professor of Old Testament at Luther Northwestern Theological Seminary (ELCA), St. Paul, Minnesota.

The first books of the Old Testament appear to be a weaving together of different strands of material. Genesis 1 introduces the priestly, or "P" strand. . . .[1]

The point to be made is that in identifying two versions here, "J" and "P," we gain a better understanding of how the material fits together and what it means.[2]

2) *Search. Unit 9. Deuteronomy, Joshua, Judges,* Leader's Guide, Dr. Terence E. Fretheim.

Fretheim is professor of Old Testament at Luther Northwestern Theological Seminary (ELCA), St. Paul, Minnesota.

Where did the book of Deuteronomy come from? A brief look at its contents will help answer this question. The form of Deuteronomy is that of a sermon given by Moses to Israel just before he died and they entered into the promised land. . . . While the sermons are attributed to Moses, most scholars [liberal scholars] think that it comes from a period long *after* Moses, at least in its present form. Why then is Moses so prominent? The reason is quite simple. The *authors* were making a conscious effort to recapture the faith and spirit of the age of Moses, which they believed had been neglected. . . . The book of Deuteronomy is thus the product of a revival document.[3]

3) *Search. Unit 8. Exodus 19-40, Leviticus, Numbers,* Leader's Guide, David B. Kaplan.

Kaplan is listed on the clergy roster of the ELCA, Maryland Synod.

III. Consecration and theophany (Ex. 19:7-25)—The remainder of Exodus 19 seems confusing and hard to follow. Moses appears to go up and down the mountain several times. His precise location and the people's location are not easily determined. When we encountered such confusion in Exodus 1-18, we observed that the existing text is usually a composite of different *sources* representing different perspectives.[4]

---

[1]James Limburg, *Search. Unit 3. Genesis 1-17,* Leader's Guide (Minneapolis: Augsburg Publishing House, 1983), p. 21.

[2]Ibid., p. 54.

[3]Terence E. Fretheim, *Search. Unit 9. Deuteronomy, Joshua, Judges,* Leader's Guide (Minneapolis: Augsburg Publishing House, 1985) pp. 18, 19.

[4]David B. Kaplan, *Search. Unit 8. Exodus 19-40. Leviticus, Numbers,* Leader's Guide (Minneapolis: Augsburg Publishing House, 1985), p. 18.

In order to understand why the historic critics reject Moses' authorship of the Pentateuch (the first five books of the Old Testament), you have to remember that they do not believe anything supernatural is possible and that they *begin* with the notion that God could not have verbally inspired the biblical writers to write what they wrote. The same thing applies to the next chapter on Old Testament prophesy and authorship.

In the case of the Mosaic authorship, since they reason that God didn't verbally inspire the biblical writers, they infer that much of the material presented in the Pentateuch involves concepts too advanced to have originated at the time of Moses. They make this judgment primarily on the basis that archaeologists do not find such advanced materials in their archaeological investigations of surrounding peoples and civilizations from the same era as Moses. They reason that since the biblical people *must* have borrowed these more advanced concepts from their neighbors, an assumption without a shred of supporting *scientific* evidence, Genesis through Deuteronomy must have been written after these various concepts were in evidence among Israel's neighbors.

The obvious solution to their puzzle is the solution that they cannot accept, namely, that the biblical materials are advanced for their time precisely because they *did* originate among the *chosen* people who were led and inspired by God himself, and that it took some time before Israel's neighbors began to imitate *them*.

The best and most logical *documentary* evidence for the conservative position[5] is found in the one source that the arbitrary presuppositions of the historic critics will not allow, the Holy Scriptures themselves. The Scriptures, given that supernatural events are possible, support the historic Christian position.

In the *Search* quotation, (2) above, Fretheim, after alleging that Deuteronomy was written long after the time of Moses, attempts to answer the obvious question of why the figure of Moses was so prominent in the book of Deuteronomy if Moses was not the author and if it wasn't from his time? He proposes that "the reason is quite simple" and then proceeds to give an answer that is neither simple nor obvious. He suggests that Deuteronomy was written "long after Moses" as a "revival document" and that "The authors were making a conscious effort to recapture the faith and spirit of the age of Moses." This would be tantamount to someone in our day attempting

---

[5]The conservative Lutheran positions concerning the authorship of the books of the Bible is presented in John Schaller's *Book of Books: A Brief Introduction to the Bible* (Milwaukee: Northwestern Publishing House, 1990).

to "recapture" the spirit of the Reformation by fabricating a theology book with Luther's name appearing prominently and with his apparent authorship and then presenting it to the scholarly world as a lucky discovery.

Such an explanation for the authorship of the book of Deuteronomy (and the other books of the Pentateuch) would also assure that the authors were frauds and deceivers. Consider the contents and nature of these books as well as that of the other books of the Bible. They are all books of impeccable moral teaching, of intricate and highly developed theology that consistently agree with and complement the theology of each other book without contradiction.

The notion that such books were written by frauds and deceivers is psychologically, sociologically, and historically inconceivable. Considering such internal evidence honestly and without bias lends itself only to the conclusion that all was divinely, verbally inspired.

If those who hold the historic Christian faith are right, then the historic critics are left to grapple in the dark for every imaginable answer except the only actually *true* and sufficient answer, the one answer they will not tolerate, the plain answer of God's Word, the Holy Scriptures.

In their zeal to bring the church along with them in their error, the historic critics have become like the Greek sophists who were known for fabricating arguments to support their faulty notions. In the process, they destroy the faith among the lay people.

8.

THE OLD TESTAMENT —
PROPHECY AND AUTHORSHIP

Position A

The Old Testament prophets foretold the coming of Jesus Christ, God's Son, the Savior of the world. Whatever the New Testament teaches about the authorship of the books of the Old Testament is true. The books of Isaiah and Daniel were written by Isaiah and Daniel, respectively. Jesus Christ himself bore witness to this fact.

1) The Bible.

> And I will put enmity between you and the woman, and between your offspring and hers; he will crush your head. and you will strike his heel (Genesis 3:15). (Cf. Romans 16:20.)

> Therefore the Lord himself will give you a sign: The virgin will be with child and will give birth to a son, and will call him Immanuel (Isaiah 7:14). (Cf. Matthew 1:23.)

> In my vision at night I looked, and there before me was one like a son of man, coming with the clouds of heaven. He approached the Ancient of Days and was led into his presence. He was given authority, glory and sovereign power; all peoples, nations and men of every language worshiped him. His dominion is an everlasting dominion that will not pass away, and his kingdom is one that will never be destroyed (Daniel 7:13,14). (Cf. Matthew 24:30.)

> Jesus appears to the disciples: "He said to them, 'This is what I told you while I was still with you: Everything must be fulfilled that is written about me in the Law of Moses, the Prophets and the Psalms'" (Luke 24:44).

Even after Jesus had done all these miraculous signs in their presence, they still would not believe in him. This was to fulfill the word of Isaiah the prophet: "Lord, who has believed our message and to whom has the arm of the Lord been revealed?" For this reason they could not believe, because, as Isaiah says elsewhere: "He has blinded their eyes and deadened their hearts, so they can neither see with their eyes, nor understand with their hearts, nor turn—and I would heal them." Isaiah said this because he saw Jesus' glory and spoke about him (John 12:37-41).

Position B

There are no prophecies in the Old Testament that actually refer to the man Jesus Christ. Whatever the New Testament says about the authorship of the books of the Old Testament is not necessarily true. Isaiah and Daniel were written, at least in part, by others. Our Lord either accommodated himself to error or he did not know better.

The liberal scholars explain away the miracle of prophecy by assigning the Old Testament books to *unknown* authors who supposedly wrote *after* the occurrence of the predicted events. For example, the book of Daniel, written by the prophet Daniel in the sixth century B.C., is said to have been written by someone else around 160 B.C. We know that the prophet Isaiah wrote the book of Isaiah in the eighth century B.C. and that chapters 40-66 speak about the coming of Jesus. The liberals believe that these chapters were written by an unknown author, or possibly two authors, who spoke of Israel's hope for rescue from the exile and Babylonian captivity rather than the predictive prophecy of the coming of Christ.

1) *The Lutheran Standard,* Dr. William A. Poovey.

The Lutheran Standard was the official magazine of the former American Lutheran Church (ALC). Poovey is a retired ALC seminary professor and the author of many books. A reader wrote to *The Lutheran Standard* and asked the following question concerning the first messianic prophecy recorded in the Old Testament: "Is Genesis 3:15 a prophecy of the coming of Christ?" The following quotation is taken from Poovey's response.

It long has been regarded as messianic, although it is not cited in the New Testament as a fulfilled prophecy, and it was not related to the promised Messiah until late in the Old Testament period—if at all. . . . But we must be careful

75

not to read our New Testament understanding into Old Testament passages![1] (cf. Romans 16:20 KJV)

2) *Christian Dogmatics,* Braaten/Jenson, the *primary* theology textbook used in all seminaries of the Evangelical Lutheran Church of America (ELCA).

The prophet responsible for Isaiah 56-66 (so-called "Third Isaiah") introduces a new element into the creation witness. . . . [2]

When we come to Second *Isaiah,* the *destruction* of *Jerusalem* is *history.* . . . Though the messianic element of the victorious king is not lacking in Second Isaiah's description of the suffering servant, the prophet did not dare to identify him with an historic figure.[3]

As stated earlier, there was only one Isaiah and he spoke *before* the destruction of Jerusalem. Liberals refer to three Isaiahs and date the prophecies after the predicted events.

3) *Affirm Series, Old Testament,* Teacher's Guide. Catechism materials for seventh-and eighth-grade children.

The exiles waited about 50 years, wondering if God would act to save them. . . . The prophet *2* Isaiah is thought to have written the portion of Isaiah from Chapter 40 to the end of the book. . . . Four servant songs tell of this emerging mission: Isaiah 42:1-9; 49:1-7; 50:4-11; 52:13; 53:12. In these passages we read that God's glory will be revealed through a servant. . . . We do not know who the particular servant was of whom Isaiah writes.[4]

The four servant songs listed in the preceding quotation have long been accepted as clear prophecies of Jesus.

4) *The Interpreter's Dictionary of the Bible.*

This is a recommended resource book for *Search* and *Word and Witness,* two primary ELCA adult Bible-study programs.

---

[1]William A. Poovey, "Question Box," *The Lutheran Standard,* March 2, 1984, p. 28.

[2]Philip J. Hefner, *Christian Dogmatics,* 2 vols., eds. Carl E. Braaten and Robert W. Jenson (Philadelphia: Fortress Press, 1984), 1:287.

[3]Hans Schwarz, *Christian Dogmatics,* 2:487-490.

[4]Stephen Ringo, *Affirm Series. Old Testament,* Teacher's Guide, eds. Susan Miemi Tetlie and Lori L. J. Rosenkvist (Minneapolis: Augsburg Publishing House, 1984), pp. 35, 36.

Our author played fair by the standards of his day, for he did not create his message, but received it from the *tradition* of the apocalyptic movement. This tradition he handed on through the medium of the character he had *created,* Daniel, and, unhampered by our ideas of identity and authorship, gave his message in all good faith to those who stood in sore need of it.[5]

Our concluding remarks for Chapter 7 can be applied here as well. In addition, since the historic critics do not believe that God has planned out and executed history according to his immutable will, but that all history unfolded purely by chance, the prophets could not possibly have foretold of future persons and events. Having rejected the one vital fact in the matter, the critics *must* conclude that prophesies of persons and events that eventually occurred were written after the fact.

The historic critics think that they are salvaging Christianity by attempting to hold onto some "essence" while letting go of the historic foundation upon which it rests.

---

[5]*The Interpreter's Dictionary of the Bible,* 4 vols., ed. Emory Stevens Bucke (Nashville: Abingdon Press, 1962), 3:768.

9.

THE WORDS OF JESUS

Position A

Jesus Christ really made all the statements attributed to him and recorded in the New Testament.

1) The Bible.

> For even the Son of Man did not come to be served, but to serve, and to give his life as a ransom for many (Mark 10:45).

> This is my blood of the covenant, which is poured out for many for the forgiveness of sins (Matthew 26:28). (Cf. Mark 14:24.)

> He began to teach them that the Son of Man must suffer many things . . . that he must be killed and after three days rise again (Mark 8:31ff).

Please note that the above words of Jesus Christ were chosen as an example because they are the very same words referred to in the first quotation under *Position B,* which follows.

Position B

Many, if not all, of the statements attributed to Jesus Christ in the New Testament were not made by Jesus but were added by the early church.

1) *Christian Dogmatics,* Braaten/Jenson, the *primary* theology textbook used in all seminaries of the Evangelical Lutheran Church in America (ELCA).

> Mark 10:45 has Jesus say that the Son of Man came to give his life "as a ransom for many," and the accounts of the Last

Supper speak of Jesus' blood as his "blood of the covenant, which is poured out for many" (Mark 14:24) and "my blood of the covenant, which is poured out for many for the forgiveness of sins" (Matthew 26:28). Such passages, in their present form at least, are usually regarded as having come *not from Jesus himself* but from later interpretative traditions. The same is true of the instances where Jesus predicts his own death and resurrection, such as Mark 8:31ff and 9:31, and parallels in the other Synoptics. They are interpretations attributed to Jesus after the fact. But aside from such scanty references, the Synoptics even in their final form afford *little explicit interpretation* of Jesus' work.[1]

2) *Search. Unit 5. Matthew 1-16,* Leader's Guide, Dr. Donald H. Juel.

Search is a primary ELCA adult Bible-study program. Juel is associate professor of New Testament at Luther Northwestern Theological Seminary (ELCA), St. Paul, Minnesota.

The picture we have of Jesus' life is made of bits and pieces taken from various Gospels, with generous portions of *imagination* added.[2]

BISHOP CHILSTROM RECOMMENDS . . .

3) *What Christians Believe,* Dr. Hans Schwarz.

Schwarz is a professor of systematic theology. He served at Trinity Lutheran Seminary (ELCA), Columbus, Ohio; is a faculty member at the University of Regensburg, Regensburg, Germany; and is listed in the *1991 ELCA Yearbook* as a visiting professor at Lutheran Theological Southern Seminary (ELCA), Columbia, South Carolina. He remains on the clergy roster of the ELCA and is one of the authors of *Christian Dogmatics.*

What Christians Believe was listed as a main selection of the April 1988 list of the Augsburg Reading Club. Bishop Herbert W. Chilstrom provided the following endorsement: "Schwarz's well-written book would be helpful for both congregational groups and individual readers. . . . He draws the reader into the heart of the issues so that one can wrestle with them. I heartily recommend this book."

---

[1]Gerhard O. Forde, *Christian Dogmatics,* 2 vols., eds. Carl E. Braaten and Robert W. Jenson (Philadelphia: Fortress Press, 1984), 2:12, 13.

[2]Donald H. Juel, *Search. Unit 5. Matthew 1-16,* Leader's Guide (Minneapolis: Augsburg Publishing House, 1984), p. 17.

In the following quotation Schwarz casts doubt concerning statements attributed to Jesus:

> Modern historical science has given us two important facts about Jesus of Nazareth. First, through careful study of the available sources and through critical comparison with his contemporaries, Jesus has emerged as an actual historical figure who has passed through the acid test of historical study. . . . Second, beyond these reliable conclusions about the historical figure of Jesus, modern science has also shown us that this information is not sufficient to write a biography of Jesus with all details included. Many of the stories about Jesus presented by the evangelists must be recognized as narratives and *not* as reports. They were written with the intention of showing how important and significant Jesus is. They are *not* neutral and unbiased *factual* reports.[3]

4) *Jesus in the Church's Gospels*, Dr. John Reumann.

Reumann, a professor at Lutheran Theological Seminary at Philadelphia (ELCA), Philadelphia, Pennsylvania, served as a member of the Commission for the New Lutheran Church. He was recently named to chair a panel that will conduct a major study of ministry for the ELCA.[4] Reumann is also the New Testament author of *Word and Witness,* another primary ELCA adult Bible-study program.

> There are many books about Jesus of Nazareth—what he did and what he said—and more are being written every year. This one is offered in order to suggest why it should no longer be possible to present as serious history the traditional "lives" of the sort which deal with Jesus "from the cradle to the grave"—and to indicate why even the *teachings attributed* to *Jesus* need to be sifted critically so as to separate what might actually have been spoken by Jesus from that which stems from the early church.[5]

5) The Jesus Seminar.

The Jesus Seminar is a group of 125 New Testament scholars and seminary professors from almost all of the mainline denominations. They have been meeting since 1985 to determine if Jesus actually

[3]Hans Schwarz, *What Christians Believe* (Philadelphia: Fortress Press, 1987), p. 40.

[4]Jean Caffey Lyles, "Reumann to Chair Ministry Task Force," *The Lutheran,* August 10, 1988, p. 20.

[5]John Reumann, *Jesus in the Church's Gospels* (Philadelphia: Fortress Press, 1968), p. vii.

said all of the words attributed to him in the Bible. After much debate, seminar members reached agreement as to the authenticity of Jesus' words by the process of *voting*.

An article about the seminar in *The Lutheran* (ELCA) states that "only three of a dozen 'blessings' and 'woes' in the Gospels of Matthew and Luke were deemed to have derived from Jesus."[6] The article also points out that "they have hesitated to broadcast the assured results of *historical-critical* scholarship out of fear of public controversy and political reprisals."

As a result of additional meetings *seminar members* concluded that Jesus did not speak the words of John 3:16, the parable of the "Rich Man and Lazarus" (Luke 16:19-31), the "Wicked Tenants" (Mark 12:1-11), or the seven final words from the cross. Nor did he speak of the end of the world or of his Second Coming. Furthermore, there was no Jewish trial of Jesus nor was any Jewish crowd involved in his condemnation.[7] At a meeting in Atlanta, Georgia, on October 14, 1988, seminar members decided that the Lord's Prayer was written years after the crucifixion by early Christians, not by Jesus.[8] In the planning stages is a movie tentatively titled "Christ the Man," in which Jesus would perform miraculous healings; but he would not walk on water, there would be no reference to a virgin birth, nor would there be any hint of a resurrection.[9]

The sixth meeting of the seminar was held at Luther Northwestern Theological Seminary (ELCA) in St. Paul, Minnesota, on the weekend of October 17, 1987.[10] Since that event, seminar members have published their first book, *The Parables of Jesus: A Report of the Jesus Seminar*.[11] Listed among the "Fellows of the Jesus Semi-

---

[6]"Scholars' Vote on the Sayings of Jesus," *The Lutheran*, January 15, 1986, p. 17.

[7]Clark Morphew, "Did Jesus Actually Say That? Scholars Scrutinize the Bible," *St. Paul Pioneer Press Dispatch*, Oct. 17, 1987. *Christian News*, Nov. 1, 1987, p. 22.

[8]Gustav Niebuhr, "Liberal Scholars Assert That Jesus Did Not Compose the Lord's Prayer," *Religious News Service*, October 17, 1988. *Christian News*, October 24, 1988, p. 1.

[9]Gustav Niebuhr, "Watch Out, Martin Scorcese! 'Christ the Man' Being Planned," *Religious News Service*, Nov. 8, 1988. *Christian News*, Nov. 21, 1988, p. 1.

[10]Willmar Thorkelson, "Scholars Debating Jesus' Sayings Spell Trouble for Lutheran Seminary," *Religious News Service*, Oct. 27, 1987. *Christian News*, Nov. 2, 1987, p. 22. Thorkelson is also a reporter for *The Lutheran*.

[11]Robert W. Funk, Bernard Brandon Scott, and James R. Butts, *The Parables of Jesus: A Report of the Jesus Seminar* (Sonoma: Polebridge Press, 1988).

nar," pp. 94-97, are ELCA professors Dr. Arland Jacobson, assistant professor of religion, Concordia College, Moorhead, Minnesota, and Dr. Richard L. Jeske, professor of New Testament, and Dr. Robert D. Kysar, professor of New Testament, Lutheran Theological Seminary at Philadelphia.[12]

The same assumptions that lead the historic critics to reject the Mosaic authorship of the Pentateuch, the reality of prophesy, and, as we shall see in the chapters ahead, the miracles, the deity of Christ, the Trinity, the Atonement, and a myriad of other things, lead them to conclude that "the man Jesus" simply could *not* have said much or most of what the Bible reports him as saying. Since they believe that he was not the virgin born prophesied Messiah and Savior, and that he had no consciousness of himself as being the Savior or as being God, he *could not* have said any of the things that would in substance contradict their presuppositions. Again, false presuppositions force them to stumble over the truth.

It seems significant that the historic critics invariably refer to our Lord as "Jesus" rather than as "Jesus Christ," "the Christ," or "the Lord." This small detail signifies their attitude toward the Savior. Jesus, derived from the Hebrew *Yeshua,* was his given name, *Christ* was his title. Christ derives from the Greek equivalent of the Hebrew *Messiah,* which meant *anointed* and signified the one chosen by God as Savior of the world. The Messiah of prophesy was to be Immanuel, God with us (Isaiah 7:14). Isaiah also calls the Messiah "Wonderful Counselor, Mighty God, Everlasting Father, Prince of Peace" (Isaiah 9:6). Why do the critics avoid the messianic title of our Lord Jesus Christ? They simply have moved through a progression of denials, including the denial of Jesus' real deity, that leaves "the person Jesus" unqualified for the title *Christ.*

When they begin to discover what the historic critics are proposing in the place of Christianity, faithful Christian lay people invariably ask, "Well then, what *do* these people believe?" The critics claim that they believe "the gospel," although the "gospel" that they propose is not recognizable as the gospel of the historic Christian faith, the faith of the Lutheran Confessions. In their zeal to "demythologize" the Bible, they would obliterate every vestige of "the faith that was once for all entrusted to the saints" (Jude 3).

It is comforting to know that despite the critics, God's Word, the words of Jesus [Christ] will never pass away. "Jesus Christ is the same yesterday and today and forever" (Hebrews 13:8).

---

[12]Herman Otten, "Voices of Jesus Seminar Scholars Adopted at Roman Catholic and Protestant Seminaries," *Christian News,* January 2, 1989, p. 1.

10.

MIRACLES

Position A

All miracles recorded in the Old and New Testaments actually and historically occurred.

1) Miracles—a definition.

A miracle is an act which transcends human powers of accomplishment and human ability of explanation. It is not an unnatural occurrence, but a supernatural one. At times it may be exactly like a natural event; but the conditions under which it takes place are such that we classify it as a miracle, for instance, when rain comes in answer to prayer, as in the case of Elijah, 1 Kings 18:41ff; James 5:17f. When a miracle takes place, God Himself intervenes and makes His presence felt in a special manner. . . . The Bible is full of reports of miraculous happenings. The chain of such events begins on the first page, in the story of the creation of the world, and it continues to the last page, where the message of an angel who brought revelations to John is recorded, Rev. 22:8. These miracles are of many different kinds, some occurring in inanimate nature, others, on and in man; some visible, others invisible; some bringing health, others bringing punishment; some performed without human agents, others, through prophets, Apostles, etc. If we take everything miraculous out of the Bible, how little will there be left![1]

---

[1]William Arndt, *Bible Difficulties* (St. Louis: Concordia Publishing House, 1932), pp. 25, 26. *Bible Difficulties* and *Does the Bible Contradict Itself* (also by Arndt) have been revised and combined into *Bible Difficulties & Seeming Contradictions,* eds. Robert G. Hoerber and Walter Roehrs (St. Louis: Concordia Publishing House, 1987).

2) Martin Luther.

> . . . although God ordained and created all these things by His Word, nevertheless He is not thereby so bound to these rules that *He* cannot change them according to *His Will*.[2]

Position B

"Miracles" found in the Bible must be understood as ways of conveying spiritual truths, not as actual historical events.

1) *Christian Dogmatics,* Braaten/Jenson, the *primary* theology textbook used in all seminaries of the Evangelical Lutheran Church in America (ELCA).

> According to the biblical witnesses, miracles are intrinsically related to the work of salvation. At the high points of God's salvation-history, we are confronted with miracles; the parting of the Red Sea, the virginal conception of Jesus, his resurrection as the Christ. Of course, one could object that miracles are literary devices to underscore the reality of God's salvational activity. Thus there might be no historical reality that pertains to them. Yet today even the severest critics of the New Testament sources admit that Jesus did indeed perform acts that his contemporaries regarded as miraculous and that we still consider highly unusual. . . . We must concede the possibility that miracles must have been attributed to people simply to enhance their status, that is, their special relationship to the gods. Each claim to the truth must be carefully analyzed, and it should not be excluded *a priori* that some of the miracles attributed to Jesus may have no historical basis and serve only to emphasize his exceptional status (author's emphasis).[3]

> The exaltation of Jesus Christ moves from his resurrection on the third day through the forty days of his self-manifestation to the day of his "ascension." The mythical features of this trajectory of exaltation are obvious the moment we ask where Jesus went when he ascended to heaven. Christian art has depicted the ascension as a visible movement of Jesus' body through the clouds, with the disciples standing by, looking up and watching him disappear. In some realistic

---

[2]*What Luther Says,* ed. Ewald M. Plass, 3 vols. (St. Louis: Concordia Publishing House, 1959), 2:953. Now available in a one-volume edition.

[3]Hans Schwarz, *Christian Dogmatics,* 2 vols., eds. Carl E. Braaten and Robert W. Jenson (Philadelphia: Fortress Press, 1984), 2:282, 283.

paintings all one can see is the feet, the rest of the body having been enveloped by clouds. The need to demythologize the story should not, however, weaken our sense for the message it contains. . . . The end of Jesus' time on earth is like the beginning. It is a mystery clothed in the language of *myth* and *symbol*. History does not give us a key to unlock it.[4]

2) *Search. Unit 1. Acts 1-8,* Leader's Guide, Dr. David Tiede.

Search is a primary ELCA adult Bible-study program. Tiede is the president of Luther Northwestern Theological Seminary (ELCA), St. Paul, Minnesota.

Many of the stories told in Acts were probably well known to most of the readers. The author wastes no effort trying to prove that these things really happened. A few of the stories may have even seemed strange to Luke. The miracles performed by those who carried handkerchiefs away from Paul's body and the evil spirit that beat up the traveling exorcists (Acts 19) seem to be simply part of the lore about Paul.[5]

3) *Search. Unit 8. Exodus 19-40. Leviticus, Numbers,* Leader's Guide, David B. Kaplan.

Kaplan is listed on the clergy roster of the ELCA, Maryland Synod.

Some interpretive helps are necessary for this passage. *Above everything else Numbers 22-24 should be looked at as a story.* It may contain historical data, but like a parable its point or truth is not dependent upon the historical accuracy of the events it describes. For instance, we'll miss the thrust of 22:21-30 entirely if we get locked into a debate about whether Balaam's ass really talked. The passage, like many others in the story, *is intended as humor* with an ironic twist: the ass is smarter than its owner.[6]

4) *Search. Unit 10. Ruth, 1 & 2 Samuel, 1 & 2 Kings,* Leader's Guide, Dr. Terence E. Fretheim.

Fretheim is professor of Old Testament at Luther Northwestern Theological Seminary (ELCA), St. Paul, Minnesota.

---

[4]Carl E. Braaten, *Christian Dogmatics,* 1:552, 553.

[5]David Tiede, *Search. Unit 1. Acts 1-8,* Leader's Guide (Minneapolis: Augsburg Publishing House, 1983), p. 6.

[6]David B. Kaplan, *Search. Unit 8. Exodus 19-40, Leviticus, Numbers,* Leader's Guide, p. 85.

The picture of the ministry of Elisha is not as clear and consistent as that of Elijah. The beautiful story of the healing of Naaman the leper (2 Kings 5) stands beside other stories which call his ministry into question (for example 2 Kings 2:23-25). The *miraculous* element sometimes seems to have been greatly *exaggerated* (cf. 2 Kings 6:1-23). Probably the word for many of these stories is *legend*. They have an historical nucleus, but they have been exaggerated later in order to stress the power and authority of the prophet.[7]

5) *The Comings of God,* Dr. Richard Simon Hanson.
Hanson is professor of religion at Luther College (ELCA), Decorah, Iowa.

The *heavenly host* is the Biblical way of talking about the *stars* in the sky. . . .[8]

6) *Word and Witness,* Leaders Guide, edited by Frank W. Klos and Donald R. Richaske.
Word and Witness is a primary ELCA adult Bible-study program.

Move now to the crossing of the Red Sea. Use the map to indicate that scholars are fairly well agreed that the sea in question is what was known as the Reed Sea, probably a shallow, watery marshland choked with rushes. A stiff wind could clear a passageway through for people afoot leading their animals. The wind growing into the intensity of a violent storm could cause heavy chariot wheels to sink through the mucky bottom while the churning water swirled over the drivers.[9]

The authors of the above quotation contradict the clear words of Scripture, which says that the waters were *divided*, that they went into the midst of the sea on *dry* ground, and that the waters were a wall on their *right* hand *and* on their *left*.

Then the Lord said to Moses, "Why are you crying out to me? Tell the Israelites to move on. Raise your staff and

---

[7]Terence E. Fretheim, *Search. Unit 10. Ruth, 1 & 2 Samuel, 1 & 2 Kings,* Leader's Guide, p. 84.

[8]Richard Simon Hanson, *The Comings of God* (Minneapolis: Augsburg Publishing House, 1981), p. 98.

[9]James L. Barkenquast, John Stevens Kerr, Frank W. Klos, and Donald R. Pichaske, *Word and Witness,* eds. Frank W. Klos and Donald R. Pichaske, Division for Parish Services (Philadelphia: Lutheran Church in America, 1977), pp. 140, 141.

stretch out your hand over the sea to divide the water so
that the Israelites can go through the sea on dry ground.
. . ." Then Moses stretched out his hand over the sea, and all
that night the Lord drove the sea back with a strong east
wind and turned it into dry land. The waters were divided,
and the Israelites went through the sea on dry ground, with
a wall of water on their right and on their left (Exodus
14:15,16,21,22).

The comments we have made at the conclusion of the last several
chapters about the effect of the radical anti-supernatural presupposition of the historic critics applies singularly to the reality of miracles.
Nothing more clearly epitomizes and portrays the basic difference between the historic critics and historic Christians than the affirmation
or the denial of the real occurrence, the historicity, of the *miracles* of
the Bible. The world views represented by each position are light
years apart.

The God of orthodox Christianity is a God who planned and willed
everything, including his miracles, before all time. The God of the
historic critics neither works miracles nor intervened in history or in
the natural processes of nature and has no plan for history and inspires no Scripture. As such, he is little more than an unseen benign
observer. There is no indication that this God is malevolent or benevolent, since he neither plans or wills anything nor intervenes in the
affairs of man or the natural order of things. When all things are
considered, the "God" of those who would "demythologize" the Bible
is, for all practical purposes, *mythological.*

The denial of miracles by the critics reaches its most wretched
pinnacle in the next chapter: the denial of the Virgin Birth and of
God's Fatherhood of his only begotten Son, Jesus Christ.

11.

THE VIRGIN BIRTH

Position A

We believe that the Virgin Birth is a biological miracle as taught in the Holy Scriptures. Jesus Christ did not have a human father.

1) The Bible.

> This is how the birth of Jesus Christ came about: His mother Mary was pledged to be married to Joseph, but before they came together, she was found to be with child through the Holy Spirit (Matthew 1:18).

> The angel answered, "The Holy Spirit will come upon you, and the power of the Most High will overshadow you." So the holy one to be born will be called the Son of God (Luke 1:35).

2) The Lutheran Confessions, *The Book of Concord*—Formula of Concord.

> Mary, the most blessed virgin, did not conceive a mere, ordinary human being, but a human being who is truly the Son of the most high God, as the angel testifies. He demonstrated his divine majesty even in his mother's womb in that he was born of a virgin without violating her virginity. Therefore she is truly the mother of God and yet remained a virgin.[1]

3) The Apostles, Nicene, and Athanasian creeds; the three universal or ecumenical creeds found in most Lutheran hymnals, which represent the basic core of the Christian faith.

---

[1] *The Book of Concord,* trans. and ed. Theodore G. Tappert (Philadelphia: Fortress Press, 1959), Formula of Concord, Solid Declaration, Art. VIII., 24, p. 595.

a. I believe in God the Father Almighty, Maker of heaven and earth. And in Jesus Christ, His only Son, our Lord; who was conceived by the Holy Ghost, born of the Virgin Mary . . . (Apostles Creed).

b. I believe . . . in one Lord Jesus Christ, the only begotten Son of God, begotten of the Father before all worlds . . . who for us men, and for our salvation, came down from heaven, and was incarnate by the Holy Ghost of the Virgin Mary, and was made man . . . (Nicene Creed).

c. Furthermore, it is necessary to everlasting salvation that he also believe faithfully the incarnation of our Lord Jesus Christ. For the right faith is, that we believe and confess that our Lord Jesus Christ, the Son of God, is God and Man; God of the Substance of the Father, begotten before the worlds; and Man of the substance of His mother, born in the world; Perfect God and perfect Man, of a reasonable soul and human flesh subsisting (Athanasian Creed).

4) The Virgin Birth—its importance.

Jesus Christ was born of the Virgin Mary—The doctrine of the Virgin Birth of Christ is a *fundamental* article of our faith, the denial of which makes saving faith in Christ impossible.

A true child of God finds it no harder to believe this miracle than any other. If God in the beginning institutes natural conception through the union of husband and wife, the same almighty power enables Him to use other means. "With God nothing shall be impossible" (Luke 1:37).

If we do not believe this, but regard Jesus as the true, natural son of Joseph and Mary, then we are compelled by Holy Scripture to regard Jesus as having been born in sin like all the other sons of men (John 3:6; Eph. 2:3). The Virgin Birth was God's way of producing a holy child, who was also the Son of God and therefore able to fulfill the Law perfectly, suffer our punishment, and thus bring about everlasting atonement and reconciliation of the world to Himself (2 Cor. 5:19). Our Savior was God and man in one person; that fact makes our redemption certain.[2]

---

[2] Otto E. Sohn, "What's the Answer?" *Lutheran Witness*, April 9, 1957.

Position B

Jesus Christ was not born of a virgin. We are not sure who his physical father was—perhaps Joseph or an itinerant Roman soldier. The early church honored Jesus by pretending his only father was God.

1) *Christian Dogmatics,* Braaten/Jenson, the *primary* theology textbook used in all seminaries of the Evangelical Lutheran Church in America (ELCA).

> . . . the story of the descent of the Son of God to earth and his ascent into heaven *cannot* be taken *literally.* The question is whether the meaning of the *myth* of the incarnation can be saved without taking it literally yet without getting rid of its mythic structure.

> . . . Finally, the history and phenomenology of religions have called our attention to the *mythic* character of the incarnation. The *notion* of the pre-existent Son of God becoming a human being in the womb of a virgin and then returning to his heavenly home is bound up with a *mythological* picture of the world that clashes with our modern scientific world view.

> The primary interest of dogmatics is to interpret the virgin birth as a *symbol* and not as a *freakish* intervention in the course of nature.

> The main statements of the *Apostles Creed* are so bound up with its *mythological* form that to get rid of the myth would destroy the creed in toto. Can modern people still be expected to accept the creed, with its mythological elements?[3]

2) *Search. Unit 9. Deuteronomy, Joshua, Judges,* Leader's Guide, Dr. Terence E. Fretheim.

Search is a primary ELCA adult Bible-study program. Fretheim is professor of Old Testament at Luther Northwestern Theological Seminary (ELCA), St. Paul, Minnesota.

In the following quotation, note the subtle reference to the historical account of Jesus' birth within the context of *doubt* concerning the historical accuracy of the battle of Jericho.

> Joshua and the battle of Jericho. . . . Many people are profoundly bothered by this story. . . . The story of the battle of

---

[3]Carl E. Braaten, *Christian Dogmatics,* 2 vols., eds. Carl E. Braaten and Robert W. Jenson (Philadelphia: Fortress Press, 1984), 1:529, 527, 546, 528, 529.

Jericho is told in terms of religious ceremony. . . . Because of the liturgical casting of the narrative, it is very difficult to determine what it is that *actually* happened at Jericho. Did the event take place just as the chapter tells it, or (like many liturgical celebrations of the *Christmas story*) do we have to read between the lines to find out what actually happened?[4]

3) *The Interpreter's Dictionary of the Bible.*

This is a recommended resource book for *Search* and *Word and Witness*, two primary ELCA adult Bible-study programs.

Later Christian doctrine laid great emphasis upon the virgin birth; but for the gospels, and the NT writings generally, and their writers, it had *little* significance, and was probably *unknown*.[5]

4) *Jesus in the Church's Gospels,* Dr. John Reumann.

Reumann is a professor at Lutheran Theological Seminary at Philadelphia (ELCA), Philadelphia, Pennsylvania, and served as a member of the Commission for the New Lutheran Church. He was recently named to chair a panel that will conduct a major study of ministry for the ELCA. Reumann is also the New Testament editor of *Word and Witness,* another primary ELCA adult Bible-study program based on the historical-critical method. The following quotation is an example of casting doubt on a basic doctrine of the Christian faith.

The traditional Christmas story cannot be the starting point for telling the life of Jesus historically or of his development psychologically, since what Matthew and Luke report about his birth and infancy was not, during his ministry, public knowledge (cf. Luke 2:19, 51b). . . . Christmas and Christmas customs, we need to remember, have always been subject to many romantic influences and have tended to assimilate pagan practices. . . . The whole New Testament insists on the full humanity of Jesus and assumes he was born, grew up, etc. on earth, though no details are given. (Galatians 4:4, "born of woman," refers to his birth as a human being, *not* to a virgin birth). . . . Matthew and Luke do present material about the birth which deserves atten-

---

[4]Terence E. Fretheim, *Search. Unit 9. Deuteronomy, Joshua, Judges,* Leader's Guide (Minneapolis: Augsburg Publishing House, 1984), pp. 80, 81.

[5]*The Interpreter's Dictionary of the Bible,* 4 vols., ed. Emory Stevens Bucke (Nashville: Abingdon Press, 1962), 2:880.

tion. It derives from the special *sources* of Matthew and Luke, *M* and *L* respectively. If one seeks for historical origins, it is usually said that—*if* there are firsthand sources to be reckoned with—Mary conveyed the information to Luke, though Luke also seems to have had a series of stories about John the Baptist which he has woven in with those about Jesus; moreover, the origin of some of the hymns in Luke 1-2 has been much debated. All the stories show a heavy influence from the Old Testament and doubtless bear the stamp of countless retellings within Christian circles. . . . The nativity stories thus tell readers who Jesus is. To this extent, all the nativity stories seek to describe what early Christians believed about Jesus. The stories might be called "Christology in picture form."[6]

5) *Invitation to Faith,* Dr. Paul Jersild.

Jersild is academic dean, director of admissions, and professor of ethics at Lutheran Theological Southern Seminary (ELCA), Columbia, South Carolina. He is also one of the translators of the *Evangelical Catechism,* which is used in the ELCA for adult instruction.

As a part of Christian tradition which expresses this discontinuity, the virgin birth is a *story* that is rightly revered and celebrated by Christians. But it is also *misused* when some maintain that without a virgin birth Jesus could not have been the chosen one of God.[7]

6) Dr. Michael Root, in response to a letter concerning the Virgin Birth and the Resurrection.

Root is associate professor of systematic theology at Lutheran Theological Southern Seminary (ELCA), Columbia, South Carolina. He has taken a leave of absence to accept a three-year appointment at the Institute for Ecumenical Research in Strasbourg, France. Root will participate in researching and writing an ecumenical study project requested by a board composed of Lutheran church leaders from around the world.[8]

The following quotations are taken from a letter written by Root in response to a letter received from Dr. Gregory Jackson, a former

---

[6]John Reumann, *Jesus in the Church's Gospels* (Philadelphia: Fortress Press, 1968), pp. 139-141.

[7]Paul Jersild, *Invitation to Faith* (Minneapolis: Augsburg Publishing House, 1978), p. 94.

[8]"Faces," *The Lutheran,* June 1, 1988, p. 42.

pastor of the Lutheran Church in America (LCA).[9] The letter is dated December 17, 1986. Jackson wrote to Lutheran Southern Seminary to inquire if there were any professors who still believed in the Virgin Birth or the Resurrection of Christ. Root responded in part:

> Your letter about the virgin birth and the physical resurrection of Jesus was passed on to me a few weeks ago. . . . I have enclosed the sections on the virgin birth and resurrection from Carl Braaten and Robert Jenson's *Christian Dogmatics*. These are written by Braaten. They are *typical* of the attitudes I have encountered among colleagues at the seminaries.
>
> I think the Braaten text also represents the fairly common perception that the resurrection is decisive for Christian faith in the way that the virgin birth is *not*. While I have not encountered a seminary professor who would deny the virgin birth (after all, all things are possible with God), I have not encountered many who think much rides on asserting it as a biological, historical *fact* in the modern sense. Theologically, one can say all that tradition has said about the person and work of Christ without mention of the virgin birth (as one cannot *without* mention of the resurrection). If one is not assuming that the transmission of original sin is somehow linked to sexual intercourse (a doctrine with dubious biblical basis), then *nothing* theologically significant depends on the assertion of a sexual [virgin] conception. Biblically, the birth narratives in Matthew and Luke seem to me to call for a symbolic or mythical reading. Reading them symbolically seems to me truer to the text than reading them as historical descriptions.

In contrast to Root's words concerning the significance of the Virgin Birth in relation to having a saving faith in Christ, please refer back to Position A in this chapter.

BISHOP CHILSTROM RECOMMENDS . . .

7) *What Christians Believe,* Dr. Hans Schwarz.

Schwarz is a professor of systematic theology. He served at Trinity Lutheran Seminary, Columbus, Ohio; is a faculty member at the University of Regensburg, Regensburg, Germany; and is listed in the

---

[9]Jackson is now a member of the conservative Wisconsin Evangelical Lutheran Synod and is serving as a parish pastor. He left the LCA in 1987 because of the liberal theology. (cf. "Pastor-Scholar Leaves The Lutheran Church in America," *Christian News Encyclopedia,* 4 vols., ed. Herman Otten [Washington: Missourian Publishing Co.], 3:2195).

1991 ELCA Yearbook as a visiting professor at Lutheran Theological Southern Seminary, Columbia, South Carolina. He remains on the clergy roster of the ELCA and is one of the authors of *Christian Dogmatics*.

What Christians Believe was listed as a main selection of the April 1988 list of the Augsburg Reading Club. Bishop Herbert W. Chilstrom says of the book, "Schwarz's well-written book would be helpful for both congregational groups and individual readers. . . . He draws the reader into the heart of the issues so that one can wrestle with them. I heartily recommend this book." In the following quotation Schwarz casts doubt upon the Virgin Birth:

> In the first centuries after Christ the affirmation of the virgin birth was something quite common for most people. A virgin birth was, so to speak, a *status symbol.* Everybody who had special significance was born by a virgin. Even someone like Alexander the Great, whose biological parents were well-known, was thus said to be born of a virgin. This means that a virgin birth was *not* always understood as a strictly biological fact but rather was an indication that the person thus born was of special significance. If we were to interpret the confession of the virgin birth of Jesus in a similar way, we would in no way violate the context in which this confession is to be understood and evaluated.[10]

8) "The Confession of a Former Liberal LCA Pastor," Dr. J. Kincaid Smith.

Smith is a conservative pastor in the Evangelical Lutheran Synod (ELS).

> I was trained in the "new thinking" at Hamma School of Theology, now merged with Capital and called Trinity. . . . When I graduated in 1973, to the best of my knowledge, none of my classmates, nor I, believed in any of the miraculous elements in the Bible, in anything supernatural. . . . One of my New Testament profs was moved to write a poem for the occasion of his receiving tenure. It was read at the service at Wittenberg University Chapel. In it he speculated that Jesus' father was an *itinerant Roman soldier.* He flatly denied the real deity of Christ.[11]

---

[10]Hans Schwarz, *What Christians Believe* (Philadelphia: Fortress Press, 1987), p. 46.

[11]J. Kincaid Smith, "The Confession of a Former Liberal LCA Pastor," *Christian News Encyclopedia,* 4 vols., ed. Herman Otten (Washington: Missourian Publishing Co., 1988), 3:2165.

The next chapter addresses the deity of Jesus Christ, the deity of him who is the second person of the Trinity. The deity of Christ is radically dependent upon the miracle of the *Virgin* Birth of Christ. If the Holy Spirit was not the one who conceived Jesus in Mary's womb so that he was "of *one substance* with the Father," as the ancient Nicene Creed so painstakingly states, Jesus couldn't have done what the whole 2,000-year history of the Christian church has held and taught as necessary for our salvation. He could not have lived out the life of perfect obedience by which we are declared righteous. He could not have paid the price for the sins of the whole world, God his Father meting out to him the punishment we deserve. As a mere man, he would be without the real Fatherhood of God and he would surely be no fit object of our worship.

As we shall see in the chapters that follow, these concerns pose no difficulty for the historic critics.

12.

THE DEITY OF CHRIST

Position A

Jesus Christ is God. His true deity is clearly taught in Scripture.

1) The Bible.

In the beginning was the Word, and the Word was with God, and the Word was God. He was with God in the beginning. Through him all things were made; without him nothing was made that has been made (John 1:3).

But when the time had fully come, God sent his Son, born of a woman . . . (Galatians 4:4).

Thomas said to him, "My Lord and my God!" (John 20:28)

I and the Father are one (John 10:30).

Simon Peter answered, "You are the Christ, the Son of the living God" (Matthew 16:16).

2) The Lutheran Confessions, *The Book of Concord*—Small Catechism.

I believe that Jesus Christ, true God, begotten of the Father from eternity, and also true man, born of the virgin Mary, is my Lord. . . .[1]

---

[1]*The Book of Concord,* trans. and ed. Theodore G. Tappert (Philadelphia: Fortress Press, 1959), Small Catechism, Creed 6, p. 345.

3) The Apostles, Nicene, and Athanasian creeds, the three universal or ecumenical creeds found in most Lutheran hymnals, which represent the basic core of the Christian faith.

    a. I believe in God the Father Almighty, Maker of heaven and earth. And in Jesus Christ, His only Son, our Lord; who was conceived by the Holy Ghost, born of the Virgin Mary . . . (Apostles Creed).

    b. I believe . . . in one Lord Jesus Christ, the only begotten Son of God, begotten of the Father before all worlds . . . who for us men, and for our salvation, came down from heaven, and was incarnate by the Holy Ghost of the Virgin Mary, and was made man . . . (Nicene Creed).

    c. Furthermore, it is necessary to everlasting salvation that he also believe faithfully the incarnation of our Lord Jesus Christ. For the right faith is, that we believe and confess that our Lord Jesus Christ, the Son of God, is God and Man; God of the Substance of the Father, begotten before the worlds; and Man of the substance of His mother, born in the world; Perfect God and perfect Man, of a reasonable soul and human flesh subsisting (Athanasian Creed).

Position B

The doctrine of the deity of Jesus Christ is not taught in the Bible but was developed by pious early Christians.

1) *Christian Dogmatics,* Braaten/Jenson, the *primary* theology textbook used in all seminaries of the Evangelical Lutheran Church in America (ELCA). Braaten writes:

The history of the development and refinement of the historical-critical method covers the last two centuries and is very complex, so we can only highlight several of its main features. The first *premise* is that the orthodox doctrine of inspiration has no heuristic validity at all in the scholarly study of the Bible. The investigation must proceed without prejudice concerning the special authority of this book. The biblical writings are products of two thousand years of history and must be examined as are all other literary remains from antiquity. The startling *discovery* was that the ecclesiastical dogmas are not to be found in the Bible, but are products of a later time. In the age of Christendom, the dogmas of the Trinity and of Christ, as formulated in the Nicene and Athanasian creeds, were necessary to believe for salvation. Now the biblical critics could apply the Scripture-principle of Protestantism to show that these dogmas cannot be required for faith, since they lack solid biblical support (author's emphasis).[2]

Neither the conservative denial of myth in the New Testament nor the liberal approach of demythologizing has proven adequate for constructive Christian theology. A third approach is possible: an interpretation of the myth as story, without taking its symbolic elements literally but also without eliminating its historical aspects. Rudolf Bultmann was right in his observation that the New Testament kerygma [message] was proclaimed within the framework of mythology. . . . The story of Christ in the Gospels is a mixture of historical events and mythological symbols. The purpose of the myth is to interpret the significance of the events. . . . Myth and its symbols are indispensable to express the reality of God in the person of Jesus. Myth is an appropriate form of language for expressing the events and meanings of God's revelation in history.[3]

2) *The Interpreter's Dictionary of the Bible.* This is a recommended resource book for *Search* and *Word and Witness,* two primary ELCA adult Bible-study programs.

Jesus did *not* proclaim his messiahship. Unlike some other religious leaders of the time, and unlike the portrayal in John, Jesus (according to the Synoptics) does *not* make himself the center of his teaching or demand submission or loyalty to himself as a condition of acceptance or admission to the kingdom of God.[4]

3) *Jesus in the Church's Gospels,* Dr. John Reumann.

Reumann is a professor at Lutheran Theological Seminary at Philadelphia (ELCA), Philadelphia, Pennsylvania, and served as a member of the Commission for the New Lutheran Church. He was recently named to chair a panel that will conduct a major study of ministry for the ELCA.[5] Reumann is also an author of *Word and Wit-*

---

[2]Carl E. Braaten, *Christian Dogmatics,* 2 vols., eds. Carl E. Braaten and Robert W. Jenson (Philadelphia: Fortress Press, 1984), 1:71.

[3]Ibid., 1:528, 529.

[4]*The Interpreter's Dictionary of the Bible,* 4 vols., ed. Emory Stevens Bucke (Nashville: Abingdon Press, 1962), 2:892.

[5]Jean Caffey Lyles, "Reumann to Chair Ministry Task Force," *The Lutheran,* August 10, 1988, p. 20.

ness, a primary ELCA adult Bible-study program based on the historical-critical method. *Jesus in the Church's Gospels* is a resource highly recommended by the authors of *Word and Witness.*

> We thus repudiate the possibility of recovering his "messianic consciousness" or even his particular "self-consciousness," but we can hope to see something of his understanding of life—how he looked on existence under God and life in a time when God's reign was drawing near.[6]

4) *Invitation to Faith,* Dr. Paul Jersild.

Jersild is academic dean, director of admissions, and professor of ethics at Lutheran Theological Southern Seminary (ELCA), Columbia, South Carolina. He is also one of the translators of the *Evangelical Catechism,* which is used in the ELCA for adult instruction.

> What do Christians mean today when they confess (in the words of the Nicene Creed) that Jesus Christ "came down from heaven . . . and was made man"? When we no longer understand the universe to consist of heaven "up above," the earth in the middle, and an "underworld" beneath us, it is at least difficult and more likely *impossible* for Christians to take this language literally.

> But what does it mean to speak of Jesus as "divine"? Does not this word also call for some interpretation? Theologians *today* are concerned to interpret the divinity of Jesus in a manner which *avoids* turning him into a bizarre, mythological creature who contains both a divine nature and a human nature.[7]

Jersild, in his last amazing statement, attacks one of the most central concepts of Christian theology, the concept of the two natures of Christ, the divine nature and the human nature. He says that they ("theologians today") are concerned to avoid it, that it would turn Jesus into "a bizarre mythological creature."

Confessional Lutheran theology, accurately drawn from the Scriptures, teaches that the two natures of Christ, the divine nature and the human nature, are joined in what is called the *personal union.* This is what comprises what the Christ is and sets the bounds of what he can be.

---

[6] John Reumann, *Jesus in the Church's Gospels* (Philadelphia: Fortress Press, 1968), p. 138.

[7] Paul Jersild, *Invitation to Faith* (Minneapolis: Augsburg, 1978), pp. 99, 100.

Because of its central and vital importance, the study of the two natures of Christ, or *Christology,* is a part of Christian theology upon which faithful confessional Lutherans spend much time during their seminary studies.

All three of the great ecumenical creeds included in the Lutheran Confessions were written essentially in defense of the church's teaching of the two natures of Christ. They were formulations martialed against the unrelenting attacks of the heretics of their day.

There is no other issue in all the writings of the early church fathers over which they were more vigilant, or over which they labored more diligently, than the teaching of the church concerning the two natures of Christ.

The careful study of the two natures of Christ was paramount in the writings of Luther and of the Lutheran fathers who followed him. Martin Chemnitz, the primary author of *The Formula of Concord,* which comprises the final part of the Lutheran Confessions as contained in *The Book of Concord,* wrote the great Lutheran classic *The Two Natures of Christ,* an exhaustive treatment of this vital doctrine that Jersild and company would caricature and "avoid."

Every great heresy that has plagued the church has essentially been an attack upon the person of Christ, usually attacking one or the other of the two natures of Christ.

Jersild, by his statement, has rightly placed himself and his colleagues in the company of all the other enemies of Christ and His church. In the final analysis, in avoiding the issue of the *two* natures of Christ, they have, by default, denied the *deity* of Christ.

The next chapter deals with the concept by which faithful Christians of all times have judged all confessions of faith, the doctrine of the Trinity. If a church is judged by its teachings, its creeds (statements of what it believes), and its confessions to no longer be *Trinitarian,* then it has always been judged to be no longer Christian.

Even before we examine what the historic critics of the ELCA *formally* say about the concept of the Trinity, it should be evident that with the denial of the deity of Christ, there is no *Trinity* left to deny.

13.

THE TRINITY

Position A

The doctrine of the Trinity is clearly taught in Scripture.

1) The Bible.

Therefore go and make disciples of all nations, baptizing them in the name of the Father and of the Son and of the Holy Spirit . . . (Matthew 28:19).

May the grace of the Lord Jesus Christ, and the love of God, and the fellowship of the Holy Spirit be with you all (2 Corinthians 13:14).

Peter, an apostle of Jesus Christ, to God's elect, strangers in the world, scattered throughout Pontus, Galatia, Cappadocia, Asia and Bithynia, who have been chosen according to the foreknowledge of God the Father, through the sanctifying work of the Spirit, for obedience to Jesus Christ and sprinkling by his blood: Grace and peace be yours in abundance (1 Peter 1:1,2).

You, however, are controlled not by the sinful nature but by the Spirit, if the Spirit of God lives in you. And if anyone does not have the Spirit of Christ, he does not belong to Christ (Romans 8:9).

2) The Lutheran Confessions, *The Book of Concord*—Apology of the Augsburg Confession.

This asserts our faith and teaching that there is one undivided divine essence, and that there are nevertheless, three distinct and coeternal persons of the same divine essence, Father, Son, and Holy Spirit. We have always taught and defended this doctrine and we believe that the Holy Scriptures testify to it firmly, surely, and irrefutably. We steadfastly maintain that those who believe otherwise do not belong to the church of Christ but are idolaters and blasphemers.[1]

3) The Apostles, Nicene, and Athanasian creeds, the three universal or ecumenical creeds found in most Lutheran hymnals, which represent the basic core of the Christian faith.

Whosoever will be saved, before all things it is necessary that he hold the catholic [i.e., universal, Christian] faith. . . . And the catholic faith is this, that we worship one God in Trinity and Trinity in Unity, neither confounding the Persons nor dividing the Substance (Athanasian Creed).

4) A note of importance.

The Virgin Birth, the deity of Christ, and the Trinity are all intrinsically related to one another. To deny one is to deny all three and subsequently deny the entire Christian faith.

Position B

The doctrine of the Trinity is not taught in the Bible but was developed by pious early Christians and made a later addition by the church.

1) *Christian Dogmatics,* Braaten/Jenson, is the *primary* theology textbook used in all seminaries of the Evangelical Lutheran Church of America (ELCA).

Truly, the Trinity is simply the Father and the man Jesus and their Spirit as the Spirit of the believing community.[2]

2) *Invitation to Faith,* Dr. Paul Jersild.

Jersild is academic dean, director of admissions, and professor of ethics at Lutheran Theological Southern Seminary (ELCA), Columbia, South Carolina. He is also one of the translators of the *Evangelical Catechism,* which is used in the ELCA for adult instruction.

The formulation of the Trinity as a doctrine is *not* found in the New Testament. It was hammered out during the fourth century in what is called the Trinitarian Controversy . . . *nor*

---

[1]*The Book of Concord,* trans. and ed. Theodore G. Tappert (Philadelphia: Fortress Press, 1959), Apology of the Augsburg Confession, Art. I, 1, p. 100.

[2]Robert W. Jenson, *Christian Dogmatics,* 4 vols., eds. Carl E. Braaten and Robert W. Jenson (Philadelphia: Fortress Press, 1984), 1:155.

is the language of the fourth century dogma to be regarded as sacred and absolute.[3]

In reference to the preceding quotation: The Trinitarian Controversy was itself a *defense* of the true deity of Christ, under attack by the liberals of the 4th century.

At the end of the last chapter we noted that the Christian church has always judged all creeds and confessions of faith, whether they are to be considered *Christian,* by their treatment of the doctrine of the Trinity.

When these confessions and creeds are judged to be no longer Trinitarian, the church has always judged those who hold such confessions and creeds as having departed from the Christian faith, as no longer being Christian church bodies. Thus there has been agreement over the past years among all of the various Christian (Trinitarian) denominations that such groups as the Mormons, the Jehovah's Witnesses, the Christian Scientists, and more recently, *The Way,* the Unification Church, and the World Wide Church of God, have all been judged on the basis of their own writings, particularly in the area of their view of Christ, as having placed themselves outside the pale of Christ's Church. Each of these groups denies Christ's true deity and his position within the Trinity.

We cannot see into men's hearts to know whether genuine Christian faith is there, so we are not to judge individuals. Scripture clearly teaches, however, that we are to judge what men teach and say. St. Paul tells us in Romans 16:17: "Mark those who cause divisions in the doctrine which you learned and avoid them."

Conservative Lutherans have always said that at the point at which the statements of the *official* position of a church body are no longer Trinitarian, that church body should be pronounced to be no longer *Christian.* In the quotation from the Apology of the Augsburg Confession (2), the writer states regarding those who do not believe that there is "one divine undivided essence . . ." and "three distinct and coeternal persons . . ." and "We steadfastly maintain that those who believe otherwise do not belong to the church of Christ but are idolaters and blasphemers." The Confessions don't pull their punches.

Is the ELCA still Christian?

The words of the new constitution of the ELCA sound Trinitarian, but what do they mean? The *meaning* of a statement is comprised of

---

[3]Paul Jersild, *Invitation to Faith* (Minneapolis: Augsburg Publishing House, 1978), pp. 130, 131.

the *meaning*, that the one writing the statement, holds, the *meaning* he intends to communicate by his spoken or written words. The *official position* of a church body is that which the *officials mean* by the words they write in their official statements, the same meaning they teach in all their seminaries, schools, and colleges. That, by all reasonable understanding, ought to be the way one determines the *official position* of a church body. Surely we should use the same dictionary in interpreting their statements that they used in writing them.

Suppose it were possible to submit the two volumes of Braaten and Jenson's *Christian Dogmatics,* the *Search Bible Study,* and other books by which we have documented the case against the liberal teachers and theologians to a panel comprised of Martin Luther, Philip Melanchthon, Martin Chemnitz, and the other writers of the *Book of Concord.* Suppose we requested that they thoroughly study these documents and report to us their judgment as to whether the church body that produced them, and encourages their use throughout their church, could possibly be judged a Christian church. What would their answer be? Luther nearly judged the theology of Zwingli and Calvin not to be Christian merely on the basis of their insistence that the human nature of Christ did not share the attributes of his divine nature. What would he say of these men who deny the Virgin Birth and the real divinity of Christ? They would declare that such a church is not Christian.

The next chapter addresses the issue of the doctrine of the atonement. The chief doctrine of the Christian faith is the doctrine of justification. This doctrine teaches us that God declared all men righteous before God because of the obedience unto death of his Son, Jesus Christ (Romans 5:19). Without the atonement, Christ receiving upon himself the punishment for the sins of the world, there could be no justification of the sinner before God. Even if the liberals believed in the real deity of Christ and all of the other things they deny but still denied the doctrine of atonement, they still would not be Christians.

The progression of doctrinal error reaches its pinnacle in the next two chapters, the denial of the atonement and of the resurrection. Everything that follows documents the devastating effect that the denial of the heart of the faith must inevitably have on all those things that flow from the faith, life, and mission of the church.

14.

THE ATONEMENT

Position A

Jesus Christ died for the sins of the world. God took his anger for our sins out on his Son to save us and thus revealed a Father's heart toward us. He is not angry with us anymore; we are forgiven and reconciled to him because of Jesus. This action of God through Jesus is called substitutionary atonement or propitiation and is the heart and center of the Christian faith.

1) Atonement or propitiation—a definition.

> Dr. Robert D. Preus, a former president of Concordia Theological Seminary (Lutheran Church-Missouri Synod), Ft. Wayne, Indiana, defines atonement as: Christ's work of satisfying the wrath of God the Father by His perfect obedience to the divine law and His innocent death as our Substitute.[1]

2) The Lutheran Confessions, *The Book of Concord*—Apology of the Augsburg Confession.

> . . . by undergoing the punishment of sin and becoming a sacrifice for us, the sinless Christ took away the right of the law to accuse and condemn those who believe in him, because he himself is their propitiation, for whose sake they are now accounted righteous.[2]

---

[1]Robert D. Preus, *Getting Into the Theology of Concord* (St. Louis: Concordia Publishing House, 1977), p. 89.
[2]*The Book of Concord,* trans. and ed. Theodore G. Tappert (Philadelphia: Fortress Press, 1959), Apology of the Augsburg Confession, Art. IV, 179, p. 131.

3) The Bible.

A. The need for atonement:

For just as through the disobedience of the one man [Adam] the many were made sinners, so also through the obedience of the one man [Christ] the many will be made righteous (Romans 5:19).

B. God's wrath over man's sin:

But God demonstrates his own love toward us in this: While we were still sinners, Christ died for us. Since we have now been justified by his blood, how much more shall we be saved from God's wrath through him! (Romans 5:8,9)

C. The shedding of blood for forgiveness:

In fact the law requires that nearly everything be cleansed with blood, and without the shedding of blood there is no forgiveness (Hebrews 9:22).

. . . and the blood of Jesus, His Son, purifies us from all sin (1 John 1:7b).

D. Jesus as a sacrifice:

God presented him as a sacrifice of atonement . . . (Romans 3:25).

4) Martin Luther.

God "Made him to be sin for us" (2 Corinthians 5:21). Christ is the one who stepped into the place of our sinful nature, loaded upon Himself, and appeased for us all, the wrath of God which we had deserved by all our works.[3]

Position B

Jesus Christ "died for us" in the sense of a man dying for his friends, not in the sense of God punishing him for the sins of others. Such would portray an unjust God. God has always loved us. Jesus has shown us this.

Once the biblical absolutes are abandoned, there is no longer a clear-cut standard of right and wrong, no real sense of sin; and therefore, no place in liberal thinking for a God who is "wrathful." After all, if there is no real sin, only human weakness, what has God to be

---

[3]*What Luther Says,* 3 vols., ed. Ewald M. Plass (St. Louis: Concordia Publishing House, 1959), 3:1418.

angry about? This new view of sin has led the liberals away from the historic Lutheran understanding of atonement into the concept of a kindly, benevolent God who just wants everyone to be happy, merely winks at sin, and simply loves, loves, loves us all.

1) *Christian Dogmatics,* Braaten/Jenson, the *primary* theology textbook used in all seminaries of the Evangelical Lutheran Church in America (ELCA).

> But what is the import of this tradition? Put in its most *crass* form, this view would hold that Jesus' death is a sacrifice in which he is a substitute for us who pays the divine justice that is due for human sin and/or appeases the divine wrath. As we shall see, there is a long tradition, especially among Western conservative Christians which has taken this line. There seems to be a virtual consensus among contemporary biblical scholars, however, that this tradition finds little support in the Scriptures, either in the Old or New Testament. Scripture *never* speaks of God as one who has to be satisfied or propitiated before being merciful or forgiving.

> Jesus himself, though he *might* have and quite *possibly* did reckon with a violent death at the hands of his adversaries, seems not to have understood or interpreted his own death as a sacrifice for others or ransom for sin. Such interpretation apparently came as the result of later reflection. Even in their final redaction [editing] the synoptic Gospels contain little direct or explicit interpretation of Jesus' work.[4]

> The meaning of the historical cross was transmitted in the suprahistorical language of *mythological* symbolism. The cross is *not* a fact of history that interprets itself. The New Testament writers used a rich variety of symbols taken from the world of ancient Jewish and Gnostic mythology to interpret the meaning of the cross.[5]

> Jesus dies for us and not for God. There is not just a little perversity [contrary to the evidence] in the tendency to say that the sacrifice was demanded by God to placate the divine wrath. We attempt to exonerate ourselves from the terrible nature of the deed by blaming it on God. The theology

[4]Gerhard O. Forde, *Christian Dogmatics,* 2 vols., eds. Carl E. Braaten and Robert W. Jenson (Philadelphia: Fortress Press, 1984), 2:14, 15, 2:12.

[5]Carl E. Braaten, *Christian Dogmatics,* 2 vols., eds. Carl E. Braaten and Robert W. Jenson (Philadelphia: Fortress Press, 1984), 1:547.

of sacrifice becomes part of our defense mechanism. This must now cease. Nothing in the Scriptures warrants it. Jesus' sacrifice for us cannot be explained in that fashion. A new understanding of the nature of that sacrifice is demanded. This new understanding must arise from the event itself and not impose previously constructed theories on it.[6]

2) *The Evangelical Catechism.*
This book is used for adult instruction in ELCA congregations.

The church's message concerning justification has also suffered from *overly-literal* explanations of how Christ has atoned for human sin. When metaphors and images of the atonement are taken too concretely, they distort our understanding of God. For example, God has sometimes been seen as paying a debt to the devil, or as requiring the bloody sacrifice of his Son in order to satisfy his wrath. When such language is used it often contradicts other things we know about God from the Scriptures, including his power over evil and his steadfast love and forgiveness.[7]

3) *Affirm Series. New Testament,* Teacher's Guide, catechism materials for seventh-and eighth-grade children.

Jesus was crucified and raised as a friend of sinners. His enemies thought it fitting that if Jesus insisted on being the friend of sinners he would have to suffer the consequences. And so he was crucified.

The New Testament repeatedly asserts the fact of redemption through Christ, but nowhere does it give one simple, dogmatic explanation of it. As a result, throughout church history several theories about atonement have emerged. Some of these are:

Jesus' death as ransom—This view, held by the early church leaders, suggests that because of sin, the human race fell under the domination of the devil. Jesus' death is the ransom paid to purchase human freedom.

"Satisfaction" theory—This was the dominant view of the Middle Ages. According to this view, human sin is an infi-

---

[6]Ibid., 2:82.
[7]*The Evangelical Catechism,* American Edition, trans. Lawrence W. Denef (Minneapolis: Augsburg Publishing House, 1982), pp. 209-211.

nite offense against God; this infinite offense requires infinite satisfaction. It was necessary for God to become human. Thus Jesus, who was perfect, died to satisfy the offense created by human sin.

Other theories—Other theories have been suggested from time to time. One such theory is that Jesus' death is the supreme example of God's love which is intended to produce in us a similar love. Another is that Jesus' death is the final sacrifice, bringing all forms of animal sacrifice to an end. Some have thought that Jesus atones by means of his teaching more than by his death. Other theories have similarly chosen to emphasize only one aspect of New Testament thought.

In regard to how the work of Christ redeems us, we must be content to assert the reality and realize that there are some ambiguities.[8]

4) "The Confession of a Former Liberal LCA Pastor," Dr. J. Kincaid Smith.

Smith is a pastor in the conservative Evangelical Lutheran Synod (ELS).

I was trained in the "new thinking" at Hamma School of Theology, now merged with Capital and called Trinity. . . . When I graduated in 1973, to the best of my knowledge, none of my classmates, nor I, believed in any of the miraculous elements in the Bible, in anything supernatural. . . . The heart and center of our *denials* was that which lies at the heart and center of the Christian faith, the Gospel. And no one talked more of "the Gospel" than we. Here again is the *double-speak*. We denied true blood atonement, in the very clear sense of propitiation. That central concept is the chief doctrine of the Church, that God took his horrible wrath against our sins out on his only begotten Son. We preached about Jesus "dying for us" but this was him dying for his friends, not propitiation, just kind of a very special good guy.

I remember the day when this difference dawned on me. I finally realized what the prof had been trying to get through

---

[8]Marshall D. Johnson, *Affirm, The Apostles Creed,* Teacher's Guide, eds. Irene Getz, Susan Niemi Tetlie, and Gretchen L. Weidenbach (Minneapolis: Augsburg Publishing House, 1984), pp. 22, 23.

our heads. I was in Dr. Frank Seilhammer's class. He was later the president of Hamma and then the provost at Trinity. As the light dawned, I said, "Well then why did Christ have to die on the cross, Frank?" His eyes lit up as only a profs eyes can when a student finally sees the light. He said, "Ah ha, Kin, now you're going to have to completely *rethink* your Christology." (Your understanding of who and what Christ was and what he was about).[9]

It is significant that the liberal Lutheran theologians never quote the Lutheran Confessions when they lay out their assertions of what the doctrine of the atonement is not (Position B, [1]). The position they describe as being "crass" is actually an accurate description of the scriptural doctrine of the atonement as found in the Lutheran Confessions. They say: "Put in its most *crass* form, this view would hold that Jesus' death is a sacrifice in which he is a substitute for us who pays the divine justice that is due for human sin and/or appeases the divine wrath."

What would happen among their readers if, after calling that understanding of atonement "crass," they then said: "The Apology of the Augsburg Confession says regarding atonement: '. . . by undergoing the punishment of sin and becoming a sacrifice for us, the sinless Christ took away the right of the law to accuse and condemn those who believe in him, because he himself is their propitiation [satisfying God's wrath against us], for whose sake they are now accounted righteous' " (Position A [2] above).

If they did this, it would be easy for people to see that the position that they are calling "a crass form" of the doctrine of the atonement was none other than the position that the Lutheran Confessions take. Instead they say: "As we shall see, there is a long standing tradition, especially among western *conservative Christians* which has taken this *line.*" The implication is that "western conservative Christians" are perhaps fundamentalists or some other group of Protestants. Why weren't they honest enough to say that the whole tradition of Lutheran theology up until recently held that precise position?

Why didn't they say that many Lutherans today, several Lutheran synods in the United States and some Lutherans in foreign lands, still hold with that thoroughly confessional, thoroughly biblical position? They don't say this because, if they did, it would be clearly seen

---

[9]J. Kincaid Smith, "The Confession of a Former Liberal LCA Pastor," *Christian News Encyclopedia*, 4 vols., ed. Herman Otten (Washington: Missourian Publishing Co., 1988), 3:2165.

how they have severed themselves from the historic stream of confessional Lutheranism.

The same observation can be made about their handling of each of the doctrines with which we have dealt. Considering the long-range strategy of the liberals to carefully remold the thinking of the constituency of their church body, to slowly move them over into the new thinking, it is very important that the constituency continue to see them as faithful *Lutheran* pastors, professors, bishops, and teachers. This gives them the great advantage of the high level of trust, esteem, and credibility in which Lutheran lay people have historically held their pastors and teachers, trust earned by more faithful pastors of the past. The liberals set themselves up as the *real* Bible scholars and purposely ignore the Confessions.

Lutherans have a way of testing their teachers that people in other denominations do not have: the Lutheran Confessions. The Lutherans are the only body of Christians in the world who have historic confessions that have stood the test of time and that are faithfully adhered to today by a significant number of its constituents.

These are the three ecumenical creeds (Apostles, Nicene, and Athanasian), the Augsburg Confession, the Apology of the Augsburg Confession, the Smalcald Articles, the Treatise on the Power and Primacy of the Pope, the Small Catechism, the Large Catechism, and the Formula of Concord.

By historic definition, to be a *Lutheran* is to *subscribe* (confess full agreement with) the Lutheran Confessions. Faithful Lutherans subscribe to the Confessions *because* we believe them to be accurately drawn from the inerrant Holy Scriptures. The liberals know that in order to call themselves *Lutheran,* they, too, must *subscribe* to the Confessions. Their "subscription," however, is not the same as the subscription, the full acceptance of the Confessions, which is gladly declared by faithful conservatives. The liberals "subscribe" to the Confessions, not "because" they are accurately drawn from Scriptures, but "in so far as" they are in agreement with Scriptures. But the "Scriptures" to which the liberals compare the Confessions are whatever is left when they have demythologized them and sifted them through their historical-critical screen. They so qualify what they concede as "valid" in the Scriptures, that in their "subscription" to the Confessions they are bound to nothing but their own theologically bankrupt notions.

As *confessional* Lutherans we can take our stand and point to the Lutheran Confessions and say: "This is what we believe, these Confessions are *our* confession of faith. Your argument is not with us, it

111

is with the Confessions, with Luther and company, *and* with the Scriptures upon which they are soundly grounded."

The attitude of the liberals toward the Lutheran Confessions is illustrated by a seminary classroom incident involving Dr. Daniel F. Martensen at Hamma School of Theology, an LCA seminary in Ohio.

Martensen expressed his concern that the seminary was not teaching the Lutheran Confessions. His concern was not that the students become confessional, quite the opposite. He said that unless they studied and thoroughly understood the Confessions, the students would not be able to really free themselves from the archaic and limiting theological concepts and patterns in which they, as Lutherans, had been immersed and entangled. They were to study the Lutheran Confessions in order to free themselves from them.[10]

This professor was then the chairman of the theology department at the seminary. Significantly, he is now the head of the Office for Ecumenical Affairs at the headquarters of the ELCA.

Without rancor, faithful Lutherans can wish that these men would "free themselves" from the entanglements and bonds of the Confessions. We can hope that they would succeed in their "ecumenical" efforts to merge with other liberal Protestant and Catholic bodies and no longer use the title Lutheran.

---

[10]This incident occurred in a class attended by co-author J. Kincaid Smith, then a seminary student at Hamma School of Theology, where Dr. Martenson taught.

15.

THE RESURRECTION

Position A

The resurrection of the body will occur on the last day of history. The souls of all who died in faith will be reunited with their glorified bodies to live forever in heaven with Jesus Christ. Jesus actually *physically* rose from the dead and *physically* showed himself to the disciples. The tomb was empty on Easter morning.

1) The Bible.

Jesus answered them, "Destroy this temple, and I will raise it again in three days" . . . but the temple he had spoken of was his body (John 2:19, 21).

The angel said to the women, "Do not be afraid for I know that you are looking for Jesus, who was crucified. He is not here; he has risen, just as he said. Come and see the place where he lay. . . . Suddenly Jesus met them. "Greetings," he said. They came to him, clasped his feet and worshiped him (Matthew 28:5,6,9).

Then he said to Thomas, "Put your finger here; see my hands. Reach out your hand and put it into my side. Stop doubting and believe" (1 John 20:27).

Jesus appears to the disciples. . . ."Look at my hands and my feet. It is I myself! Touch me and see; a ghost does not have flesh and bones, as you see I have. . . . Do you have anything here to eat?" They gave him a piece of broiled fish, and he took it and ate it in their presence (Luke 24:39, 41, 42).

2) The Lutheran Confessions, *The Book of Concord*—Formula of Concord.

Fourthly, concerning the doctrine of the resurrection, Scripture testifies that precisely the substance of this our flesh, but without sin, shall arise, and that in eternal life we shall have and keep precisely this soul, although without sin.[1]

3) Martin Luther.

Thus we honorably carry the dead to the grave . . . and we together with them, will rise on Judgment Day and . . . the bodies will not be different bodies, although they will be constituted differently, and transfigured.

This article has suffered and still suffers the most opposition and is most difficult to believe. . . . Hence it is difficult to believe that man, who dies and perishes in so many different ways, is to live again; that his members, so widely scattered, reduced to dust and ashes in fire, water, and soil, are to be gathered again; that his soul is again to live in the same body in which it lived before; and that he is to have the same eyes, ears, hands and feet, except that the body together with its members, is to have a different manner of existence. . . . If you ask reason to explain this, you will never believe it. But then God will prove his divine power and majesty. Thus he did when he created heaven and earth out of nothing. He spoke only one word, and immediately they stood there. So it will be at the time of the resurrection.[2]

Position B

It is doubtful what the "body" is. The corpse that is buried is not the body. Therefore, "resurrection" concerns some kind of "spiritual body," not our earthly remains. The tomb was not empty on the first Easter morning. Jesus did not "physically" rise from the dead. Perhaps we may speak of some "spiritual" resurrection.

1) *Christian Dogmatics,* Braaten/Jenson, the *primary* theology textbook used in all seminaries of the Evangelical Lutheran Church in America (ELCA).

Mythological symbolism contributed to the interpretation of the event of the resurrection. The question has become acute in modern theology whether in the resurrection we

---

[1]*The Book of Concord,* trans. and ed. Theodore G. Tappert (Philadelphia: Fortress Press, 1959), Formula of Concord, Solid Declaration, Art. I, 46, p. 516.

[2]*What Luther Says,* 3 vols., ed. Ewald M. Plass (St. Louis: Concordia Publishing House, 1959), 3:1215-1218.

are dealing only with a *myth* or with a truly historical event.[3]

Since we are endowed neither with divine qualities nor with an immortal soul in the Platonic or gnostic sense, meaningful existence beyond death must be a resurrection of the dead. This hope is expressed in the Apostles Creed, where we say that we believe "in the resurrection of the body." This does *not* mean a biological revivification, such as is found in the case of the young man in the village of Nain (Luke 7:15) or Lazarus (John 11:44).

Contrary to other "resurrection" stories in the Bible, Jesus is *not* perceived as having returned to *this* life. His resurrection was not a resuscitation indicating that in certain exceptional instances people can be returned to their former state of life.[4]

2) *Search. Unit 6. Matthew 17-28,* Leader's Guide, Dr. Donald H. Juel.

Search is a primary ELCA adult Bible study program. Juel is associate professor of New Testament at Luther Northwestern Theological Seminary (ELCA), St. Paul, Minnesota.

The Gospels include only a small portion of what we know was a large collection of Easter *stories*. . . . The texts pose historical questions that are difficult to answer. . . . There is no reason to feel obliged to conceal the differences among the various accounts of Easter in the New Testament. They are there, part of God's word. The problems need not pose a threat to faith, however, when we bear in mind the fact that the writers of the various accounts were *not* aiming to serve as historians in the way we think of them. They were telling the good news for their particular audience. These accounts are *not* meant to be journalistic reports of facts.[5]

In response to Juel's statement that the Easter accounts are not intended to be taken as "journalistic reports of facts," we would like to make the following point. The faith of these earliest Christians, including the Gospel writers, was built upon eyewitness accounts (their

---

[3]Carl E. Braaten, *Christian Dogmatics,* 2 vols., eds. Carl E. Braaten and Robert W. Jenson (Philadelphia: Fortress Press, 1984), 1:549.

[4]Hans Schwarz, *Christian Dogmatics,* 2:566, 567, 2:558.

[5]Donald H. Juel, *Search. Unit 6. Matthew 17-28,* Leader's Guide (Minneapolis: Augsburg Publishing House, 1984), pp. 75, 76.

own and those of others). It is inconceivable that people with this common historical experience would have understood or tolerated any kind of mythological or poetic treatment of the historical events that were the very foundation of their common faith.

Juel refers to the differences in the New Testament Easter accounts in the preceding quotation and throughout the entire *Search* lesson. The liberals often cite these differences to prove that the Bible has errors. In 1984, while members of the American Lutheran Church, several Lutherans Informed for Truth (L.I.F.T.) members participated in a merger study group[6] within their congregation. The group was given a paper comparing the Easter accounts in the four gospels. The paper, prepared by the pastor and the vicar, was used in an attempt to prove to the study-group members that the Bible contains errors. Resources presenting the conservative view of the differences were not provided. Later research by L.I.F.T. members revealed that although conservative Lutherans agree that the Bible contains difficult passages that, upon first inspection, seem to contradict each other, they also know that most of these passages can be harmonized.

Dr. William Arndt points out that to harmonize these differences one must approach them with the prior assumption that the Bible is free from error. In this way, the differences will not be exaggerated. Where an apparent contradiction seems to defy all efforts to solve it, Arndt reminds us that "some things that seemed baffling to our ancestors no longer perplex us. It may well be that succeeding generations will have no difficulty in solving some things that are obscure to us today."[7]

3) *A Theological Word Book of the Bible,* Alan Richardson.

This is a recommended resource book for *Search* and *Word and Witness,* two primary ELCA adult Bible-study programs.

> (1 Cor. 15:50)—What Paul means is *not* that there is to be a restoration of the *fleshy* particles of the deceased, but that each individual will have bestowed upon him, as God sees fit (1 Cor. 15:44), a *spiritual* body—that is, a body of another order than flesh and blood.

---

[6]Patsy A. Leppien, "An Open Letter to the Laity of the ALC," *Christian News Encyclopedia,* 4 vols., ed. Herman Otten (Washington: Missourian Publishing Co., 1988), 3:2166. This article describes experiences of the L.I.F.T. members that led to their departure from the ALC.

[7]William Arndt, *Bible Difficulties & Seeming Contradictions,* eds. Robert G. Hoerber and Walter R. Roehrs (St. Louis: Concordia Publishing House, 1987), pp. 124-131.

(1 Cor. 15:35-54)—Paul does *not* teach the *crude* rabbinic doctrine of the rehabilitation of these our present physical bodies.[8]

4) *Affirm Series, The Apostles Creed,* Teacher's Guide, catechism materials for seventh- and eighth-grade children.

Many questions about the resurrection have been raised. How can there be a resurrection of the flesh when Paul says that "flesh and blood cannot inherit the kingdom of God" (1 Cor. 15:50)? . . . All such questions miss the essential point Paul makes in 1 Cor. 15:35-50—namely, God will transform us into a glorified existence freed from all forms of evil. What is involved in believing in the resurrection of the body is simply that we are saved as individuals and do not lose our individuality in the next life.[9]

5) *The Lutheran,* the official magazine of the former Lutheran Church in America (LCA). "Morning Has Broken," John R. Brokoff.
The author is an ELCA pastor and professor emeritus of homiletics, Emory University, Candler School of Theology, Atlanta, Georgia.

How many Christians really understand what happened on the first Easter—the meaning of resurrection? Resurrection is often confused with resuscitation. If believers refer to nature coming into bloom in the spring as evidence of the resurrection, they are mistaken. . . . Nature throughout winter was not dead, only dormant. When Jesus raised Lazarus from the dead, it was a case of resuscitation, because Lazarus had to die again. Resurrection is a radical transformation. Life is turned into eternal life. One who is resurrected never dies again. . . . Resurrection is not a case of a return of life to the physical body. It is destined to return to the earth. The resurrected body is a new, spiritual, glorified body which may have characteristics of the physical body but it is not the same, for flesh and blood do not inherit the kingdom of heaven.[10]

---

[8]*A Theological Word Book of the Bible,* ed. Alan Richardson (New York: MacMillan & Co., 1950), pp. 35, 108.

[9]Marshall D. Johnson, *Affirm Series, The Apostles Creed,* Teacher's Guide, eds. Irene Getz, Susan Niemi Tetlie, and Gretchen L. Weidenbach (Minneapolis: Augsburg, 1984), p. 43.

[10]John R. Brokoff, "Morning Has Broken," *The Lutheran,* April 18, 1984, p. 4.

Again, notice the use of the word resuscitation. According to Brokoff, Lazarus was not really dead, only "dormant" like the flowers and shrubs! And yet John 11:17, states "On his arrival, Jesus found that Lazarus had already been in the tomb *four days.*" By ignoring the fact that Lazarus had been dead for four days and equating Jesus' miracle to a mere "resuscitation," the author not only denies the miracle but casts doubt on Christ's own *bodily* resurrection, as well as ours. Brokoff is right when he states that Lazarus was not "resurrected," in the sense that he had to die again and await the final Resurrection. He is also right in that the resurrected body will be changed so that it will never die again. But he denies the actual *physical* resurrection when he says that "resurrection is *not* a return to life of the physical body." The entire quotation is another example of the subtle mixing of truth with error and the casting of doubt.

6) *We Believe and Teach,* Dr. Martin J. Heinecken.

Heinecken is professor emeritus at Lutheran Theological Seminary at Philadelphia (ELCA), Philadelphia, Pennsylvania. He is named among the finest of the LCA theologians.[11]

> It is the entire person, therefore, who shall live again at God's call. This resurrection of the body does *not* mean a re-assembling of the chemical particles that have constituted our bodies here.[12]

7) Dr. Michael Root, in response to a letter concerning the Virgin Birth and the Resurrection.

Root is associate professor of systematic theology at Lutheran Theological Southern Seminary (ELCA), Columbia, South Carolina. He has taken "a leave of absence to accept a three-year appointment at the Institute of Ecumenical Research in Strasbourg, France. Root will participate in researching and writing ecumenical-study projects requested by a board composed of Lutheran church leaders from around the world.[13]

The following quotation is from a letter written by Root in response to a letter received from former LCA pastor Dr. Gregory Jackson.[14]

---

[11]Timothy F. Lull, "LCA, A Church Called Lutheran," *The Lutheran,* December 1987, p. 13.

[12]Martin J. Heinecken, *We Believe and Teach* (Philadelphia: Fortress Press, 1980), p. 119.

[13]"Faces," *The Lutheran,* June 1, 1988, p. 42.

[14]Jackson now serves as parish pastor in the conservative WELS. He left the LCA in 1987 because of the liberal theology. (cf. "Pastor-Scholar Leaves the Lutheran Church in America," *Christian News Encyclopedia,* 4 vols., ed. Herman Otten [Washington: Missourian Publishing Co., 1988], 3:2195.)

The letter is dated December 17, 1986. Jackson wrote to Lutheran Southern Seminary to inquire if there were any professors who still believed in the Virgin Birth or the Resurrection of Christ.

Your letter about the virgin birth and physical resurrection of Jesus was passed on to me a few weeks ago. . . . I have enclosed the sections on the virgin birth and resurrection from Carl Braaten and Robert Jenson's *Christian Dogmatics*. These are written by Braaten. They are *typical* of the attitudes I have encountered among colleagues at the seminaries. . . . I have never met a Lutheran seminary professor who denied the bodily resurrection. (In light of I Cor. 15:44, 46, 50, I think we should avoid the phrase "physical resurrection.") Most theologians are skeptical about any precise definition of what sort of body the Risen Christ had and has, but that seems absolutely appropriate.

8) "The Confession of a Former LCA Pastor," Dr. J. Kincaid Smith. Smith is now a pastor in the Evangelical Lutheran Synod.

I was trained in the "new thinking" at Hamma School of Theology, now merged with Capital and called Trinity. . . . When I graduated in 1973, to the best of my knowledge, none of my classmates, nor I, believed in any of the miraculous elements in the Bible, in anything supernatural. . . .

One reason lay-people have such a hard time accepting what I am saying is that most of them are not aware of hearing much or any of this from their pastors. You have to understand a very peculiar thing which has happened. As this change, the metamorphosis, has taken place over the years the *language* was *revamped*. When I got out of sem we used the same words as our conservative counter-parts, but we meant something quite different by them. Thus I might speak of the "empty tomb" on Easter but I would not have meant that I believed that Jesus actually, physically rose from the dead. If you had specifically asked me, something lay-people are extremely reticent to do, what I meant by "empty tomb" I would have squirmed.[15]

In quotation (3) of Position A, Luther says: "This article (the doctrine of the physical resurrection) suffered and still suffers the most

---

[15]J, Kincaid Smith, "The Confession of a Former Liberal LCA Pastor," *Christian News Encyclopedia*, 4 vols., ed. Herman Otten (Washington: Missourian Publishing Co., 1988) 3:2165.

opposition and is most difficult to believe." What Luther says here goes right to the very heart of the problem of liberalism.

Remember that the real underlying presupposition of the whole *historical-critical method* is the assumption or conviction that the *supernatural* is *not possible*. If the reader grasps that point, he will be able to understand why the liberal scholars *must* deny all the underlying essentials of the faith.

The most critical elements of the Christian faith, the lynch pins that virtually hold the whole scheme of things together, are all things that are truly *impossible* under the laws of natural science and are, therefore, indeed "most difficult to believe."

Miraculous things are, by their very nature, *contrary* to nature; they are *super*-natural, *above* nature. If, therefore, human reason is informed by the observation of nature alone, or if the observation of nature is given precedence over the special and unique *revelation* given to us in Scripture, then the miraculous must be denied.

When, on the other hand, it is believed that with God all things are possible, then reason gladly takes its position subservient to God's Word, the God whose ways and hidden counsels are as far above our ways and thoughts as the heavens are above the earth (Isaiah 55:8,9).

The doctrine of the physical resurrection of Christ is integrally related to, tied up with, the doctrine of the physical resurrection of our own bodies. The liberal critics recognize this connection and so in the same way that they ultimately deny the real physical resurrection of Christ, they also deny the future real physical resurrection of *our* bodies in the Resurrection of the dead.

There are few things more difficult for man to imagine than how God will manage to raise us from the dead in our own (though changed) flesh. Christians, as Luther stated, have been lost or buried at sea and eaten by the fishes. Millions in time past have been buried in the earth, and their bodies have long since decayed to dust that has scattered. How all these will stand (with Job) before the Lord, in eternity, in their very own flesh, is indeed a profound mystery.

There *are,* however, many things that the historic critics deny that are even more difficult than the doctrine of the physical *resurrection* of *this* body. God *created* everything in the universe, including the very dust that makes up these our bodies. He *created* all that exists, *spoke* it all into being out of *nothing*. "By faith we understand that the universe was formed at God's command, so that what is seen was not made out of what was visible" (Hebrews 11:3). It is by *faith* that *we* understand.

Therein lies the very crux of the ultimate issue, the issue of faith itself and that which must provide the *basis* for that faith. Is it, as the critics would have it, only that which appears, the things that can be explained within the natural order, the things that reason can grasp, upon which faith is to be established? Or is the foundation for faith found in the Word that tells us of those events that by their very nature are beyond the natural explanation of reason, those things contained in the special revelation of Scripture, things that can only be grasped by the mind of faith. St. Paul gives us a doxology suitable for this chapter:

> Oh the depth of the riches of the wisdom and knowledge of God! How unsearchable his judgments, and his paths beyond tracing out! "Who has known the mind of the Lord? Or who has been his counselor?" (Romans 11:33,34)

Who indeed has been his counselor?

In concluding this chapter, let us consider the words of St. Paul, who has pointed us to the deadly seriousness of the matter at hand, the real resurrection of our Lord and subsequently our own real resurrection, when he wrote to the church at Corinth against the detractors of God's Word in *his* day:

> But if it is preached that Christ has been raised from the dead, how can some of you say that there is no resurrection of the dead? If there is no resurrection of the dead, then not even Christ has been raised. And if Christ has not been raised, our preaching is useless and so is your faith. More than that, we are then found to be false witnesses about God, for we have testified about God that he raised Christ from the dead. But he did not raise him if in fact the dead are not raised. For if the dead are not raised, then Christ has not been raised either. And if Christ has not been raised, your faith is futile; you are still in your sins. Then those who have fallen asleep in Christ are lost. If only for this life we have hope in Christ, we are to be pitied more than all men (1 Corinthians 15:12-19).

Thanks be to God for these faith-assuring words. Thanks be to God indeed, for these words, along with all of Scripture, were inspired by the Holy Spirit for our assurance and comfort.

The next chapter examines a matter intimately connected with the issue of the bodily resurrection, the immortality of the soul.

16.

THE IMMORTALITY OF THE SOUL

Position A

We believe, as the Bible teaches, that man has a soul that survives temporal death. At death the soul of the Christian believer goes to heaven, while the unbeliever's soul goes to hell.

1) The Bible.

And the dust returns to the ground it came from, and the spirit returns to God who gave it (Ecclesiastes 12:7).

Jesus said to the thief on the cross: "I tell you the truth, today you will be with me in paradise" (Luke 23:43).

While on the cross Jesus said: "Father, into your hands I commit my spirit" (Luke 23:46).

When Stephen was about to die he said: "Lord Jesus, receive my spirit" (Acts 7:59).

Paul said: "We are confident, I say, and would prefer to be away from the body and at home with the Lord" (2 Corinthians 5:8).

2) *Luther's Catechism with an Explanation,* Joseph Stump.

Years ago this was the standard catechism book used in the former Lutheran Church in America (LCA). It was also used in many of the American Lutheran Church congregations.

He will raise up me and all the Dead at the Last Day. The bodies of all men shall be raised from the dead and re-united with the souls from which they were parted at death. . . . The impenitent and unbelieving shall be cast into eternal torment, and shall suffer indescribable pain and misery forever.[1] (Cf. Daniel 12:2 and John 5:28, 29).

Position B

We should not speak of the soul, because the Bible does not teach that we have an immortal soul. We really cannot speak of what may be beyond death. Perhaps in some sense we may "be with Jesus."

1) *Christian Dogmatics,* Braaten/Jenson, the *primary* theology textbook used in all seminaries of the Evangelical Lutheran Church in America (ELCA).

> In recent years, especially under the impact of a renewed listening to the biblical documents, the idea of an immortal soul has become increasingly *suspect.* A human being is again seen as a unity. Karl Barth perhaps over-stated the case when he claimed that the notion of immortality is a typical thought engendered by fear. Karl Rahner puts the issue more correctly when he states that there is no rectilinear continuation of our empirical reality beyond death. In this regard death puts an end to the *whole man.*[2]

2) *Search. Unit 11. 1 Corinthians,* Leader's Guide, Dr. Stanley N. Olson.

Search is a primary ELCA adult Bible-study program. Olson was assistant professor of New Testament at Luther Northwestern Theological Seminary (ELCA), St. Paul, Minnesota, and is now serving as a parish pastor.

> *Bible Background*—The Christian and Jewish beliefs, however, have little in common with those religions or philosophies, ancient or modern, which believe that human nature justifies a belief that death is not the end. These theories suggest that some portion or essence of the person is not mortal and will survive death. Christians have sometimes talked about the immortality of the soul in this way, but to do so is *inappropriate.* The Christian belief focuses on the power of God, not on something about us as persons (for example, 1 Cor. 15:52). As in the New Testament, we can appropriately speak of the soul as a way of describing God's constant relationship with us, *not* as a description of some

---

[1]Joseph Stump, *Luther's Catechism with an Explanation* (Philadelphia: United Lutheran Publishing, 1907), pp. 115, 116.

[2]Hans Schwarz, *Christian Dogmatics,* 2 vols., eds. Carl E. Braaten and Robert W. Jenson (Philadelphia: Fortress Press, 1984), 2:566.

part of a human being. When we breathe our last, we are really dead, as Jesus was really dead. And, like Jesus, we will be raised by God.

A study of funeral services may reveal that some place more stress on the power of God than others. Some may even talk in terms of immortality of the soul, which this session's "Bible Background" section has suggested is *unhelpful* or, at least, *ambiguous*. Be careful about criticisms of the practice of a particular church. Ask if the words can be *interpreted* in an *appropriate* manner.[3]

3) *Beyond the Gates of Death, A Biblical Examination of Evidence for Life After Death,* Dr. Hans Schwarz.

Schwarz is a professor of systematic theology. He served at Trinity Lutheran Seminary, Columbus, Ohio; is a faculty member at the University of Regensburg, Regensburg, Germany; and is listed in the *1991 ELCA Yearbook* as a visiting professor at Lutheran Theological Southern Seminary, Columbia, South Carolina. He remains on the clergy roster of the ELCA and is one of the authors of *Christian Dogmatics.*

Immortality would be the final jewel in our crown of self-conceit. We are too good to perish but if we should die, our soul will live forever. . . . Death puts an end to our *total* existence, body, *soul,* and everything.[4]

4) *The Lutheran,* the official magazine of the former LCA. "Morning Has Broken," John R. Brokoff (LCA).

The author is an ELCA pastor and professor emeritus of homiletics, Emory University, Candler School of Theology, Atlanta, Georgia.

Christians need to understand that immortality is not the same as eternal life. The *pagan* view is that the soul is immortal. According to this view the soul has an inherent quality of immortality. Just because Christians are human does not mean that they live forever.[5]

5) *We Believe and Teach,* Dr. Martin J. Heinecken.

---

[3]Stanley N. Olson, *Search. Unit 11. 1 Corinthians,* Leader's Guide (Minneapolis: Augsburg Publishing House, 1985), pp. 85, 88.

[4]Hans Schwarz, *Beyond the Gates of Death: A Biblical Examination of Evidence for Life After Death* (Minneapolis: Augsburg Publishing House, 1981), p. 20.

[5]John R. Brokoff, "Morning Has Broken," *The Lutheran,* April 18, 1984, p. 4.

Heinecken is professor emeritus at Lutheran Theological Seminary at Philadelphia (ELCA), Philadelphia, Pennsylvania. He is named among the finest of the LCA theologians.[6]

> Individual destiny—Concerning the individual, we have *rejected* the notion of an *immortal soul* and have spoken instead of the resurrection of the body. Our hope for life hereafter rests upon Christ's victory over death and God's power to bring life out of death, not upon an indestructible soul within us. It is the entire person, therefore, who shall live again at God's call. This resurrection of the body does not mean a reassembling of the chemical particles that have constituted our bodies here.[7]

What a frightening thing death must be to those who have no one to offer them hope. What comfort can a pastor who does not know and believe that we have a soul that at death "puts on immortality" (1 Corinthians 15:53,54) give to the dying? What does he have to say to the husband or wife of one who has died in the faith? What comfort can he give to children when they ask their pastor, "Where is my father now?" or "Pastor, is my mother in heaven now?" How could a pastor answer such a child, a pastor who has been taught and believes that "death puts an end to our *total* existence, body, soul, and everything" (Hans Schwarz, [3])?

The humanistic liberalism that comprises the "new thinking" is at this point surely the most bankrupt of all "religions." Even pagan religions, perverted as they are, attempt to hold out some kind of "hope" of eternal life.

With the conclusion of this chapter there is nothing left of the Christian faith, no real Christ, no real atonement, no real resurrection, and now not even a soul to go to heaven.

In the next chapter we begin taking up the issues that result from the devastating assault of the liberals upon the historic Christian faith, the "new" morality. The remainder of the subjects covered in section one of this book document the natural results of the denial of the authority of God's Word and the consequent denial of the Christian faith.

---

[6]Timothy F. Lull, "LCA, A Church Called Lutheran," *The Lutheran,* December 1987, p. 13.

[7]Martin J. Heinecken, *We Believe and Teach* (Philadelphia: Fortress Press, 1980), p. 119.

17.

THE NEW MORALITY

Position A

Moral absolutes are clearly taught in Scripture. Moral teaching in the Bible is clear and does not allow for exceptions dependent upon the situation. Extramarital and premarital sexual relations are sins clearly condemned in the Holy Scriptures. Homosexuality, both the act and the thought (lust), are sin and are condemned in Scripture. As with any sin, the repentant fornicator, adulterer, and homosexual have forgiveness and the grace that can change their lives.

1) The Bible.

A. Jesus speaks clearly concerning the *absolute* standards of sexual morality:

> Haven't you read, he replied, "that at the beginning the Creator made them male and female" and said, "For this reason man will leave his father and mother and be united to his wife, and the two will become one flesh"? So they are no longer two but one. Therefore what God has joined together, let man not separate (Matthew 19:4-6). (Cf. Genesis 2:18-22.)

> It was said: "Whoever divorces his wife, *must give her a divorce paper*," but I tell you that everyone who divorces his wife, except for the fact that she has been sexually unfaithful, causes her to be looked upon as an adulteress, and whoever marries a divorced woman is looked upon as an adulterer (Matthew 5:31,32 NET).

> You have heard that it is said, "Do not commit adultery." But I tell you that anyone who looks at a woman lustfully has already committed adultery with her in his heart (Matthew 5:27,28).

B. Paul also leaves no doubt as to what constitutes sexual sin or its consequences:

> Because of this, God gave them over to shameful lusts. Even their women exchanged natural relations for unnatural ones. In the same way the men also abandoned natural relations with women and were inflamed with lust for one another. Men committed indecent acts with other men, and received in themselves the due penalty for their perversion (Romans 1:26,27).

> Do you not know that the wicked will not inherit the kingdom of God? Do not be deceived: Neither the sexually immoral nor idolaters nor adulterers nor male prostitutes nor homosexual offenders nor thieves nor the greedy nor drunkards nor slanderers nor swindlers will inherit the kingdom of God. And that is what some of you were. But you were washed, you were sanctified, you were justified in the name of the Lord Jesus Christ and by the Spirit of our God (1 Corinthians 6:9-11). (Cf. 1 Timothy 1:10 and Jude 7.)

C. The Old Testament is equally clear:

> Before they had gone to bed, all the men from every part of the city of Sodom—both young and old—surrounded the house. They called to Lot, "Where are the men who came to you tonight? Bring them out to us so that we can have sex with them" (Genesis 19:4,5). (Cf. Genesis 18:20—19:25 and 2 Peter 2:6-9.)

> Do not lie with a man as one lies with a woman; that is detestable (Leviticus 18:22).

> If a man lies with a man as one lies with a woman, both of them have done what is detestable. They must be put to death; their blood will be on their own heads (Leviticus 20:13). (Cf. Leviticus 18:1—20:27, Judges 19:22-27 and 1 Kings 19:21-24.)

2) Martin Luther.

Since Paul says (1 Cor. 6:9) that fornicators and adulterers will not possess the kingdom of God, it is astounding to find people to this day who ask whether simple fornication is a mortal sin. To such inquirers I say that they should themselves read what has been written. If they want me to be the

127

judge, I certainly cannot judge any differently from what *Scripture* says.[1]

Note: The term "fornication" refers to any sexual relations that occur outside of marriage, including adultery, and is used frequently in the King James Version of the Bible. The New International Version of the Bible and other versions use "sexual immorality," etc.

> The vice of the Sodomites is an unparalleled enormity. It departs from the natural passion and desire, planted into nature by God, according to which the male has a passionate desire for the female. Sodomy craves what is entirely contrary to nature. Whence comes this perversion? Without a doubt it comes from the devil. After a man has once turned aside from the fear of God, the devil puts such great pressure upon his nature that he extinguishes the fire of natural desire and stirs up another, which is contrary to nature.[2]

3) A Christ-like approach to homosexuality.

> Jesus said to the woman caught in adultery, "Woman, where are they? Has no one condemned you?" "No one, sir," she said. "Then neither do I condemn you," Jesus declared. "Go now and leave your life of sin" (John 8:10,11)

> . . . the blood of Jesus, his Son, purifies us from all sin (1 John 1:7).

There is forgiveness for all sins—sexual or otherwise. Many are urging Christians to tolerate homosexuality as a valid lifestyle and ignore what the Holy Scriptures teach. A Christ-like approach involves accepting the person without condoning the sin. We must not let our acceptance of the person slip into overlooking or even accepting the sin. Rather, we must behave in such a manner as to lead that person to seek Christian counseling; come to repentance; and through faith, put off the sin.

CONSEQUENCES OF APOSTASY

4) *Speaking the Unspeakable! Homosexuality—A Biblical and Modern Perspective*, Richard Starr.

---

[1] *What Luther Says*, 3 vols., ed. Ewald Plass (St. Louis: Concordia Publishing House, 1959), 1:133.
[2] Ibid., 1:134.

Starr is a pastor of the Wisconsin Evangelical Lutheran Synod (WELS) who is presently serving in the WELS foreign mission field. At the time this book was written, he was a parish pastor in Worthington, Ohio, and a part-time campus pastor at Ohio State University in Columbus. In his book, Pastor Starr carefully addresses the issue of homosexuality on the basis of God's Word. His discussion includes all of the Bible verses listed at the beginning of this chapter and sharply contrasts with the Position B documentation concerning the same Bible verses. We highly recommend Pastor Starr's book as an excellent study of homosexuality that will help the reader answer those who advocate homosexuality as a God-pleasing alternate lifestyle. The following quotation is an appropriate conclusion to the documentation of Position A.

> Sexual degradation always follows apostasy—the abandoning of the true faith. Sexual perversion and immorality run wild without God. The stench of sexual deviation is always evident when man rejects God's control over his life. It was that way in the days of Sodom and Gomorrah, in St. Paul's day, and today. Look at Main Street America: massage parlors, adult bookstores, adult theaters, homosexual bars and baths, adult motels where you pay not by the night but by the hour, and pornographic magazines sandwiched between *Time* and *Good Housekeeping*. Besides that, most of the "adult" world is open twenty-four hours a day, seven days a week. Indeed, the sun never sets on America's smut. We are supposed to accept all of this as normal and natural.
>
> No matter how loudly and long a person says he believes in God, if he willfully rejects God's will and continues to live in sin, then he is not really a Christian but an unbeliever.[3]

Position B

Many questions of moral behavior must responsibly take all circumstances in a given situation into account. Narrow, rigid application of moral values would be legalistic and inconsistent with the precept of love in the Gospel. Extramarital and premarital sexual relations are not always sinful but must be judged by the situation and the precept of love. Homosexuality in the life of a responsible loving Christian should be acknowledged as a valid lifestyle. Even if viewed as sin, homosexuality is no worse than any other sin.

[3]Richard Starr, *Speaking the Unspeakable! Homosexuality—A Biblical and Modern Perspective* (Milwaukee: Northwestern Publishing House, 1987), p. 23.

While the documentation of Position B focuses primarily on homosexuality, it also includes evidence of a breakdown in moral standards relating to the other sexual sins condemned in Scripture.

1) *The Bishop of the Evangelical Lutheran Church in America* (ELCA). "A Pastoral Letter: The Church and the Homosexual Person," Herbert W. Chilstrom, Bishop, Minnesota Synod, Lutheran Church in America (LCA), 1979.

The following quotations illustrate the subtle application of the historical-critical method to the Holy Scriptures. It should be noted that the documentation in Position A includes all of the Bible references that appear in the quotations from Bishop Chilstrom's letter. These passages of Scripture very clearly condemn all forms of sexual sin. At this point it will be helpful to remember that those who accept the historical-critical method deny the absolute authority of Scripture and believe that the Scriptures are conditioned by the time and the culture in which they were written. Because those ancient cultures no longer exist and times change, these people conclude that these verses of Scripture are no longer applicable to today's modern "scientifically enlightened" society. Therefore, a "new" understanding must be found.

REINTERPRETING SCRIPTURE

Bishop Chilstrom demonstrates the manner in which this new understanding is found—by reinterpreting Scripture to mean something entirely different. His method is typical of the teaching of many religious leaders and scholars in most of the mainline denominations. Presented in a seemingly reasonable and persuasive manner, this wrongful interpretation of Scripture is responsible for the change in thinking that has led many people into believing that homosexuality is "a gift from God" to be accepted and practiced as a God-pleasing alternate lifestyle. Chilstrom writes:

> Those who cannot think of a homosexual person in any terms other than "pervert," "freak" and "sinner" will not find these pages helpful since what I have to say is aimed precisely at one of the most prejudicial attitudes to be found in our church and society today. . . . The section of the paper devoted to biblical references to homosexuality will probably cause much discomfort for those who interpret these passages literally or who believe that every Scripture must bear equal weight in making applications to our contemporary world (p. 1).

Genesis 19, the Sodom account, often comes to mind because it is set before us in the form of a story. The people of this inhospitable city demand they be given Lot's guests, seemingly for sexual purposes . . . if we consider Sodom from the standpoint of subsequent reference, we find no suggestion that homosexual acts were the essence of their sin. Instead, it is clear that lack of hospitality is seen as the basic issue. . . . *Leviticus 18:22 and 20:13* need not occupy our attention to any large extent since they are part of the Levitical code designed specifically for Israel in its infancy. . . . *In the Gospels* there is no clear references to homosexuality. If Jesus had an opinion on the subject, he either did not express it or else the Gospel writers did not consider it of enough importance to preserve it for us. To argue from this that Jesus approved homosexual behavior is, or course, ridiculous. We must simply agree that we do not know the mind of Christ on this matter (p. 4).

Romans 1:26,27 condemns women and men who "exchange natural relations for unnatural" and who are "consumed with passion for one another. . . . " It can be seen that both here and again in 1 Corinthians 6, sexual perversion is grouped with a number of social sins. . . . I will continue to understand Paul to mean that homosexual acts, along with numerous other social sins, are contrary to God's intended order for believers and unbelievers alike. This then settles the issue, does it not? If one believes that Paul includes homosexual behavior in a catalog of sins, it is also safe for us to condemn it. Right? Wrong! Or at least we must say, "not necessarily." Even a strict fundamentalist— though he or she may not admit it— does not take the Bible literally. . . . Just as we acknowledge that added knowledge and a changed social order have altered our view of divorce and the role of women, so we may have to take a new look at homosexuality. In order to do so, we will have to call upon the deeper currents of the gospel as well as our evangelical tradition.

There may be some who cannot accept the possibility of a reconsideration of homosexuality. For them, it may be well to recall that the ethical prescriptions of the New Testament are drawn from a wide variety of sources, including the Old Testament, the teachings of Jesus, first century Judaism, Hellenistic moral codes, and the experience of the early church. Unlike the Pharisees, Christians do not (or should not) compile a list of New Testament commandments comparable to the 613 rules of the Torah, all held to be forever binding. The New Testament foundation for ethics is agape [unconditional love]. We live with a freedom which allows us to reexamine a particular issue with the possibility that the Spirit of God may lead us to a new or different understanding of that issue.

As I forewarned you in the introduction, those who tend to biblical literalism will of necessity have to part company at this juncture. If every passage of Scripture is thought to have equal application for Christian ethics, there is no room for further discussi.on. But for those who accept the fact that all of life stands under both judgment and grace and that the Spirit continues to work in the Church to help us understand the mind of Christ, there is room for exploration and new insight (pp. 5,6).

In this 14-page letter, Bishop Chilstrom makes reference to the studies of various contemporary scholars, both conservative and liberal, and eventually draws some conclusions of his own.

What I propose is that at this point in time in the debate over homosexuality we may have little choice in the church except to say that we accept the person, but question the behavior. Note that I avoid using the terms "sinner" and "sin." The LCA statement on "Sex, Marriage and Family" states that "persons who engage in homosexual behavior are sinners only as are all other persons . . . alienated from God and neighbor." I am completely at ease with our LCA position (p. 9).

Bishop Chilstrom later makes application of the LCA position to church membership of homosexuals by stating that "the sexual orientation of a homosexual person should be as incidental for his or her membership as that of a heterosexual person." He supports this by referring to a report to the 1978 convention of the former LCA by then President Robert Marshall. Dr. Marshall began his remarks with the LCA statement that those who engage in homosexual behavior are sinners only as are other persons. He maintained that the consequences of this position:

should lead congregations to receive homosexuals into the Christian fellowship without any qualifications. The (LCA) statement calls for the right and privacy and equal opportunity for homosexuals. While some associate homosexuality with the exploitation and abuse of others, it must be remembered that the accusation would apply to only some homosexuals and that some heterosexuals are equally guilty of the exploitation of others (p. 11).

Bishop Chilstrom goes on to express disapproval of those who are "promiscuous, immoral, lacking in commitment, and those who may prefer younger boys [in the case of males] and have no qualms about perverting the adolescent" and then makes a distinction concerning those who are living in a committed homosexual relationship.

But what about the person who has chosen to maintain a sexual relationship with someone of the same gender? Here I would make another distinction. . . . I have in mind the individual who has a profound sense of devotion to a single person of the same gender. This person would no more think of being unfaithful or promiscuous than would a heterosexual person with a sense of devotion to his wife or her husband. Furthermore, in the case of a male, the thought of perverting a young boy is absolutely out of the question. Contrary to popular notion, there are such people. Not long ago I met a man who lived with his first partner for eight years until his friend died of leukemia.

His grief for his friend and partner was genuine. Since then he has lived with another partner with whom he will soon celebrate the 25th anniversary of their relationship. He is actively involved in the affairs of his church and community, currently serving as director of an important social ministry program for a major metropolitan area.

How should we deal with homosexual persons of this kind? My inclination would be to treat these persons quite differently from promiscuous homosexual persons. I would inform them of the position of the LCA. I would point out the basically non-judgmental nature of our stance. I would also forewarn them of the resistance they are likely to face in the church if they intend to speak openly about their sexuality and try to ascertain if they are prepared to deal with it constructively. I would urge them not to make their sexual preference an issue in the life of the congregation other than in settings where the total question of sexuality is being considered (p. 10).

Bishop Chilstrom admits that not all pastors will agree with his stand but asks for understanding and tolerance.

> I realize that some pastors cannot now—and probably never will—accept the idea that one can be Christ-confessing and a practicing homosexual person at the same time. I don't ask that you change your view. I only ask that you be patient, considerate and understanding when other pastors choose to be more open on this matter (p. 11).

Bishop Chilstrom is obviously one of the pastors who has decided to be more "open on this matter." We quote now his position on the ordination of homosexual persons into the ministry.

> . . . I believe that a celibate homosexual person who meets all other requirements should be allowed ordination. I believe that an avowed, practicing homosexual person, regardless of all other qualifications and consideration, should not be allowed ordination (p. 11).

The preceding material is a good example of the kind of thinking that takes place once the authority of Scripture—God's absolutes—are denied. Without God's absolutes there is no clear and certain difference between right and wrong—no real definition of sin. Those who deny inerrancy and the absolute authority of God's Word fall victim to their own error. Uncertainty and confusion are the result, as the following quotations illustrate.

2) The Bishop of ELCA.

Bishop Chilstrom allowed the video and audio recording of an informational meeting held at Our Redeemer's Lutheran Church in Williston, North Dakota, on June 15, 1987, under the sponsorship of the Williston Conference. The following quotations are from the two audiotapes. Bishop Chilstrom began his remarks with the view that heterosexuals have no choice about their sexual orientation and that this is also true of many homosexuals. He stated that he formerly held a more conservative view of homosexuality, but after talking with a group of 25 homosexual males his thinking began to change. One should add here that perhaps Bishop Chilstrom's view of Scripture made him more vulnerable to the homosexuals' viewpoint. Bishop Chilstrom was asked if he believed that homosexuals should remain celibate—"I mean, is it *wrong* or *not?!*" (speaker's emphasis). Bishop Chilstrom responded:

> *I don't know.* I know people like definite answers, especially from bishops, but quite frankly, *I do not know* (speaker's emphasis).

After reviewing Old Testament Scripture and pointing out that there is no clear answer, he continued:

> Now some would say—"Okay, that may not be clear but you interpret Scripture with Scripture"—so you go to the New Testament to Romans and 1 Corinthians 6:18 and the book of Jude and there it's very clear that homosexuality is condemned! Well, the best scholarship, in my judgment, would raise questions about that. I think the finest book *I* have seen is called—*Homosexuality in the New Testament* by Robin Scroggs. He did what a good scholar ought to do. He went back and studied literature from New Testament times, Greek literature because the Bible was written in Greek. The point Scroggs makes is that he believes that the New Testament is silent about adult, consenting relationships. And that isn't very satisfying because he ends up as I just said a moment ago—"I don't know." But, I *don't*. And *I don't know* what the Apostle Paul had in mind when he talked about sexual perversion (speaker's emphasis).

It should be noted here that when liberal scholars compare Scripture with secular literature they treat both as uninspired.

3) *Homosexuality in the New Testament,* Dr. Robin Scroggs.

Scroggs is professor of New Testament at Chicago Theological Seminary, Chicago, Illinois. He taught a summer course at Trinity Lutheran Theological Seminary, Columbus, Ohio, in 1986. His book has been favorably reviewed by many ELCA theologians, including Dr. Paul Jersild (see earlier quotations). Scroggs states in his concluding remarks:

> The conclusion I have to draw seems inevitable: *Biblical judgments against homosexuality are not relevant to today's debate.* They should no longer be used in denominational discussions about homosexuality, should in no way be a weapon to justify refusal of ordination, *not because the Bible is not authoritative,* but simply because it does not address the issues involved (author's emphasis).[4]

GAY CERTIFICATION FOR ORDINATION

4) "Western Bishops Back Action on Gays," *The Lutheran,* the official magazine of the ELCA.

---

[4]Robin Scroggs, *Homosexuality in the New Testament* (Philadelphia: Fortress Press, 1983), p. 127.

Eleven western bishops of the Evangelical Lutheran Church in America came to the support of Pacific Lutheran Seminary faculty after a report surfaced that three "openly gay" students at the school had been certified for ordination. Bishops of the church's two western regions issued a statement jointly with faculty members during a Jan. 21-22 conference at the school in Berkeley, Calif. . . . The statement declares that faculty members *heeded church pronouncements* on ordination and homosexuality when they voted to certify gay seminarians for call and ordination. . . . In their document, the bishops and faculty members said they *"reaffirmed* the current statements and practices of the Lutheran church that to be admittedly homosexual in orientation does not in and of itself preclude ordination. The policy of the church is that practicing homosexuals will not be ordained." The statements adds, "In the bishops' judgment, the seminary faculty acted consistently with the church's statements in that students were informed that being a practicing homosexual would bar them from ordination."

The bishops' action was prompted by a press release sent out by *Lutherans Concerned,* an unofficial national caucus that conducts "a Christian ministry for lesbian and gay understanding."[5]

The attitude of the bishops, faculty, and students can be seen in the following quotations concerning the certification of the three seminary students (i.e., Jeffrey Johnson, James Lancaster, and Joel Workin).

The Rev. Stanley Olsen, former bishop of the LCA's Pacific Southwest Synod, said he was present and voting when that synod's credentials committee approved Johnson and Lancaster. "They are single and committed to a celibate life style," he said. . . . "As far as we were concerned," he continued, "they were judged on their total qualifications for ministry. It was incidental that they were of a sexual orientation that was homosexual. . . ."

In a telephone interview, Lancaster, 25, of Westminster, Calif., said, "I presented myself to the committee as a gay person called to ministry. . . . It was simply said in the com-

---

[5]Jean Caffey Lyles, "Western Bishops Back Action on Gays," *The Lutheran,* March 16, 1988, p. 23.

mittee meeting that the church expects its ministers to be morally circumspect across the board. . . . "

Johnson, 25, of Lancaster, Calif., said, "I went before the professional preparation committee as an openly gay candidate. It wasn't a real big issue for them or for me. . . . "

Workin, 26, of Walcott, N.D. [said], "Everything has gone according to church policy. To my knowledge, this is the first time that any candidate has gone through the process being openly gay and that it has been OK for that to be a matter of public knowledge."[6]

Edgar R. Trexler, editor of *The Lutheran,* has this to say:

Lutherans [i.e., liberal Lutherans] and others, have ordained homosexuals for years. Gays wanting to be ordained kept their sexual orientation quiet. . . . It is unclear if the certifying committees asked these seminarians whether they are "practicing" homosexuals. . . . Denunciations of homosexual acts, especially in the Holiness Code in Leviticus, may refer, in the words of a 1986 Lutheran Church in America study, "to the imposition of sex by one man upon another". . . . Data increasingly suggests that same-sex orientation is biological, not learned, raising the questions of whether it is *fair* to expect gays *not* to act out their sexuality.[7]

The certification of Johnson, Lancaster, and Workin created great interest and was reported by the media in newspapers across the country and in later issues of *The Lutheran.* It also prompted another pastoral letter by Bishop Chilstrom that was sent to all 11,000 pastors of the ELCA.

THE BISHOP SPEAKS AGAIN

5) *A Pastoral Letter,* Bishop Herbert W. Chilstrom, ELCA, March 20, 1988.

This letter is much shorter but very similar in content to the letter Bishop Chilstrom wrote in 1979, particularly in his view of Scripture, and supports the quotations documented in this chapter. The closing paragraph recommends the 1979 letter as a resource that is available from the main offices of the ELCA. The following statements by Bishop Chilstrom concern the three seminary students:

---

[6]Ibid., p. 24.
[7]*The Lutheran,* ed. Edgar R. Trexler, March 16, 1988, p. 50.

Let me begin by stating that the issue is not new. Persons of known homosexual orientation were ordained by our prede-cessor churches and were retained on their rosters. . . . In our predecessor churches no official *policy* was adopted to ad-dress this specific question. There grew up, however, a *prac-tice* among bishops that was uniform across the three prede-cessor churches: *persons of known homosexual orientation were told that they could not be ordained or be retained on the roster of ordained ministers unless they refrained from homosexual practice.*

It is clear from reports I have read that none of the three seminary students is involved in homosexual practice. It is also clear to me, however, that they were not asked at the time of their certification if they would refrain from such re-lationships in the future. On March 24 bishops of the region and leaders from the churchwide office will meet with the three students. At that time this question will be asked of each of the students. If they refuse to make such a commit-ment, it is my recommendation to the bishops of the area that they not recommend them for call to a congregation (author's emphasis) (p. 1).

Subsequent articles reported that all three students refused to promise that they would remain celibate and have been denied or-dination.

NEW GUIDELINES

6) *The Lutheran* (ELCA).
The ELCA has come up with the following "new interim guide-lines" concerning this issue:

The appropriate setting for sexual intercourse and other erotic expressions of sexual intimacy is marriage. A *pattern* of behavior that substitutes promiscuous behavior or the sexual abuse of another for that of a relationship of commit-ment and care is conduct that is inappropriate and is reason for a person to be removed from candidacy in the ELCA.

There is a distinction between homosexual orientation and homosexual behavior. A pattern of behavior that includes homosexual erotic activity is conduct that is inappropriate and is reason for a person to be removed from candidacy in the ELCA.

The Rev. Craig Settlage, director for candidacy for ordained ministry, said the statement's wording allows committees to make a distinction between an isolated incident and a pattern of behavior. There is also *leeway* in the first guideline, Settlage said, "for an engaged couple to grow in sexual intimacy leading to marriage."[8]

Contrary to what is stated above, God makes no distinction between homosexual orientation and homosexual behavior. Both the desire (lust) and the act of any sexual sin are wrong (Matthew 5:28).

THE YOUTH—CLAY TO BE MOLDED

The following material again illustrates the more open approach used in teaching the ELCA youth as opposed to the more careful and subtle approach used with adults. When one stops to realize that these young people are the future pastors and leaders of the church, the very people who will shape the thinking of future generations of Christians, there is much cause for alarm.

7) *Gay and Lesbian Ministry in the ELCA,* Verlyn O. Smith.

This article was featured in *Entree* (ELCA), the official magazine of the National Lutheran Campus Ministry, which is sent to all chaplains and students. Smith formerly served as Metropolitan Campus pastor in the Twin Cities and as western regional director, National Lutheran Campus Ministry. He is now pastor of Grace University Lutheran Church, Minneapolis, Minnesota. In the following quotations, Smith shares his beliefs about homosexuality and God's Word.

An observation

The acid test of inclusiveness is homosexuality. . . . Already in the brief history of the Evangelical Lutheran Church in America we have seen how dangerously real is the prediction made some years ago that homosexuality may be the issue that splits the Christian Church.[9]

Concerning sin

Church statements that call for equal legal rights have no meaning, if at the same time they declare gay and lesbian people guilty of sin simply because they are gay and lesbian.

---

[8]Lyles, "Guidelines for Sexual Conduct OK'd," *The Lutheran,* October 12, 1988, p. 23.
[9]Verlyn O. Smith, "Gay and Lesbian Ministry in the ELCA," *Entree,* October 1988, p. 4.

Jesus warned us against judging one another, not as an arbitrary rule, but because he knew that a judgmental attitude hurts people. . . . We must as a total church get past our need to be judgmental of gay and lesbian people. We must reach the point we have reached regarding racism. . . . We must declare anti-gay attitudes and actions as sin and denounce them as vigorously as we do racism, sexism, ageism, and classism.[10]

The Bible

But some are asking, "What about the Bible? Does it not say that homosexuality is a sin?" Many Lutherans struggle with that issue, and let us recognize that it is not an easy one. We rightly regard the Bible as Holy Scripture and as a guide to faith and life. But what needs to be demonstrated is that faithfulness to the Bible and acceptance of gay and lesbian people are not mutually exclusive.

I often say to people that if they would like to be set free from their need to believe gayness is a sin out of regard for the Bible, I would like to help them—adding also, that, if they do not want to be set free, I have little to say. I try to make it clear that the process will take some time and patience. Some stay long enough to work it through and our approach goes something like this:

First, I ask what they understand the Bible to say about homosexuality. Usually they do not know explicitly but have some sense that the Bible says it is wrong. They are invariably surprised to learn that there are only seven passages in the entire Bible that even the most "homophobic" person can use against gays and lesbians. [He then lists all of the Bible passages in Position A]. . . . They are also surprised to learn that not one word can be quoted from the lips of Jesus against homosexuality, and, while an argument from silence is never conclusive, it is difficult to understand why Jesus had nothing to say about what some consider to be such a heinous sin.

Whatever else can be said, it is clear that we have Scripture passages that are often taken out of context and whose meanings are at least debatable. There is no recognition in these verses that for some people the "natural" sexual ex-

---

[10]Ibid.

pression is the same-sex; that discovery is of much more recent vintage. There is also no reference to the possibility of a loving, committed same-sex relationship. I try to show that it really is not our business as Christians to make judgments about the lives of other people unless we have very good reason to do so. Jesus made that clear both by word and example. We have to decide whether a few scattered passages, subject to a variety of interpretations, is sufficient basis for labeling homosexuality, in and of itself, a sin. It is probably accurate to say that the Bible generally is a heterosexual book, that is, the biblical authors seem to see life that way. But it is also a male dominant book, and it is a human *slavery* book. Certain conditions prevailed in the world out of which the Bible emerged and were seen as normative. The question is whether attitudes descriptive of *that* world must be taken as prescriptive for all time.[11]

"Blessing" gay couples

Yet as a heterosexual I have to admit that I have the advantaged place. There is a Catch-22 for gays: Our church statements say that sexual activity outside of marriage is a sin, yet there is no marriage or anything similar for same-sex people. Church and society bless and support heterosexual relationships; neither is willing to do the same for gay and lesbian relationships, however long or loving they may be. It is difficult to understand why clergy are not encouraged to administer "blessings" to committed gay and lesbian relationships. It would seem that in the church we would want to encourage loyal and lasting loving relationships, whether heterosexual or homosexual. So the truth is that both church and society operate with what is clearly a double standard.[12]

Ordination

The same thing is true with regard to ordination, an issue very much visible now in the ELCA. Why do certification committees feel it is okay to probe the sexual life of people suspected to be gay in a way that they generally do not with people assumed to be beyond suspicion? And I thought celibacy as a pre-requisite to ordination went out with the Reformation.[13]

---

[11]Ibid , p. 5.
[12]Ibid., pp. 5, 6.
[13]Ibid., p. 6.

Gay advocacy

. . . one of the best ways to demonstrate your hospitality is to become an advocate for the gay and lesbian cause. Gay and lesbian people need to hear in sermons and read in newsletters that this representation of the Church is with and for them, even if it means some risk. It is generally true that a minority will not develop majority acceptance, unless people from the majority become their advocates. The congregation I serve as pastor is a Reconciled in Christ (RIC) congregation. This means that we have formally committed ourselves to welcome explicitly people of all sexual orientations—unconditionally. We need more RIC ministries.[14]

RESOURCES

Smith encourages his young adult readers to contact two very active gay Lutheran advocacy groups, Wingspan and Lutherans Concerned—Reconciled in Christ. Included in the list of recommended resources are Bishop Chilstrom's 1979 and 1988 Pastoral Letters and the book *Embodiment* by Dr. James Nelson. Documentation from this book and the two advocacy groups follow the next quotation.

Youth—congregational level

8) *Ministries with Young Adults,* Division for Congregational Life (ELCA).

This publication is for young adults at the congregational level.

The spring 1989 issue of *Ministries with Young Adults* was devoted to the preceding article from *Entree* by Verlyn O. Smith, including the list of resources. Following are a few of the editorial comments that accompanied the reprint of the article.

One of the most difficult issues facing the Church today is homosexuality. This issue of *Ministries with Young Adults* focuses on this concern, in particular, on ministry with gay and lesbian persons. Verlyn Smith, a former campus pastor, addressed the issue directly and with understanding. Suggestions are given at the end of the article for discussing it with a group of young adults. . . . It is recommended that resource persons be asked to participate in the discussion to provide factual information and the perspective of their particular field or concern. These persons might be psycholo-

---

[14]Ibid.

gists or counselors, doctors, pastors, and local representatives from groups such as Parents of Gays and Lesbians, Lutherans Concerned, or Reconciled in Christ congregations. Make copies of the article for distribution before the scheduled discussion. You might also make available some of the resources noted in the article. . . . [15]

A list of suggested questions for the discussion is provided and the following two Bible verses are recommended for use in advocating the acceptance of persons of homosexual orientation.

Come to me, all you who are weary and burdened, and I will give you rest (Matt. 11:28).

Here there is no Greek or Jew, circumcised or uncircumcised, barbarian, Scythian, slave or free, but Christ is all, and is in all (Col. 3:11).

9) *Embodiment,* Dr. James B. Nelson.

This textbook is widely used in ELCA seminaries and appears frequently as a recommended resource in *many* ELCA publications. It was listed as a resource book in the *1984-1985 Luther League Theme Manual* (American Lutheran Church [ALC], p. 27), and in the previously cited article by Verlyn Smith. Nelson is a clergyman of the United Church of Christ and has been a lecturer at Luther Northwestern Seminary (ELCA), St. Paul, Minnesota. His book allows for premarital and extramarital sex, homosexual marriages, and ordination of homosexual clergy. The following representative quotations illustrate what the youth are being exposed to under the disguise of *Christian* education!

Concerning premarital and extramarital sex

Traditional marriage will remain one of the options for many people, but there will be others, options that permit different types of relationships for different stages of life, and different living arrangements according to the nature of the relationships. . . . In the face of considerable anxiety about change, however, I believe it needs reiteration that no single form of institutional life on earth, marital or otherwise, ought to be considered final. . . . We have heard the arguments on both sides. Where are we left? First, I believe that the case of those who would reinterpret the traditional

---

[15]Smith, "Gay and Lesbian Ministry in the ELCA," *Ministries with Young Adults*, Division for Congregational Life, Spring 1989, pp. 1-4.

meanings of fidelity and monogamy ought not be too quickly dismissed. . . . I believe that the case for the redefinition of marital fidelity cannot be summarily dismissed. Openness to the *possibility* that this might reflect a viable Christian marriage for some, then, I think is appropriate. . . . For most of us the better rule is marital genital exclusivity. But, I would argue, this rule (as is any other) is a "presumptive" rule which can admit exceptions. . . . To put the matter this way and thus leave the possibility that there *may* be morally-justifiable acts of intercourse before marriage is vastly different from an endorsement of "recreational sex" or "fun-sex" (whose advocates are not difficult to find). (Author's emphasis.)[16]

Concerning homosexuality and homosexual marriages

I came to believe that nothing less than full Christian acceptance of homosexuality and of its responsible genital expression adequately represented the direction of both gospel and contemporary research. . . . A "Blessing of Union" rite (by whatever name), for example, might function for gays in ways fully parallel to the marriage rites. Such an ordinance would convey the Christian community's recognition, affirmation, pledge of support, and prayer for divine blessing to the gay couple whose intention is lasting fidelity.[17]

Concerning homosexual ordination into the ministry

It was not until 1972 that a major American denomination, the United Church of Christ, ordained a publicly-avowed gay candidate. . . . The recommendation made by the United Church's Executive Council to its ordaining bodies is worthy of consideration by other denominations: "that in the instance of considering a stated homosexual candidacy for ordination, the issue should not be his/her homosexuality as such, but rather the candidate's total view of human sexuality and his/her understanding of the morality of its use."[18]

---

[16]James B. Nelson, *Embodiment* (Minneapolis: Augsburg Publishing House, 1978), pp. 142-157.
[17]Ibid., pp. 199, 208.
[18]Ibid., p. 207.

ADVOCACY GROUPS—WITHIN THE CHURCH

One can see the strides being made by the homosexual movement in this country simply by reading the daily newspapers. Not only is the movement making progress in the secular world, but it has invaded the church as well. Nearly every mainline denomination has homosexual groups working diligently toward the ultimate, unrestricted acceptance of their lifestyle, including full access to every area of the church. The ELCA is no exception.

Misguided ministry

10) Wingspan, a Gay-Lesbian ministry within the ELCA.

The *Concord* of Luther Northwestern Seminary featured a favorable article concerning this group. The article stated that this ministry was founded in 1982 through the combined efforts of the members of St. Paul-Reformation Lutheran Church in St. Paul, Minnesota; their pastor, Paul Tidemann; a gay member, Leo Treadway; Bishop Chilstrom; and other church leaders.[19]

Wingspan's mission emphasis is described as follows:

> As the Wingspan Ministry has evolved it has clearly become not only a ministry within the congregation, but also a mission within the wider church. Wingspan's stated functions are: *Pastoral Care and Counseling* for Gay men, Lesbians and their families and for others wrestling with the issue; *Education and Outreach* for our members and the wider church, as well as within the Gay and Lesbian communities; *Witness and Advocacy* in the structures of society, including legislative matters and areas of law enforcement which will uplift the situation in life for Gay and Lesbian persons.

> Clearly, without the understanding and counsel of Bishop Chilstrom and other synodical and church-wide staff our Wingspan Ministry would be infinitely more difficult. We have also felt the spiritual and material support of other congregations and agencies who have been with us as we strive to do God's will in a new area of transcultural ministry.[20]

Pastor Paul Tidemann and the congregation were the topic of an article in *The Lutheran* (LCA).

---

[19]"Martin Luther King Jr.—A Dream Lives on—Local Congregation Risks Keeping Dream Alive," *Concord* (Luther Northwestern Seminary), January 12, 1988. *Christian News,* February 8, 1988, p. 24.

[20]Ibid.

> *Pastor agrees to end homosexual blessings*—A concern for
> the lack of stability in relationships within the homosexual
> community motivated the council of St. Paul-Reformation
> Church, St. Paul, Minnesota to authorize services of "bless-
> ings" for the union of gay or lesbian couples. After publicly
> blessing one union, the Rev. Paul Tidemann, pastor, was
> asked by Minnesota Synod Bishop Herbert Chilstrom to re-
> frain from blessing any more. Tidemann agreed. Tidemann
> had conferred with Chilstrom before starting the "blessing."
> Chilstrom said that in his judgment the Lutheran Church in
> America has no policy on such blessings. "It's a matter of
> personal conscience at this time," Chilstrom said.[21]

Because Smith recommends this ministry as a resource for young
adults in his article, the teaching carried out by representatives of
this ministry will be of particular interest to the reader.

Twisting Scripture

Words of Life, the publication of Living In Freedom Eternally
(L.I.F.E.), a "non-denominational Christian ministry which proclaims
freedom from homosexuality through Jesus Christ,"[22] reports on a
three-day Lutheran (LCA) conference on gay/lesbian ministry held in
1987. The L.I.F.E. member in attendance summarized the main
thrust of a speech given by Wingspan member Leo Treadway. Following is a small portion of her summary:

> After a particularly heart-rending statement about the con-
> dition of the homosexual person in the church, Mr. Treadway
> began a section of his address called "Reclaiming Scripture."
> He likened it to women cutting through the "male" Bible and
> blacks cutting through the "white" Bible. Then he said there
> were people like gay/lesbian people in the Bible—people
> such as Ruth and Naomi, David and Jonathan, Jesus and
> John, Centurion and the slave. Were all of these gay and les-
> bians? He says the Bible does not allow him to say yes or no.
> (What heresy!) I could hardly stay in my seat but we were
> pledged to try to speak in love. Then he likened "coming out"
> to Joseph "coming out" to his brothers, Jesus "coming out"
> on the road to Emmaus (blasphemy!) and (I could hardly

---

[21]William L. Thorkelson, "Pastor Agrees to End Homosexual Blessings,"
The Lutheran, April 4, 1984, p. 22.

[22]Joanne Highley, "Prancing White Horse," *Words of L.I.F.E.,* December
1987, p. 3.

contain myself) Lazarus "coming out" of the grave, and when he did there was a "great stench just as when a homosexual comes out." He even said Esther spoke to people that were "closeted" and "perhaps for this reason God made you a Queen." This was done in seriousness. . . . The study of issues put out by the Lutheran Church in America is a slanted, pro-gay misinterpretation of Scripture. I pray that they may repent and see the truth.[23]

Of additional significance is the fact that the author of the above quotation comes from a homosexual background herself, has been free for 29 years, is happily married, and has counseled people in this area for more than seven years.

Acid test of inclusiveness—gay is ok

11) Lutherans Concerned/North America, (LC/NA).

The LC/NA is a gay advocacy group that describes itself as "a society of gay and non-gay Christians that is working to foster, within our church, a climate of understanding, justice and reconciliation among all women and men, regardless of their affectional preference."[24] In 1985 the LC/NA published a document titled *A Call for Dialogue.* According to a front-page article in *Vanguard,* this document was prepared by the Lutherans Concerned Task Force on Theology, which includes several ordained people. Additional input came from members, theologians, and church leaders.

Human sexuality, without distinction based on sexual orientation, is a gift of God, not only for procreation, but also for learning and expressing love and affection. . . . Human sexuality manifests itself in a variety of gender orientations, from exclusively heterosexual to exclusively homosexual. . . . All sexual orientations are gifts of God and are to be honored as such. . . . While sexual orientation may be distinguished from sexual expression, we reject the argument that would divide the two in order to condone one while condemning the other.[25]

Originally started with a $2,000 grant from the ALC in 1974, the LC/NA claims as members both homosexuals and heterosexuals. The

---

[23]Ibid.

[24]*Concord,* newsletter of Lutherans Concerned/North America (LC/NA)—A Christian Ministry for Lesbian and Gay Understanding, 1990:2, p. 2.

[25]Lutheran Concerned Task Force on Theology, "Lutherans Concerned Issues 'A Call for Dialogue,' " *Vanguard* (Lutheran Human Relations Association), May 1986, pp. 4-6.

May 23, 1975, issue of *Christianity Today,* in an article titled "Dollars for Disobedience," charged the ALC with "the dubious distinction, apparently, of being the first denomination officially to make a cash grant to a 'gay' caucus within its ranks."

Support grows

Support of the LC/NA within the ELCA and its predecessor bodies has continued to grow. Since its beginnings in 1974, various prominent leaders have served as preachers or speakers at LC/NA local chapters and international conferences. The *Concord,* the organization's official newsletter, reports on two of the more recent gatherings:

> . . . in December the LC/Chicago Chapter will have John Tietjen [vice president of the former Association of Evangelical Lutheran Churches], Bishop-Elect of the Metro Chicago Synod [ELCA] as preacher.[26]

> The keynote speaker at the Assembly [1983 International Conference in Toronto] was Barbara Lundblad, famous in American Lutheran churches as the woman to be nominated for the position of Bishop of the Evangelical Lutheran Church in America. She came in third, thus narrowly missing becoming the first woman to head a major Christian denomination in America. . . . Lundblad challenged women clergy in particular to "speak up for gays and lesbians even at the risk of being called lesbian."[27]

The LC/NA carries out its work through an educational program whose principal mailings are received by all Lutheran churches.[28] At its 1988 International Conference in Toronto, Canada, the LC/NA passed a resolution that created a speaker's bureau. The stated purpose of this bureau is to enable the three openly gay seminarians, Jeff Johnson, Jim Lancaster, and Joel Workin, to speak at Lutheran colleges, seminaries, and universities.[29] The LC/NA seeks to spread its influence and realize its goals through the following program.

Swaying congregations

12) Reconciled—In Christ (RIC).

The RIC is a "program of Lutherans Concerned/North America which seeks to identify Lutheran congregations engaged in ministry

---

[26]*Concord,* op. cit., 1987:3, p. 2.
[27]Ibid., 1988:3, p. 1.
[28]Ibid., 1989:1, p. 7.
[29]Ibid., 1988:3, p. 5.

inclusive of lesbian and gay people."[30] RIC congregations accept gays by "affirmation of faith and expect and encourage them to share in the sacramental and general life of the church."[31] The sexual orientation of church members is not an issue.

The RIC congregations ministry to gays and lesbians includes making contact with other gays and their supporters in nearby congregations. The intent is to add these new congregations to RIC membership through education of the laity—the educational materials being of the same variety as that contained in the preceding quotations. As of January 1989, the RIC contained 41 member congregations. The following quotation demonstrates the RIC's methods and the influence of two of the newer chapters, LC/Baltimore and LC/Washington, D.C.

Gays march on Washington

Representing ten chapters from around the country, LC/NA members joined in a secular march on Washington in fall 1988 to "demonstrate the need for full lesbian and gay civil-rights legislation."

> *Lutherans Concerned Participate*
> *in March on Washington!*

[October 1988]. . . . Holding our banners high, LC/NA marched proudly on Sunday, singing Lutheran hymns, with occasional outbreaks of high-spiritedness from our young seminarians. . . . Capping the emotion-filled day, the LC participants joined together Sunday night for worship with Holy Communion, just two blocks from the Capitol at Reformation Lutheran Church. They processed into the sanctuary carrying the chapter banners from the March. . . . Dr. Carl Mau, Associate Pastor at Reformation Church and former General secretary of the Lutheran World Federation [1975-1986] was the celebrant.[32]

Progress

Lutherans Concerned is excited and gratified to learn that Lutheran Church of the Reformation, Washington, D.C., has joined the growing list of Reconciled in Christ (RIC) Congregations. . . . A spokesperson for the LC/Metro Washington Chapter reports that "the process which led to Reformation's

---

[30]Ibid., p. 2.
[31]Ibid.
[32]Ibid., 1987:4, pp. 1, 6.

participation in RIC were the efforts of Jon Lackey, LC/MW, who is also a member of Reformation." Of note also are Dr. Arnold Keller, Pastor and *Dr. Carl Mau,* pastor of the Public Affairs Ministry. Dr. Keller's and Dr. Mau's strong interest in this issue resulted in Reformation's speedy enrollment in RIC. The addition of Lutheran Church of the Reformation is a great boost to the RIC Program. It is a large and respected congregation among the churches of the Washington area and now is our second RIC congregation in the Metro Washington area.[33]

Influence in high places

On April 8, 1989, the Metropolitan Washington Synod of the Evangelical Lutheran Church in America will be holding a day-long "Educational Convocation" on "Jesus, Gay People, and the Church," at the Church of the Reformation in Washington D.C. ELCA Bishop E. Harold Jansen will greet the assembly. . . . "A Holy Eucharist" is scheduled for 4 p. m. . . . Eugene C. Root, a leader of the pro-homosexual Lutherans Concerned/ Metro Washington, comments: "Due to the efforts of many faithful and devoted people the Metropolitan Washington Synod will have the extraordinary opportunity to learn the truth about gay and lesbian people in the church. On April 8 an impressive collage of people will present their views, insights, and experiences. . . . at a convocation called by the Bishop of the Synod."[34]

The following quotation from the *Concord* illustrates the continuing influence of the LC/NA. In the quotation, Kathy Crary, the LC/NA's co-chairperson, reports on the presence of the LC/NA at the first ELCA Churchwide Assembly.

Being present, and not acting apologetic, afraid or powerless, characterizes LC/NA's participation at the LCA churchwide assembly in August. Lutherans Concerned/North America, as part of the Justice Network of the Lutheran Church (JNLC) shared "alternative space" immediately adjacent to the plenary hall. Together with *Namibia Concerns, Pension Members for Justice, Independent Lutheran Press,* and more, we reminded delegates INSIDE that there were more things

---

[33]Ibid., 1989:1, p. 3

[34]David Becker, "ELCA Still Promoting Homosexuality," *Christian News,* April 3, 1989, p. 17.

going on OUTSIDE than many would ever imagine. LC/NA, Wingspan and Lutheran Lesbian/Gay Ministry Bay Area (LLGM) occupied one corner of the alternative space (author's emphasis).

We held three workshops, two on ordination and one basic— *we're gay/lesbian people, ask 1,000 questions.* Jeff Johnson [one of the three gay men certified for ordination in the ELCA as mentioned earlier in this chapter], Region 1 & 2 Director and part of LLGM, and I were invited to speak to 150 youth delegates at a lunch meeting. That event alone made the trip worth it. Another highlight was doing a two-hour radio show with Barbara Lundblad (author's emphasis).[35]

The influence of ELCA leadership also continues. As of 1990, RIC membership consisted of 62 member congregations, including 13 ELCA campus ministries and 4 ELCA synods.[36] The LC/NA reports:

Two years ago, we were not ready to believe that we might have RIC synods by 1990. There are four. We hoped for 50 RIC congregations, and there are 62. . . . Welcome to the Sierra Pacific Synod ELCA, Northern California/Northern Nevada (Rev. Lyle Miller, Bishop). The synod adopted the RIC affirmation by a wide margin as a resolution at its June assembly in Sparks, NV. This is the fourth RIC synod![37]

The LC/NA lists the other three member synods as Metropolitan Washington D.C., Eastern North Dakota, and Eastern Washington-Idaho. Special emphasis is given when noting the following new member congregations:

Our Savior's Atonement Lutheran Church, New York, NY (Rev. Barbara Lundblad). Rev. Lundblad brought the RIC information back home after giving her wonderful keynote addresses at Assembly '88 in Toronto.[38]

Real love

13) A God-pleasing approach

We leave with the reader this final thought concerning the sin of homosexuality and the real Christian approach. To quote David Barnhart, a former LCA pastor:

---

[35]*Concord,* op. cit., 1989:4, p. 3.
[36]Ibid., 1990:3, inserted page.
[37]Ibid., p. 3.
[38]Ibid.

The liberals often accuse Bible-believing Christians of being unloving toward homosexuals because we call their activities sinful. They view our position as a condemnation of the homosexual himself. May God forbid that we are ever rightly accused of such an attitude to homosexual persons. Truly it is the liberal's false interpretation of Scripture regarding homosexuality that is unloving. Love points the sinner to his sin in order that he may be cleansed and made whole. Those who tell the homosexual that his immoral acts are accepted in God's sight bear the responsibility for the homosexual's spiritual death. . . . In my 22 years of ordained ministry, I have seen men delivered from homosexuality. I have personally counseled with many who were shackled by this satanic bondage. Our God is faithful. Not one of His precious promises "falls to the ground." No person who ever trusted in Him went away in disappointment. This includes the repenting homosexual who turns to Jesus for salvation and deliverance [39]

FURTHER EROSION OF MORAL VALUES

14) Lutheran Social Services of Minnesota (LSSM).

The documentation of the ELCA's move away from the moral absolutes of Scripture would not be complete without at least some mention of the pornographic films in use by the LSSM in its treatment program for youthful sex offenders. These films are a part of the University of Minnesota's Program on Human Sexuality, which was started in 1971 through the combined efforts and funding of the former ALC, the Playboy Foundation, University of Minnesota Medical School, and others.[40] The *Chicago Tribune* reported on the ALC's involvement:

Support for pornographic films in a church-sponsored program on human sexuality at the University of Minnesota has been reaffirmed by the American Lutheran Church whose Board for Service and Mission in America voted to continue its $10,000 annual investment.[41]

---

[39]David Barnhart, "The Church's Desperate Need for Revival" (Minneapolis: Abiding Word Ministries Inc., 1986), pp. 102, 103.

[40]"Playboy Foundation and ALC Funding Same Anti-Christian Sex Program," *Christian News*, October 11, 1976, p. 7.

[41]"Support porno films," *Chicago Tribune*, October 2, 1976. *Christian News*, October 11, 1976, p. 7.

The efforts of a group of pastors and laity in the former ALC and LCA to end the use of these films is thoroughly described by Barnhart in his book about liberalism in the Lutheran church, *The Church's Desperate Need for Revival*. The reinstatement of these films by the LSSM in its counseling program was the last straw that led Pastor Barnhart to leave the LCA. He is now a pastor in the conservative Association of Free Lutheran Congregations (AFLC) and the director of Abiding Word Ministries. The following quotations from Barnhart's book describe the films and point out the significance of their reinstatement:

> In May 1984, the board of directors of Lutheran Social Services of Minnesota officially, and in full violation of Scripture and church doctrine, reinstated the showing of sexually explicit films. *Sexually explicit* is a euphemism for pornography. We are told that these films are principally for the therapy of juvenile sex offenders. Yet we know that entire families, including innocent young children, are subjected to watching this filth. And of course, many reason it must be proper because the church has now officially sanctioned it.

> In these films, men and women are shown engaging in various sex acts, acts of immorality. How do I know since I have not personally seen the films? Five eyewitnesses have shared with us out of their personal experience in this program the detailed contents of these films. In addition, I have in my possession the complete list of revised films now used by LSS, and I have an order catalog with detailed descriptions of these films. Not only did we receive the catalog upon our request; we also received with it ads for various sex books and sexual paraphernalia. The catalog assured us that they would accept our check and a variety of credit cards. We were told by an LSS official that acquiring these films was as difficult as "getting gold out of Fort Knox." If that be true, I suggest someone run quickly to check the status of our gold reserves.

> The decision to reinstate these pornographic films is most ominous and distressing for several reasons: First of all, multiplied thousands of Lutherans have expressed their outrage and objections to such practices. Their outrage and objections are being ignored. Secondly, some of the finest counselors in the country, including Dr. James Dobson, have disputed the value and justification of such treatment proce-

dures. Thirdly, protests have gone up from many pastors and organizations within the church, including the threatened withdrawal of both districts of the Lutheran Church-Missouri Synod from Lutheran Social Service of Minnesota. Fourthly, and what I believe to be the most ominous sign of all—every single bishop of all the involved Lutheran bodies is a member of the LSS board of directors. The decision to reinstate the films was made at the highest echelons of church leadership. I am firmly convinced that the decision could not have been carried out without the approval of the bishops. These actions reveal how far from scriptural truth we have strayed and the degree to which false teaching is practiced and tolerated in our Lutheran church.[42]

15) "The Victims of Pornography"—analysis by the ALC Office of Church in Society (1985).

This final piece of documentation is from the concluding statements of the above document.

> Human sexuality itself is a gift from God; portrayals of respectful, even *erotically explicit,* sexual encounters may be edifying.[43]

The reader at this point should be enlightened if not "edified" by this very long section. This section is long for an important reason. Nothing demonstrates the total theological and spiritual bankruptcy of the *new thinking,* with its resultant depravity, better than a thorough review of its *new morality.*

Today's society exemplifies the disastrous results of the "morality" of these "new theologians," the "morality" of the *new thinking* that has so thoroughly pervaded our society.

The pervading morality of a people is of necessity the direct outgrowth, the fruit, of its pervading belief system.

The moral decay that is evident around us, with its breaking down of the social fabric, is the *direct* result of the abdication of the historic Christian faith with its biblically-based morals, ethics, and values, first by the theologians of the mainline churches, then trickling down, being slowly accepted within their constituencies and finally permeating throughout the broader society.

Christianity's moral absolutes, upon which all of western civilization was built, have, over the last several decades, been quietly dis-

---

[42]Barnhart, op cit., pp. 54, 55.
[43]"The Victims of Pornography," analysis by the ALC Office of Church in Society, 1985.

placed by the anarchy of the moral relativism and situation ethics of the theologians of the *new thinking*.

Situation ethics or moral absolutes

The field of ethics deals essentially with the question of what is right and wrong, good and bad; it seeks to establish a body of moral principles and values.

The supreme problem of ethics is the problem of authority. Who (or what) is to be the ultimate and final authority in the matter of morality? In order to carry out his role, the *ethicist* must find an adequate *authority* as a basis from which to determine right from wrong.

The obvious, but problematic, question of ethics is "How does one *know*?" That question involves something called *epistemology,* the study of *knowing* itself, which asks, "How can we *know* anything with certainty, and consequently, how can we *know* what is right and what is wrong?"

The possibility of some basis, some authority upon which to found our beliefs, morals, and ethics, could conceivably come from one of only *two* possible sources. One source is what man thinks. The only other possibility is what God thinks.

Therein lies the heart of the historical critics' problem as far as determining right from wrong or, for that matter, determining belief in any other area of the faith. The critic has decided for himself that God did not inspire the Scriptures to be written, let alone preserve them for us down through history in the church. The only other authority the critic can turn to is himself or other men. Ultimately, since even the notions of other men are acceptable to him only if they fit within his own scheme of things, the critic himself is ultimately his *own* final authority in all matters. That means that ultimately he is his own *god*.

The essential nature of sin as independence from God, and its resultant self-determinacy, can be traced to the garden of Eden. There Eve, through Satan, was enticed by the attractive fruit of the forbidden tree, the tree of the knowledge of good and evil. Satan's lie was that if Eve partook of the apple she wouldn't die and that she would be like God—she would know good and evil. Satan suggested that she know for herself (apart from God) what makes for *good* and for *evil*. In effect, she would be her own authority in matters of *ethics* and morality.

In this self-centered, ethical self-sufficiency, we have the perfect picture of the essence of sin. It is nothing less than a complete self-determination, which is nothing short of *self-deification,* making oneself to be god. As Satan had said: "You shall be as gods" (Genesis 3:4).

Solomon's proverb precisely pinpoints the futility of man given his fallen, blind nature, determining for himself what makes for right and wrong. To quote Proverbs 14:12, "There is a way that seems right to a man, but in the end it leads to death." Solomon instructs and directs us throughout Proverbs to avoid sin which he directly ties to going one's own way, and enjoins us to seek the right path through faith in the Lord and trust in his Word.

He says in Proverbs 9:10: "The fear of the Lord is the beginning of wisdom, and knowledge of the Holy One is understanding." This "knowledge of the Holy One" involves the Hebrew word *ya-dah,* to *know* someone in a personal and intimate sense. The "wise" man *knows* God, personally through faith in Christ; and then, to the extent that he is subservient to God's Word, he *knows* the truth and thus right and wrong. By "God's Word," we mean the objective *written* Word of God, the Holy Scriptures.

As we have seen, the ultimate problem of ethics *is* the problem of determining and knowing good from evil. The ultimate problem for the liberal ethicist in determining right and wrong (whether he knows or acknowledges it or not) is that he himself has a fallen or sinful nature which, apart from faith in Christ and reliance on God's inerrant Word, *cannot* adequately determine good and evil. Only God, through his inerrant written Word, can distinguish for us between good and evil. Even then, faithful men can, and do, err in their interpretation, understanding, and application of God's Word.

Adam and Eve *knew good* before they disobeyed God because they *knew God.* They were perfectly *moral.* When they sinned, they died spiritually and no longer *knew God*; consequently, they no longer *knew good* and became immoral. In and through Christ we have the beginnings of the restoration of our *knowing God* and, consequently, of our *knowing good.* Through faith in Christ, as "new creatures" (2 Corinthians 5:17) we have a restored capacity for right moral behavior, though we remain imperfect because of our "old Adam," our sinful nature that continues to cling to us until death.

Because even the Christian still has the old sinful nature, he must have an objective "guide" in order to know right from wrong. The only *objective* guide that man could have, outside of himself or other men (who are likewise sinners), would be God's *written, inerrant* Word.

Here again the liberal, because of his low view of Scripture, is left without any *objective* basis upon which to found his judgments of moral right and wrong. Most of the liberal theologians we have cited believe that the Bible was written by well-intentioned, pious men, but not actually inspired or given by God himself. It is on this basis that they consider their own "enlightened" views superior to those of the biblical writers.

Even if some think that part, or even most, of the Bible was truly inspired by God, how would they determine which teachings were from God and which were from man?

The liberals insist that the "Word of God" *is* their only guide and norm, but their insistence that this "Word of God" is merely Christ himself, or the "gospel" itself and not the *written* Word, leaves them with no objective basis for determining anything let alone moral right and wrong. In addition, the "Christ" and the "gospel" that they teach is quite a different Christ and is certainly a different gospel.

Yet another problem for the liberal

Yet another problem remains for the liberal. Only those whose faith is grounded in the *historic* gospel are enabled to live a Christian moral life.

It is one thing to *know* what comprises right moral behavior; it is quite another to *live* it. Moral law, even if acknowledged as truly being *God's* moral law, cannot bring about what it demands of us. This is Paul's whole argument in Chapter 7 of Romans and in the book of Galatians. It is the *gospel* that brings about, in a growing way, the right behavior, which the law can only demand.

Luther and the other 16th century Lutheran theologians understood this and passed it on to us in the Confessions and their other writings. Understanding that it is gospel (the *real* gospel) and not law that brings about right, moral living (sanctification) in the life of the Christian is one of the great strengths of confessional Lutheranism. The Reformed Churches, the Catholics, and, it would seem, the liberal Lutherans have never understood this biblical truth.

Lutherans alone teach that it is the gospel—the good news of our justification before God because of Christ's life of obedience and his substitutionary death for sins—which, as the means of grace, brings about faith itself and right, moral, or righteous living as a result of that faith.

No means of grace, no faith, no true morality

When the gospel as the *means of grace* is not present and active in lives, or if, as with the liberals, it is stripped of its true content (and thus its power), there can be no changed life, no *sanctification* of life, no truly *moral* life.

The liberals, in effect, having denied the real gospel, have left themselves with no *means of grace,* no means by which genuine faith can be worked and life changed.

The Christian life with its high morality (Christ living *his* life in us) is only possible when the historic gospel is believed. That is the very nature of the Christian faith, and subsequently the very nature of the Christian life.

The decadence of the "New Morality"

The kind of moral behavior described in this chapter has been referred to in ages past as *decadence*. The *new morality* of the historic critics, through the eyes of Christian faith and in light of God's inerrant Word, is nothing less than the *old immorality* dressed up in the euphemistic and seductive language of the false teachers of the new thinking.

In the next chapter, "The Way to Heaven," the doors of the church have been thrown open to any and all manner of doctrine and the doors of heaven thrown even wider.

The chapter could have been called "Universalism," the theological doctrine that teaches that all men will eventually be saved. The ELCA has clearly embraced this doctrine, virtually placing it in doctrinal agreement with the Unitarians.

With their denial of the Virgin Birth and the deity of Christ, the doctrine of the atonement, the physical resurrection of Christ, and the biblical and historical doctrine of the Trinity, ELCA theologians act with theological consistency in embracing the doctrine of Universalism.

18.

THE WAY TO HEAVEN

Position A

Jesus Christ is the only way to heaven. Those who die without faith in him are lost in hell.

1) The Bible.

A. Jesus Christ is the only way to heaven:

> For God so loved the world that he gave his one and only Son, that whoever believes in him shall not perish but have eternal life (John 3:16).

> I am the way and the truth and the life. No one comes to the Father except through me (John 14:6).

> Then Peter, filled with the Holy Spirit, said to them. . . . Salvation is found in no one else, for there is no other name under heaven given to men by which we must be saved (Acts 4:8,12).

> In my Father's house are many rooms; if it were not so, I would have told you. I am going there to prepare a place for you. And if I go and prepare a place for you, I will come back and take you to be with me that you also may be where I am (John 14:2,3).

B. Those who die without faith in Christ are lost in hell:

> Whoever believes in the Son has eternal life, but whoever rejects the Son will not see life, for God's wrath remains on him (John 3:36).

> Depart from me, you who are cursed, into the eternal fire prepared for the devil and his angels. . . . Then they will go

away to eternal punishment, but the righteous to eternal life (Matthew 25:41,46).

2) Martin Luther.

Hell—Now and Later. I am as yet not too sure what hell really is like before the Last Day. . . . To be sure, however, matters will take a different turn on the Last Day. Then hell will be a particular place, where those will be who are condemned to hell or to the eternal wrath of God[1]

Position B

Jesus Christ is not the only way to heaven. Sincere followers of non-Christian religions may also get to heaven. We must allow for the possibility of Universalism.

In contrast to the preceding clear words of Scripture, the "new thinking" denies the biblical reality of heaven and hell and allows for the possibility of Universalism, the doctrine that somehow all people will be saved regardless of what they believe. This chapter reveals the fact that theologians and professors of the Evangelical Lutheran Church in America (ELCA) have written articles and books stating that Christians are "too dogmatic about who is going to hell or who is going to heaven"[2] and that they need to give up their "one-wayism"[3] concerning salvation. Not only are we to study non-Christian religions for "new ideas and inspirations for renewal of the church,"[4] but we are to be open to the possibility that the sincere followers of these false religions may also get to heaven. This opening of the door to the acceptance of Universalism, in reality the rejection of the entire Christian faith, should not shock the reader. As has been carefully documented in the preceding chapters, leading ELCA theologians and professors have already denied or cast doubt upon every basic doctrine of the Christian faith; and in so doing, they have already rejected the Christian faith, whether they admit it or not.

1) Dr. Martin E. Marty, a noted ELCA historian, author, and professor.

---

[1]*What Luther Says,* 3 vols., ed. Ewald M. Plass (St. Louis: Concordia Publishing House, 1959), 2:625.

[2]Paul Jersild, *Invitation to Faith* (Minneapolis: Augsburg Publishing House, 1978), p. 72.

[3]Norman Beck, "A New Future for Jews, Christians, and Muslims," *Dialogue,* Spring 1984. Reprinted in *Christian News Encyclopedia,* 4 vols., ed. Herman Otten (Washington: Missourian Publishing Co., 1988), 3:2171.

[4]George Hall, "A Religion of Grace," *Augsburg Adult Bible Studies,* July/August 1987, p. 9.

Marty was numbered among those who were seriously considered as candidates for becoming the first bishop of the ELCA.[5] In the article "Whatever Happened to Hell?" Marty made the following statements:

> One of the great events in modern Roman Catholic history is the decline of purgatory and hell. . . . A *Catholic Digest* poll in 1952 found that 42 percent of the American public, including Catholics, did not believe in hell, and few who did saw it as a threat to them; "only a little more than one out of eight adults regarded hell as a possible future alternative. . . ." In 1983 *U.S. Catholic* polled its readers and found that only 1 percent pictured the possibility of going to hell as real for them; only 3 percent thought of hell as fire; only 22 percent were ready to picture Hitler in hell. . . . Lutheran councils do not and will not take up the issue of how to take hell off the books. They just put it in corners of indices. Six fine and major Lutheran theologians recently published two pounds and 1,189 pages of *Christian Dogmatics*. If the index-maker had not worked with the principle of a vacuum cleaner to pick up everything, hell would have shot by unnoticed.
>
> The biblical scholars [liberal] have another burden. They have to ask exactly what *does* the Bible teach about the hell that at the moment and perhaps henceforth seems less available? They have been busy. They remind us that the images of hell in the Bible are often but that: images. They develop, contradict each other. When Jesus tells about the rich man and Lazarus, he is not imparting [sic] information about the detail of an afterlife he elsewhere tells us we cannot imagine. He simply repeats a folkloric story of the rabbis and gives it a new twist. . . . Much of our "hell" has come not from Bible and theology but from *Faust* and cartoons, from folklore and popular cathedral art. The theologians also will tell you that hell connects with other teachings that they are wrestling with today. Some discuss the possibility of "universal salvation," for which there are a biblical clue or two (Acts 3:21 and 1 Corinthians 15:22, for example), but about which they have to be tentative.[6]

---

[5]"Marty Has Bishop Support," *The Lutheran,* April 2, 1986, p. 21.

[6]Martin E. Marty, "Whatever Happened to Hell?" *The Lutheran,* April 2, 1986, pp. 15-17.

2) *Affirm, The Apostles Creed,* Teacher's Guide , catechism materials for seventh- and eighth-grade children.

> Jesus' descent to the dead. *Lutheran Book of Worship* gives an option for this part of the Creed; Jesus descended "into hell" or "to the dead." In fact this phrase is the latest addition to the Creed, added probably in the sixth century A.D. The original meaning is no longer certain. It could mean simply that Jesus died; he went to the place where the dead go. It has become customary to link this assertion of the Creed with the statement in 1 Peter 3:18-19 that Jesus "in the spirit . . . went and preached to the spirits in prison." 1 Peter does not actually say that this was done in the interval between Jesus' death and resurrection. Some scholars believe that the intent of the passage is to assert that Jesus, *after* the resurrection, preached to the spirits of the other world. In any case, Luther interpreted this belief to mean that Jesus triumphantly announced his victory over death to those who had previously died (author's emphasis).[7]

3) *Invitation to Faith,* Dr. Paul Jersild.

Jersild is academic dean, director of admissions, and professor of ethics at Lutheran Theological Southern Seminary (ELCA), Columbia, South Carolina. He is also one of the translators of the *Evangelical Catechism,* which is used in the ELCA for adult instruction.

Concerning heaven and hell:

> We do not take the devil seriously, but we are impressed with dimensions of life which can best be described as demonic, or "devilish." It is this sense of the power of evil in human experience which provides the meaningful context for any reference to the devil, but many Christians today see little if any value in bringing the devil into the discussion. . . . The church's teaching about the devil constitutes *no* article of *belief,* such as belief in God. There is no witness to a revelation of the devil in Scripture *nor* even a developed teaching concerning the devil, and the Christian tradition has never recognized an ontological or cosmological necessity to the devil as we find in arguments for the existence of God. Belief in the devil was common in previous centuries—*Jesus* him-

---

[7]Marshall D. Johnson, *Affirm, The Apostles Creed,* eds. Irene Getz, Susan Niemi Tetlie, and Gretchen L. Weidenbach (Minneapolis: Augsburg Publishing House, 1984), p. 17.

self *reflects his times* in talking about Satan. . . . The church has generally spoken *too dogmatically* about who is going to hell or who is going to heaven. The importance of these terms is their recognition that we are responsible for our lives, and that God is sovereign in his judgment of us. But our destiny remains a *mystery* which Christian faith awaits with expectation.[8]

Concerning other religions:

But the question must be asked whether there is not more to revelation than the experience of Christians. Is it not *audacious* to define revelation in terms of Jesus of Nazareth, a historical figure of whom millions have never heard? What about other religions of the world, such as *Hinduism, Buddhism, and Islam?* . . . Too often the church has been guilty of a *graceless imperialism* when it has claimed an *exclusive* truth in Jesus. The church needs both a sense of self-criticism and the ability to listen to the truth to which *others* give witness.[9]

4) *A New Future for Jews, Christians, and Muslims,* Dr. Norman Beck.

Beck is professor of theology at Texas Lutheran College, Sequin, Texas. His article appeared in *Dialogue,* a theological journal published quarterly through the efforts of 25 to 30 influential ELCA theologians and professors, including four of the six authors of *Christian Dogmatics.* In his article, Beck calls upon Christians to give up their "one-wayism" in Christ.

. . . we cannot limit God's power and grace to any single religious tradition or statement of faith. As individuals and corporately we as Christians should boldly and joyfully acknowledge that other religious traditions, most of all those of our Jewish and Muslim neighbors and relatives, are also fully valid forms of spirituality through which God has been and is active with power and grace. . . . We should recognize that our various religions are merely houses in which we live, vehicles in which we travel through life, that they are not absolutes, that we must continually remodel, overhaul, and reform them for optimum service in a changing world.

---

[8]Jersild, op. cit., pp. 66-72.
[9]Ibid., pp. 45-47.

Therefore, we as Christians are called upon to be sufficiently mature individually and corporately to give up our claims of religious exclusivism, of the religious "one-way-ism" which has contributed to the defamation and destruction of millions of other people.

. . . within our lifetime in some Christian circles including our own, considerable progress is being made in bringing Christianity toward a more *mature* position in which *Judaism, Islam,* and *other* forms of spirituality are recognized as valid expressions of God's power and grace.[10]

5) *Augsburg Adult Bible Studies,* Teacher's Guide .

This is an adult Bible-study series that was produced jointly by the former American Lutheran Church (ALC) and Lutheran Church in America (LCA). This edition contains an article by George Hall titled "A Religion of Grace," which not only teaches Universalism but connects it with God's grace. In addition, it states that the use of non-Christian religious practices is God's way of renewing his church.

We must know in our hearts that every person we meet and serve is already in the community of the faithful, one of the elect, chosen to be a saint. Our call is to let others know that they already belong in Christ's own flock. Does it matter that they are of another faith, or *not* Christian at all? *No.* They are not enemies but part of the flock prepared by God in God's own way to become eventually a pillar in the Christian faith. What they bring with them in culture and from their own religious backgrounds is God's way of *renewing* the church by bringing into the church *new ideas* and *inspiration.* . . . The church is the flock of grace. We do not have the right to put fences around God's grace and limit it just to those we think fulfill criteria for the same.[11]

6) *The Invasion from the East,* Dr. Howard A. Wilson.

Wilson has served as professor of religion at Capital University, Columbus, Ohio. He is a specialist in Asian religions and is a member of the Association for Asian Studies. The following paragraph from the book's cover is consistent with the general content of the book:

Dr. Howard A. Wilson evaluates the impact of Eastern religions on the West, describing ideas and practices of the Hin-

---

[10]Beck, loc. cit.
[11]Hall, op. cit., pp. 9, 10.

du, Buddhist, and Zen traditions. He expresses concerns Christians have about the Eastern influence and outlines how we can learn from Oriental religions.[12]

In the concluding chapter, "What Christians Can Learn from the Resurgence of Religion," Wilson promotes the use of non-Christian religious practices.

> God has not left himself without a witness in the great religious traditions of Asia, which form so large a part of the human family. Perhaps they can lead us to rediscover dimensions of meaning in the Christian faith that have been long neglected and ignored.[13]

Christians may use *yoga* and *Eastern meditative techniques* or any other techniques that focus the mind on spiritual matters.

> The practice of meditation and contemplation will vary widely among Christians because individual aptitudes vary widely. There is no one prescribed set of methods to use. For some body/ mind techniques like *yoga* are effective; for others the Christian contemplative tradition; for others the indirect methods of *Zen;* for others reading the Bible; for others the discipline of *logic* and hard intellectual thinking about the faith; for still others the contemplation of great Christian art and music. There are degrees of understanding and attainment, and Christians should use what is most natural to their temperament. They may eventually learn to use *all* of these techniques at different times because *each possesses* some part of the *truth*. Instruction of *all* of them should be available in *congregations*.[14]

A clear picture emerges then of how Christians may meet the present challenge of the invasion from the East. They can: Rediscover the rich tradition of Christian *mysticism* and its practice, and *teach it* to other mystics as a further *stage* to be reached. . . . Recognize that there are *diverse paths* of *salvation,* and so meet a broader spectrum of people's needs. . . . Frame a more optimistic doctrine of humanity, and teach Christian self-transcendence to those Westerners attracted by the religions of the East.[15]

---

[12]Howard A. Wilson, *The Invasion from the East* (Minneapolis: Augsburg Publishing House, 1978), cover.

[13]Ibid., p. 135.

[14]Ibid., pp. 149, 150.

[15]Ibid., p. 156.

Dr. J. Kincaid Smith is a former liberal who was himself involved in forms of these Eastern religions as a seminary student at what is now Trinity Lutheran Seminary, Columbus, Ohio, and then later as an LCA pastor. He has this to say about Wilson's conclusions:

> The basic belief system underlying the mind-techniques recommended by Dr. Wilson is *pantheism* which holds in effect that the only reality that exists is God and the aim in these exercises is to look within oneself and come to the realization that *we are God!* This is the heart of all forms of Eastern meditation which cannot be separated from pantheism. Nothing could be more utterly *opposed* to the Christian faith than this! These religions comprise the very essence of Satan's suggestion to Eve that "you shall be as God" (Genesis 3:5).[16]

The implication of the liberal position in this chapter is abundantly clear. The new thinkers, having led us systematically through a step-by-step dismantling of the foundation and structure of the Christian faith, would now lead us out of the "graceless" limitation of narrow-minded "one-wayism" into the "freedom" of Universalism.

One way is narrow and the other is broad. Our Lord and Savior Jesus Christ, in the Sermon on the Mount, urges us:

> Enter through the narrow gate. For wide is the gate and broad is the road that leads to destruction and many enter through it. But small is the gate and narrow [strait] the road that leads to life, and only a few find it (Matthew 7:13).

Norman Beck, on the other hand, one of the apostles of the new thinking, urges the church to take the *broad* road, he counsels us to "give up our 'one-wayism.' " Beck's fellow apostle, Martin Marty, says that the theologians (the historic critics), having "wrestled" with other doctrines (the basic doctrines of the faith), see the doctrine of hell connected with these other doctrines (which they have rejected) and that this has led them to Universalism. Given their assumptions (i.e., the denial of all the basic tenets of the Christian faith), their conclusion that there is no hell should, of necessity, follow.

Who needs hell?

With the open bounds of their "situation ethics," the liberal theologians have effectively neutralized any real guilt and responsibility for sin. Sin, as Christians have biblically and historically understood

---

[16]J. Kincaid Smith, L.I.F.T, Vol. 1, No. 14, p. 5.

it, has, with their redefinition, all but disappeared. Whatever is still acknowledged (reluctantly) as sin is removed beyond the threat of any consequence since "all is covered by the precept of love . . ." (love without the need of Christ's atonement or man's repentance). The inescapable effect is that there is simply no need of hell. There is no one left to go there.

Universalism must always be the final theological destination of all who deny the deity of Christ (and thus the Trinity) and have no absolute code of morality.

Islam, and Orthodox Judaism, both have a closer semblance to biblical morality, each having moral absolutes, than do other eastern religions. Both, however, reject the notion of Universalism. Both teach "one way" only, albeit without grace and consequently without salvation. On the other hand, Hinduism and Buddhism, with which most of the liberal theologians are enamored, has neither Christ nor moral absolutes but, like liberal theology, would teach us that "there are many paths, many ways to heaven."

The book by Paul Jersild under Position B is titled *Invitation to Faith*. He indeed invites us to "faith," but it is not an invitation to faith in the Christ, who said "I am the way and the truth and the life. No one comes to the Father except through me" (John 14:6). Jersild would invite us to faith in Buddha and the thousands of gods that are worshiped in Hinduism.

Jersild considers it "audacious (reckless and arrogant) to define revelation in terms of Jesus of Nazareth. . . ." He says, "The church is guilty of a *graceless imperialism* when it has claimed an exclusive truth in Jesus."

How "audacious" these words must appear to faithful Christians. These men refuse to acknowledge the divine authorship of God's Word, the Holy Scriptures, but run after the "revelation" of other gods and urge Christians to follow them.

Jersild's book, in effect, calls what amounts to the central and most vital teachings of the Christian faith "graceless" ("graceless imperialism"), and Norman Beck urges upon us that other religions have "God's power and grace."

Beck suggests that we Christians "should boldly and joyfully acknowledge that other religious traditions . . . are also *fully valid* forms of spirituality through which God has been and is active with power and grace." We are called upon to be "mature" and to "give up claims of religious exclusivism."

In the last part of Beck's quotation he notes that "considerable progress" is being made in bringing Christianity into this more "mature" position (the merging of Christianity with Hinduism and others). Sad to say, Beck's observation is correct. The liberal theologians have already moved into the very forms of "spirituality" that comprise the mystical religions of Hinduism and Buddhism. Some minor adjustments of terminology and modes of expression are even now being worked out as the "considerable progress" of their love affair with eastern religion continues.

The other difficult task that these false teachers face is to continue leading lay people down the *broad* path straight into the darkness that comes when the light of Christ has been extinguished.

The theologians of the "new thinking" are running after strange gods and working feverishly to drag the unsuspecting with them in their headlong plunge toward the hell that they blithely dismiss as the fantasies of Faust and folklore.

The purpose and whole aim of this book is to warn and wake up the dear people who have been led down that awful path, people who sense that something is missing, that they aren't hearing what they heard from their pastors of years ago.

It is an ancient warning. Our Lord Jesus Christ, at the very beginning of his public ministry, warned us:

> Watch out for false prophets. They come to you in sheep's clothing, but inwardly they are ferocious wolves. *By their fruit you will recognize them.* Do people pick grapes from thornbushes, or figs from thistles? Likewise every good tree bears good fruit, but a bad tree bears bad fruit. A good tree cannot bear bad fruit, and *a bad tree cannot bear good fruit.* Every tree that does not bear good fruit is cut down and thrown into the fire. Thus by their fruit you will recognize them (Matthew 7:15-20).

The Christian who trusts in Christ and cleaves to his word *can* recognize them by their fruit, *can* see clearly enough the audacious denial of the faith encompassed within these chapters, documented in the writing of these Lutheran theologians of the ELCA.

The next chapter is on "Missions." It is significant, and yet thoroughly consistent with the direction that the liberal theology has taken, that the zeal for *missions* in the ELCA has almost entirely evaporated in recent years.

Dr. Wayne Ewing, a seminary professor at Hamma School of Theology (now merged and in the ELCA) once told a class on "missions" that he had apologized to a Buddhist scholar for Christian missionary efforts to convert Buddhists and adherents of other [non-Christian] religions. He assured his Buddhist friend that he believed that

Buddhism was a faith equally as valid as Christianity and that Christians had much to learn at the feet of Buddha.[17]

In light of the above, the reader might better understand the strange and alien directions in which the ELCA missionary enterprise has drifted.

---

[17]Dr. Ewing taught missiology at Hamma School of Theology (LCA) at Springfield, Ohio, in the early 1970s. This incident occurred in a class attended by co-author J. Kincaid Smith.

19.

MISSIONS

Position A

The primary mission of the church is the proclamation of the saving gospel of Jesus Christ. Genuine Christian love, of course, will always result in ministering to the earthly needs of people as well.

1) The Bible.

A. Scripture clearly teaches what Christ has done for us and that the only way to eternal life is through him only.

> For God so loved the world that he gave his one and only Son, that whoever believes in him shall not perish but have eternal life (John 3:16).

> I am the way, the truth, and the life. No one comes to the Father except through me (John 14:6).

> Then Peter, filled with the Holy spirit, said to them. . . . Salvation is found in no one else, for there is no other name under heaven given to men by which we must be saved (Acts 4:8,12).

B. Salvation is solely dependent upon faith in Christ and his redemptive work. Therefore, the primary mission of the church is the preaching of the saving gospel of Christ. Jesus himself commands it.

> Therefore go and make disciples of all nations, baptizing them in the name of the Father, and of the Son and of the Holy Spirit, and teaching them to obey everything I have commanded you (Matthew 28:19, 20).

C. Along with preaching the gospel, Christians will be moved by the love of Christ to be concerned for the welfare of their neighbors.

This is how we know what love is: Jesus Christ laid down his life for us. And we ought to lay down our lives for our brothers. If anyone has material possessions and sees his brother in need but has no pity on him, how can the love of God be in him? Dear children, let us not love with words or tongue but with actions and in truth (1 John 3:16-18).

2) The spiritual mission of the church.

The primary mission of the church is spiritual. Although the love of Christ will lead Christians to minister to the material needs of others, concern for the improvement of man's existence here on earth must not be allowed to take priority over concern for man's spiritual needs and eternal salvation. The greatest missionary emphasis of Christians must always be focused on reaching people with the gospel message so that they may come to faith in Christ and obedience to God's will. The importance of maintaining a balance in ministering to both the spiritual and material needs of man is emphasized by Oswald Skov, a conservative pastor in the Lutheran Church—Missouri Synod.

It is natural for true Christians to be moved by the love of Christ to feed the hungry, clothe the naked, etc., Matt. 25:35. Every failure to show this concern should be deplored, for such neglect is tantamount to being out of step with the love and will of God, 1 John 3:16-18. Such passages, however, do not make social welfare the primary goal or overwhelming activity of church organizations. Jesus had compassion on those who fainted for lack of food. He came to the rescue by feeding them miraculously. But when they gave no heed to His spiritual activity, and thought only of making Him a bread-king, He withdrew from the area. When they caught up with Him, wondering how He had escaped them, He sternly reproved them: "Labor not for the food that perishes, but for the food that endures unto everlasting life," John 6:27; and then continued with the lengthy discourse on "The Bread of Life."

Instead of following the Biblical example, many clergymen and church members have brought the Gospel much disrespect by their conduct to procure social change. What lawful and ethical influence we can exert, of course, should not be neglected. Then also we should take every opportunity to give material assistance in order to spearhead the proclamation of the Gospel. Such as medical missions, literacy training, distribution of food and clothing and the like. The point is this: The church is not carrying out its assignment when it spends time and energy on social welfare without an attempt in bringing people to faith and obedience to God's will. What good does it do to make man's brief life on earth somewhat better, if his name is not written in the Book of Life? Or as Jesus states it: "What shall it profit a man if he gain the whole world and lose his own soul?" Mark 8:36. Let us therefore put the emphasis where it belongs and give high priority to our resources in carrying out Christ's commission to "make disciples of all nations" by baptizing and teaching, Matt. 28:19,20.[1]

When the church fails to strike a balance in ministering to both the spiritual and material needs of man and allows the improvement of man's existence here on earth to take priority over his spiritual needs and eternal salvation, we have what is commonly called the *Social Gospel*. The error of the Social Gospel cannot be fully understood without a clear understanding of the proper roles of the church and the state as taught in the Scripture and the historic Lutheran faith.

3) The church and the state.

The following quotation states the orthodox Lutheran position concerning the proper roles of the church and the state:

We believe that not only the church, but also the state, that is, all governmental authority, has been instituted by God. "The authorities that exist have been established by God" (Rom. 13:1). Christians will, therefore, for conscience' sake be obedient to the government that rules over them (Rom. 13:5) unless the government commands them to disobey God (Acts 5:29).

We believe that God has given to each, the church and the state, responsibilities that do not conflict with one another. To the church the Lord has assigned the responsibility of calling sinners to repentance, of proclaiming forgiveness through the cross of Christ, of encouraging believers in their Christian living. The purpose is to lead the elect of God through faith in Christ to eternal salvation. To the state the Lord has assigned the keeping of good order and peace, the arranging of all civil matters among men (Rom. 13:3,4). The

---

[1]Oswald Skov, *What is Truth* (Northridge, CA: Oswald Skov, n.d.), p. 35.

purpose is "that we may live peaceful and quiet lives in all godliness and holiness" (1 Tim. 2:2).[2]

The orthodox Lutheran position concerning the role of the individual Christian in both of these institutions is stated by Armin W. Scheutze, professor emeritus of the Lutheran Confessions at Wisconsin Lutheran Seminary, Wisconsin Evangelical Lutheran Synod (WELS):

> The Christian citizen finds himself involved in both of these institutions of God. He is a member of Christ's church; he is a citizen of a particular state or country. He has responsibilities in each. Yet these need not conflict as long as the Christian, the church, and the state all remember their assigned roles.

> The Christian will not look to his church to correct the ills of government. He will not seek governmental help to carry on the functions God has assigned to the church. Nevertheless, as a faithful Christian, he will in his prayers remember his government and those vested with authority (cf. 1 Timothy 2:1,2). He will use his influence as a citizen to persuade his government to pass laws that are just and good. He will conscientiously do all that is expected of loyal citizens "for the Lord's sake". The fact that he is a Christian will mean that he is a good citizen.

> In this way the state will be benefited by the presence of the church in its midst. As the church trains faithful Christians, the state too will profit through the God-fearing concern and loyalty which Christian citizens will show toward their government.[3]

Position B

Once the shift in our thinking takes place and we see behind the mythical notions of the divinity of the man Jesus Christ, primitive ideas of spreading a message about a spiritual, other-worldly redemption from sin can be seen as missing the authentic message of the man Jesus. Jesus must be seen as the man for others, especially the poor and downtrodden. His chief concern was the elimination of poverty and oppression.

---

[2]WELS, *This We Believe* (Milwaukee: Northwestern Publishing House, 1980), pp. 21, 22.

[3]Armin W. Schuetze, *Basic Doctrines of the Bible* (Milwaukee: Northwestern Publishing House, 1986), pp. 82, 83.

Christians should not seek to "convert" sincere followers of other religions that also teach love and concern for mankind. Instead, we should join our efforts with theirs in the true spirit of Jesus. Other religions sincerely followed are equally as valid as Christianity.

The preceding chapters of this book have documented the fact that some leading theologians and professors of the Evangelical Lutheran Church in America (ELCA) have gone so far in their acceptance of the liberal theology that they attack the deity of Christ and the Biblical reality of heaven and hell and allow for the possibility of Universalism, the doctrine that somehow all men will be saved regardless of what they believe. It naturally follows that if Christianity is no longer seen as the only hope for man, there is no need to channel the church's efforts into reaching the entire world with the saving gospel of Jesus Christ. Concern for man's spiritual needs becomes of secondary importance. This new way of thinking has changed the mission emphasis of the ELCA and has led to a deep involvement in a wide variety of social and political issues designed to improve man's earthly conditions—namely the Social Gospel.

While the documentation in the remainder of this chapter deals with the ELCA, the shift in the church's mission emphasis is not confined to the ELCA. The Social Gospel movement began much earlier in the so-called mainline denominations. It originated with the liberal theologians of Europe and is the result of spiritual depletion. This fact is brought out by Dr. Edmund W. Robb and Julia Robb in their book, *The Betrayal of the Church: Apostasy and Renewal in the Mainline Denominations,* which documents "the alarming story of how the leaders of the mainline denominations have abandoned the gospel in favor of the religious and political ideology of the Left."

A growing percentage of Christian leadership has abandoned its role as spiritual shepherd because it no longer considers humanity's spiritual welfare its greatest concern. A great many bishops have rejected winning souls in favor of influencing political issues. . . . The transformation from classical Christianity to political advocacy has occurred gradually during the last twenty years and is the result of spiritual depletion. Christian leadership, for the most part, no longer believes that eternity is of prime significance. The emphasis is now on this world. . . . The inequities of society disturb churchmen, and rightly so. But as statists, they seem to believe that government should remedy all injustice in this imperfect world. They have discarded the ancient

Christian belief that hearts must be changed before societies can be reformed.[4]

Sadly, the vast majority of lay people do not understand what is happening in their churches. Still believing in the basic doctrines of the Christian faith, they innocently follow along and out of sincere Christian love for their fellow man, they support the social-political agenda of their churches with their time and financial contributions.

THE ELCA AND THE SOCIAL GOSPEL

Evidence of the drift of the ELCA away from the historic Lutheran understanding of the church's mission to the Social Gospel can be easily seen through the official ELCA publications. Any issue of *The Lutheran* contains an abundance of articles that deal with the social-political agenda that now dominates ELCA mission endeavors. In addition, ELCA Sunday school materials, adult Bible-study courses, and books and articles are filled with endless references to poverty, freedom, peacemaking, justice concerns, liberation, the oppressed, and so forth.

Further proof of the drift into the social-political realm is provided by the publication *Working for Justice: A 1988 Directory of Lutheran Ministries*. This publication lists "fifty Lutheran-affiliated groups, organizations, networks, agencies, coalitions, projects and programs oriented toward justice concerns" and describes the Justice Network in the Lutheran Church (JNLC) as a "network of organizations gathered to ensure that justice is central to the life and mission of the Lutheran Church." (The ELCA's definition of "justice" appears later in this chapter.) This publication is a recommended resource for leaders in ELCA congregations.[5]

Following are just a few of the 50 agencies listed in the directory:

1. *Center for Global Education*—sponsors trips to foreign countries to increase awareness of other cultures, inform debate on foreign policy, include perspectives on the poor and study dynamics of social change. Program of Augsburg College—ELCA.
2. *ELCA Commission for Church in Society*—responsible for preparation of the ELCA social statements, carries out the

---

[4]Edmund W. Robb, Julia Robb, *The Betrayal of the Church: Apostasy and Renewal in the Mainline Denominations* (Westchester, IL: Crossway Books, 1986), pp. 12-14.

[5]*Seeds for the Parish*, Commission for Communication, ELCA, Chicago, May 1988, p. 5.

ELCA's advocacy to national and international governmental bodies to influence legislation.

3. *Justice Network in the Lutheran Church*—grassroots network of justice agenda organizations in the church centering on racial, sexual, economic justice, and global justice and peace.

4. *Lutheran Coalition on Latin America*—to involve more Lutherans in the Latin American liberation struggles.

5. *Lutherans Concerned*—a Christian ministry for lesbian and gay understanding that seeks to unite gay/lesbian Lutherans and their non-gay supporters for education and affirmation.

6. *Wingspan Ministry*—a ministry with and on behalf of gay and lesbian people and their family members in the Minneapolis/St. Paul area.[6]

The work of Lutherans Concerned North America and Wingspan Ministry was well-documented in Chapter 17, "The New Morality."

Soon after the ELCA was formed, an incident made national news that is indicative of how deeply the leadership of the ELCA is involved in governmental business. A *Religious News Service* article[7] stated that more than half of the denomination's synodical bishops (37)—including Bishop Herbert W. Chilstrom, head bishop of the ELCA—were part of a nondenominational group of 300 religious leaders that signed a letter to Congress opposing aid to the Nicaraguan contra rebels. The bishops received much criticism, perhaps most clearly stated by one critic who wrote to *The Lutheran:*

> As a Lutheran and political scientist I must challenge the decisions of so many ELCA bishops in lending their names and church offices to a political campaign by an interreligious group to attack U.S. foreign policy in the name of morality. No one objects to the bishops expressing personal opinions on any subject, but to use their official church positions to enter the political arena is unbecoming to their Lutheranism.[8]

An editorial comment following the letter stated that the bishops had been authorized to "do their advocacy work on the basis of prior church-body statements."[9] It was then pointed out that the American

---

[6]*Working for Justice: A 1988 Directory of Lutheran Ministries* (Chicago: Justice Network in the Lutheran Church, 1988), pp. 5, 10, 19, 22, 36, 49.

[7]Gustav Spohn, "New ELCA Grapples with Question of Identity, Authority, and Teaching," *Religious News Service,* April 22, 1988. *Christian News,* May 2, 1988, p. 1.

[8]"Letters," *The Lutheran,* April 20, 1988, p. 49.

[9]Ibid.

Lutheran Church (ALC) and the Lutheran Church in America (LCA) had in convention "supported efforts for peaceful negotiated settlement to the conflicts in Central America and have opposed all forms of foreign military intervention."[10] The interreligious group referred to in the previous quotation is the Washington Interreligious Staff Council, a coalition of religious groups that counts the ELCA among its member organizations.

LIBERATION THEOLOGY

One cannot write about the Social Gospel without some mention and explanation of the movement's most dangerous development—liberation theology. Liberation theology is another result of the historical-critical method of Biblical interpretation, which attacks and denies the deity of Christ. Jesus is now seen as the "man" for others, especially the poor and downtrodden, whose chief concern was the elimination of poverty and oppression. This new view of Jesus and his message is the foundation of liberation theology.

The danger of liberation theology cannot be overestimated. It denies the true identity and message of Jesus and consequently perverts the true mission of the church—that of proclaiming the saving gospel of Jesus Christ for all the world to hear. Instead, another gospel is preached—that of the kingdom of God on earth. The ultimate mission of liberation theology goes beyond personal religious beliefs. Its real goal is to change the political-economic structure of the entire world. This goal may be more easily understood if we take a look at the real message of liberation theology as described by Dr. William R. LeRoy, who served as a missionary in Brazil for more than 25 years:

> The message of liberation theology is very simple. Salvation means political liberation. It is liberation from every form of oppression (defined by them) that could prevent man from true and full humanization. Sin and guilt are basically social in their definition and origin. If their definition of sin is synonymous with social oppression and "injustice" of any kind, then it only follows that liberation from "sin" becomes possible only by the overthrow of those oppressive social structures. Sin becomes externalized and finds its origin only in a social contextual framework. The point of reference for conversion is no longer the sinful heart of man which is in a state of rebellion against a holy God; but now the point of reference for conversion refers to that which is external, such as social structures.

---

[10]Ibid.

> The theologians of liberation are convinced that socialism is the necessary pre-condition for the construction of a just and humane society. Only the social appropriation of the means of production will pave the way to a new order in which the needs of all the people can be met.

> Gustavo Guitierrez [a Roman Catholic priest, a leading thinker, and one of the founders of Liberation Theology] from Peru offers the meaning of the message of liberation when he writes, "It is a theological reflection born of the experience of shared efforts to abolish the current unjust situation, and to build a different society, freer and more human" (*A Theology of Liberation,* Gustavo Guitierrez, Orbis, 1973, p. ix).[11]

Another very real danger that many sincere followers of this false theology have perhaps failed to recognize is the fact that liberation theology is consciously being used in Christian Third World countries to spread communism. Liberal Roman Catholic priests and nuns who were deeply involved in liberation theology began to use it in Latin America, a stronghold of Roman Catholicism, in the early 1970s. Its impact is now felt worldwide and involves all the mainline denominations.

One of the most qualified persons to speak on the issue of liberation theology and its impact on Latin America is Humberto Belli. A native Nicaraguan, lawyer, and sociologist, Belli was a Marxist and active member of the Sandinista front until 1975.

He was later editorial page editor of the independent Nicaraguan newspaper *La Prensa* until full censorship in 1982 forced him to quit. In 1977, Belli converted to the Christian faith. He has been in the United States since 1982, informing the American people about the true situation in Latin America. The following quotation is from an article that reports Belli's message at a gathering of conservative Roman Catholics in June 1984:

> Belli called liberation theology "the best ideological weapon ever designed" to spread Communism in Christian Third World countries.

> "Liberation theology started in the 60s after Vatican II stated its concerns for justice," he said, adding that the first political group to espouse it was Christians for Socialism in

---

[11]William R. LeRoy, "Liberation Theology," *Christian News Encyclopedia,* 4 vols, ed. Herman Otten (Washington: Missourian Publishing Co., 1988), 2:1133.

Chile. Until that time, Communism in Latin America had known only failure. But with liberation theology, it gained the potential to sow confusion among Catholics, especially students who heard it taught in schools by apparently knowledgeable theologians.

The 38-year-old exile outlines the story of liberation theology which the theologians present to students as follows: "If we love Jesus, we have to love the poor. But to be effective in our love for the poor, we have to destroy the structure which oppresses the poor. This is done through social-political action and it calls for revolution to change the system and create a new world. Scientific Marxism tells us the best scientific means to achieve revolution."

The theologians no longer talk or preach about personal sin, Belli explains; instead, they talk about "social sin," meaning capitalism, which, they say, oppresses the poor. Christians must fight against capitalism, according to these theologians. The revolutionary party becomes the messiah, the new Christ, freeing the people from social sin, and the kingdom of God is socialism in this ideology. Conversion is getting connected with "The People" and working for revolution. Christ is not denied, but Christ is transformed into a guerrilla fighter, Belli noted. The revolution is God.

Belli pointed out that when the Communists in the past had openly denied the existence of God, they made no headway with the Latin Americans. But this subtle false theology is confusing to Catholics, especially naive students impressed with the prestige of their professors. And they get caught up in the cause. (Belli himself was a Marxist for some time.) The liberation theologians tell the students that true Christians must be revolutionaries.[12]

THE ELCA TEACHES LIBERATION THEOLOGY

1) *The Bible As Liberating Word—An Introduction to Liberation Theology,* Dr. Phyllis Anderson.

Liberation theology is now officially taught at the congregational level in the ELCA. The ALC (now part of the ELCA) published An-

---

[12]Frank Teskey, "Belli Denounces Liberation Theology in Nicaragua," *Christian News Encyclopedia,* 4 vols., ed. Herman Otten (Washington: Missourian Publishing Co., 1988), 4:2554.

derson's book as a course of study for congregations in 1986. The book was written and published under the auspices of the Division for Life and Mission in the Congregation and the Board of Publication of the ALC. The author is the director for theological education, Division for Ministry, in the ELCA. The following documentation is another example of the subtle mixing of truth with error for the purpose of changing a student's way of thinking. In fact, the introduction to the book clearly states that this is the purpose of the course of study:

> *The Bible as Liberating Word* is an introduction to liberation theology. In this study, participants will learn what liberation theology is—a theology that interprets God as the one who frees people from all conditions of life that enslave. Participants will also learn some of what the experiences of the poor have been as the poor tell their own stories. . . . Introduce is not a neutral word. It implies more than exposure. It means "to lead into." The intent of this study has been to lead you into a particular understanding of the Christian faith that may be new to you, having arisen out of circumstances very different from your own (author's emphasis).[13]

Throughout the five sessions of study, the Christian faith is mentioned and seven Bible passages are quoted; but in every instance, the Bible passages are interpreted to support the liberation theologians' emphasis on man's material needs and the kingdom of God on earth. The following examples serve as an illustration:

> *Welcoming the Kingdom*—Liberation theologians assert that following Jesus means being open to God's future and obedient to the call of the kingdom that Jesus proclaimed.

> It is commonly thought that the kingdom of God is equal to the popular conception of heaven. But that is not so, either in the New Testament or in liberation theology. In parable after parable, Jesus described the kingdom of God not as the place where people go when they die but as a future reality that with the coming of the Messiah was beginning to impinge upon the earth. The kingdom of God is not just a state of mind but a physical, social, and political realm in which God rules and God's will for justice and peace prevails.

---

[13]Phyllis Anderson, *The Bible as Liberating Word: An Introduction to Liberation Theology* (Minneapolis: Augsburg Publishing House, 1986), p. 2, 27.

What is the Nature of Human Sin?—But Jose David went on to say that now he understood sin as something bigger and more dangerous than the sins the nuns had caught him at [as a youth in school]. Through the discussion at Meribah, he had become aware of how the selfish desire to want more, even at the expense of others, was not only an individual sin, but the evil principle on which his society and its economy was founded. . . . More and more, Jose David and his community were thinking of sin as a power that controlled their lives, for which they were not responsible and from which they gained only grief.

What is Salvation?—. . . Maria began by slowly reciting her favorite Bible passages with her eyes closed.

"I came that they may have life, and have it abundantly" (John 10:10).

"Blessed are you poor, for yours is the kingdom of God. Blessed are you that hunger now, for you shall be satisfied. Blessed are you that weep now, for you shall laugh" (Luke 6:20-21).

"The Spirit of the Lord is upon me, because he has anointed me to preach good news to the poor. He has sent me to proclaim release to the captives and recovering of sight to the blind, to set at liberty those who are oppressed, to proclaim the acceptable year of the Lord" (Luke 4:18-19).

Maria's eyes opened and sparkled. She said to her friend: "I believe Jesus' promise. He died for us and rose again. He won, friends, he won. He broke the hold of the evil ones. He took their power. "Jesus came to save us from our sins, yes, but not only that. He came to save us from the sin in our world, in our government, in our church, in the way things are arranged, the sin that oppresses us. . . ." His kingdom is coming here in our neighborhood where people don't have jobs, and children don't have shoes to wear or milk to drink. Life is going to be different. It already is different. You have water now, and you never did before. That is a little piece of salvation. But there is so much more. "The spirit of Jesus is alive among us with power to transform our lives and the structures of society so that we can be free at last."[14]

---

[14]Ibid., pp. 20-24.

It will be helpful at this point to re-read the preceding quotations by LeRoy and Belli. Note especially the manner in which liberation theologians re-interpret Christ's identity, his message of salvation, and the meaning of sin and guilt. Anderson continues:

> Our politics cannot be separated from our faith. Our church-es should be places where we consider how our voting records reflect God's "preferential option for the poor." We should not be surprised to hear talk about economics from the pulpit. Having seen the seriousness with which God regards the poor, we can expect that our Bible classes, like the Bible itself, will dwell on the theme of justice.[15]

In the above quotation, Anderson fails to note the biblical Lutheran teaching concerning the proper roles of the individual Christian, the church, and the state (see Position A, "The Church and the State," at the beginning of this chapter). This is demonstrated again in the following quotation as Anderson writes:

> Liberation theology has come under attack from both the church and secular sources because it has borrowed two of its key methodological principles from the philosophy of Karl Marx. The first of these is the Marxist concept of eco-nomic determinism, which views society and its problems in concrete, materialistic terms. Human suffering is largely attributed to the unfair distribution of wealth. This under-standing of reality leads to an analysis of society in which conflict between economic classes, or between the oppres-sors and the oppressed, is seen as the basic nature of the human dilemma. Liberation theologians, like many poor people, have found that this analysis accurately reflects their experience. It frees them to imagine that society could be organized differently. . . . The theory of economic deter-minism and the methodological mix of theory and practice are not necessarily wrong simply because Karl Marx [an atheist] introduced them. It is possible to make use of some Marxist ideas without endorsing atheism or Soviet-style communism.[16]

Once again, Anderson fails to point out that man's real dilemma is sin and that it is the gospel message that frees us from the sin's slav-ery and Satan's captivity.

---

[15]Ibid., p. 26.
[16]Ibid., pp. 30, 31.

2) "The Confession of a Former Liberal LCA Pastor," Dr. J. Kincaid Smith.

Interest in the philosophies and principles of Karl Marx is not new to the leadership of the now merged ELCA. Smith, now a pastor in the Evangelical Lutheran Synod, relates an incident that occurred while he was a seminary student at Hamma School of Theology (now merged with Trinity Lutheran Seminary [ELCA], Columbus, Ohio):

> In 1970 Hamma invited a Marxist from Uraguay, Dr. Mario Utzis, to come as a visiting professor. He taught a course called Marxism, Christianity and Revolution. The course put forth violent Marxist revolution as the acceptable way of bringing about social change. He was praised at every turn in this seminary and his viewpoint was coveted at convocations because we always wanted to hear the "Marxist perspective." Mario went back to Uruguay after his stay with us and participated in revolutionary activities there. He was later once more welcomed, as rather a hero, and stayed for a brief visit.[17]

3) *Christians and the Many Faces of Marxism,* Wayne Stumme, editor.

This book, the work of ten influential ELCA theologians and seminary professors, reflects an ongoing interest in the "Marxist perspective." The authors include the editor, Wayne Stumme, as well as Paul Jersild; Will L. Herzfeld, bishop of the former AELC; Faith E. Burgess; James M. Childs, Jr.; Marc Kolden; Timothy F. Lull; Paul V. Martinson; Russell B. Norris, Jr.; and Ronald F. Thiemann.

The events leading up to the publication of the book are stated in the foreword by Paul A. Wee:

> At its Sixth Assembly in Dar es Salaam, Tanzania in 1977, moreover, the LWF [the Lutheran World Federation] affirmed "the need for radical change in the world's economic system as one essential step toward attaining peace." The message was not antagonistic, but it was certainly clear: the Lutheran churches in North America should reexamine their own policies, as well as those of their governments, to determine if they help or hinder the realization of the dignity, freedom, well-being, and peace which the Lord intends

---

[17]J. Kincaid Smith, "The Confession of a Former Liberal LCA Pastor," *Christian News Encyclopedia,* 4 vols., ed. Herman Otten (Washington: Missourian Publishing Co., 1988), 3:2165.

for all people. . . . It was in response to this challenge that the Lutheran World Ministries Commission [the U.S. branch of the LWF], on the recommendation of its Standing Committee on Studies, called a major consultation in 1983 on the theme, "The Challenge and Necessity of the Christian-Marxist Dialogue" and commissioned the writing of study material for the laity, pastors, congregational groups, and students to help them become better equipped to deal with the many types of Marxism and the challenges they pose to the church.[18]

In reference to the LWF, mentioned in the preceding quotation, it is important to note that the LWF is made up of liberal Lutheran church bodies. As such, its mission emphasis also centers on the Social Gospel.

The ten essays contained in the book support earlier quotations of Anderson's, which defend the selective use of Marxist principles and methods in bringing about political and economic change. The central message of the book is summed up by Jersild. (See previous chapters for additional quotations from Jersild):

The Christian-Marxist Dialogue—Many Christians in the United States would regard dialogue between Christians and Marxists as utterly impossible. There would appear to be no common ground on which the two sides could meet. Many would assume that the only possible purpose of these kinds of meetings would be to convert the Marxists to Christianity. However, such a viewpoint fails to recognize that the very *purpose of dialog* is to help both sides to break out of that mentality which slices the world into opposing camps, refusing to allow for possibilities of understanding and recognition of mutual goals. To engage in genuine dialogue is to be willing to acknowledge that our own side has something to learn. It demands openness to the possibility that Christians as well as Marxists can be guilty of self-interest which prejudices our view of the other side and prevents us from really understanding their aspirations. It is to recognize that they are human beings too, moved by their own vision of the future and what they hope to do for their society and the larger world.[19]

---

[18]*Christians and the Many Faces of Marxism,* ed. Wayne Stumme (Minneapolis: Augsburg Publishing House, 1984), p. 13.

[19]Ibid., Paul Jersild, p. 104.

To appreciate the significance of Jersild's statement, one must understand the true meaning of the word *dialogue* and the way in which liberal theologians apply it—not only in relation to Marxism, but also as a tool to be used in reaching agreement in all areas of doctrine and theology.

Both the liberal theologians and Karl Marx, the father of Marxism, trace their philosophical roots back to the *dialectical* method of G. F. Hegel. This philosophy holds that all of reality is in a continuous state of flux or change. There are no absolute or unchanging truths—no definite standards of right and wrong.

The practical application of the dialectical method is carried out through a process called dialogue. The word dialogue itself is derived from the word dialectic. For Hegel's followers, it means to meet together for the purpose of presenting to one another opposing ideas—thesis and antithesis—with the intention of each side moving to a new position and forming a new philosophy—synthesis. Smith explains why this dialectical approach, used by the liberals, is so hard for conservative pastors and lay people to deal with:

> It involves an entirely different way of *thinking*. I have said many times to my conservative friends: "You don't understand, they think in an entirely different way. You think in terms of one thing which is *true* and the opposite which is *false*. They have adopted a "dialectical" way of thinking in which there is no true and false, only thesis, antithesis, and synthesis. They have effectively adopted Hegel's dialectical way of thinking. There truly are no *absolute* truths within their system. They will discuss things with conservatives in a way that gets their opponent to think that they are discussing which of two positions is *right*. All the while the real issue for them is that there is no certain answer. This is why they get so exasperated with us when we will not move from our position.[20]

LOOKING BACK

As a closing to this chapter, Smith reflects on the theological position that he held before his conversion to orthodox Lutheranism:

> Looking back now, I would have to say that given what I was taught and had come to believe as a student in a liberal Lutheran seminary, I was little more than a humanist

---

[20]Smith, loc. cit.

dressed up in the garb of Christian language. Politically I was virtually a Marxist, although I would not have called myself that at the time—I don't think that I could have admitted that even to myself.

In the big shift that our theology had taken, the foundation for our beliefs had completely changed without our wanting to recognize it. Instead of being based on God's Word, our beliefs had shifted around until they finally leaned entirely on the same philosophies upon which Karl Marx had built his "house."

There were consequently some very critical blind spots that were built into our way of understanding the nature of man, the world, and society.

It is important to say that we *did care* about people and about society. This caring is evident in the writing of the liberation theologians. For example, as we consider the writing of Dr. Phyllis Anderson, it is obvious that she is a person of deep feeling and compassion, moved with genuine concern for the plight of the poor and downtrodden. The genuineness of her concern, however, is not the issue. We ought all to be concerned for suffering people everywhere.

Considering my own former position in retrospect, it was because certain vital elements were *missing* in our scheme of things that we were completely obstructed from being able to recognize the real problem in society. As a result, our proposals of what the church's mission to the world should be were utterly ill-conceived and misguided. We were crippled in our capacity to access the nature of the real root problem, because vital truths that are found only in the Bible had gotten lost in the historical-critical shuffle.

What was missing?

One cannot approach the problems in the world, understand them, and propose action unless one knows:

1. How things got the way they are.
2. What the purpose of history is and where it is going.

As liberation theologians, we were like aliens dropped from space into a different world, completely ignorant of how the conditions we found there had come about and the plan that was unfolding and leading that world in a certain determined direction with a precise culmination planned for the end of its history.

If the Bible is God's Word, then it is only from the Bible that we can learn and believe that *God* created man and *planned our* history; that history had its beginning in the creation, and that God has a precise purpose for its whole span in time and for its end when Christ will come again.

In the Bible, we find out what man is really like—that he is not a product of mere chance and evolution but a creature of God, created perfect but then fallen into sin.

The world today is consequently a fallen world and as such it is *not* perfectible. In his fall into sin, man turned away from his creator. He turned to himself and to his own way. The nature of man since the fall is sinful and self-centered and because of this, man is not capable of bringing about the perfect peaceful utopian society that we as liberation theologians so hopefully proposed. We were like men trying to plan and construct a building while having a totally wrong understanding of the nature and strength of the building materials and of the purpose of the building itself.

Having obliterated the truth, we always proposed programs that could never work. Blind to certain *realities* that are revealed only in the Scriptures, we were unfit as workmen. We were utterly incapable of proposing a *mission* for the Church of Christ.

If the Bible *is* the Word of the sovereign God who planned and created the world, laid out its history, and is leading it toward its end and ultimate future, then only from God's Word, the Bible, can we find the vision to be able to rightly comprehend the true problem of society and to know what the mission of the church should be.

Only in God's Word can we find the true nature of *the* problem, *sin* as disobedience to God. Here also we find *God's* solution to the fatal illness of sin. He sent His virgin-born Son, Jesus Christ, to redeem the world through the shedding of his blood. Only here can we discover what the true mission of the church should be—spreading the good news of this redemption in a fallen world until the day of his coming.[21]

---

[21]J. Kincaid Smith, "Reflections," unpublished paper, October 1989.

A FOOTNOTE OF HISTORIC IRONY

It is a great irony of history that the liberation theologians are reaching the height of their movement toward a synthesis with Marxism at a time when most of the governments of the Communist block nations are openly admitting the bankruptcy of their Marxist systems. While this book was being written, the Berlin Wall was being torn down and most of the Warsau Pact Nations as well as Russia were electing noncommunists to their parliaments. What must the Marxist professors in our American colleges and seminaries be thinking of all this?

20.

THE NATIONAL COUNCIL
OF CHURCHES
AND
THE WORLD COUNCIL
OF CHURCHES

Position A

Lutherans should not join the National Council of Churches or the World Council of Churches. Not only are these organizations not Lutheran, but their primary emphasis is political and leans heavily on Marxism.

The political-social agenda of the National Council of Churches (NCC) and the World Council of Churches (WCC) and their Marxist leanings has created a great deal of interest and much concern among pastors and laity alike in all denominations. Many books and articles have been written that thoroughly document this subject. It would be impractical to use the limited space in this book to attempt to duplicate the work of so many others. Therefore, this chapter will summarize the work of these two organizations through the introduction of several resources. These resources will provide an excellent starting point for the reader interested in additional research and study.

It should be noted that the authors of these resource books are Reformed, not Lutheran. Therefore, the authors do not hold the conservative Lutheran position of separation of church and state (Martin Luther's doctrine of the two kingdoms) as defined in the preceding chapter. The authors do not object to the church's involvement in the affairs of the government; rather, they are concerned with the radical direction this involvement has taken over the last few years. Nevertheless, their observations and insights are valuable and important as an aid in understanding Position A's beliefs on this subject.

MEMBERSHIP OF THE NCC AND WCC

The NCC is composed of 31 communions—Protestants, Orthodox, and Anglican church bodies—with a combined membership of approximately 40 million Christians. The NCC includes nearly all of the so-called mainline denominations, as well as many smaller church bodies, and depends on member churches for its income.[1]

The WCC is made up of more than 300 church bodies in more than 100 countries with one-third of its funding coming from the United States.[2]

These two bodies derive their theological and mission emphasis from their member churches, which have all been influenced by the historical-critical method of biblical interpretation. As a result, most of the member churches are involved to some degree in the Social Gospel, as defined in Chapter 19, and suffer from the "spiritual depletion" described by Dr. Edmund W. Robb and Julia Robb in the following resource book.

1) *The Betrayal of the Church: Apostasy and Renewal in the Mainline Denominations,* Dr. Edmund W. Robb and Julia Robb.

Edmund W. Robb, an ordained minister of the United Methodist Church, is chairman of the Institute on Religion and Democracy, Washington, D.C. Julia Robb, his daughter, is an author and a journalist:

> A growing percentage of Christian leadership has abandoned its role as spiritual shepherd because it no longer considers humanity's spiritual welfare its greatest concern. A great many bishops have rejected winning souls in favor of influencing political issues. . . . The transformation from classical Christianity to political advocacy has occurred gradually during the last twenty years and is the result of spiritual depletion. Christian leadership, for the most part, no longer believes that eternity is of prime significance. The emphasis is now on the world.[3]

---

[1] National Council of Churches literature.

[2] "The World Council of Churches," *The Presbyterian Layman,* September/October 1987, p. 7. World Council of Churches literature.

[3] Edmund W. Robb, Julia Robb, *The Betrayal of the Church: Apostasy and Renewal in the Mainline Denominations* (Westchester, IL: Crossway Books, 1986), p. 12.

The results of the Social Gospel, with its emphasis on man's material needs rather than spiritual needs, as well as its involvement in governmental affairs, has left the church wide open to an ever-increasing involvement in the matters of this world. This is demonstrated in the following quotation, in which the Robbs describe the creation of the "religious left":

> *The Creation of the Religious Left*—When people reflect on the Christian church they generally picture a fellowship of believers whose focus is on spiritual growth, spreading the faith, and good works. These were the church's primary goals until the last few decades. There is a wide gulf, however, between yesterday's goals and today's agenda. The American mainline churches—the most prominent of which are the United Methodists, the United Church of Christ, the Presbyterian Church (USA), the Episcopalians, the American Baptists, many Catholic leaders and orders, and the Lutheran Church in America [now part of the ELCA]—have realigned their priorities in a frighteningly political direction. . . . Church bureaucracy now neglects traditional missions in favor of lobbying for political causes. In fact, certain sectors of the church now make it their primary business to manufacture, widely distribute, and finance a radical agenda by which they hope to save the world. In doing so, they have created the Religious Left.

> Main components of the Religious Left are organizations financed by the church. These organizations, such as Clergy and Laity Concerned (an anti-American, prodisarmament group), lobby the secular world and the American government on behalf of the Religious Left agenda. Unfortunately, church members are rarely aware of these organizations or their denomination's spending practices and would probably disapprove if they did know.

> The Religious Left is a result of the cooperation between these church-created organizations and mainline denominational bureaucracies (such as the United Methodist General Board of Global Ministries, the United Church of Christ Board for Homeland Ministries, the Presbyterian General Assembly Mission Board and the Presbyterian Peacemaking Program), mainline church leadership, and the National and World Council of Churches. The cooperation among these groups is not planned, but is the product

of mutual agreement among allies on what they consider true and important.[4]

The Robbs illustrate the cooperation among the groups listed in the preceding quotation through their coverage of such topics as:

1. The National Council of Churches and the Soviet Union (Chapter 5).
2. The World Council of Churches and African Terrorism (Chapter 9).
3. Liberation Theology: What It Is and What It Does (Chapter 6).
4. Attitudes Toward Democratic Capitalism and Totalitarianism (Chapter 4).
5. The Attack on Free Enterprise (Chapter 3).

The reader no doubt noticed that the Lutheran Church in America (LCA) was listed in the preceding quotation as a mainline denomination involved in the Religious Left. The documentation provided by the Robbs supports that in Chapter 19, "Missions."

The next resource provides documentation concerning the WCC. The mainline church bodies listed by the Robbs belong to the NCC and the WCC. A resource book by Dr. Ernest W. Lefever examines the interaction of these groups.

2) *Nairobi to Vancouver: The World Council of Churches and the World, 1975-1987,* Dr. Ernest W. Lefever.

Lefever, the founding president of the Ethics and Public Policy Center, Washington, D.C., has a B.D. and a Ph.D in Christian ethics from Yale University and is the author of several books. The following quotation from the cover of the cited book is consistent with its general content:

> In this sequel to his 1979 study *Amsterdam to Nairobi: The World Council of Churches and the Third World,* Ernest Lefever examines the behavior of the WCC since 1975 and the reasons for its continuing revolutionary stance. He finds that its official pronouncements on international issues— from Afghanistan and nuclear arms to Nicaragua and southern Africa—have much more closely reflected the aims of the Soviet Union than those of the West. It has used a persistent double standard: supporting, condoning, or apologizing for Soviet policies or those of Soviet-backed regimes while harshly criticizing less repressive governments allied with the United States and the West. It has given nearly $7 million to revolutionary causes.

---

[4]Ibid., pp. 11, 12.

Lefever concludes that the WCC has lost sight of its original spiritual and social vision. Having failed to preach a morally sound and politically responsible approach to world problems, it has seriously damaged its credibility as an authentic voice of the Christian moral tradition.[5]

Lefever offers an explanation as to why the WCC's official pronouncements on international issues more closely reflect the aims of the Soviet Union than those of the West:

Does this mean that the WCC staff in Geneva and other key Council leaders were taking orders from Moscow? Hardly. There has been, of course, increasing Soviet influence, even pressures on Council deliberations at every level since the Russian Orthodox Church was admitted to membership in 1961. . . . The USSR was also successful in increasing the number of the Soviet and Soviet bloc staffers at the WCC Geneva headquarters, where key policy decisions on the international agenda are made. In a real sense, the development of the World Council of Churches parallels that of the United Nations General Assembly and Secretariat. In both institutions the influence of the Soviet bloc states and their Third World friends has dramatically increased since the 1950's, when Western members could command a majority vote on any important issue. Now, through coalition politics based on the number of member states, a Soviet-Third World alliance can insure a majority vote. At Vancouver [1983], as noted in Chapter 1, there were 336 delegates from the West, compared to 511 from the Soviet bloc and the Third World. At Nairobi [1975], there were approximately 300 Western delegates and 350 from the Soviet bloc and the Third World. Generally, most delegates from Asia, Africa, and Latin America supported the Soviet view along with many from Western countries.[6]

The geographical distribution of assembly delegates is not the only explanation for the WCC's revolutionary stance. The NCC has taken positions similar to those of the WCC's despite the fact that the NCC does not include Soviet or Third World denominations. Dr. Lefever points to a common denominator—*Liberation Theology:*

---

[5] Ernest W. Lefever, *Nairobi to Vancouver: The World Council of Churches and the World, 1975-1987* (Washington: Ethics and Public Policy Center, 1987), dustcover.

[6] Ibid., pp. 80, 81.

> *Triumph of Liberation Theology*—No simple "devil theory of
> history" takes into account the reality of multiple causation.
> The geographical distribution of Assembly delegations alone
> cannot explain the WCC's revolutionary stance, which came
> to flower before the 1975 Nairobi Assembly and has flour-
> ished ever since. After all, the U.S. National Council of
> Churches, which has no Soviet or Third World member de-
> nominations, takes positions almost identical to those of the
> WCC. In both cases, the councils have been profoundly influ-
> enced by the canons of "liberation theology" developed by
> Gustave Gutierrez, a Peruvian Catholic priest, in his book *A
> Theology of Liberation,* published in 1973. He and other lib-
> erationists differ somewhat among themselves, but in
> essence liberation theology as understood by Catholic and
> Protestant adherents alike is an operational doctrine that
> ties Christian salvation to liberation from political repres-
> sion and economic bondage in this world. In practical terms,
> this doctrine calls for a class struggle against feudalism,
> multinational corporations, and Western imperialism along
> the lines of V.I. Lenin's pregnant dictum: "Imperialism is the
> last stage of capitalism." As such, liberation theology identi-
> fies itself closely with the Marxist-Leninist doctrine and
> practice of "national liberation," which insists that unjust po-
> litical and economic structures (capitalism and imperialism)
> can be eliminated only by protracted pressure including rev-
> olutionary violence.[7]

In his epilogue, Lefever refers to an earlier book he wrote and to
other developments that precipitated critical evaluations of both the
WCC and the NCC:

> Does the WCC have or deserve to have a future? In my
> study *Amsterdam to Nairobi: The World Council of Churches
> and the Third World,* published in 1979, I concluded, as I
> have in the present volume, that the WCC's political stance
> since the mid-1960's has been profoundly misguided. Then I
> harbored the hope that the Council could be reformed, that
> it could return to a realistic and non-utopian understanding
> of the world, recognizing both human limitations and hu-
> man possibilities, and thus become an authentic voice of the
> great Christian moral tradition for our troubled times.

[7]Ibid., p. 81.

There is considerable evidence that the earlier book had an impact in both religious and secular circles. Some WCC critics said the book "shook the Council to its foundations." This turned out to be an exaggeration. The book certainly irritated Council stalwarts, but it did not lead to significant reform.

The modest study, along with the founding of the Institute on Religion and Democracy [see (1), Dr. Edmund W. Robb] in 1981 and other developments, did help, however, to precipitate a critical evaluation of both the World Council of Churches and the U.S. National Council of Churches. The results included a revealing CBS-TV "Sixty Minutes" program (January 23, 1983) that exposed a pattern of ecumenical support for violent revolutionary movements. That same month there was also a critical *Reader's Digest* article by Rael Jean Isaac.[8] The Salvation Army withdrew from the WCC and several churches suspended their membership. Countless church members and local congregations in the United States and elsewhere have withheld funds from the WCC or its Program to Combat Racism, the agency that has provided almost seven million dollars to revolutionary causes on four continents.[9]

Included in the Lefever book are six appendices that contain official WCC resolutions and statements from 1948 to 1983. In addition, the book contains two lists of WCC grants and the names of their recipients. The figures are drawn from official WCC records and show the grant totals by year and by region. Both the Lefever and Robb books are well-documented and provide the reader with ample resources for additional study.

3) *On Thin Ice: A Religion Reporter's Memoir,* Roy Howard Beck.

Beck is Washington, D.C. bureau chief for *Booth* newspapers. *On Thin Ice* is an account of the years (1980-86) that Beck spent covering the world of religion for the *United Methodist Reporter.* During this time, he won virtually every award given by church-press or-

---

[8]Ibid., p. 133. Author's endnote. Citation reads: See transcript of "Sixty Minutes" program, "The Gospel According to Whom?" broadcast by the Columbia Broadcasting System (CBS-TV), New York City, January 23, 1983. See also Rael Jean Isaac, "Do You Know Where Your Church Offerings Go?" *Reader's Digest,* January 1983, pp. 120-125. See also *A Time for Candor: Mainline Churches and Radical Social Witness* (Washington: Institute on Religion and Democracy, December 1983).

[9]Ibid., pp. 86, 87.

ganizations for journalistic excellence. Beck speaks of his invitation to join the staff of the *Reporter* and introduces the reader to the *Reporter,* himself, and the general content of the book:

> My call came at 11:30 p.m. in late August 1980 without warning or expectation. . . . Would I be interested in leaving the Cincinnati *Enquirer* after a decade with various daily newspapers to cover the world of religion for the *United Methodist Reporter?* The voice belonged to Spurgeon Dannam III, the editor. I was only vaguely aware of the *Reporter,* although I would learn it was the largest-circulation weekly religious paper in the world. . . . Jumping from "pure journalism" into a specialty publication was not an easy decision. But the church was a familiar place. I was a lifelong, regular churchgoer. . . . I found journalism and the church had many similarities in their imperfect pursuits of truth. . . . I soon found myself with the *United Methodist Reporter* covering all kinds of people and church organizations worldwide dealing with the issues of our Mainstream Class. Their struggles—and mine—are the tales of this book.
>
> *The Reporter,* based in Dallas, Texas, was serving more than a half-million households and reaching a million people each week. Soon after I got there, we started an interdenominational weekly called the *National Christian Reporter* and later took over the operation of the 50-year-old *Religious News Service* that provides daily interfaith wire coverage to public and church publications nationwide. . . . My stint with the *Reporter* afforded me an extraordinary observation post to witness the challenges, joys, tensions and pitfalls of some of the hottest Christian social action episodes of the 80's.[10]

Beck went into his work as a religion reporter with a positive attitude and an open mind and was shocked by what he discovered. His reporting concentrated largely on his own denomination, the United Methodist Church, as well as the wider mainline Protestant community, and on social stances similar to his own. The entire book is fascinating reading, including his disturbing account of homosexual activism at NCC headquarters. For our purposes, the most valuable section concerns his investigation into the affairs of the NCC as a result of the stir created by the *Reader's Digest* article and the CBS-TV

---

[10]Roy Howard Beck, *On Thin Ice: A Religion Reporter's Memoir* (Wilmore, Kentucky: Bristol Books, 1988), pp. 1, 2.

"Sixty Minutes" program. His research, carried out at NCC head-quarters in New York under the auspices of the *Reporter's* staff, largely confirms the concerns raised by the media and the Institute on Religion and Democracy.

Position B

Lutherans should join the National Council of Churches and the World Council of Churches.

The first Churchwide Assembly of the ELCA voted decisively to remain in the NCC and the WCC. The *Religious News Service* reported on this memorable event:

> Mainline religion scored a victory August 25 when the Evangelical Lutheran Church in America voted decisively to remain inside two heavily criticized ecumenical bodies. Only scattered opposition arose among delegates to the 5.2 million-member denomination's first Churchwide Assembly here [Chicago] as the ELCA voted to maintain its ties with both the National Council of Churches and World Council of Churches. . . . Only one of the three predecessor bodies [the LCA] of the Evangelical Lutheran Church in America, which began operations in January 1988, belonged to both the National Council and World Council. The new church's constituting convention in 1987 moved to keep the denomination in association with both councils until membership could be reviewed and voted on at this assembly.[11]

After three, one-hour sessions in which WCC General Secretary Emilio Castro and NCC President Patricia McClurg urged continued membership in both councils, the 1,000-plus delegates to the convention voted to remain. The article continues with a description of the voting process:

> The World Council membership question sailed through a convention plenary session without any debate, with only a handful of the 1,000-plus delegates voting against continued participation in that body. Membership in the National Council was debated for less than a half hour, with fewer than two dozen delegates voting against membership. The assembly also easily beat back a bid to delay the vote another two years. . . . Dues and related services in the WCC will

[11]Daniel J. Lehmann, "ELCA Lutherans Vote to Remain in National, World Council of Churches," *Religious News Service*, August 25, 1989. *Christian News*, Sept. 11, 1989, p. 6.

cost the ELCA $761,700 this year, with $867,934 going to the NCC. The ELCA is undergoing a financial crisis, having finished its first fiscal year $15.8 million in debt, and money worries seemed to cast a pall over the gathering here.[12]

In the opening paragraph of this chapter, one of the reasons given for not joining the NCC and WCC was the fact that they are "not Lutheran." Both of these organizations are made up of churches of many denominations, all of which teach doctrines in conflict with those of historic Lutheranism. Lutherans who join organizations such as these violate the biblical doctrine of fellowship. It is the incorrect understanding of this doctrine that lies at the heart and center of the modern Ecumenical Movement—the final subject of our comparison column.

The next chapter will define the Biblical doctrine of fellowship and provide the reader with a clear understanding of what it means to say "I am Lutheran." It will lay the foundation for subsequent chapters that deal not only with the fundamental error of the ecumenical movement, but also those factors and events essential to understanding what has gone wrong among both Lutheran church bodies and those of other denominations.

Please note a departure from our usual procedure of presenting both Positions A and B of our comparisons in the same chapter. As noted above, the final subject of our comparison column is the ecumenical movement (see Chapter 1). Position A will be presented at the beginning of the next chapter, while Position B will not appear until Chapter 28. Also, since each of the remaining chapters build upon the preceding chapters, it is important that they be read in sequence.

---

[12]Ibid.

Section II

THE GREAT
STRENGTHS
OF LUTHERANISM

21.

WHAT IT MEANS TO BE A LUTHERAN

Position A

All doctrines of the Bible are important and provide foundation and support for the chief doctrine, the gospel. While God's Word commands our fellowship in the body of Christ, that fellowship is to be the outward expression of unity in faith and doctrine. Therefore, Lutherans should join in fellowship with those church bodies that subscribe to the Lutheran Confessions and whose teaching and practice is consistent with their confession.

We will begin this chapter by defining the words fellowship, faith, and doctrine as they are used in the preceding statement.

> *Fellowship:* a relationship that exists among those who hold something in common.

> *Faith:* Trust in Christ; receiving Christ and his atoning work; knowledge of Christ and his benefits (his work of salvation).[1]

> *Doctrine:* What we, or a church body, believe and teach concerning our faith.

Unity in faith

As thus defined, fellowship is a relationship that exists among those who hold something in common. For Christians, faith in Christ is the common bond that creates fellowship—fellowship with God and with one another. This is clearly taught in Scripture:

---

[1]Robert D. Preus, *Getting Into the Theology of Concord* (St. Louis: Concordia Publishing House, 1977), p. 87.

> You are all sons of God through faith in Christ Jesus, for all of you who were baptized into Christ have clothed yourselves with Christ. There is neither Jew nor Greek, slave nor free, male nor female, for you are all one in Christ Jesus (Galatians 3:26-28).

> But if we walk in the light, as he is in the light, we have fellowship with one another, and the blood of Jesus, his Son, purifies us from all sin (1 John 1:7).

It is God who has established this fellowship among his children and it is his desire that we show and practice it for the mutual strengthening of our faith and for the purpose of witnessing to Christ.

> Let us not give up meeting together, as some are in the habit of doing, but let us encourage one another—and all the more as you see the Day approaching (Hebrews 10:25).

> But you will receive power when the Holy Spirit comes on you; and you will be my witnesses in Jerusalem, and in all Judea and Samaria, and to the ends of the earth (Acts 1:8).

Unity in Doctrine

God-pleasing fellowship is to include agreement in doctrine. Unity in doctrine assumes that the members of a church, or a denomination, are in agreement on *all* of the doctrines they teach and confess concerning their common faith. This, too, is commanded by Scripture:

> I appeal to you, brothers, in the name of our Lord Jesus Christ, that all of you agree with one another so that there may be no divisions among you and that you may be perfectly united in mind and thought (1 Corinthians 1:10).

SOURCE OF LUTHERAN DOCTRINE

Sound doctrine must begin with a firm foundation—the Bible. The Lutheran Church is a Bible church. This fact is most eloquently expressed in the words of the late Dr. Paul E. Kretzmann, a noted Lutheran Church—Missouri Synod (LCMS) theologian and scholar:

> To this very hour the Lutheran Church, following in the footsteps of its great teacher, cherishes the lesson which Luther expounded to the world. Her motto is to this day: *Sola Scriptura,* the Bible alone. By the grace of God the Lutheran Church has remained the Bible Church. There is no duty which she urges more than that of searching the

Scriptures; there is no task which she performs more devoutly and conscientiously than that of teaching the Bible; there is no distinction which she covets more than that of being faithful to the Bible; there is no principle for which she would shed her blood more willingly than for that of *Sola Scriptura* (author's emphasis).[2]

"Everything we need to believe and do as Christians is told us in the Scriptures." So states Dr. Robert D. Preus, a noted scholar and theologian in the LCMS, in his book *Getting Into the Theology of Concord:*

> *Scripture is Divinely Authoritative*—The average Lutheran layman today may not know any Latin, but he probably knows what the phrase *Sola Scriptura* (Scripture alone) means. It means that we Lutherans base our theology solely on the Scriptures of God and nothing else, not tradition, not human speculation, not modern scholarship, not our experiences or feelings or anything else. *Sola Scriptura* is a watchword, a guide for action, for every true Lutheran, pastor or layman. This was the position and practice of Luther. . . . This is the spirit in which our great Lutheran Confessions speak. Everything we need to believe and do as Christians is told us in the Scriptures. Just as our Lord Jesus was a man of one Book and drew all His teaching from that one divine source and submitted Himself to it utterly in all He said and did, so we too who are His disciples today place ourselves joyfully under the prophetic and apostolic Word (author's emphasis).[3]

The doctrine of Sola Scriptura is in keeping with the teaching of Scripture itself:

> If anyone speaks, he should do it as one speaking the very words of God. If anyone serves, he should do it with the strength God provides, so that in all things God may be praised through Jesus Christ. To him be the glory and the power for ever and ever. Amen (1 Peter 4:11).

> To the Jews who had believed him, Jesus said, "If you hold to my teaching, you are really my disciples. Then you will

---

[2]Paul E. Kretzmann, *Popular Commentary of the Bible, The New Testament* (St. Louis: Concordia Publishing House, 1923), Vol. 1, p. iii, Foreword.
[3]Preus, op. cit., p. 20.

know the truth, and the truth will set you free" (John 8:31,32).

If anyone teaches false doctrines and does not agree to the sound instruction of our Lord Jesus Christ and to godly teaching, he is conceited and understands nothing (1 Timothy 6: 3, 4).

And beginning with Moses and all the Prophets, he explained to them what was said in all the Scriptures concerning himself (Luke 24:27).

To the law and to the testimony! If they do not speak according to this word, they have no light of dawn (Isaiah 8:20).

This doctrine is also taught in the Confessions. On the authority of Scripture the Lutheran Confessions state:

The Word of God is and should remain the sole rule and norm of all doctrine, and that no human being's writings dare be put on a par with it, but . . . everything must be subjected to it.[4]

We pledge ourselves to the prophetic and apostolic writings of the Old and New Testaments as the pure and clear fountain of Israel, which is the only true norm according to which all teachers and teachings are to be judged and evaluated.[5]

The Word of God shall establish articles of faith and no one else, not even an angel.[6]

THE LUTHERAN CONFESSIONS

Scripture reminds us that Christians should be prepared at all times to give an account of the reasons for their faith. The apostle Peter exhorts:

But in your hearts set apart Christ as Lord. Always be prepared to give an answer to everyone who asks you to give the reason for the hope that you have (1 Peter 3:15).

---

[4]*The Book of Concord,* trans. and ed. Theodore G. Tappert (Philadelphia: Fortress Press, 1959), Formula of Concord, Solid Declaration, Rule and Norm, 9, p. 505.

[5]Ibid., 3, pp. 503, 504.

[6]Ibid., Smalcald Articles, Part II, Art. II, 15, p. 295.

Being prepared also includes the ability to state clearly the doctrinal position of the church body to which we belong. When a Lutheran is asked "What does the Lutheran Church teach?" or "What do you as a Lutheran believe?" he can refer the inquirer to the Lutheran Confessions. The Lutheran Confessions are found in the *Book of Concord* (1580), along with the three ecumenical creeds, (Apostles, Nicene, and Athanasian), which together summarize the doctrinal position of historic Lutheranism. Dr. Wilhelm W. Petersen, president of Bethany Lutheran Seminary, Evangelical Lutheran Synod (ELS), emphasizes the fact that all who claim the name "Lutheran" should have a working knowledge of the Confessions. He responds to the question, "Why is it so important that our people be acquainted with the Lutheran Confessions?"

> It is so important because the Confessions are a correct exposition, or interpretation, of the Bible and it is in our confessions where we as a Lutheran Church publicly confess our faith before the world and confidently declare: "This we believe, teach, and confess." They are also the banner under which we march and by which we identify one another as brethren. I believe that it is fair to say that if it were not for our Confessions the Lutheran Reformation would not have gotten off the ground and, consequently, there would be no Lutheran Church today. It is also fair to say that if we depart from our confessions, as many have, the time may come when there will be no true Lutheran Church.

> Our attitude today should be that of the original signers of the Augsburg Confession on June 25, 1530, who said, "This is just about a summary of the doctrines that are preached and taught in our churches for proper Christian instruction, the consolation of consciences, and the amendment of believers. Certainly we should not wish to put our own souls and consciences in grave peril before God by misusing His name or Word, nor should we wish to bequeath to our children and posterity any other teaching than that which agrees with the pure Word of God and the Christian truth" (Tappert p. 47).[7]

As Peterson states above, the Confessions are a correct exposition, or interpretation, of the Scriptures. They are derived solely from the

[7]Wilhelm W. Petersen, "Pastor, I Have A Question," *The Lutheran Sentinel*, February 1985, p. 4.

Bible. One might be led to ask, "What is the most important reason that the Lutheran Confessions were written?" Preus responds:

> Our great Lutheran Confessions were written for the sake of the Gospel. The Augsburg Confession, Luther's cate-chisms, the Formula of Concord were not written just to blast or correct abuses in the Roman Church, or to defend Lutheran theology against the attacks of papists, or to per-petuate party spirit. . . . A reading of our Confessions will reveal that they all sprang from an urgent need to give ar-ticulation to the Gospel of Jesus Christ and to teach and give witness to this Gospel.[8]

This is also the spirit in which this book has been written.

Preus describes the statement in the Confessions concerning the gospel as being perhaps "one of the most important and formative statements in our Lutheran Confessions because it is the most com-plete and beautiful definition of the Gospel to be found in them."[9] The Confessions read:

> The Gospel, however is that doctrine which teaches what a man should believe in order to obtain the forgiveness of sins from God, since man has failed to keep the law of God and has transgressed it, his corrupted nature, thoughts, words, and deeds war against the law, and he is therefore subject to the wrath of God, to death, to temporal miseries, and to the punishment of hell-fire. The content of the Gospel is this, that the Son of God, Christ our Lord, himself assumed and bore the curse of the law and expiated and paid for all our sins, that through him alone we re-enter the good graces of God, obtain forgiveness of sins through faith, are freed from death and all the punishments of sin, and are saved eternally.[10]

To those who suggest that Lutherans put the authority of the Con-fessions above that of Scripture, Preus says:

> Are there, then, levels of authority? Yes. Precisely. Specifi-cally there is a threefold tier of authority in the church, ac-cording to our Confessions. . . . Scripture, the Confessions, other good Christian literature! Scripture's authority is di-

---

[8]Preus, op. cit., pp. 24, 25.

[9]Preus, op. cit., p. 24.

[10]*The Book of Concord,* op. cit. Art. V, 20, p. 561.

vine and absolute. The Confessions' authority is derived from their agreement with Scripture and is binding for everyone who professes to be a Lutheran. Other Christian writings are authoritative and useful too when they agree with Scripture and the Lutherans Confessions.[11]

TRUE AND FALSE CHURCHES

Position A states: "Lutherans should join in fellowship [only] with those church bodies who subscribe to the Lutheran Confessions and whose teaching and practice is consistent with their confession." What is meant when one speaks of the *true* or *orthodox* church? The late Dr. Edward W. A. Koehler, noted theologian and scholar in the LCMS, explains in his book *A Summary of Christian Doctrine:*

> The question whether or not a church is the true church may not be determined on the basis of the personal faith and the sincerity of its members, but on the basis of its public doctrine, as laid down in its official Confessions. If these agree with the Scriptures, then that church is a true church. . . . A true church, then, is one which in all its doctrines adheres strictly to the Word of God. . . . On examination we find that the doctrines of the Lutheran Church, as they are laid down in the Book of Concord of the year 1580, agree with the Word of God in every respect. Therefore those church bodies, no matter what their names may be, which actually teach, and adhere to, these doctrines [this means in their practice as well] are to be regarded as the true, or orthodox, visible church. . . . When we say that the Lutheran Church is the true, or orthodox church, we do not mean to say that it is the only saving church, or that all its members are true Christians and will unfailingly be saved. Membership in the Lutheran Church is not identical with membership in the invisible Church whose membership is known only to God. But we do mean to say that all its official teachings agree with the Word of God and are, therefore, positively true, and that all doctrines differing from them are heterodox and false.[12]

---

[11]Preus, op. cit., p. 22.

[12]Edward W. A. Koehler, *A Summary of Christian Doctrine* (St. Louis: Concordia Publishing House, 1971), pp. 246, 247.

Having defined the true or orthodox church, it is necessary also to define the *false* or *heterodox* church. Koehler continues:

> A false church is one which in one or more points departs from the teachings of the Word of God. . . . Those church bodies which, besides teaching some true doctrines, confessedly uphold and defend erroneous teachings, must be regarded as heterodox churches. . . . When we say that other churches are false churches, we do by no means wish to insinuate that there are no Christians in those churches, or that it is impossible for any one to be saved in them. We are passing judgment, not on the personal faith of their members, branding them hypocrites and heathen, but only on those public doctrines, which do not agree with the Word of God.[13]

TRUE AND FALSE DOCTRINE

The importance of holding to correct doctrine cannot be overemphasized. Koehler clearly states this:

> If the truth of God's Word is to accomplish its divinely intended purpose, it must be taught and accepted as it is revealed in Holy Scriptures. Any change or corruption of these teachings will necessarily affect the influence they have on the hearts and the lives of men. Guided by wrong information, man will go wrong. Only the right doctrine can create the right faith in our hearts and lead us in the right way through life. . . . Our faith must not be built on what men say, but on what God says in His Book; only in this way can our hearts be established (Heb. 13:9).[14]

Martin Luther shows the danger of allowing even a little false doctrine:

> Doctrine is our only light. It alone enlightens and directs us and shows the way to heaven. If it is shaken in one quarter (*in una parte*), it will necessarily be shaken in its entirety (*in totum*). Where that happens, love cannot help us at all.[15]

> In philosophy an error that is small at the beginning becomes very great in the end. So a small error in theology overturns

---

[13]Ibid.

[14]Ibid., pp. iii, iv, Foreword.

[15]*What Luther Says,* 3 vols., ed. Ewald M. Plass (St. Louis: Concordia Publishing House, 1959), 1:414.

the whole body of doctrine. . . . That is why we may not sur-
render or change even an iota (*apiculum*) of doctrine.[16]

Scripture itself issues the strongest warning of all:

A little yeast works through the whole batch of dough (Galatians 5:9).

Watch out for false prophets. They come to you in sheep's
clothing, but inwardly they are ferocious wolves. By their
fruit you will recognize them (Matthew 7:15,16).

I urge you, brothers, to watch out for those who cause divisions and put obstacles in your way that are contrary to the
teaching you have learned. Keep away from them. For such
people are not serving our Lord Christ, but their own ap-
petites. By smooth talk and flattery they deceive the minds
of naive people (Romans 16:17,18).

Among the fruits of false doctrine are disunity and division. This
will be observed in the next chapter, which examines the major divisions in the Christian church resulting from doctrinal errors.

---

[16]Ibid., 3:1365.

22.

DISUNITY AND DIVISION IN THE CHURCH

EARLY DISUNITY

False doctrine has caused disunity and division in the Christian church since its early beginnings. Dr. Herbert J. A. Bouman, a professor emeritus of systematic theology in the Lutheran Church—Missouri Synod (LCMS), states that the "spirit of factionalism has manifested itself throughout the church's history, even in the days of the apostles." In his book, *A Look at Today's Churches—A Comparative Guide,* Dr. Bouman states:

> The New Testament, especially in the letters of the apostles, teems with admonitions to Christians to avoid all that would jeopardize their unity and to be diligent about all that would serve to preserve and strengthen it. That is the ideal that has never been realized in the history of the church and certainly is not so today.

> Christendom is divided into literally hundreds of church groups maintaining separate names and separate existence. . . . There have not always been as many divisions as there are now, but the spirit of the factionalism has manifested itself throughout the church's history, even in the days of the apostles. St. Paul attacks this spirit in the church at Corinth: "I appeal to you, brethren, by the name of our Lord Jesus Christ, that all of you agree and that there be no dissensions among you. . . . each one of you says, 'I belong to Paul,' or 'I belong to Apollos,' or 'I belong to Cephas' or 'I belong to Christ.' Is Christ divided?" (1 Cor. 1:10-13). Among the works of the flesh are listed strife, dissension, and party

spirit (Gal. 5:20). In the early church there soon developed groups which separated from the main church because of divergent interpretations or emphases with regard to the Christian message.[1]

Dr. Lewis W. Spitz, a professor emeritus of systemic theology in the LCMS, describes the dangers that threatened the early church and outlines the havoc wrought by the false prophets who have influenced the church since the days of the apostles. In his book *Our Church and Others* he writes:

Where the church is planted, the devil is not idle. He tries to curb the preaching of the Gospel. To do this he resorts to persecutions and false doctrine. Jesus predicted that the devil would do this (John 16:1,2). He was persecuted, so His disciples had to expect the same treatment, for "the servant is not greater than his lord" (John 15:20). Jesus warned His disciples against false prophets. He said: "Beware of false prophets, which come to you in sheep's clothing, but inwardly they are ravening wolves" (Matthew 7:15).

All of the Lord's disciples, excepting John, died a martyr's death. The New Testament shows that the Lord's warning against false prophets was very much in order even in the days of the apostles. Paul, for example, found it necessary to defend the doctrine of salvation by grace against Judaizing teachers who insisted that the Christians must continue to keep the ceremonial laws of the Old Testament in order to be saved.

Persecutions raged and false prophets abounded in the early church. During the first three centuries the church was subjected to ten major and many less bloody persecutions. Still it kept on growing. . . . When the fury of the earlier centuries quieted down, false teachers became more daring in proclaiming their errors. . . . These false teachers stirred up bitter controversies in the church; but though the church was divided in these theological battles, it was not defeated. In fact, these controversies compelled the church to formulate its creeds and to defend those which had already been formulated.[2]

[1]Herbert J. A. Bouman, *A Look at Today's Churches: A Comparative Guide* (St. Louis: Concordia Publishing House, 1980), pp. 8, 9.
[2]Lewis W. Spitz, *Our Church and Others* (St. Louis: Concordia Publishing House, 1960), pp. 12-14.

THE FIRST MAJOR DIVISION

Despite the influence of many false teachers and the bitter controversies they created, the church remained essentially united until 1054. Spitz describes the first major division:

> Though the ecumenical creeds [Apostles, Nicene, and Athanasian] served as symbols or confessions around which all true Christians could rally in the confession of their faith, they did not prevent the tragic schism, or split, which divided the *Eastern,* or Greek, Church from the *Western,* or Latin, Church. . . . Personal rivalries, conflicting church practices and doctrinal concerns, differences in culture—all combined in the course of centuries to lead to the final division in 1054. . . . The final break may, however, be attributed to a clash between the patriarch of Constantinople and the pope of Rome.[3]

The modern church bodies that trace their origins back to this split are the Eastern Orthodox Church and the various churches in the Western Catholic tradition (Roman, Lutheran, Anglican, etc.). The remaining documentation concerning the history of the church will address future developments within the Western church—the historical roots of the Reformation and Lutheranism.

THE WESTERN CHURCH

After the break with the Eastern Church, the Western Church grew under the leadership and expanding power of the bishop of Rome. Spitz describes his influence and development of false doctrine:

> As the power of the western part of the Roman Empire declined, that of the bishop of Rome and his prestige as a leader increased. . . . The monks who went out to convert the unbelievers did much to expand the pope's power. . . . Unfortunately the pope did not use his expanding power to keep the church faithful to the truth of Christ's Word. Though he regarded himself as the successor of Peter, who was to feed the Lord's sheep, he permitted the food which he gave them to be adulterated. In the course of centuries errors of various kinds crept into the teachings of the church. So-called reform councils, which met during the first half of the fifteenth century, failed to correct the evils in the church.[4]

---

[3]Ibid., pp. 15, 16.
[4]Ibid., pp. 16, 17.

THE REFORMATION AND
THE SECOND MAJOR DIVISION

By the time Martin Luther appeared on the scene in the 16th century, the church was in great need of a reformation. Spitz describes its beginning and the manner in which it spread throughout Germany and other European countries:

> A reformation is a change back to a former normal condition. The Reformation inaugurated by God through Martin Luther aimed to restore the church, deformed in the course of centuries by false doctrine and wrong practice, to its early normal condition.

> Luther, seeking the answer to the question: "How do I obtain a gracious God?" found it in the words of St. Paul, Rom. 1:17: "The just shall live by faith." These words told him that the sinner is not saved by his own good works but receives the forgiveness of his sins only through faith in Jesus Christ as his Savior. Luther had tried works and failed to find peace with God. St. Paul taught him to rely solely on the grace of God, who through faith imputes to [bestows upon] the penitent sinner the righteousness of Jesus Christ. This conviction made Luther the Great Reformer of the church, for what he believed, he taught.

> When Luther found that the people were misled by the sale of indulgences to trust in a false way of salvation, he challenged this practice of gathering money, inviting debate on the famous 95 Theses nailed to the door of the castle church in Wittenberg. The posting of these theses, Oct. 31, 1517, may be regarded as the dawn of the Reformation.

> Despite the opposition of the papacy, the Reformation spread rapidly, entering various lands chiefly through Luther's writings. By 1540 it covered all of northern and most of middle Germany. All of the Scandinavian countries turned to Lutheranism. In the states bordering on Germany or inhabited by Germans most of the people welcomed it.[5]

Martin Luther was not the only one leading people away from Rome. Spitz names two other men whose reformation efforts led to an unfortunate division in the Protestant ranks and briefly outlines the progress of their doctrines into other areas of Europe:

----

[5]Ibid., pp. 17, 18.

In Switzerland Ulrich Zwingli (d. 1531) and John Calvin (d. 1564) led the people away from Rome. Unfortunately they also caused a division in the Protestant ranks by departing from some of Luther's doctrines. Their doctrines spread into southern Germany and followed the Rhine into the Netherlands.

The Huguenots in France were followers of Calvin. John Knox introduced Calvin's doctrine and church polity in Scotland. England separated from Rome for rather worldly reasons but soon leaned toward Protestantism, favoring the doctrines of Calvin.

In the schism of the eleventh century the church divided itself into an Eastern and a Western church (or, more accurately, into a group of Eastern churches and a Western church). The Reformation divided the Western Church into a Roman Catholic Church and a number of Protestant churches.

The two main divisions of the Protestant churches may be designated as Lutheran and Calvinist, or Reformed. The latter represents the followers of Zwingli and Calvin. In a general way these include the Episcopalians, the Presbyterians, the Dutch Reformed, the Baptists, and various other religious groups. Why so many divisions? It would take many pages to answer this question. Some of the divisions are due to differences in doctrine; some are due to differences in practice.[6]

Spitz answers his own question by devoting the remaining pages of his book to a description of the differences in doctrine and practice responsible for the huge variety of church groups in existence today. While a lengthy study of these differences is not possible in this book, it is important for the reader to understand the foundation from which these differences arose. This is essential to understanding the biblical doctrine of fellowship and recognizing the error of the modern ecumenical movement. The starting point in our brief study is the three-way split that occurred during the time of the Reformation.

THE THREE MAJOR DIVISIONS
OF WESTERN CHRISTENDOM

As Spitz notes, the Reformation inaugurated by God through Martin Luther aimed to restore the church to its early normal condition.

---

[6]Ibid., p. 19.

By the 16th century the truth of the Gospel and salvation had been all but lost in a sea of error and false teaching. The Reformation was needed to restore the Bible to its proper position and to bring back the truth about salvation. As pointed out in Chapter 21, Martin Luther set us on a course of following Scripture alone as the sole source for doctrine and practice and returned us to the pure teaching of God's Word. It was a return to the teaching of the earliest or apostolic church, the church of historic Christianity.

However, not everyone agreed with Luther's view of Scripture. Thus the Reformation divided Western Christendom into three major divisions; the *Lutheran* churches, the *Roman Catholic Church*,[7] and the churches of the *Reformed* tradition. The fundamental differences between these three groups lies in their approach to the interpretation of Scripture and the role that *reason* plays in each approach.

Because of the Bible's unique status as a sole authority, historic Lutheran doctrine has always insisted on Scripture's self-interpretation. Authoritative and inerrant in all that it says and teaches, it is the only resource needed. Thus, the Bible is taken as a whole, and since the Bible does not contradict itself, clear passages of Scripture are used to interpret less clear passages, the very passages that are most vulnerable to misinterpretation.

In the Lutheran Church the role of reason in the interpretation of Scripture is subordinate to the plain words of Scripture. Reason is placed below Scripture and made to serve Scripture.[8] This will be explained and illustrated in Chapter 24 in a comparison between Luther and Calvin on the interpretation of Scripture.

Chapters 23 and 24 examine the Roman Catholic and Reformed approach to Scripture and compare them to Lutheranism.[9] This comparison begins with some of the fundamental doctrines of the Roman Catholic Church and the Roman Catholic approach to Scripture that shaped the development of these doctrines—doctrines that led to the need for a reformation.

---

[7]Eastern Orthodox churches, formed as a result of the split in 1054, have generally been classified doctrinally with the Roman Catholic Church.

[8]Siegbert W. Becker, *The Foolishness of God: The Place of Reason in the Theology of Martin Luther* (Milwaukee: Northwestern Publishing House, 1982), pp. 235, 236.

[9]Recommended resources for further study on the Lutheran approach to interpreting Scripture are: J. Kincaid Smith, *Interpreting the Scriptures: Twelve Guiding Principles* (unpublished manuscript), and Roland C. Ehlke, *Understanding the Bible* (Milwaukee: Northwestern Publishing House, 1977).

23.

THE ROMAN CATHOLIC
APPROACH TO SCRIPTURE

SOURCE OF DOCTRINE

In contrast to the Lutheran approach (Scripture interprets Scripture), the Roman Catholic Church interprets Scripture by papal authority. The pope, not the Bible, is the chief authority on all matters pertaining to faith and doctrine. Dr. Lewis W. Spitz, a professor emeritus of systematic theology in the Lutheran Church—Missouri Synod (LCMS), draws attention to this fact in the following quotation:

> The pope has become the chief cornerstone of the Roman Catholic Church. . . . The pope is supreme. He claims to have jurisdiction even over those whom he regards as heretics—indeed over all mankind. In the bull *Unam Sanctam,* which is accepted as church law today, Pope Boniface VIII clearly and emphatically states the papal claim to supreme power in both church and state. He insists. . . . "It is necessary to salvation that every man should submit to the pope. . . . The supremacy of the pope, even in temporal things, is to be enforced."[1]

It should be noted that the Roman Catholic Church has always claimed to be infallible or free from error. The doctrine of papal infallibility simply moved this doctrine to the office of one person—the pope. It was not a new doctrine as some have come to believe.[2]

---

[1]Lewis W. Spitz, *Our Church and Others* (St. Louis: Concordia Publishing House, 1960), pp. 48, 49.

[2]Otto W. Heick, *The History of Christian Thought,* 2 vols. (Philadelphia: Fortress Press, 1966), 2:312.

In addition to papal authority, two other sources determine the doctrinal stance of the Roman Catholic Church—the Bible and *tradition*. The following statement is taken from an official Roman Catholic document, *The Documents of Vatican II:*

> It is not from sacred Scripture alone that the Church draws her certainty about everything which has been revealed. Therefore both sacred tradition and sacred Scripture are to be accepted and venerated with the same sense of devotion and reverence.[3]

UNBIBLICAL DOCTRINES

The combination of papal authority, the Bible, and tradition have led the Roman Catholic Church to develop doctrines and practices that are not taught in the Holy Scriptures. Spitz briefly sums up some of the results of this combination:

> The Holy Catholic Apostolic Roman Church is often referred to as the Latin Church in order to distinguish it from the Greek Orthodox Church. The designation is appropriate because Latin is its official language. . . . For the sake of brevity we shall hereafter frequently refer to this denomination as Rome, inasmuch as Rome plays such an important role in its history.

> Like the Eastern Orthodox churches, Rome names two sources of doctrine: the Bible and Divine Tradition. Rome defines the Bible as the collection of inspired writings of the Old and New Testament. In the writings of the Old Testament, Rome includes the apocryphal books, ascribing to them the same divine authority as the canonical books. Rome needs the Apocrypha to support her doctrine of intercession and masses for the dead (2 Maccabees 12:42-45). It should be noted, however, that the New Testament writers nowhere make use of the Apocrypha as they do the canonical writings of the Old Testament. Rome's official Bible is not the original Hebrew and Greek text but the Vulgate, a Latin version by St. Jerome, which contains various false translations, for example, in Gen. 3:15, where the woman is said to crush the ser-

---

[3]"Dogmatic Constitution on Divine Revelation" (1956), *The Documents of Vatican II* (American Press, 1966), p. 117. Cited in David Jay Webber, "Catholic Doctrine and the Authority of Scripture," *Lutheran Synod Quarterly,* December 1988.

pent's head. English versions [of the Vulgate] contain explanations so that the reader will understand the Bible in the Roman Catholic sense, for Rome regards it her exclusive right to decide on the true sense and the correct interpretation of the Holy Scriptures. For Roman Catholics not the Bible but the church (actually the pope) is the rule of faith.

Tradition is defined as doctrines handed down without being put in writing. Divine Tradition, according to Rome, was given to the church by Christ and His apostles only by word of mouth, though later it was put in writing by the fathers of the church. Tradition is regarded as of equal authority with the written Word of God in the Bible. In fact, the Bible must be understood in the light of tradition. In the final analysis, however, Rome makes use of the idea of tradition whenever she finds it necessary to defend a new doctrine or practice. Such doctrines as the immaculate conception of Mary [not to be confused with the virgin birth], purgatory, and the infallibility of the pope are based on tradition.[4]

THE ROLE OF REASON

The Roman Catholic traditions are, for the most part, the carrying down of errors that resulted from man's imposition of reason upon the Scriptures in the past. The role of reason in the development of Roman Catholic doctrines became more prominent with the emergence of the scholastic movement in the Western Church. Scholasticism developed over a long period of time but took form during the Middle Ages in the Western universities around 1054 and continued until the Reformation.[5] The church scholars had read the works of Aristotle, the Greek philosopher, and liked his principles and methods of thinking and reasoning. To their way of thinking, Aristotle's methods seemed more logical and organized than those of the ancient church fathers, and so they made Christian theology fit his philosophical framework. Reason became the standard by which Scripture was interpreted. The result was the distortion of much of Christian doctrine.

ADDITIONAL DOCTRINAL ERRORS

Among the many distortions of Christian doctrine by the Roman Church that led to the Reformation efforts of Luther and the other

---

[4]Spitz, op. cit., pp. 43, 44.

[5]Bengt Hagglund, *History of Theology*, trans. Gene J. Lund (St. Louis: Concordia Publishing House, 1968), p. 163.

reformers, the doctrine of justification, in particular, needs to be mentioned. Scripture teaches that we are saved by *grace* through *faith* in Christ: "For it is by grace you have been saved, through faith—and this not from yourselves, it is the gift of God—not by works, so that no one can boast" (Ephesians 2:8,9). The Roman Catholics believe that salvation is by grace through faith and *good works*. Spitz makes the following comparison:

> Rome is ready to admit that we are saved by grace, but she does not mean grace through faith (Eph. 2:8,9). According to Scripture grace is God's infinite love and undeserved mercy toward sinners for Jesus sake (Rom. 3:24; 4:4; 2 Cor. 8:9). According to Rome grace is a spiritual quality infused by God into the soul which enables man to merit eternal life by doing good works. This grace is infused through the sacraments, which put man in possession of the supernatural powers whereby his works become meritorious. Rome combines grace and works in its efforts to earn heaven. The Scriptures combine grace and faith in Christ in offering heaven as a free gift of God.[6]

Much of Roman doctrine is based on work-righteousness—man cooperating with God in his salvation. The late Dr. John Theodore Mueller, a noted conservative scholar and professor in the LCMS, notes this fact about the Roman Church in his book *My Church and Others*. He writes:

> Throughout, the doctrinal content is dominated by rationalism, and the whole system of teaching, with all its antiscriptural tenets, like saint worship, purgatory, the mass, extreme unction, additional sacraments and sacramentals, is based upon work-righteousness.[7]

A HETERODOX CHURCH

As Spitz continues his study of the Roman Church with a listing of additional sources of Roman doctrine, he points out that despite the extra sources the church does teach much that is true:

> The doctrines of the Roman Catholic Church are found in the ecumenical creeds, in the decisions of the general councils, particularly in the Tridentine and Vatican decrees, the

---

[6]Spitz, op. cit., p. 52.

[7]John Theodore Mueller, *My Church and Others* (St. Louis: Rudolph Volkening, 1968), p. 70.

authorized catechisms, the papal bulls and letters, the Roman Missal and the Roman Breviary, and in books which have the approval of the respective bishop and the censor.

Inasmuch as the Roman Catholic Church accepts the ecumenical creeds, it teaches much that is true. It teaches the doctrine of the Holy Trinity, the deity and the incarnation of Jesus Christ, and His suffering and death for the redemption of the fallen human race. But the truth is hard to find in the maze of Roman error which sprang up in the Middle Ages, to which Rome still clings and to which she has added other unscriptural doctrines in modern times.[8]

While the mixing of truth and error in the Roman Church classifies her as a "heterodox" church, Lutherans readily acknowledge that there are many Christians to be found within her constituency. The Lutheran Confessions speak very clearly to this fact:

We ought not assume immediately that the church of Rome accepts everything that the pope or cardinals or bishops or some theologians or monks advance. To the prelates their own authority is obviously more important than the Gospel of Christ. . . . It is also obvious that the theologians have mingled more than enough philosophy with Christian doctrine. Their authority ought not seem so great as to end all argument, when there are so many manifest errors among them. . . . The Scriptures, the holy Fathers, and the judgment of all the faithful are consistently against them. Therefore the knowledge of Christ has remained with some faithful souls.[9]

A SUMMARY OF DIFFERENCES

In concluding his study of the Roman Church, Spitz sums up some of the differences between Romanism and Protestantism that continue to cause division in today's world:

True Protestantism bases its theology solely on the Bible as the Word of God; Romanism bases its theology largely on human tradition. Protestantism bases its hope firmly on the promises of the Gospel; Romanism bases its promises on

---

[8]Spitz, op. cit., pp. 45, 46.

[9]*The Book of Concord,* trans. and ed. Theodore G. Tappert (Philadelphia: Fortress Press, 1959), Apology of the Augsburg Confession, IV, 390, pp. 166, 167.

man's ability to keep the commandments, especially also the commandments of the church. Protestantism is a religion of grace; Romanism of works and human merit. Protestantism inspires confidence in God's mercy; Romanism instills fear of God's justice. The Romanist asks: Have I done enough to meet the demand of the church? The Protestant knows that Jesus has done enough and that heaven is his through faith in his Savior's works and merits.[10]

Martin Luther and the Reformation corrected the doctrinal errors of the church of Rome. Unfortunately, yet another source of error soon rose up in Christendom—that of the newly developing churches of the Reformed tradition (Chapter 22).

The Reformed branch of Christendom has often brought a great amount of influence to bear on Lutheranism, beginning in the early years of the Reformation and continuing into the present day. It is for this reason that the next chapter examines the doctrinal errors of the churches of the Reformed tradition in greater detail than those of the Roman Catholic Church.

It is also hoped that as we complete our doctrinal comparison between the Roman Catholic, Lutheran, and Reformed churches, the reader will recognize the unique position and strengths of orthodox Lutheranism.

---

[10]Spitz, op cit., p. 60.

24.

THE REFORMED
APPROACH TO SCRIPTURE

SOURCE OF DOCTRINE

The Reformed approach to the interpretation of Scripture varies from that of both the Lutherans and the Roman Catholics. While the conservative (or traditional) Reformed agree with the Lutherans that the Bible is the Word of God and the only source and authority for doctrine, they do not hold strictly to the Lutheran principle that Scripture alone must interpret Scripture—the principle that less clear passages are to be interpreted in light of clear passages. Furthermore, although the Reformed usually hold that the Bible is to be taken "literally," they do not hold to Luther's biblical teaching of the *perspicuity* (clarity) of Scripture—the teaching that all the doctrines of Christian faith are taught in the Scriptures in plain clear words. In addition they, like the Roman Catholics, rely on other sources.

For the conservative churches in the Reformed tradition, Scripture must be understood in the light of *reason, experience,* and for many, *emotions.* A brief look at each of these sources, as well as several other contributing factors, will be helpful in understanding some of the reasons for the hundreds of church groups that exist today under the general heading of Protestantism. It will also serve to illustrate the words of Luther already cited (Chapter 21): "In philosophy an error that is small at the beginning becomes very great in the end. So a small error in theology overturns the whole body of doctrine."[1] In this instance the error in theology is the misguided use of reason, which divided Protestantism into many branches and planted the

---

[1]*What Luther Says,* 3 vols., ed. Ewald M. Plass (St. Louis: Concordia Publishing House, 1959), 3:1365.

seeds for later acceptance of the historical-critical method and the ecumenical movement.

THE REFORMED ROOTS

The hundreds of church bodies in existence today trace their roots back to the split that occurred in the Protestant ranks during the later years of the Reformation under the leadership of Martin Luther (1483-1546), Ulrich Zwingli (1484-1531), and John Calvin (1509-1564). As a result of this split, Protestantism was divided into two camps, with Martin Luther emerging as the leader of the "Lutheran" Reformation and John Calvin as the leader of the "Reformed" movement. Zwingli was also a leader among the Reformed but in a lesser role.

Zwingli's Reformation efforts were limited to Switzerland and, in contrast to the theology of Calvin, his influence was rather limited.[2] His life-work had strong political overtones with one of his major goals being that of uniting the Protestants politically against Roman Catholic suppression. He was so intent on achieving political unity among the Protestants, he was willing to overlook differences in doctrine. In this he demonstrated the same spirit that prevails among today's advocates of ecumenism—that of doctrinal compromise. Zwingli lost his life fighting with a Swiss army against Emperor Charles. After Zwingli's death, the Swiss Protestants found a new spiritual leader in John Calvin.[3]

The above division, a result of Zwingli's and Calvin's departure from some of Luther's biblical doctrines, was the first of many divisions for the Reformed. These resulted from disagreement in doctrine and practice and are so numerous and interrelated that they have been the subject of many books, some of which are listed among our resources for further study. However, we will only examine those doctrines that relate to the subject of this chapter and the overall message of the book.

FURTHER DIVISION

The next major division among the Reformed came to a head in Holland at the Synod of Dort (1618-1619). Early in the 17th century, a group of people led by Jacob Arminius (1560-1609), soon to be

---

[2]Bengt Hagglund, *History of Theology,* trans. Gene J. Lund (St. Louis: Concordia Publishing House, 1968), p. 259.

[3]Victor H. Prange, *Why So Many Churches?* (Milwaukee: Northwestern Publishing House, 1985), pp. 20, 25.

223

known as Arminians, disagreed with five main points of Calvinist theology and countered with five of their own. While the theology of the Arminians was condemned by the Synod of Dort, it nevertheless spread rapidly and became a dominating view in various Reformed churches. As a result of the division, the Reformed are commonly referred to as the Calvinist Reformed and Arminian Reformed churches.[4]

Current denominations predominately in the *Calvinist* tradition are the Presbyterians, Dutch and German Reformed, Episcopalians (Anglicans), Baptists, and Congregationalists. Those in the *Arminian* tradition are the Methodists, the Holiness groups (Nazarenes, Assemblies of God, and Pentecostals), and the Salvation Army. However, these names do not represent a clear-cut distinction because some denominations, such as the Baptists and Episcopalians, have churches in both traditions. Nor does this listing indicate complete doctrinal agreement among the churches of each group. Not all Calvinist Reformed agree with all of Calvin's doctrines, nor do all Arminians accept every teaching within the Arminian tradition. To complicate matters further, the multitude of smaller Reformed groups that emerged from these main branches were born, for the most part, out of doctrinal disagreements and tend to derive their doctrines from both traditions.[5] Due to this blending of doctrines, it is difficult today to find a pure Calvinist or pure Arminian denomination or group.

REASON—THE COMMON DENOMINATOR

The common denominator, or fundamental error, in all of these doctrinal controversies was the misguided use of reason. As we have seen, the use of reason in the Roman Catholic Church led to error, but it did not divide the church. It remains to this day institutionally united as one worldwide church body. The same is not true of the Reformed. While both Roman Catholics and the Reformed make reason the norm by which Scripture is to be interpreted, there has been a major difference in their approach to its use.

In the Western or Roman Catholic Church, reason was applied collectively. The church theologians worked together as a group under the authority of the pope. With the pope as the final and "infallible" authority in the interpretation of Scripture and the determina-

---

[4]Lewis W. Spitz, *Our Church and Others* (St. Louis: Concordia Publishing House, 1960), p. 67.

[5]Ibid., pp. 70-96.

tion of doctrine the Roman church was spared doctrinal diversity[6] and division.

In contrast, the Reformed used reason on an individualistic basis, with each man acting as his own "pope." Used in this manner, reason produced an infinite variety of doctrines and caused the division that characterizes the churches of the Reformed tradition.

NO BINDING CONFESSIONS

With so many different Reformed doctrines, one can see the difficulty involved in writing confessions that could be held as binding and serve as a single standard in uniting the various churches into one denomination.

Among the church groups that, in a general way, can be called Calvinists, more than 60 confessions have been written. However, because of their number and variety and the fact that they do not agree on all points of doctrine, the Calvinists do not attach the same degree of importance to them that Lutherans place on theirs. In fact, some Calvinist groups have rejected all denominational confessions and insist that only the Bible is their creed. An example of this can be found among the Baptists. Both the Calvinist and Arminian Baptists have an aversion of creeds. As a result, they have produced a greater diversity of teaching than any other church body.[7]

Among those church bodies listed as Arminian, there is even less emphasis on confessions and creeds. John Wesley, the founder of Methodism, wrote a few doctrinal statements, but they are not binding on the Methodists or remaining Arminian church bodies that emerged from these roots. In the following quotation, Dr. Lewis W. Spitz, a professor emeritus of systematic theology in the Lutheran Church—Missouri Synod (LCMS), emphasizes the importance of confessions and creeds concerning Methodism's lack of doctrinal standards:

> Actually Methodism does not consider itself bound by any doctrinal standards. It started as a movement to improve the life of the church, not its teaching. Its slogan could, therefore, very well be: "Deeds, not creeds." But creeds ex-

---

[6]The use of historical criticism has become more prominent among Roman Catholic theologians. Pope Pius XII's "Divino Afflante Spiritu" and the *Dogmatic Constitution on Divine Revelation*, II, 12, *The Documents of Vatican II* (New York: Herder and Herder, 1960), supports this, as does E. Michael Jones, *Is Notre Dame Still Catholic?* (South Bend: Fidelity Press, 1989).

[7]Spitz, op. cit., pp. 64, 70, 73.

press what Christians believe. Faith in the Gospel and obedience to God's Commandments go together as cause and effect, or as a good tree and its fruit (John 8:31,32; 15:4-8;
Phil. 1:9-11). It is impossible to improve the life of the
church without a sincere concern for the doctrine of Scripture as revealed in the Gospel.[8]

REASON—LUTHER AND CALVIN

The role of reason in the development of doctrine in the churches
of the Reformed tradition will be more clearly understood if we look
at a comparison between Luther and Calvin. In the following quotations, David Jay Webber,[9] a pastor in the conservative Evangelical
Lutheran Synod (ELS), compares Luther's understanding of the
proper place of reason in the interpretation of Scripture with that of
Calvin in his article "Luther and Calvin on the Interpretation of
Scripture." He writes:

> Regarding the authority of Holy Scripture, Luther and the
> other Lutheran reformers taught that "the Word of God shall
> establish articles of faith and no one else, not even an
> angel."[10] Calvin and his associates also claimed that they de-
> sired "to follow Scripture alone as rule of faith and religion,
> without mixing with it any other thing which might be de-
> vised by the opinion of men apart from the Word of God . . ."[11]
> Why, then, have Protestants in the Reformed tradition and
> Lutherans never agreed in all their teachings? If both sides
> look to the same Scriptures as the only source of doctrine,
> why do they not hold to the same belief? The answer is that
> those who follow Luther's principles of interpretation and
> those who follow Calvin's principles of interpretation ap-
> proach the Scriptures with *different presuppositions and as-
> sumptions* (author's emphasis).

[8]Spitz, op. cit., p. 83.

[9]Pastor Webber was raised in an LCA congregation and received his theological education in the LCMS Ft. Wayne Seminary. He was ordained into the
ELS and is presently serving an ELS congregation.

[10]David Jay Webber, "Luther and Calvin on the Interpretation of Scripture," *Lutheran Synod Quarterly,* December 1988, p. 77. Author's endnote. Citation reads: Smalcald Articles II, II:15, *The Book of Concord,* trans. and ed.
Theodore G. Tappert (Fortress Press, 1959), p. 295.

[11]Ibid., p. 77. Author's endnote. Citation reads: Genevan Confession, 1,
Calvin: Theological Treatises, trans. and ed. J. K. S. Reid (Westminster
Press, 1954), p. 26.

Martin Luther believed that the Holy Scriptures are to be interpreted according to their literal sense (except when the context itself indicates a figurative interpretation), and that "Man is to render his reason captive and to submit to divine truth."[12] According to Luther: "The knowledge of lawyers and poets comes from reason and may, in turn, be understood and grasped by reason. But what Moses and the prophets teach does not stem from reason and the wisdom of men. Therefore, he who presumes to comprehend Moses and the prophets with his reason and to measure and evaluate Scripture according to its agreement with reason will get away from the Bible entirely. From the very beginning all heretics owed their rise to the notion that what they had read in Scripture they were at liberty to explain according to the teachings of reason."[13]

Because "the foolishness of God is wiser than man" (1 Cor. 1:25), Luther was willing to believe whatever the Scriptures taught, even if it seemed to run contrary to his own human reason and experience. As a student of God's Word, Luther remembered what the Lord Himself had declared to His people: "For as the heavens are higher than the earth, so are My ways higher than your ways, and My thoughts higher than your thoughts" (Isaiah 55:9).

In contrast, John Calvin believed that "the Lord has instituted nothing that is at variance with reason."[14] According to Calvin: "Reason and faith are not opposed to each other. Hence we maintain that we must not admit anything, even in religious matters, which is contrary to right reason."[15]

Calvin may have looked to the Scriptures as a course of Christian doctrine, but he assumed beforehand that they would not teach him anything which did not agree with his preconceived standard of "reasonableness." Calvin used his

---

[12]Ibid. p. 78. Author's endnote. Citation reads: Sermon on Luke 2:21, *What Luther Says,* ed. Ewald M. Plass (Concordia Publishing House, 1959), p. 1165.

[13]Ibid. Author's endnote. Citation reads: Sermon on Luke 24:13-35, *What Luther Says,* p. 1163.

[14]Ibid. Author's endnote. Citation reads: Geneva Catechism, *Calvin: Theological Treatises,* p. 134.

[15]Ibid. Author's endnote. Citation reads: *Institutes of the Christian Religion,* I, VIII:2, F. E. Meyer, *The Religious Bodies of America* (Concordia Publishing House, 1954), p. 203.

own human reason and experience as a "screen" through which he filtered the statements of Holy Scripture. Whenever the literal sense of a passage ran contrary to his "reason," Calvin would automatically impose a figurative interpretation on that portion of God's Word or otherwise twist the meaning of the text until it became "reasonable."[16]

THE DENIAL OF THE REAL PRESENCE

Webber continues his comparison by demonstrating the way in which Calvin's method of interpretation led Calvin and his followers to deny the Real Presence of Christ in the sacrament of the Lord's Supper. This denial was one of the major departures from Luther's biblical doctrines, which led to the first split in the Protestant ranks. To this day it continues to be a critical difference separating Lutherans from the Reformed.

This basic difference in methodology between Luther and Calvin is best illustrated by the way in which each interpreted Christ's words of institution in the Lord's Supper. Luther wrote: "Let a hundred thousand devils, with all the fanatics, rush forward and say, 'How can bread and wine be Christ's body and blood?' Still I know that all the spirits and scholars put together have less wisdom than the divine Majesty has in his little finger. Here we have Christ's word, 'Take, eat; this is my body.' 'Drink of it, all of you, this is the new covenant in my blood,' etc. Here we shall take our stand and see who dares to instruct Christ and alter what he has spoken."[17]

However, Calvin and his allies understood Christ's words in an entirely different manner. They declared; "We repudiate as preposterous interpreters, those who in the solemn words of the Supper, 'This is my body, this is my blood,' urge a precisely literal sense, as they say. For we hold it to be indisputable that these words are to be accepted figuratively, so that bread and wine are called that which they signify."[18]
Calvin, on the basis of his rationalistic principles, thought

---

[16]Ibid., p. 79.

[17]Ibid. Author's endnote. Citation reads: Large Catechism V:12,13, *The Book of Concord*, p. 448.

[18]Ibid, pp. 79, 80. Author's endnote. Citation reads: Consensus Tigurinus, Francis Pieper, *Christian Dogmatics*, Vol. III (Concordia Publishing House, 1953), p. 295.

that Luther was "preposterous" because he accepted Christ's sacred words at face value. Because Calvin could not comprehend how bread and wine could be the true body and blood of Jesus Christ, he simply would not believe it.[19]

THE DOCTRINE OF THE INNER WORD

It is important to note that an additional factor is involved in the Reformed view of not only the Lord's Supper but the sacrament of Baptism as well. It is the addition of a doctrine that originated with Ulrich Zwingli. As stated earlier, Zwingli's reformation efforts in Switzerland were carried out about the same time as Luther's in Germany. Like Luther, Zwingli was a priest in the church of Rome. He had become antagonistic toward the medieval sacramental systems in which the grace of God (forgiveness and salvation) was supposed to gradually filter down through the use of the seven sacraments established by the church. He also objected, and rightly so, to the veneration (holding in respect or awe) of relics at a shrine dedicated to Mary in the town where he served as a priest. In an overreaction to the beliefs and practices of the church of Rome, he decided that God did not need any external means in his dealings with man and declared, "The Holy Spirit needs no vehicle."[20] Thus he created the Reformed doctrine, which teaches that the Holy Spirit works directly on man *apart* from, or independent of, the Word and the Sacraments—a doctrine that John Calvin built upon. Spitz explains:

> Like Luther, Calvin believed that the Bible is the divinely inspired and inerrant Word of God and the only source of doctrine. However, Calvin distinguished between the outward word of the Bible, in which God speaks to all men, and an inner word by which the Holy Spirit speaks only to the elect. Only by their own inner religious experiences and feelings can people discover whether or not the Holy Spirit is speaking by the inner word. The belief that God, or the Holy Spirit, speaks directly to men by an "inner word" is known as enthusiasm. Misled by this false spirit of enthusiasm, some Calvinistic sects have discarded the Bible as their source of doctrine in favor of their own visions, dreams, revelations, or emotions.[21]

[19]Ibid., p. 80.

[20]Herbert J. A. Bouman, *A Look at Today's Churches: A Comparative Guide* (St. Louis, Concordia Publishing House, 1980), p. 29.

[21]Spitz, op. cit., p. 63.

The doctrine of the inner word is contrary to the plain teaching of Scripture and the Lutheran Confessions:

> Faith comes from hearing the message, and the message is heard through the word of Christ (Romans 10:17).

> In these matters, which concern the external, spoken Word, we must hold firmly to the conviction that God gives no one his Spirit or grace except through or with the external Word which comes before.[22]

> Accordingly, we should and must constantly maintain that God will not deal with us except through his external Word and sacrament. Whatever is attributed to the Spirit apart from such Word and sacrament is of the devil.[23]

> Likewise we reject and condemn the error of the Enthusiasts who imagine that God draws men to himself, enlightens them, justifies them, and saves them without means, without the hearing of God's Word and without the use of the holy sacrament.[24]

The combination of reason and the doctrine of the inner word led the Reformed to an understanding of the sacraments that is in opposition to that of the Lutherans. Spitz compares the two viewpoints:

> To the Reformed the sacraments are not means of grace in the Lutheran sense. Lutherans believe that God converts man and keeps him in the saving faith through the Word and only through the Word (John 17:17,20; Rom. 1:16; 1 Cor. 1:18). This same Word is connected with the water in Baptism and with the true body and blood of our Lord Jesus Christ under the bread and wine in the Sacrament of the Altar (Matt. 28:19; 26:26-28; Mark 14:22-24; Luke 22:19,20; 1 Cor. 11:23-25). Calvin denied that the sacraments are means or instruments through which God creates and preserves faith. He regarded Baptism and the Lord's supper merely as symbols and outward ceremonies of what the Holy Spirit does in the heart directly and immediately without means. According to Calvin, Baptism signifies but does not bestow or give new life, or forgiveness of sins. In Reformed

---

[22]*The Book of Concord,* trans. and ed. Theodore G. Tappert (Philadelphia: Fortress Press, 1959), Smalcald Articles, Part III, Art. VIII, 3, p. 312.

[23]Ibid., 10, p. 313.

[24]Ibid., *Formula of Concord,* Epitome, Art. II, 13, p. 471.

theology the Lord's Supper is merely a memorial of Christ's death—this it certainly is—and a public profession of faith in Christ's sacrifice, which it also is. But to Lutherans it is much more: a blessed means of grace![25]

By regarding the sacraments of Baptism and the Lord's Supper as merely symbols, the Reformed have denied that the sacraments are means of grace, just as they deny that the Word itself is a means of grace, the instrument through which the Holy Spirit works faith. The effects of this fundamental error in doctrine are far-reaching.

THE DOCTRINE OF SYNERGISM

One Arminian doctrine in particular has been instrumental in shaping the theological emphasis of virtually all of the churches of the Reformed tradition. It is the doctrine of *synergism*. This teaching holds that man cooperates with God in his conversion by his own free will. The following statements by some well-known, contemporary, Reformed evangelists illustrate this doctrine.

Dr. Billy Graham, a conservative Southern Baptist clergyman, writes in his book *How To Be Born Again:*

> In order not to be condemned you must make a choice—you must choose to believe. . . . Faith in Christ is also voluntary. A person cannot be coerced, bribed, or tricked into trusting Jesus. God will not force his way into your life. . . . The Holy Spirit will do everything possible to disturb you, draw you, love you—but finally it is your personal decision. God not only gave His Son on the cross where the plan of redemption was finished, He gave the law as expressed in the Ten Commandments and the Sermon on the Mount to show you your need for forgiveness; He gave the Holy Spirit to convict you of your need. He gives the Holy Spirit to draw you to the cross, but even after all of this, it is your decision whether to accept God's free pardon or to continue in your lost condition.

> So faith is not just an emotional reaction, an intellectual realization, or a willful decision; faith is all-inclusive. It involves the intellect, the emotion, and the will. . . . If you are willing to make this decision and have received Jesus Christ as your own Lord and Savior, then you have become a child of God in whom Jesus Christ dwells.[26]

---

[25]Spitz, op. cit., p. 69.
[26]Billy Graham, *How To Be Born Again* (New York: Warner Books, Inc., 1977), pp. 193, 194, 202.

Dr. Bill Bright, a layman and founder of Campus Crusade for Christ International, writes in his evangelism booklet "Have You Heard of the Four Spiritual Laws?":

> Just as there are physical laws that govern the physical universe so are there spiritual laws which govern your relationship with God. . . . Law Four: We must individually *receive* Jesus Christ as Savior and Lord; then we can know and experience God's love and plan for our lives. . . . We receive Christ by personal invitation. . . . We receive Jesus Christ by faith, as an act of the will (author's emphasis).[27]

Bright's position is further stated in a transcript of a talk by Bright during an hour-long television special:

> But it is not enough to believe that He [Christ] is the Son of God, not enough to believe that He's been raised from the dead, not enough to be baptized and active in the church, read your Bible and pray. All these things are important but that's not enough. You must receive Jesus Christ as an act of faith. You must as an act of the will ask Him to come into your heart.[28]

Dr. D. James Kennedy, a conservative Presbyterian clergyman, gives an example of how to present the gospel to a non-Christian in his book *Evangelism Explosion:*

> Rene, would you like to ask Jesus Christ to come into your life as your Savior today? . . . Are you willing to yield your life, to surrender your life, to him, out of gratitude for the gift of eternal life? . . . Are you willing to repent of your sins and follow him? . . . All right, Rene. The Lord is here right now. We can go to him now in prayer and we can tell him that you want to cease trusting in your own striving and you want to put your trust in Christ the Lord for your salvation and receive him as your personal Savior. Is this *truly* what you want (author's emphasis)?

> If you really want eternal life will you say to him aloud: Lord Jesus, I want you to come in and take over my life

---

[27]Bill Bright, "Have You Heard of the Four Spiritual Laws?" (San Bernardino: Campus Crusade for Christ, 1965), pp. 2, 8, 9.

[28]Transcript of "Here's Life," Nov. 27, 1976, at 3:00 p.m., Channel 5. *Christian News Encyclopedia,* 4 vols., ed. Herman Otten (Washington: Missourian Publishing Co., 1983), 1:297.

right now. (She repeats each phrase), I am a sinner. I have been trusting in myself and my own good works. But now I place my trust in you. I accept you as my own personal Savior. I believe you died for me. I receive you as Lord and Master of my life. Help me to turn from my sins and to follow you. I accept the free gift of eternal life. I am not worthy of it but I thank you for it. Amen.[29]

The lay evangelist is then taught some methods based on "the laws of selling":

There are five great laws of selling or persuading: attention, interest, desire, conviction, and close. It does not matter whether you are selling a refrigerator or persuading men to accept a new idea or philosophy, the same basic laws of persuasion hold true. . . . We should familiarize ourselves with these laws of persuasion and use them to critique our presentation of the gospel to help detect places of weakness. We should ask ourselves such questions as: Did I confront the person clearly with his need to make a decision for Christ and to commit his life to him in repentance and faith?[30]

The doctrine of synergism is contrary to the plain teaching of Scripture and the Lutheran Confessions:

For it is by grace you have been saved, through faith—and this not from yourselves, it is the gift of God—not by works, so that no one can boast (Ephesians 2:8,9).

You did not choose me, but I chose you and appointed you to go and bear fruit—fruit that will last. Then the Father will give you whatever you ask in my name (John 15:16).

For it is God who works in you to will and to act according to his good purpose (Philippians 2:13).

I believe that by my own reason or strength I cannot believe in Jesus Christ, my Lord, or come to him. But the Holy Spirit has called me through the Gospel, enlightened me with his gifts, and sanctified and preserved me in true faith. Luther-Small Catechism.[31]

---

[29]D. James Kennedy, *Evangelism Explosion* (Wheaton: Tyndale Publishers, 1970), pp. 42, 43.

[30]Ibid., pp. 46, 47.

[31]*The Book of Concord,* Small Catechism, Creed, Art. III, 6, p. 345.

Thus, according to Scripture, man does not, indeed cannot, decide to believe or come to faith. He cannot "make a decision for Christ" nor "invite Jesus into his heart." Man does not cooperate with God in his conversion (Romans 3:10-12; 8:7; 1 Corinthians 2:13ff.). Faith is a gift of God, created and preserved by the Holy Spirit working through the Word and sacraments. The plain, clear words of Scripture, the objective[32] Word of God, communicate a certainty or assurance for faith and, consequently, a confidence in one's salvation that is completely independent of any action on the part of man's will (Romans 1:17). When faith seems to waver or uncertainty knocks on the door, the Christian need only turn to Scripture for reassurance and certainty.

It is different for the Reformed. Their belief that the Holy Spirit speaks only to the elect by an "inner word," and their insistence that man's will cooperates with God in his conversion robs them of certainty of faith, forgiveness, and salvation. They are left facing many questions. How can they be sure they *are* one of the elect, let alone be certain they really have faith, that they have cooperated sufficiently to *gain* forgiveness and salvation? In the only addition, in their failure to recognize the Word and Sacraments as the only *means* of *grace,* they have robbed themselves of the power found only in the promises of the objective Word of God. They search for certainty for their faith and salvation within themselves, shifting their focus and attention from the one thing that works and sustains faith, the Word and Sacraments. They have moved from the objective to the *subjective,*[33] the subjective that can never provide an adequate basis for certainty.

Whether acknowledged or not, for the synergist the shifting sands of each man's reason, experience, and emotions become the primary basis for "certainty."

FAITH AND FEELINGS

One often hears those of the Reformed persuasion speak of "head" knowledge and "heart" knowledge. They make a distinction between what Scripture clearly states and how they feel. They must "feel"

---

[32]The objective Word of God may be defined as the external truth, or facts, that are independent of any personal notions or feelings; the absolute authoritative Word of God.

[33]Subjective means having to do with a person's own ideas, opinions, experiences, feelings, and emotions (that which goes on inside the person). Truth or facts are objective (that which is outside of the person), such as the Word of God. Truth and facts are sometimes denied or ignored, and actions or beliefs are sometimes based upon the subjective.

that they have faith, forgiveness, and salvation to be certain. For Lutherans, head and heart knowledge are joined together. The objective promises of God, as plainly stated in Scripture, are the means by which certainty is brought about. Lutherans simply can know, by the objective Word, that they have faith, as well as forgiveness and salvation, regardless of how they feel at any given moment. They realize that feelings are at best transient and unreliable and ultimately lead to the undermining of the message of the objective Word of God when relied upon for certainty of faith. Luther himself spoke to this issue:

> If you are not ready to believe that the Word is worth more than all you see or feel, then reason has blinded faith. So the resurrection of the dead is something that must be believed. I do not feel the resurrection of Christ but the Word affirms it. I feel sin [guilt] but the Word says that it is forgiven to those who believe. I see that Christians die like other men, but the Word tells me that they shall rise again. So we must not be guided by our own feelings but by the Word.[34]

Luther, in an exposition of Psalm 130:7, also tells us that "after all, everything depends on how God feels towards us, not on how we feel toward God" and points out that this insight "comes to us from the Word alone." He explains what he means by this statement:

> *Faith and Feeling Are Not Synonyms:* We must not judge by what we feel or by what we see before us. The Word must be followed, and we must firmly hold that these truths are to be believed, not experienced; for to believe is not to experience. Not indeed that what we believe is never to be experienced but that faith is to precede experience. And the Word must be believed even when we feel and experience what differs entirely from the Word. Therefore when in calamities our hearts think that God is angry with us, does not care for us but hates us, faith is nevertheless convinced that God harbors neither wrath or hatred nor vindictiveness against us nor imputes our guilt [God no longer holds us guilty because of Christ. We are forgiven]. . . . To this conclusion I have come, not by way of my feelings or my present circumstances but through the Word, which says that the mercy of the

---

[34]Luther, "Sermon on 1 Cor. 5:1ff," March 31, 1519, Adolf Koeberle, *The Quest for Holiness,* p. 79. Cited in *Sanctification: Christ In Action,* Harold L. Senkbeil (Milwaukee: Northwestern Publishing House, 1989), pp. 116, 117.

Lord is over me and all who believe, that His Wrath is over all who do not believe. Therefore I shall overcome my thoughts by the Word and shall write this promise in my heart, that after I have come to faith in Jesus Christ and do not doubt that my sins are forgiven me through His blood, I shall not be put to shame though all my senses and my experience speak a different language. Within myself I feel the wrath of God; the devil vents on me his hatred and the world its extreme fury. But the Holy Spirit tells no lies. He bids me hope; for "with the Lord there is mercy, and with Him is plenteous redemption" (Ps. 130:7).[35]

As Luther points out, this is not to deny the validity of religious experiences or emotions. Both the Reformed and Lutherans admit to their existence. The difference is in the importance placed upon them. For many of the Reformed they tend to be, whether consciously or unconsciously, a foundation upon which their theology is based. For Lutherans they are a natural outcome of a faith based on the objective Word of God.[36]

THE REFORMED EMPHASIS ON LAW

Another important factor is involved in the doctrinal differences separating Lutherans from the churches of the Reformed tradition. It is the Reformed emphasis on God's law.

Calvinist emphasis

For the followers of Calvin, emphasis on God's law originated with Calvin and his view of God. Calvin was originally a student of law in France and had a legal and logical mind. His knowledge of Luther and his teachings were gained primarily through literary means and through contact with people talking reform in the church in France. Unlike Luther and Zwingli, who had been priests in the Roman church, Calvin had no pastoral experience[37] and his theology was largely self-taught.[38]

The dominant thought in Calvin's theology was the sovereignty of God. Calvin tended to view God through a lawyer's eyes, with emphasis on God as the sovereign ruler and judge with man as his ser-

---

[35]*What Luther Says,* 1:513.

[36]Harold L. Senkbeil, *Sanctification: Christ in Action* (Milwaukee: Northwestern Publishing House, 1989), pp. 116, 117.

[37]Prange, op. cit., pp. 27-29.

[38]Hagglund, op. cit., p. 263.

vant. Calvin emphasized *law*. In contrast, Luther, while fully recognizing the sovereignty of God, saw him as a loving and forgiving Father and us as his children. He emphasized God's mercy and love as exhibited in the atoning work of his Son, Jesus Christ. Luther emphasized *gospel*. Luther understood the vital importance of making the proper distinction between law and gospel. This fundamental difference between Luther and Calvin is further explained by Spitz in the following comparison:

> *God's Sovereignty*—The dominant thought in Calvin's theology is the infinite and transcendent sovereignty of God. The Scotch Confession of Faith (1560) put it thus: "All things in heaven and earth, visible and invisible, have been created, are preserved, ruled and guided by His inscrutable providence to such end as His eternal wisdom, goodness and justice have appointed them, to the manifestation of His own glory" (Art. I). Lutherans miss in this statement an equal emphasis on the grace and mercy of God.
>
> Luther also believed in the infinite and transcendent sovereignty of God, but he did not make it the central thought of his theology. For Luther the grace of God in Jesus Christ was the heart of the Christian faith. This difference in emphasis largely explains the difference between Lutheran and Calvinistic theology. Lutherans like to think of their relation to God as that of a dear child to his dear father. In Calvinistic theology God is primarily the Master, man His servant. For Lutherans the Bible is chiefly the letter of a loving Father to His dear children; for Calvinists it is chiefly a code of rules and regulations for good behavior to the glory of the Master.[39]

Calvin's view of God and his law is further described by Lutheran historian Bengt Hagglund of the Church of Sweden. He writes:

> There was a tendency in Calvin to make sanctification the purpose of justification. Sanctification, in turn, was thought of as a means to increase the glory of God. Man is to live in strict agreement with divine law and thus to testify to his faith and strengthen the certainty that he is one of the elect. It is the law, therefore, which is the norm [or standard] of the sanctified life. God's law is eternal and a direct expression of His will. It must therefore concern even those who

---

[39]Spitz, op. cit., p. 65.

have been born again, and serve as the norm for their lives. Conformity to God's will is the goal of sanctification.[40]

For Calvin and his followers, certainty of faith and salvation were largely dependent upon how well they kept God's law. Keeping the Law dutifully and earnestly was seen as proof of one's faith—both as an inward and outward sign. As stated by Hagglund, "man is to live in strict agreement with divine law and thus to testify to his faith and strengthen the certainty that he is one of the elect." As a result, Calvin's followers strive to keep themselves in faith by strict adherence to the Law. They seek diligently to live the Christian life and often speak of this as "being obedient" and "working to keep in the center of God's will." Thus the Calvinists, like the Arminians, cooperate with God by relying on their own strengths and abilities for certainty of faith as well as for spiritual growth and living a Christian life.

Arminian emphasis

Those churches of the Reformed tradition that follow the theology of the Arminians trace their emphasis on God's law back to John Wesley (1703-1791), an ordained clergyman of the Church of England (Anglican) and the founder of Methodism, and his brother Charles (1708-1788). As clergymen in the Church of England, the Wesleys' theology was shaped by Arminianism, which was introduced in the church 100 years earlier through the efforts of Archbishop William Laud (1573-1645).[41] By the time the Wesleys came upon the scene the church had, for various reasons, suffered doctrinal erosion, with the real content and message of the Christian faith having been largely lost. It was to this situation that the Wesleys and their followers reacted and out of which Methodism was born. In the following quotation, Dr. Herbert J. A. Bouman, a professor emeritus of systematic theology in the Lutheran Church—Missouri Synod (LCMS), describes the role of the Wesleys and the emphasis on God's law in the development of Methodism:

> The Wesleyan movement arose within the Church of England as a protest against the cold formalism of the church and the moral laxity of the people. . . . The Wesley brothers were ordained clergymen of the Church of England and had no desire to separate themselves from it. . . . All they wanted was to revitalize the nation's religion, stimulate a genuine heartfelt faith, and induce the people to lead sanctified lives.

[40]Hagglund, op. cit., p. 259.
[41]Spitz, op. cit., p. 80.

The Wesleys came to their ideas early in life. They were reared in a very large parsonage family, where sheer necessity compelled the gifted and resourceful mother to adopt rules and regulations for the maintenance of domestic order. At Oxford University [where they were preparing for priesthood in the Church of England] the Wesleys were appalled by the worldliness of the students and determined to counteract it by strict methods of Bible-study, prayer, and admonition. In derision their fellow students called this group "Holy Club" or "Methodists." The basic elements of Wesley's system were the attainment of holiness, or perfection, or entire sanctification, through methodical observance of rules and regulations under the supervision of other Christians. . . . For Wesley the principal concern was life rather than doctrine.[42]

EXPERIENCE AND EMOTIONS—THE WESLEYS

The Wesleys and their followers not only emphasized divine law, but they combined it with experience and emotions. This combination is pointed out by Victor H. Prange, a pastor in the conservative Wisconsin Evangelical Lutheran Synod (WELS), in his book *Why So Many Churches?* He writes:

The Wesleys were sons of an Anglican priest. In their home they learned the value of prayer and Bible-study, moral values and frugal living. Their mother, Susanna, was a woman of very strong character who ruled the children through a benevolent despotism. From their father they learned to value the sacraments but also to cherish inward religion. "The inward witness, son, the inward witness, that is the proof, the strongest proof of Christianity"—these were Samuel Wesley's dying words to his son John.

The members of the Oxford "Holy Club" . . . had no interest at that time in reforming society. Their only interest was to experience personal spiritual assurance of salvation and a corresponding reform of life. . . . Wesley's goal was to attain perfect love of God and neighbor. . . . The importance of living a holy life was a constant theme. . . . In his sermons and tracts Wesley seldom points to the cross of Jesus Christ as the basis for one's certainty of salvation; rather he stresses the inner witness of the Spirit of Christ. Not right teaching

---

[42]Bouman, op. cit., pp. 40-42.

but inner assurance of salvation and a striving for perfect love form the core of Wesley's message.[43]

The emphasis on emotional experiences, or "inner witness" as it is referred to above, as proof of faith and salvation is based on John Wesley's doctrine of "sure salvation" or "assurance salvation." Spitz explains:

> According to Wesley's doctrine of "sure salvation" the sinner must feel in his own consciousness the certainty of his salvation. He called this the witness of the Spirit. Salvation must be felt. Hence, said Wesley, only those are truly converted who, like him, have passed through a serious struggle under the conviction of sin and have suddenly experienced the inward assurance that they have passed from death to life. Wesley's doctrine of "sure salvation," like his doctrine of "free salvation," contributed to the emotional excesses of later Methodist revivalism [in America]. With exciting music and singing, shouting and the like, revivalists aimed to bring on a psychological state in the sinner, a form of hysteria, which they identified with the witness of the Spirit.[44]

The above-mentioned Wesleyan doctrine of "free salvation" is based on the Arminian doctrine of synergism or "making a decision for Christ." This doctrine is a result of Wesley's reasoning that if man possesses the ability to accept Christ, he can be helped along in the decision-making process by the above-described emotional means.[45]

For the churches of the Reformed tradition, the combined errors of the Calvinists and Arminians have had far-reaching effects. In many instances, the Reformed say they remember when they "asked Jesus into their heart" and they came to believe and their lives changed. Having been led through the experience of synergism, they do not realize that their faith came not through what they themselves did, but by what the Holy Spirit accomplished working through their hearing of the objective Word of God. Along with this "change of heart," this new faith, came many blessings that enriched their lives. Unfortunately, because they believe these blessings resulted because they asked Jesus into their heart, they are more vulnerable when calamities occur and it seems as if God is punishing them. They tend to see only blessings as proof of God's love (a view Lutherans call the "theol-

---

[43]Prange, op. cit., pp. 50, 51, 54, 55.
[44]Spitz, op. cit., pp. 85, 86.
[45]Ibid.

ogy of glory"), not the difficult things that God allows to come into their lives to strengthen their faith and the faith of others (what Lutherans call the "theology of the cross").[46] Even in the everyday struggles involved in leading a Christian life, with its spiritual ups and downs, they are at risk and many begin to doubt their faith and ask such questions as, Did I really commit my life to Christ? Am I really staying in the center of God's will? Am I really forgiven? They may reason that if they cooperate with God and strive to lead a more God-pleasing life through stringent obedience to his laws, he will bless them again. Thus the combination of law, striving after perfection, and reliance upon one's own strength and abilities becomes a heavy burden, certainty of faith is lost, and many fall away.

LUTHERANISM—LAW AND GOSPEL

The errors of the churches of the Reformed tradition will be more easily understood if we look at one of the characteristics and great strengths of Lutheranism—the proper distinction between law and gospel. Each plays a separate role in the life of the Lutheran.

It will be helpful at this point to define two familiar words—law and gospel.

Law: the immutable [unchanging] will of God, showing man how he should behave in thought, word, and deed.

Gospel: the good news that God has saved us by sending Christ to obey God's law [perfectly] and to suffer the punishment for all our sins in our stead.[47]

Lutherans find in Scripture three uses or purposes of the law. In the *first* use of the law we find the law acting as a *curb*. Because of the threat of civil punishment, the law curbs outward immoral conduct. This first use of the law is usually regarded as third in importance theologically. The *second* use of the Law Lutherans call a *mirror* because it shows us our sins and thus prepares us to recognize our need for a savior. In the following paragraphs this second use is referred to as the *primary purpose* of the law (the most important theologically). Lutherans also refer to a *third* use of the law, the law as a *guide*.

---

[46]This subject is examined thoroughly in Roland Cap Ehlke's *Faith on Trial* (Milwaukee: Northwestern Publishing House, 1980), a Bible study course on the book of Job.

[47]Robert D. Preus, *Getting Into the Theology of Concord* (St. Louis: Concordia Publishing House, 1977), p. 88.

For Lutherans, who already have certainty for their faith through the objective promises of God in Christ, the gospel, the primary purpose of the *law,* is to serve as a mirror to show man his sins, for as God's Word tells us, "all have sinned and fall short of the glory of God" (Rom. 3:23). Because the "wages of sin is death" (Rom. 6:23), it also points out his need of a savior. The primary purpose of the *gospel* is to show man his Savior, Christ the Lord. Luther explains the manner in which law and gospel are to be applied:

> *Man Must Hear the Law First. Then the Gospel*—Before receiving comfort of forgiveness, sins must be recognized [in the "mirror" of the Law] and the fear of God's wrath must be experienced through the preaching or apprehension of the Law, that man may be driven to sigh for grace [and know he needs a Savior] and may be prepared to receive the comfort of the Gospel.[48]

As just stated, this correct understanding of the proper distinction between law and gospel is one of the characteristics and great strengths of the Lutheran Church. The importance placed upon it is reflected in orthodox Lutheran preaching and teaching by her pastors, in her hymns, and in her liturgical worship services.

LUTHERANISM AND THE CHRISTIAN LIFE

The vital importance of the proper distinction between law and gospel will be further illustrated as we look at another great strength of Lutheranism—maintaining the proper emphasis and balance between justification and sanctification. These two terms are defined as follows:

Justification: God's counting lost and guilty sinners righteous because of Christ's atoning work.

Sanctification: The new life a person lives when he believes in Christ. In this new life the Holy Spirit leads him to obey the Law for Christ's sake.[49]

Lutherans maintain the proper emphasis and balance between these two important doctrines by placing justification ahead of sanctification without diminishing the importance of leading a Christian life.

As Lutherans already know, justification is brought about by God's grace through faith in Christ *apart* from any merit or works of

---

[48]*What Luther Says,* 1:738.
[49]Preus, op. cit., pp. 88, 89.

man. And, like faith, sanctification is worked by the Holy Spirit working through the means of grace, the Word and the sacraments. It is in the area of sanctification that we again see the vital need for understanding the proper use of the law. For here the law serves a *third* purpose—that of a *guide* in leading the new life in Christ. This is the third use of the law. Because Lutherans have the right understanding of the relationship between law and gospel, the gospel receives greater emphasis and justification is placed ahead of sanctification. For it is the gospel that produces right behavior, not law. Dr. C. F. W. Walther (1811-87), an orthodox Lutheran scholar considered by many to be one of the finest Lutheran theologians in American history, points this out in his book *The Proper Distinction Between Law and Gospel*. He writes:

> A preacher of the Law comes down on men with threats and punishment; a preacher of divine grace coaxes and urges men by reminding them of the goodness and mercy which God has shown them. . . . Let no minister think that he cannot induce the unwilling to do God's will by preaching the Gospel to them and that he must rather preach the Law and proclaim the threatening of God to them. If that is all he can do, he will only lead his people to perdition [eternal damnation]. Rather than act the policeman in his congregation, he ought to change the hearts of his members in order that they may without constraint do what is pleasing to God with a glad and cheerful heart. A person who has a real understanding of the love of God in Christ Jesus is astonished at its fire, which is able to melt anything in heaven and on earth. The moment he believes in this love he cannot but love God and from gratitude for his salvation do anything from love of God and for His glory.[50]

Thus, keeping God's commandments becomes something the Christian sincerely desires to do and the burden of the law has been lifted. With hearts changed by the gospel and the sure and certain knowledge of how faith is brought about, the Lutheran takes comfort in Christ alone, knowing he is a forgiven sinner. As faith grows the Christian finds himself doing more and more by grace what the law demands but cannot produce. Christian obedience flows naturally out of grace, the assurance of forgiveness through Christ. The Lutheran Christian looks to the gospel and, knowing that he is a for-

---

[50]C. F. W. Walther, *The Proper Distinction Between Law and Gospel,* reproduced from the German edition of 1897, W. H. T. Dau (St. Louis: Concordia Publishing House, 1928), pp. 388, 389.

given sinner, Christ works in him, bringing about "good works." Good works are then a natural response to the gracious love of God. Luther explains it this way:

> Oh, it is a living, busy, active, mighty thing, this faith! It is impossible for it not to be doing good works incessantly. It does not ask whether good works are to be done, but before the question is asked, it has already done them, and is constantly doing them.

> Faith is a living, daring confidence in God's grace, so sure and certain that the believer would stake his life on it a thousand times. This knowledge of and confidence in God's grace makes men glad and bold and happy in dealing with God and with all creatures. And this is the work which the Holy Spirit performs in faith. Because of it, without compulsion, a person is ready and glad to do good to everyone, to suffer everything, out of love and praise to God who has shown him this grace.[51]

As previously stated, sanctification comes about by the power of the Holy Spirit. Therefore, if there is any diligence to do anything at all, it will be a diligence to be faithful in the study of God's Word and in using the sacrament of the Lord's table. For these means of grace *alone* will bring about the good works in this life that God commands. Even this urgency to use the Word is itself brought about through the teaching of the same Word, so that Jesus alone is "author and perfecter of our faith" (Hebrews 12:2).

THE REFORMED EMPHASIS ON LIFE OVER DOCTRINE

The failure of the churches of the Reformed tradition to understand the biblical distinction between law and gospel resulted in the tendency to place more emphasis on leading the Christian life than on the doctrine that will produce it. Most preaching and teaching in the Reformed churches tends towards moralizing, stress on the law, and experience. Those of the Arminian persuasion add to this a special emphasis on emotion.

Calvinistic emphasis

Among the Reformed churches, generally identified as Calvinistic, the tendency to place greater emphasis on life than doctrine was in-

---

[51]Martin Luther, *Commentary on Romans,* trans. J. Theodore Mueller (Grand Rapids: Kregel Publications, 1976), Preface, p. xvii.

herited from Zwingli and Calvin. They had been influenced to some degree by the Roman Catholic scholar Erasmus of Rotterdam (1467-1536), Luther's old adversary. Erasmus's humanistic reform of Christianity emphasized preaching the Gospel and the ethical principles of the Sermon on the Mount (Matthew 5-7) to change individual man and, subsequently, society as a whole.[52] Erasmus's view of the law fit in particularly well with Zwingli and Calvin's theology, and the combined influence may be observed in the following quotation from *A Look at Today's Churches—A Comparative Guide,* by Herbert J. A. Bouman:

> As a humanist Zwingli was concerned principally with recapturing the life-style of the church before its degeneration through centuries of human traditions and ceremonies. He wanted to reform worship and morals rather than theology, and he strove to achieve it by means of appropriate legislation rather than through the Gospel. . . . A strong political and social activism characterized his work. . . . Zwingli died on a battlefield in 1531 . . . [and] some years later the city of Geneva became the center of great reformatory activity under the leadership of John Calvin. . . . Calvin was a man of outstanding intellect and learning, one of the most systematic thinkers of his time. With single minded devotion he set himself to the task of reforming whatever needed reforming, not only in the church but also in society, in business, and in civil government. Eventually Calvin gained complete control of Geneva and through the city council initiated laws and ordinances regulating all aspects of community life, including commercial and social matters, such as price control and amusements. . . . Calvin's influence reached far beyond Switzerland, and his view gained the support of many thousands [all over Europe]. . . . As emigrants from Great Britain and Holland colonized North America, they brought their Calvinistic theology and ethos with them . . . *and for the greater part of United States history varieties of Calvinism were the dominant factor in shaping American ideas of religion and culture.*[53]

It should be noted that while Zwingli was not overly concerned with theology, this was not true of Calvin. This may be demonstrated by the fact that during his lifetime Calvin produced many dogmatic

---

[52]Hagglund, op. cit., p. 255.
[53]Bouman, op. cit., pp. 29, 30.

books and Bible commentaries. However, Calvin's failure to understand the proper distinction between law and gospel and his emphasis on reforming society, as well as the church, opened the door to the later development of the social gospel movement, with its emphasis on life rather than doctrine (see Chapter 19).

Arminian emphasis

In the churches of the Reformed tradition, which derive their theology predominately from Arminianism, there is a much greater tendency to emphasize life over doctrine. This can be observed in the development of Methodism and the Arminian church bodies that have emerged from its roots. It is important to note that Methodism itself originated out of a church body that was already doctrinally weak. Bouman examines some of the major reasons for this weakness:

> The great movement inaugurated by Wesley was principally by way of reaction to a specific set of historical circumstances in England. In the 16th century, under Queen Elizabeth I, the Church of England was established, flexible enough in its theology, it was hoped, to permit a variety of Christians to get along in one national church. In the 17th century . . . an attempt originating in Calvinist Scotland was made to reform or "purify" the church from within. This endeavor led to the production of the Westminster Standards of the Presbyterian Church. As we know, this had no lasting effect. The Establishment, consisting of the Crown, the church, the nobility, the Tory press, and the social and economic upper class, regained control. Subsequently Deism (belief in the existence of an impersonal "Supreme Being") and rationalism (rejecting what cannot be harmonized with reason) infiltrated the theology of the church and robbed the Christian message of much of its basic content. The church became identified with the privileged class and appeared to have little to offer the great masses of the poor and underprivileged. The liturgical rubrics and forms of the Book of Common Prayer were generally observed as the clergy went through the motions of worship, but there seemed to be no life in it.[54]

THE HOLINESS AND PENTECOSTAL GROUPS

The Wesleys were right in recognizing the need for reform in the Church of England, but rather than addressing their efforts to cor-

---

[54]Bouman, op. cit., pp. 39-41.

recting the root cause of the problem, lack of doctrinal emphasis and false teaching, they set about treating the symptoms rather than the disease. As a result, they were unable to bring about change in the Church of England and were finally forced to form a separate group. The Methodist Church started out strong enough on the surface but inwardly it was weak, for the Wesleys and their followers brought with them the same Reformed errors in theology that were responsible for the weakness of the Church of England. Therefore, after a period of extensive growth, Methodism followed in the footsteps of the Church of England. This becomes clear as Prange describes the growth of Methodism and points to the emergence of the Holiness and Pentecostal groups from their Methodist roots. In his chapter concerning American churches he writes:

> Hymn singing fueled the spread of the Methodist movement. John Wesley translated a number of hymns from the German language including several by Paul Gerhardt (TLH 349: "Jesus, Thy Boundless Love to Me"). Brother Charles is said to have written over 6,000 hymns. Twelve are found in *The Lutheran Hymnal* including the familiar "Hark! The Herald Angels Sing" (TLH 94) and "Christ the Lord is Risen Today" (TLH 193). Charles Wesley often expresses the desire for "perfect love" which will drive out all fear and sin. Of the mind of Jesus he sings, "When I feel it fixed within/I shall have no power to sin." Many of his hymns are very subjective, appealing to individual feelings and emotions. They lack the objective proclamation of Christ's saving work. Only in Christ's work for us can one find the Wesleyan goal of perfect love and holiness.

> As Methodists increased in numbers, criticism arose about widespread neglect of Christian perfection. Those eager for the revival of perfectionism turned to the camp meeting as the instrument by which to revive the theological heritage of Methodism. A National Camp Meeting Association for the Promotion of Holiness was formed. . . . Many of those in this holiness movement were Methodists. Controversy flared up leading to an official statement of the church: "There has sprung up among us (Methodists) a party with holiness as a watchword; they have holiness associations, holiness meetings, holiness preachers, holiness evangelists, and holiness property. . . . We deplore their teaching and methods insofar as they claim a monopoly of the experience, practice, and advocacy of holiness, and separate themselves from the body of

ministers and disciples." Such criticism hastened the process by which individual holiness denominations emerged. Two of these are the Church of the Nazarene and the Church of God (Anderson, Indiana). Many more smaller church bodies also have links to the holiness movement.

The most significant offshoot of the holiness movement is the Pentecostal churches. They took the restoration emphasis a step further by including not only conversion and entire sanctification as essential for New Testament Christianity, but also the gift of speaking in tongues. It is not a long step from the Kentucky camp meeting to modern Pentecostal worship.[55]

Pentecostalism has indeed carried the emphasis of Methodism and the holiness movement a step further, for it is here we see the greatest emphasis upon life, experience, and emotion over and above concern for doctrine. Bouman elaborates:

But while the Holiness groups emphasize the work of the Holy Spirit in entire sanctification, the Pentecostals lay stress on the miraculous, the charismatic gifts of the Holy Spirit.

Pentecostals regard "baptism in the Holy Spirit" as far more important and effective than the water Baptism instituted by Christ. Baptism in the Spirit is said to endow those Christians fortunate enough to receive it with extra gifts not experienced by "ordinary" Christians.

There are a number of Pentecostal churches, some containing the word "Pentecostal" in their name, while others call themselves Assemblies of God, or Churches of God. Formerly the Pentecostals or "Charismatics" were not welcome in old-line churches, and for that reason they formed separate groups. In recent times, however, they have appeared in most of the churches, Roman Catholic, Episcopalian, Lutheran, etc., as forces to be reckoned with, at times even hailed as resources for revitalizing a Christianity that seems to have gone flat. This development is sometimes referred to as Neo-Pentecostalism.[56]

We shall see later how the Neo-Pentecostal development fits into the modern day ecumenical scene, but first, having completed our

---

[55]Prange, op. cit., pp. 55, 58-60.
[56]Bouman, op. cit., pp. 43, 44.

comparison between Lutheran, Roman Catholic, and Reformed doctrine, it is necessary to take a look at an important movement in the church called *pietism*. Through our study of pietism in the next chapter the reader will be able to recognize the threads of Reformed doctrine that were woven into the fabric of Lutheranism, causing weakness and division in the Lutheran Church.

25.

PIETISM

Pietism, as a movement, had its beginnings in the Lutheran Church in 17th century Germany. It is a movement that has influenced both Lutherans and Reformed. While it started through the efforts of a Lutheran pastor, its theological roots, as we shall see ahead, are really anchored in Reformed theology rather than Lutheran orthodoxy.

> Pietism was cradled in the Dutch Reformed church in the early seventeenth century. It was probably Theodore Untereyk who introduced it in Germany. It flowered in the Lutheran church. It breathed new life into a country exhausted by the Thirty Years War. . . . English Puritans and dissenters, and Dutch Calvinists, had shown this form of piety early in the seventeenth century. Philip Spener's *Pia Desideria* gave it a new direction, in the form of German Pietism, after 1675. . . . Towards the end of the seventeenth century a warm evangelical piety began to appear among Protestants. It crossed denominational and political boundaries. Protestants started to stress the importance of personal conversion, holy living and the need to tell non-Christians about Christ's saving work. . . . It caught fire among Anglicans in the early eighteenth century in the Awakening. It burned in virtually every church in the American colonies.[1]

---

[1]*Eerdmans' Handbook to the History of Christianity,* organizing ed. Dr. Tim Dowley; consulting eds. John H. Y. Briggs, Dr. Robert D. Linder, David F. Wright (Grand Rapids: Wm. B. Eerdmans Publishing House, 1977), pp. 442, 473, 474.

Pietism's greatest importance for Lutherans is based on the fact that it is the vehicle through which Reformed theology was introduced on a wide scale to Lutheran pastors and laity.

Lutheran orthodoxy has felt the influence of Reformed theology since the days of the Reformation, beginning during Luther's lifetime and continuing into the present day. Even Melanchthon, Luther's trusted right-hand man, vacillated on some important issues, as did others who followed after him. This can be seen in the teaching that developed in Luther's home territory, the University of Wittenberg in Germany. Kurt E. Marquart, a conservative theologian and professor in the Lutheran Church—Missouri Synod (LCMS), writes:

> Finally, the Formula of Concord settled a number of conflicts which had torn the Lutheran Church apart since the death of Luther. Melanchthon, Luther's scholarly friend and right-hand man, lacked Luther's depth and decisiveness. After the great Reformer's death Melanchthon himself vacillated on some important issues. Some of his followers went further, and actually formed a conspiracy in the very University of Wittenberg, to replace Lutheran with Calvinistic doctrine. They regarded Luther's belief in the Real Presence of Christ's body and blood in the Sacrament as a piece of extremism which needlessly divided the church. They themselves agreed with Zwingli and Calvin that Christ's body could only be in one place at a time and therefore could *not* be in the Sacrament, since it was now somewhere in heaven. These university professors taught their Calvinistic doctrine in their classes, but publicly assured everyone, even to the point of perjury, that they were sticking faithfully to Luther's doctrine and to the Augsburg Confession. They were not open and honest but rather were "Crypto-Calvinist"—Calvinists in secret. Had their trickery not come out into the open, so that the pious but gullible Saxon prince could finally see it, they might well have succeeded, humanly speaking, in destroying the Lutheran Church from within.[2]

In spite of the weakness of some of Luther's followers, Lutheran orthodoxy thrived and grew in Europe during the hundred years following the publication of the *Book of Concord* in 1580. Concerning this period in the history of the Lutheran Church Marquart writes:

---

[2]Kurt E. Marquart, *Anatomy of an Explosion* (Grand Rapids: Baker Book House, 1978), pp. 17, 18.

During the next hundred years the doctrinal heritage of the Reformation was elaborated and defended by the giants of the so-called Age of Orthodoxy, men like Chemnitz, John Gerhard, Dannhauer, Quenstedt . . . and Calov. . . . Few today appreciate the monumental work of these men, and even fewer know it. Yet the Swedish scholar Bengt Hagglund has paid them this high tribute: "With respect to its versatile comprehension of theological material and the breadth of its knowledge of the Bible, Lutheran orthodoxy marks the high point in the entire history of theology."[3] Lesser lights regrettably fell into a hair-splitting disputatiousness with little evidence of spiritual life and warmth. The reaction came in the form of Pietism.[4]

Climate leading to Pietism

The above reference to the "lesser lights" is descriptive of some in academic circles where there developed an over-intellectualization of religion. This, combined with several other factors, created the climate out of which the movement called pietism developed. John M. Brenner, professor of modern church history and the Lutheran Confessions at the Wisconsin Lutheran Seminary (Wisconsin Evangelical Lutheran Synod), elaborates:

Pietism was a reaction to what was perceived as a dead orthodoxism and lack of piety in the Lutheran Church of the seventeenth century. The Lutheran Church in Germany in the seventeenth century had some problems. The Thirty Years War had a horrible effect on Germany and on German morality. . . . [It] was also afflicted by caesaropapism. In other words, the church was controlled by the state. At the time of the Reformation Luther had turned to the territorial rulers for leadership in the church because they were the best trained and most capable laymen available. But in the years that followed not all the rulers of Lutheran lands proved to be pious or to have a clear understanding of Scriptural truth. Instead they used the church to foster their own political ambitions and appointed pastors to suit their own political needs. Church discipline became difficult and the morality of some of the clergy and laity left much to be desired.

---

[3]Ibid., pp. 18,19. Author's endnote. Citation reads: Bengt Hagglund, *History of Theology* (St. Louis: Concordia Publishing House, 1968), p. 303.
[4]Ibid., p. 19.

In the minds of some, Lutheranism had degenerated into the thought that you can live any way you want and it doesn't make any difference as long as you believe what is right. In some academic circles there was an over-intellectualization of religion with little concern for practical application to the lives of the common people. Confessional Lutheranism always needs to be on guard against this danger. As Prof. Balge of our Seminary warns, "There is always the danger that knowledge of right teaching will be confused with faith and that adherence to an orthodox system of doctrine will breed a self-righteous complacency that precludes personal conviction of sin and trust in the Savior of sinners."[5] Yet the early leaders of Pietism never blamed Lutheran Orthodoxy for these problems but considered themselves to be orthodox Lutherans. No one . . . can make sweeping generalization that this was an era of dead [orthodoxism] or lack of concern for personal piety. But there were some abuses. And over the years many voices had called for correction of these abuses.[6]

Philip Jacob Spener

One such voice was that of Philip Jacob Spener (1635-1705), a Lutheran pastor and founder of pietism. This movement was launched when Spener's book, *Pia Desideria* (pious wishes), was published in 1675 and has been described as "the movement in behalf of practical Christianity within the Lutheran Church in the seventeenth and eighteenth centuries."[7] Few books have exerted a greater influence on subsequent church history than this one, particularly those written by Lutheran pastors. Spener's efforts were well-intentioned. He meant only to integrate his faith into daily life. Unfortunately, while he considered himself an orthodox Lutheran, he had been influenced by Reformed theology. This is indicated in Theodore G. Tappert's introduction to *Pia Desideria*, where he writes:

An omnivorous reader from his youth, Spener's early years were . . . shaped by books which he found in his father's li-

---

[5]John M. Brenner, "Pietism, Past and Present," Southeastern Michigan Pastor/Teacher/Delegate Conference, January 23, 1989, and Northern Michigan Pastoral Conference, April 3, 1989. Author's endnote. Citation reads: Richard D. Balge, "Pietism's Teaching on Church and Ministry," *Wisconsin Lutheran Quarterly*, Vol. 82, No. 2, Fall 1985, p. 248.

[6]Ibid., p. 2, 3.

[7]Ibid., pp. 1, 2. Author's endnote. Citation reads: Samuel M. Jackson and Lefferts A. Loetscher, *The New Schaff-Herzog Encyclopedia of Religious Knowledge* (Grand Rapids: Baker Book House, 1957), Vol. IX, p. 53.

brary. Next to the Bible his favorite was John Arndt's *True Christianity,* a devotional book which later became popular in the Scandinavian countries as in Germany and was carried to America by many colonists. John Arndt (1555-1621) had asserted that orthodox doctrine was not enough to produce Christian life and advocated a mysticism which he borrowed largely from the late Middle Ages. . . . Spener also read several . . . devotional books by English puritans [Reformed] . . . critical of conventional Christianity. They advocated self-examination, an earnest quest for holiness, and other worldly standards of morality which would set the true Christian apart from his neighbor. They shared with John Arndt an emphasis on rigorous religious and moral life as over against a dogmatic intellectualism, but they were less mystical.[8]

For Spener, John Arndt was the bridge into Reformed theology. A prolific writer and author of many devotional books, Arndt contributed much of value to the Christian world. In fact, it was as a preface in his edition of sermons on the gospels that *Pia Desideria* first appeared. Nevertheless, he had come under attack for his emphasis on sanctification and emotionalism and his unhesitating acceptance of medieval and other mystics (e.g., Bernard of Clairvaux).[9]

Mysticism, as noted above, is a factor in the theological emphasis of both John Arndt and the English puritans. Mystical spiritualism has been called "objectively the most important forerunner of Pietism,"[10] carrying within it the seeds for the development of most of the movement's characteristics, which will soon be described. While it is beyond the scope of this chapter to delve deeply into mysticism, a brief definition is required. The word mysticism has never had a precise meaning. In relation to pietism, mysticism involves subjective experiences. A mystical experience may be defined as a completely subjective experience occurring within the person that is not based on any objective facts or change in surroundings. It is completely confined to the mind and is primarily an emotional *event.*[11] This is in contrast to an emotional *response* to an event, as in hear-

---

[8]Philip Jacob Spener, *Pia Desideria,* trans. Theodore G. Tappert (Philadelphia: Fortress Press, 1964), pp. 8, 9.

[9]*The Encyclopedia of the Lutheran Church,* 3 vols., ed. Julius Bodensieck (Minneapolis: Augsburg Publishing House, 1965), 1:105, 106.

[10]Ibid., 3:1901.

[11]Arthur L. Johnson, *Faith Misguided: Exposing the Dangers of Mysticism* (Chicago: Moody Bible Institute, 1988), pp. 22, 23.

ing the Word and partaking of the Sacraments. The late Dr. Hermann Sasse, a noted orthodox German/Australian Lutheran scholar and theologian, supports this definition and points out the orthodox Lutheran position concerning its use in the church. In his book *Here We Stand* he writes:

> In the Fifth Article [of the Augsburg Confession] mysticism, the great German mysticism of all the ages, including its philosophical consequences, is excluded from the church. In fact, the judgment of the old Lutheran Church is particularly severe on this point. Mysticism holds that there can be a genuine experience of God, a real encounter with the Spirit of God, *even* apart from the external word of the Gospel [the Word and Sacraments]. More than that, it maintains that this immediate experience of the presence of God is the uttermost which can fall to the lot of man.[12]

We shall see ahead the emphasis on subjective experiences by Spener and his followers as we look at the development of the pietistic movement. As we have observed in the preceding chapter, subjective experiences are one of the hallmarks of Reformed theology.

Spener was further influenced by Reformed theology when, after completing his theological studies, he spent two years traveling in Switzerland, France, and Germany. In Geneva he became acquainted with Jean de Labadie, a zealous French Reformed preacher, when Labadie was at the height of his influence and before he lapsed into his later mystical fanaticism. Spener often went to hear him speak. The impression Labadie made on his young visitor is indicated not only by the frequency of his visits, but by the fact that six years later Spener had one of Labadie's tracts published in a German translation.[13] Labadie preached not only a "strong experiential, otherworldly, mystical faith," but he also came to emphasize the importance of separation and small group meetings.[14]

Characteristics of Pietism

The infiltration of Reformed thinking into the theology and practice of Spener and those who followed after him can be easily recognized. It should be noted that in pietism, as well as in most move-

---

[12]Hermann Sasse, *Here We Stand,* trans. Theodore G. Tappert (Adelaide, South Australia: Lutheran Publishing House, 1979), p. 55.

[13]Spener, op. cit., p. 11.

[14]Robert G. Clouse, *The Church in the Age of Orthodoxy and the Enlightenment* (St. Louis: Concordia Publishing House, 1980), p. 76.

ments that begin as a protest of a situation or series of events, many
of Spener's followers carried his efforts at reform much further than
he originally intended.

As mentioned earlier, Spener meant only to speak to the abuses of
his day and to integrate his faith into daily life. He considered himself an orthodox Lutheran and did not intend to move away from correct doctrine. When asked to write the preface to Arndt's book, he
used the opportunity to point out what he felt were some of the abuses in the church and offered a six-point program for improvement.
Ernst H. Wendland, a WELS missionary to Africa and seminary professor, summarizes Spener's proposals as follows:

1. The Word of God must be more widely studied by the people.
   To this end he proposed discussion under the pastor's guidance.
2. The universal priesthood of believers needs new emphasis.
   All Christians should exercise this privilege by testifying, in-
   structing, and exhorting each other.
3. Mere head knowledge is not Christianity, but such knowledge must be translated into action.
4. More love and gentleness between the Christian denominations is needed in polemics [refuting of doctrinal error].
5. The schooling of the clergy in the universities must include
   training for personal piety as well as intellectual knowledge.
6. Sermons should be prepared with less emphasis on rhetori-
   cal art and more on the edification of the hearers.[15]

Spener's proposals were received very favorably by most people
throughout Germany, including orthodox Lutheran theologians. But
when they, and other orthodox Lutherans, realized what he meant
by what he said and the methods he would use to carry out his proposals, opposition developed.[16]

The first of many criticisms to be leveled against Spener was his
use of private meetings for the cultivation of holiness, called *collegia
pietatis* or conventicles. Brenner describes these meetings and some
of the reasons for the developing criticism:

> One of his more controversial methods was the introduction
> of the so-called collegia pietatis (gathering of the pious). The
> collegia pietatis were private gatherings of the "better"

---

[15]Ernst Wendland, "Present-Day Pietism," *Wisconsin Lutheran Quarterly,*
Vol. 49, January 1953, pp. 23, 24.

[16]Brenner, op. cit., p. 5.

members of his congregation for the purpose of Bible-study and mutual edification. Spener had advocated and introduced these conventicles even before the writing of his *Pia Desideria*. He hoped that these gatherings around God's Word would create pockets of God-fearing people in the state church congregations who would then work as a leaven for improving conditions in the church.

But instead these little churches within the church caused all kinds of problems. Pharisaism developed. For the members of these groups began to consider themselves to be better than the other members of the congregation who weren't participating in the conventicles. Instead of working as a leaven to promote ethics and morality they became disruptive, splitting churches as they separated themselves from those they considered to be unconverted or second-class Christians. Later on, pietists actually attempted to classify people according to their growth in sanctification. Because of emphasis on the universal priesthood the public ministry was disparaged.[17]

If we are to understand the negative results of the conventicles cited above, we must understand the fundamental error of pietism—the error that was to lead to many more errors. In their genuine concern for integrating faith into daily life, Spener and his followers emphasized sanctification over justification. Brenner brings attention to this fact as he writes:

The doctrine of justification . . . was for Luther the doctrine on which the church stands or falls. What Jesus has done *for* us is all-important. . . . But Pietism began to change the emphasis from what Christ has done *for* us to what Christ does *in* us. They emphasized holy living rather than the forgiveness of sins. Their theology and practice centered on sanctification . . . rather than on justification.[18]

In failing to emphasize the very thing that produces a grateful heart and holy living, they fell into a second error—that of confusing law and gospel. Brenner explains:

In their efforts to promote morality and Christian living, the pietists fell into another trap. They were disappointed with

---

[17]Brenner, op. cit.
[18]Ibid., pp. 7, 8.

the slowness of the Gospel in producing Christian living so they turned to legalism. They began to use the law for a purpose God never intended. The main purpose of the law is to show us our sins. . . . But Pietism tended to use the law not so much to convict their hearers of the depths of their sinfulness, but more to rail against the gross sins of society. Such preaching tends to turn people into Pharisees [Matt. 23] rather than crushed sinners.

When Pietism shifted the emphasis from the law as mirror (to show us our sins) to the third use of the law (as a rule or guide), legalism resulted. For the pietists the main purpose of the law was to give a set of legal requirements for Christian living. They tried to use the law to motivate Christian living. This is an improper use of the law and a characteristic of Reformed rather than Lutheran theology.

The pietists wanted to foster sanctification. But by misusing the law and de-emphasizing justification, they took away the very thing which can foster sanctification—the law and the gospel properly distinguished and applied.[19]

As a result of the cited errors, Spener and his followers moved from the certainty of faith found in the objective promises of God in the Word and Sacraments to the subjective world of experience and emotion. The importance of the means of grace was shunted into the background and emphasis was placed on repentance, prayer, and the need for a "born again" experience. Wendland explains:

The importance of the true Means of Grace was shunted into the background. . . . In their stead prayer was substituted as a means of achieving the grace of God, although this was not openly taught as a doctrine by the early pietists. The assurance of salvation was no longer objectively based upon God's word, but was to be subjectively experienced in the individual's emotional life and in the fruits of faith. A life of perfect sanctification was considered possible. Thus although Pietism in Germany protested again and again its adherence to the Lutheran Confessions, it betrayed itself through its insistence on experiential conversion or regeneration and its obscuring of objective justification based upon the Means of Grace. . . . It was denied that those who were weak in faith were truly converted. True conversion in their opinion was

---

[19]Brenner, op. cit., pp. 9-11.

rather something that the individual sinner had to achieve through a prolonged period of tearful contrition and the agonizing struggle of prayer [In this way repentance and prayer became the means of grace]. As a matter of fact, in order to know whether or not you are truly converted, you had to be able to point to the exact hour of your *Gnadendurchbruch,* an emotional experience in which you became personally convinced of the "breaking through" of God's grace. . . . One's Christianity was gauged according to the intensity of his experience. Naturally the Christianity of those who couldn't point to a similar experience was considered of dubious quality and origin (author's emphasis).[20]

The emphasis on a "born again" experience led to a greater emotional fervor among the pietists. Spener's followers encouraged this aspect of pietism by describing Christian experience as "cheerful faith," "warmed hearts," and "great joy." Other followers later came to teach that happiness and success would inevitably follow the salvation experience.[21] This, of course, is very similar to the experience-oriented "success theology" taught by most Reformed pietists today.

The emphasis on subjective proof of faith led to trying to make the invisible church visible by setting a subjective standard of outward behavior. Christians were divided into classes based on this behavior: those who had a form of godliness but did not yet meet the "standards" set for Christian living, those who had made a beginning but were not yet fully "committed," and those who met the standards set for Christian living and were fully committed to leading a godly life (a much smaller group).[22]

Bible study was emphasized, but the Bible was viewed more as a source of encouragement, warning, and consolation[23] than for the doctrine (objective truth of God's Word) that would bring about the changed heart leading to Christian living. Practical teaching in the Bible (what Christ does *in* us), or "heart knowledge," was placed over and above doctrine (what Christ did *for* us), or "head knowledge." Thus, the pietists stressed the subjective over the objective and made sanctification a "subtle form of work-righteousness."[24]

The lowered view of the means of grace and greater emphasis on lay involvement led to a blurring of the biblical distinction between

[20]Wendland, op. cit., pp. 24, 25.

[21]Clouse, op. cit. p. 96.

[22]Brenner, op. cit., p. 16.

[23]Clouse, op. cit., p. 94.

[24]Brenner, op. cit., p. 8.

the universal priesthood of believers and the public ministry.[25] Every Christian is a part of the universal priesthood and is called to share the Gospel with others, but special requirements apply to the public ministry. Of special importance are the pastor's training and responsibility for the administering of the Sacraments and safe-guarding the teaching of correct doctrine.[26] In their eagerness to serve in the church, the laity got into areas in which they did not belong, such as lay-led Bible studies without pastoral guidance. In emphasizing subjective experience over doctrine, the pastor's special training lost much of its significance and his role was modified. He was no longer primarily the "minister of the Word of God," but rather the personally accountable representative, witness, and example of spiritual life, of "godliness."[27]

The results of this combination of errors can be observed in the following quotation, which further describes the negative influence of the conventicles on the life of the church:

> Some members of the groups began to decry the church as "Babel," to denounce ministers as "unconverted," to refuse any longer to attend services of the church with the "godless," and to refrain from receiving the Lord's Supper at the hands of "unworthy" ministers. . . . Conventicles [were formed] independent of churches and ministers. In 1682 Spener tried to counteract these by changing the meeting place from private homes to churches, but he was unable to prevent the proliferation of conventicles.[28]

As the following quotation illustrates, the effects of the move into subjective experience could be observed in virtually every area of religious activity:

> The Lutheran Order of Service began to be regarded as an ossified relic of Pre-Reformation times, a legalistic strait jacket which through its prescribed prayers impeded the free outpouring of a devout heart. The ex-corde [free-flowing] prayer took precedence over the liturgical prayer [as found in the Service Book and Hymnal]. Sentimental Gospel-hymns replaced the confessional Lutheran hymn. Private confession and particularly the pronouncement of

---

[25]Brenner, op. cit., p. 26.

[26]Armin W. Schuetze, *Basic Doctrines of the Bible* (Milwaukee: Northwestern Publishing House, 1986), pp. 75-78.

[27]*The Encyclopedia of the Lutheran Church,* 3:1904.

[28]Spener, op. cit., p. 20.

absolution by the pastor was bitterly opposed, since it was claimed to presuppose a judgment as to the true repentance of an individual. . . . Meetings of smaller Bible-study and prayer meeting groups were encouraged as a leaven of the truly sanctified and a means of gaining more "truly converted" souls, which resulted in a neglect of the importance of the regular service of worship. Adiaphora or indifferent things were not recognized as existent at all, since anything that did not contribute toward spiritual edification was classed as directly harmful. Card-playing, dancing, theater-going, etc., was vigorously condemned as inherently sinful, and even all humor, fiction, and play was frowned upon as unbecoming to a pious soul. The acquiring of secular knowledge was despised, and the daily parochial school-curriculum consisted of as many as six hours of religion in varied forms and doses. In the rite of confirmation the renewal of the baptismal vow by the confirmed was stressed to the extent that every baptized child was looked upon as having fallen from the state of baptismal grace, necessitating this conscious pledge on the part of the individual as a completion of the efficacy [effectiveness] of this covenant.[29]

Doctrinal indifference

Emphasis on the sanctified life combined with subjective experience over and above doctrine led the pietists first to doctrinal neglect and then to indifference. Spener himself contributed to this drift into indifference, even though he considered himself an orthodox Lutheran. He tended to regard as important only those doctrines which played a direct part in personal religious experience.[30] Interested more in the godly life than the doctrine that produced it, Spener minimized the importance of orthodox theology:

Desiring to link salvation more closely to a godly life, Spener was led to attack the prevailing theology of his day. He felt that the intricate scholastic elaboration of theology, coupled with hostility toward those who differed even on minor points, conflicted with a life of service to others. Doctrine was to be tested not on an academic basis but rather by its effect on the lives of those who held it.[31]

[29]Wendland, op. cit., pp. 25, 26.
[30]Spener, op. cit., p. 26.
[31]Clouse, op. cit., p. 95.

261

The difference between Lutherans and the Reformed, a subject that occupied many of the orthodox Lutheran theologians, was generally played down by Spener.[32] He later came to view Calvin's erroneous teaching on the Lord's Supper as correct, thereby denying the Real Presence, and held that agreement on the doctrine of the Lord's Supper was not essential for church unity. For these reasons, Spener has been called the first "union theologian," providing a bridge between Lutherans and the Reformed.[33]

Another factor contributing to the diminished interest in doctrine was the development of fellowship among the pietists. It first included only members of individual conventicles but then, as pietism spread, it came to encompass all pietists and all conventicles wherever they might be. This spirit of fellowship also came to include a spirit of "unionism," which is the foundation of today's ecumenism:

> Pietists feel more intimately related to the "fellow believers" in other churches than to their own fellow church members. . . . The unification of all genuine Christians therefore, constituted a natural goal of pietistic endeavors. This union was said to exist, at least basically, already now inasmuch as all reborn Christians live a life of godliness. It was this somewhat naive attitude that gave some of the pietists an unprecedented magnanimity in accepting elements of Roman Catholic devotion into their own prayers and devotional books, and particularly their biographical writings.

> Among the immediate results of Pietism the rise of *ecumenicity* no doubt deserves first place. From the beginning Pietism regarded itself as an international and interconfessional movement. It diluted and dissolved the confessional consciousness of orthodoxy from within (author's emphasis).[34]

Spener and the pietists' softened stance toward the importance of doctrine and their failure to recognize the errors of Reformed theology, particularly in the area of sanctification, provided the "spade work for the church unions of the nineteenth century,"[35] as well as for today's

---

[32]Spener, loc. cit.

[33]Gregory L. Jackson, "Questions and Answers About Pietism," *Christian News,* October 16, 1989, p. 6. Author's endnote. Citation reads: Otto W. Heick, *The History of Christian Thought,* 2 vols. (Philadelphia: Fortress Press, 1966), p. 23.

[34]*The Encyclopedia of the Lutheran Church,* 3:1899, 1900, 1904.

[35]Otto Heick, *The History of Christian Thought,* 2 vols. (Philadelphia: Fortress Press, 1966), 1:23.

ecumenical movement. This will be observed in the paragraphs that follow, along with pietism's role in Herrnhut, Saxony, Lutherans in America, and Methodism. But first we will examine the manner in which pietism spread to see the reasons for its far-reaching and long-lasting influence in the Christian world, which continues today.

The spread of Pietism

Between the initial launching of pietism and the availability of pietist clergymen, pietism spread through the large circle of Spener's pupils, his numerous friends among the nobility in all parts of Germany,[36] and devotional literature.[37] Later it advanced largely through the efforts of Spener's chief disciple, August Hermann Francke (1663-1727) with the training of more than 6,000 pastors at the University of Halle, the "international center of Pietism."[38] Noted church historian James Hastings Nichols writes:

> Spener was called to Dresden as court preacher in 1686 but soon found himself in a row with the academic theologians. A. H. Francke began *collegia* at nearby Leipzig the same year. These conventicles were forbidden by the theological faculty, and both Spener and Francke were forced out of conservative Saxony at the beginning of the 90's.
>
> Frederick III offered them asylum in Brandenburg, the haven of religious refugees from all over Europe. The University of Halle, founded in 1694, gave Spener a chance at forming a center. For ten years he built the school, but after his death in 1705 it was even more successful under Francke for the two decades until his death in 1727. The University was surrounded with other institutions, a pauper school, a boy's boarding school, an orphanage, a Latin school, a printing press, a pharmacy, and a Bible Institute. Thousands of children were taught there; many became missionaries, and some six thousand pietist clergy were trained in the Halle theological faculty, which was the largest divinity school in Germany. . . . Even the Reformed pietists on the lower Rhine contributed regularly to Halle. Colonial Lutheranism in America was largely evangelized and organized from Halle (author's emphasis) [39]

[36]*The Encyclopedia of the Lutheran Church*, 3:1902.

[37]Clouse, op. cit., p. 108.

[38]Clouse, op. cit., p. 78.

[39]James Hastings Nichols, *History of Christianity 1650-1950: Secularization of the West* (New York: The Ronald Press Co., 1956), pp. 83, 84.

Francke was the major leader in Halle's emphasis on education and charity. His vision of a better world is described as involving "not only changes in the church but a reordering of all human institutions in the interest of a more just society for everyone."[40] Thus his social concerns carried out at Halle, much like Calvin's reforms in Geneva, planted the seeds for the later development of the Social Gospel movement. Also among Francke's priorities was emphasis on missionary activities. Because of his efforts in this area, pietism's influence was felt in many other parts of the world:

> Halle is often heralded as the point of origination for inner missions (ministry to social needs), foreign missions, and Jewish missions, for dissemination of the Bible and other literature, and for the spread of Pietism by young men who followed German soldiers and settlements to eastern and southeastern Europe, North America (especially Pennsylvania and Georgia), and many other parts of the world.[41]

The influence of pietism in various parts of the world was dependent upon the degree to which pietism was carried by those in a position of preaching and teaching. As in most movements that develop in protest of circumstances or events, pietism encompassed radical as well as milder elements, with many holding to an intermediate or middle position.

Radical Pietism

Those holding to the more radical forms of pietism tended to go off into a fanatic, mystical form of religion combined with a critique of church doctrine using the principles of rationalism. Included in their theology was acceptance of millennialism and criticism of the doctrine of the Atonement.[42] The rationalistic ideas of radical pietism reached maturity in the Age of Reason and the extent to which they were sometimes carried is demonstrated by the Church of the New Jerusalem (Swedenborgians). The followers of Emanuel Swedenborg (1688-1772), a radical pietist in Sweden, founded this church in London in 1787[43] after publishing his extensive personal revelations and visions concerning heaven and things below—something he was commanded to do after holding conversations with angels, devils, Luther,

---

[40]Clouse, op. cit., p. 98.

[41]Dale Brown, *Understanding Pietism* (Grand Rapids: Wm. B. Eerdmans Publishing Co., 1978), p. 31. Cited in Brenner, op. cit., p. 6.

[42]Hagglund, op. cit., p. 331.

[43]Heick, op. cit., p. 31.

Melanchthon, and Calvin. In his writings he denied all the fundamental doctrines of the Christian faith. As a result, the Church of the New Jerusalem is listed as a cult and "the religion of Swedenborgianism rests upon the doctrine of work-righteousness and is entirely unchristian."[44] As a note of interest, although Swedenborgianism "is overtly anti-Trinitarian" it is a member of the National Council of Churches[45] (see Chapter 1—*Baal or God* quotation).

Intermediate Pietism—Zinzendorf

Intermediate pietism can be observed in the Arminian branch of the churches of the Reformed tradition, beginning with Methodism. Methodism is not only an outgrowth of Arminian theology but also of pietism. Its pietistic roots go back through founder John Wesley to Count Nicholaus von Zinzendorf (1700-60).

Zinzendorf, a nobleman and godson of Spener, was the son of a cabinet minister in Saxony who died when Zinzendorf was only six weeks old. After his mother's remarriage he was brought up by his grandmother, Baroness von Gersdorf, who was a friend of Spener's and a devotee of pietism.[46]

Educated at Halle and Wittenberg, where he studied law, Zinzendorf held a position midway between the radical and milder pietists. He developed a completely subjective, highly emotional theology that centered on the contemplation of the wounds of Christ. This contemplation was seen as kindling faith as well as producing the knowledge and certainty of forgiveness.[47]

Zinzendorf blended his theology with that of a group of radical Moravian pietists, refugees from Roman Catholic oppression who were allowed to settle on his estate in Herrnhut, Saxony, in 1722. He became the leader of this group and, in 1727, organized the Moravian Brethren, a highly evangelistic movement with strong missionary emphasis.[48] The group consisted of several hundred Bohemians, Moravians, Lutheran Saxons, a few Reformed,[49] Separatists, Anabaptists, and Schwenkfelders.[50]

It is important to note at this point that Zinzendorf had become involved in church union efforts before the arrival of the Moravians.

---

[44]John Theodore Mueller, *My Church and Others* (St. Louis: Concordia Publishing House, 1968), p. 74.

[45]Jackson, loc. cit.

[46]*Eerdmans' Handbook to the History of Christianity,* p. 477.

[47]Heick, op. cit., p. 33.

[48]Nichols, op. cit., p. 86.

[49]Spitz, op. cit., p. 107.

[50]*Eerdmans' Handbook to the History of Christianity,* p. 443.

While traveling in Western Europe, he had established contact with many Reformed pietists and had been inspired with the idea of gathering together all true lovers of the Savior into one fold. In this way he became involved in the grand scheme of church union.[51] In fact, he was a "pioneer of ecumenism, and indeed was the first to employ the term 'ecumenical' in its modern sense."[52] Thus, when he recognized the religious ideas of each group as equally valid, he was in keeping with his already established unionistic views. The different ideas were combined and the Augsburg Confession was accepted as an ecumenical creed of biblical Christianity. In 1734, Zinzendorf was ordained as a Lutheran minister[53] and three years later was consecrated as a Moravian bishop. On these grounds the Moravian Brethren Church was recognized in Germany as being affiliated with the Lutheran Church. Thus, the uniting of Moravians (Episcopal), Lutherans, and Reformed created a union church within Lutheranism almost a century prior to the Prussian Union—an event that will be noted in Chapter 26.[54] It was through Moravian missionary efforts that doors opened to pietistic influence among the Methodists—said to be "the most considerable institutional consequence of the whole pietist movement; indeed, the most important ecclesiastical [in the church] development in Protestantism since Puritanism."[55]

Intermediate Pietism—Wesley

Zinzendorf's influence in Methodism came about through John Wesley. Wesley served as a missionary in Georgia from 1735 to 1738 with almost complete lack of success. On the Atlantic voyage Wesley traveled with a group of Moravian missionaries also on their way to Georgia, whose faith during a dangerous storm had profoundly impressed him. During the storm, Wesley came to realize that in spite of all his strenuous religious exercises (see preceding chapter) he was still afraid to die. This caused him to question past assumptions concerning faith and salvation, and when he returned to England he sought out the Moravians and worshiped with them for awhile. Wesley became assured of his own salvation. while listening to a reading of Luther's preface to the Epistle to the Romans concerning justifica-

---

[51]Heick, op. cit., p. 32.

[52]*Eerdmans' Handbook to the History of Christianity,* p. 477.

[53]Although ordained as a Lutheran pastor, Zinzendorf is not accepted by Lutherans because of his involvement with the Moravians and his pietistic doctrines.

[54]Heick, op. cit., pp. 32-34.

[55]Nichols, loc. cit.

tion by faith at a Moravian prayer meeting on May 24, 1738, at Aldersgate Chapel in London.[56] Of that "dated" emotional experience he reports: "I felt my heart strangely warmed. I felt I did trust in Christ, Christ alone for salvation; and an assurance was given me that he had taken away my sins, even mine, and saved me from the law of sin and death."[57]

Before explaining Wesley's experience it will be helpful to define, once again, the word faith:

> Trust in Christ; receiving Christ and His atoning Work; knowledge of Christ and His benefits (His work of salvation).[58]

Wesley's experience would be described by Lutherans as one of "illumination," an experience of deeper understanding or new insight, rather than conversion.[59] The Holy Spirit working through the means of grace, the Word and Sacraments, not only converts man but also keeps him in the faith. Growth in faith includes an increased understanding of the meaning and significance of the Gospel. Again we see how, for Lutherans, "head" and "heart" knowledge are intrinsically related (see preceding chapter). As the Holy Spirit works through the means of grace to increase one's intellectual understanding of the faith, there is also increased confidence and certainty in the truth of the Gospel. This is a gradual process that may produce an emotional response similar to that described by Wesley. However, Wesley and his followers erred in making the dramatic emotional response an essential ingredient for certainty of faith and salvation.[60]

Wesley's emotional experience became, for him, a turning point. He went to Germany and learned from Zinzendorf and the Moravians at Herrnhut, where his theology came to include emphasis on

---

[56]Summary from Nichols, pp. 85, 88, 89; Jackson, p. 6; Clouse, p. 83.

[57]*The Journal of the Rev. John Wesley*, A. M., Vol. I, ed. Nehemiah Curnock (London: Epworth Press, 1912), p. 475,476. Cited in Clouse, op. cit., p. 83.

[58]Robert D. Preus, *Getting Into the Theology of Concord* (St. Louis: Concordia Publishing House, 1977), p. 87.

[59]Gregory L. Jackson, *Liberalism: Its Cause and Cure—The Poisoning of American Christianity and the Antidote* (Milwaukee: Northwestern Publishing House, 1991), p. 86.

[60]Heinrich Schmid, *The Doctrinal Theology of the Evangelical Lutheran Church* (Philadelphia: Lutheran Publication Society, 1889), pp. 456, 457. Schmid's book is a classic compilation of orthodox Lutheran dogmatics, invaluable for pastors and theologians. Formerly published by Augsburg Publishing House, Minneapolis.

"born again" experiences, "accepting the Lord as my personal Savior," and other outward signs as proof of faith and salvation. He also taught a striving for a second blessing of the Holy Spirit, a "higher" form of Christianity that is, in one way or another, a standard for most pietists.[61] Wesley's Reformed-pietistic theology later led to the emotional excesses that marked Methodist revivalism in 19th century America and the Neo-Pentecostal movement of today.

Milder Pietism

Lutherans holding to the milder forms of pietism clung more closely to orthodox teachings of the past than did those who held to the intermediate and radical positions. In fact, the milder pietists opposed the extremes of both of these groups.[62] Nevertheless, the Reformed-pietistic influence has had lasting effects on Lutheranism, as the following chapters illustrate.

---

[61]Summary from Nichols, pp. 85, 88, 89; Jackson, p. 6; Clouse, p. 83.
[62]Hagglund, op. cit., p. 333.

Section III

AMERICAN
LUTHERANISM'S
DRIFT INTO
THE NEW THINKING

26.

LUTHERANS IN AMERICA 1634-1874

It is a notable fact that the Reformation was launched only 25 years after Columbus sailed to the American continent. Thus, the door was open into a new country for oppressed people seeking freedom of worship as well as opportunity for material gain. Early in the 17th century Protestants began the colonization of North America with settlements on the Atlantic coast. These early settlers combined their desire for freedom of worship with missionary zeal. Most of the newcomers were Calvinists.[1] Some were Lutherans.

THE EARLIEST IMMIGRANTS

Victor H. Prange, a pastor in the conservative Wisconsin Evangelical Lutheran Synod (WELS) and author of a series of articles concerning the history of Lutherans in America, traces some of the earliest Lutheran immigrants back to a Dutch settlement on the Hudson River:

> The Dutch colony of New Netherlands was founded in 1624. It is likely that some Lutherans were among these early settlers. By 1651 there were about 150 Lutheran "heads of families" in New Netherlands. These Lutherans were not permitted to hold public worship since only Reformed services were allowed. Quite different was the situation on the Delaware River where Swedish colonists established themselves in 1638; nearly all were Lutherans with pastors sent to serve them.

---

[1]*Eerdmans' Handbook to the History of Christianity,* organizing ed. Dr. Tim Dowley; consulting eds. John H. Y. Briggs, Dr. Robert D. Linder, David F. Wright (Grand Rapids: Wm. B. Eerdmans Publishing House, 1977), p. 434.

The greatest concentration of Lutherans was, however, in the colony laid out by William Penn [a Quaker]. The vast majority were Germans. Their most pressing spiritual need was for competent Lutheran pastors. The only source was Germany; but few pastors wanted to leave their homeland for the wilds of America.[2]

These German Lutherans had been settling in Pennsylvania since 1682, with the largest influx of immigrants coming between 1735 and 1745. By the middle of the century they had grown to at least 40,000, with congregations scattered over a wide area. The combined congregational membership consisted of more than 1,500 families. Beginning in 1733 they appealed to the Lutheran court preacher at London and August Francke at the University of Halle for pastors.[3] But it was not until 1741, when Count Nicholaus von Zinzendorf appeared on the scene, that any real results of the negotiations were forthcoming. The late Abdel Ross Wentz, historian of the United Lutheran Church of America (ULCA), predecessor body of the Evangelical Lutheran Church in America (ELCA), reports:

> Negotiations dragged on. But in 1741 Count Nicholas Ludwig von Zinzendorf, the Moravian, appeared in Pennsylvania posing as a Lutheran, holding interdenominational conferences, and assuming leadership among the shepherdless Lutherans of the colony. The Halle authorities were at last stirred to action. They called Henry Melchior Muhlenberg, and hurried him off to Pennsylvania. With his coming, the Lutheran church in America entered a new phase.[4]

HENRY MELCHIOR MUHLENBERG

Henry Melchior Muhlenberg (1711-87), has been called the "Patriarch of the Lutheran Church in America." After completing his theological education, he served for a time as a teacher at Halle, where he absorbed much of the theology of pietism. He arrived in Pennsylvania in 1742 and soon encountered Zinzendorf, known in public as "Mr. von Thurstein," who was still posing as a Lutheran pastor among the Germans. Before long, the two came into conflict. Al-

---

[2]Victor H. Prange, "Lutherans in America—Henry Melchior Muhlenberg," *The Northwestern Lutheran,* June 15, 1987, p. 227.

[3]Abdel Ross Wentz, *A Basic History of Lutheranism in America* (Philadelphia: Fortress Press, 1964), pp. 14-16.

[4]Ibid., p. 16.

though Muhlenberg was himself a Halle pietist, he objected to Zinzendorf's ecumenical efforts and wanted to perpetuate the Lutheran church in the colonies.[5] He also objected to Zinzendorf's intermediate brand of pietism.[6] Muhlenberg was a man of great vision who recognized the unlimited possibilities for the expansion of this new mission field. A well-organized and energetic leader, he soon found the demands on his time so great that he sent to Halle for help. In 1745 men and money arrived for the new work.[7] Thus, it could be stated that "colonial Lutheranism in America was largely evangelized and organized from Halle."[8] As a result, pietism became the dominant influence among Lutherans in North America.[9]

THE PENNSYLVANIA MINISTERIUM

The remainder of Muhlenberg's life was devoted to forwarding the task of planting the Lutheran church in America.

Under his leadership the church continued to grow and flourish, and in 1748 he organized the first permanent Lutheran synod. He observed on this occasion that "a twisted cord of many threads will not easily break. There must be unity among us. We are here assembled for this purpose, and, if God wills, we shall assemble yearly." The synod organized by Muhlenberg united ten congregations and became known as the "Pennsylvania Ministerium."[10]

The Lutheran unity sought by Muhlenberg has never been fully realized. Some of the reasons for this failure will be examined as we trace the development of the larger synodical structures of the Lutheran churches in America.

THE GENERAL SYNOD

After Muhlenberg's death, synods were organized in other states and soon voices were heard in support of uniting these various state

[5]Otto Heick, *The History of Christian Thought*, 2 vols. (Philadelphia: Fortress Press, 1966), 1:32.

[6]Lewis W. Spitz, *Our Church and Others* (St. Louis: Concordia Publishing House, 1960), p. 108.

[7]Robert G. Clouse, *The Church in the Age of Orthodoxy and the Enlightenment* (St. Louis: Concordia Publishing House, 1980), p. 104.

[8]James Hastings Nichols, *History of Christianity 1650-1950: Secularization of the West* (New York: The Ronald Press Co., 1956), p. 84.

[9]*The Lutherans in North America*, ed. E. Clifford Nelson (Philadelphia: Fortress Press, 1975), pp. 63, 64.

[10]Prange, "Lutherans in America—Henry Melchior Muhlenberg," *The Northwestern Lutheran*, June 15, 1987, p. 227.

synods into a general synod. Thus, in 1820 the "Evangelical Lutheran General Synod of the United States" was formed. However, it failed to unite all Lutherans into one body.[11] Prange explains:

> Not everyone was pleased with this new General Synod. Tennessee did not join because the constitution failed to include a firm Lutheran confessional position. On the other hand Pennsylvania soon quit because of a desire among many congregations for closer union with the nearby German Reformed rather than distant Lutherans.
>
> The lack of a firm Lutheran confessional basis for the General Synod may be traced to Muhlenberg's influence. He had absorbed much of the pietistic theology of Halle which put personal religious experience above unyielding commitment to the Lutheran Confessions. Many saw little difference between Lutheran and Reformed teachings. In 1817 a hymnal for use by both Lutheran and Reformed churches was published. A joint Lutheran-Reformed seminary was proposed.[12]

The lack of a firm Lutheran confessional basis for the General Synod may also be attributed to another group of Lutheran pietists. Lutheran pietism came to America in two stages. The first, as previously noted, came directly from the international center of pietism at Halle to colonial America with Muhlenberg. The second stage arrived when the Scandinavians fled the state church for America and freedom of religion. These immigrants had been introduced to pietism by Moravian missionaries sent to Sweden by Zinzendorf in the 1730s.[13] Concerning this group of Lutherans in America, WELS pastor Dr. Gregory L. Jackson writes:

> The second stage of Lutheran Pietism came to America in the 19th century, when Swedes, Finns, Norwegians, and Danes escaped the secularized horrors of the state church to enjoy freedom of religion in a new land. Many of these Lutherans were united by the Pietistic movement of the 19th century. The Swedes, for instance, found the problem of alcoholism in their native land a major scandal. Influenced by the Methodist George Scott, they formed conventicles to

---

[11]Ibid.

[12]Ibid.

[13]Gregory L. Jackson, *The Impact of Alvin Daniel Mattson Upon the Social Consciousness of the Augustana Synod,* doctoral dissertation, Department of Theology, Notre Dame, Indiana, May 1982, p. 1.

cultivate personal piety and avoid the temptations of the world. They founded a temperance society to deal with alcoholism and mission societies to spread the Gospel. The other Scandinavians had similar experiences.[14]

The Reformed-pietistic influence continued and it wasn't too long before the General Synod began to decline. Prange points out reasons for the decline:

In 1853 the Pennsylvania Ministerium rejoined the General Synod and by 1860 fully two-thirds of Lutheran congregations in America were part of this body. But this was to be the high point in the General Synod's history. In 1867 a new organization of synods was formed named the General Council which reduced the General Synod to half its former size.

There are several reasons for the decline of the General Synod and the founding of the General Council. First was the publication in 1855 by Gettysburg seminary president Schmucker of a revised "americanized" version of the Augsburg Confession. Among other things Schmucker rejected the real presence of the body and blood of Christ in the Lord's Supper. Although repudiated by the majority of General Synod members, Schmucker continued to head the seminary till 1864.

The action which finally split the General Synod was the admittance into membership of the Frankean Synod, a body which did not include adherence to the Augsburg Confession as part of its constitution.[15]

The Reformed influence in the General Synod can be further illustrated with an excerpt from a formal letter sent by the General Synod to the Prussian Union Church in Germany:

In most of our church principles we stand on common ground with the Union Church of Germany. The distinctive doctrines which separate the Lutheran and the Reformed Churches we do not consider essential. The tendency of the so-called Lutheran part seems to us to be behind the time. Luther's peculiar views concerning the presence of the

---

[14]Gregory L. Jackson, "Pietism in America," unpublished paper, May 1990, pp. 1,2. See also: *The Lutherans in North America,* ed. E. Clifford Nelson (Philadelphia: Fortress Press, 1975), p. 121.

[15]Victor H. Prange, "Lutherans in America—The General Council," *The Northwestern Lutheran,* September 1, 1987, p. 292.

Lord's Body in the Communion have long been abandoned by the majority of our ministers.[16]

The Prussian Union Church of Germany was itself a Lutheran-Reformed union whose history and importance to Lutherans in America will be pointed out later. But first we must note the formation of the General Council.

THE GENERAL COUNCIL

The General Council was organized in 1867 in response to a call issued by the Pennsylvania Ministerium, which had become supportive of a firm confessional Lutheran position. They wanted to unite all Lutheran synods that confessed the Unaltered Augsburg Confession.[17] However, the General Council soon became known for its ability to say nothing when questions arose regarding doctrine and practice. Some synods declined membership in the General Council and others dropped out citing unsatisfactory answers to four questions concerning: (1) the position of the General Council on the lodge, (2) the thousand-year reign of Christ on earth (millennialism), (3) whether non-Lutherans were permitted to commune at Lutheran altars, and (4) whether non-Lutheran pastors were permitted to preach in Lutheran pulpits.[18] These issues became known as the *Four Points*. Those who protested the General Council's failure to provide clear answers to these four points did so in support of confessional Lutheranism. To this day, these issues remain open questions in some segments of the Lutheran church and, therefore, require a brief explanation.

Lodge membership

Lodges are secret societies generally listed under the heading of religious cults. Dr. Lewis W. Spitz, a professor emeritus of systematic theology in the Lutheran Church—Missouri Synod (LCMS), offers the following explanation:

> Most lodges have a religious ritual and therefore come under the heading of religious cults. But inasmuch as their religion is not the Christian religion, they must be treated under the

[16]S. E. Ochsenford, *Documentary History of the General Council of the Evangelical Lutheran Church in North America* (Philadelphia: General Council Publication House, 1912), p. 63. Cited in: Kurt Marquart, *Anatomy of an Explosion* (Grand Rapids: Baker Book House, 1978), p. 22.

[17]Prange, "Lutherans in America—The General Council," *The Northwestern Lutheran*, September 1, 1987, p. 292.

[18]Victor H. Prange, "Lutherans in America—The Synodical Conference," *The Northwestern Lutheran*, October 15, 1987, p. 349.

heading of non-Christian cults. The order of Freemasons, established in England in 1717, is the oldest lodge in America. Many other lodges have in some ways copied the principles and the practices of the Freemasons.

Like the other cults . . . , the lodges may place a Bible on their altar, or table. Their meetings may be opened with the reading of some portion of the Bible. Bible verses may decorate the walls of their temple or hall. Their ritual contains texts from the Scriptures. The name of Jesus and of the Holy Trinity may be used in their religious exercises and statements. On certain occasions the members of the lodge may march to a church as a body and listen to a Christian sermon. But none of these Christian symbols and practices makes a lodge a Christian society.[19]

In fact, lodgery is in conflict with basic doctrines of the Christian faith. In the booklet *How to Respond to the Lodge,*[20] we find a review of some of the major doctrinal differences between lodges and historic Christian faith. The comparison illustrates why conscientious Christians cannot maintain membership in both their church and a non-Christian lodge. The following quotation from a periodical of the Masonic Lodge is a simple summary of the basic teaching of the lodge:

We have but one dogma, a belief in God, but this is so firmly established as the principal foundation-stone of the brotherhood that no one can ever be admitted a member of an English-speaking lodge without a full and free acceptance thereof. In all reference to the Deity, God is reverently spoken of as the Great Architect of the Universe. . . . Upon this foundation-stone we construct a simple religious faith—the Fatherhood of God, the Brotherhood of man, and the Immortality of the Soul—simple, but all-efficient. By reason of this simple creed, Freemasonry has been able to attract and accept as members of the Fraternity adherents of every religious faith in the world—Christians, Jews, Hindoos, Mohammendans, Pharisees, Buddhists, and others—atheists alone being excluded.[21]

---

[19]Spitz, op. cit., pp. 133, 134.

[20]L. James Rongstad, *How to Respond to the Lodge,* Concordia Publishing House, is one of a series of booklets comparing the teachings of cults with the Christian faith. We recommend them as an excellent and inexpensive resource for our readers.

[21]"Freemasonry—A Simple Religious Faith," *Royal Arch Mason,* Vol. V, No. 9, March 1987. Cited in: L. James Rongstad, *How to Respond to the Lodge* (St. Louis: Concordia Publishing House, 1977), p. 24.

Fundamental to the "simple, but all-efficient *religious* faith" of the lodge is its teaching concerning God:

> The first and most glaring contradiction between the lodge and Christianity centers on God. Although the lodge demands belief in a "Supreme Being," and although it uses the terms "god," "Lord," "The All-Seeing Eye," etc., and although they form a theology about their "god" as to what he does, the lodge very carefully refuses to confess the God of the Scriptures. A definition of the Person of God is avoided. There is no identification of the Father, Son, and Holy Spirit in the lodge, nor any phrase which would identify God as the Trinity. The lodge simply by omission denies the revealed God of the Bible. This offends the Christian—or it should! The Christian is taught from the Bible that there is no salvation, no god other than the Lord of Lords, the Holy Trinity, and that to be saved it is essential to believe and confess this God.[22]

The lodge not only fails to acknowledge the Trinity but, again by omission, denies Jesus as Redeemer and promotes work-righteousness. This is illustrated in the following description of the lodge-teaching concerning man and the immortality of the soul:

> Masonry teaches that man has a "rough and imperfect nature," but this is as close as they come to saying that man is originally sinful. The reason, most probably, is that if Masonry teaches the Scriptural truth of man's sinful nature, then they would also have to teach salvation by some means. The lodge would then have to deal with Jesus, the Redeemer. Rather, the lodge simply accepts the idea of salvation as something which will happen to all who live a morally upright life. It makes no attempt to identifying what is rejection of God's truth. It does say that good works are necessary for admission into the "Grand Lodge above." And it does so without any reference to Jesus, His death and resurrection, man's repentance, God's grace, and the like.

> Immortality is a lodge-teaching which had been adopted from Christianity. But that is all that has been adopted—the simple teaching of immortality. The lodge has eliminated the truth that eternal life in heaven is purely a gift of

---

[22]Ibid., p. 23.

God, that Jesus by His death and resurrection has reconciled sinful man to God, that the Holy Spirit brings men to believe and have faith in Christ as their personal Savior from all sin. Or to say it differently, the lodge is immortality, with or without Christ.[23]

In addition, the lodge denies the authority and inerrancy of Scripture. While the Bible may be displayed in the lodge and passages of Scripture used in their rituals, it is only one of many "sacred" volumes used. The religion of the majority of the members determines which "sacred volume" will be used:

Lodgery does not accept the Holy Bible as the only inspired, infallible, inerrant Word of God. It cannot. This would be unacceptable to all lodge members who were not Christian.[24]

There are other doctrinal concerns with the lodge, but these few examples are sufficient for our purpose. As Rongstad notes:

It can be summed up by saying that Masonry teaches man that he is not originally sinful, just imperfect; that if he works faithfully at keeping the principles of Freemasonry he will be welcomed into the Grand Lodge Above where the Supreme Grand Master presides. This is universalism, deism, and humanism. This denies the necessity of having a Savior. . . . Therefore, we conclude the lodge is a religion—a Christless religion—and thus a cult, a cult totally incompatible with Christianity and to be avoided by every Christian.[25]

Millennialism

Millennialism, also called chiliasm, is a word derived from Latin that means 1,000 years. Millennialists believe that there will be a thousand-year golden age, or utopia, here on earth either immediately before or after the second coming of Christ. Spitz explains:

Millennialists may be divided into postmillennialists and premillennialists. Postmillennialists hold that before Jesus returns to judge the world the church will experience a thousand years of prosperity. When these thousand years are up Jesus will come. . . . Premillennialists believe that Jesus will come to establish and rule personally in his kingdom here on

---

[23]Ibid., pp. 24, 25.
[24]Ibid., p. 25.
[25]Ibid., p. 12, 24.

earth for a thousand years and that at the end of the thousand years he will judge the world. This is the generally accepted view of the millennium. Some premillennialists are dispensationalists, who divide the history of the world into seven periods, or dispensations. Five of these, they say, have passed. We are now nearing the close of the sixth. The seventh will be the world's great "Sabbath."[26]

The idea of a millennium is not new. Ever since man's fall into sin he has yearned for a return of paradise. The Jews looked for a restoration of the kingdom of David, the golden age of Israel's history. Before Pentecost, even the disciples and followers of Jesus entertained ideas of an earthly kingdom. Elements of the Jewish hope for a millennium were carried over into the early church, with a number of theologians explicitly chiliastic. However, by the end of the fourth century most forms of millennialism had been rejected by the church as unbiblical.[27]

Not until the last 150 years or so has millennialism enjoyed a strong revival. It is a revival that crosses denominational lines and has been influenced by many factors. Dr. Herbert J. A. Bouman, a professor emeritus of systematic theology in the LCMS, writes:

> Within the last 150 years or so there has been a strong revival of chiliastic hopes and teaching. A number of factors have contributed to this resurgence. As private Bible-study and interpretation was encouraged, many of the Christian laity discovered the wealth of poetic and highly figurative sections in the writings of some of the Old Testament prophets, such as Isaiah, Ezekiel, Daniel, and others, and in the New Testament book of Revelation, and took them quite literally. Furthermore, recent eras of church history have witnessed the rise of science and interest in this world and material things, with a corresponding drop in concern for the things of the world to come. Many looked upon this universe as closed and self-sufficient, and regarded the Bible's message concerning the end of this world and its final judgment by a returning Christ with increasing skepticism. The kingdom of God, the golden age, they said, was not something to look forward to, but was being realized here and now in a general betterment of the human condition. In reaction to

---

[26]Spitz, op. cit., p. 152.

[27]Herbert J. A. Bouman, *A Look at Today's Churches: A Comparative Guide* (St. Louis, Concordia Publishing House, 1980), pp. 59, 60.

this deemphasis of eschatology [teaching concerning the "last things"] many conservative Christians began to give special emphasis to this area of the faith and even placed it into the center of their message. Major catastrophes in our century, particularly the two World Wars and the tensions between the free world and the nations under dictatorships, have heightened concern for an ultimate deliverance. Last but not least, the establishment of the state of Israel in the ancestral land of Palestine has contributed greatly to a renewed interest in what Biblical prophecy might be saying about the future of Israel.

Generally millennialism is not confined to specific denominations but often spreads to a greater or lesser degree across a number of denominational lines, being prominent in many Holiness and Pentecostal churches as well as in Baptist and fundamentalist-literalist traditions.[28]

The resurgence of interest in millennialism rode in with pietism. Spener and his followers held with a subtle form of chiliasm. Concerning this, the late Dr. Otto W. Heick, a professor of systematic theology in the Lutheran Church in America (LCA), reports:

Two peculiar doctrinal tenets of pietism should be mentioned in passing. Spener and his followers looked favorably upon a kind of subtle chiliasm. They expected a more glorious revelation of God in the future through the power of his Spirit. Johann Albrecht Bengel [a milder pietist] spent much time and effort to unlock the mystery of the Book of Revelation. He toyed with the idea of a restoration of all."[29]

Millennialism was introduced to the Lutheran Church toward the end of the 17th century by Spener and his followers. Others were also influenced by this teaching, especially a small Reformed church body, the Plymouth Brethren, which was led by John Nelson Darby (1800-82). This group came to America in about the middle of the 19th century, and Darby and his coworkers became the forerunners of modern premillennialism.[30]

Historically, most of the Christian world has rejected millennialism as unbiblical. Bouman writes:

---

[28]Ibid., pp. 60, 61.

[29]Heick, op. cit., 1:25.

[30]*Lutheran Cyclopedia,* ed. Erwin L. Lueker (St. Louis: Concordia Publishing House, 1975), pp. 109, 540.

Historically, the majority of Christians have rejected chiliasm because they could find no basis for its teachings in the Bible. They believed that the prophecies about the splendor of Christ's kingdom must be interpreted spiritually as references to the glory of the New Testament church. Specifically, these Christians believe that the Bible speaks of only one visible return of Christ to this earth, namely on the Last Day for the final judgment. They find no support in Scripture for a distinction between God's kingdom and Christ's kingdom. Nor do they see any Scriptural proof for the claim that the Jewish nation as such (all descendants of Abraham "after the flesh") will be converted *en masse*. Finally, those opposed to millennial teachings believe that emphasis on a millennial kingdom of earthly blessings and glories turns the Christian's hope away from eternal life in heaven to some earthly paradise (author's emphasis).[31]

Those who reject all forms of millennialism are called Amillennialists. Amillennialism is the position of the historic Lutheran faith. This is clear in the following quotation in which the late Dr. John Theodore Mueller, a noted conservative scholar and professor in the LCMS, cites the Augsburg Confession in his summary of the errors of millennialistic teaching:

The Lutheran Augsburg Confession rejects the entire millennialistic scheme as a system of "Jewish opinions" (Art. XVII). Christ's eschatological teachings (cf. Matt., Ch. 24) leave no room for any millennialistic or dispensational hope, nor do any of the great Christian creeds profess chiliasm. It is a product of rationalizing enthusiasm which perverts Scripture and draws the minds of men away from the doctrines of sin and grace, justification and sanctification, which must ever be stressed, as the Christian is directed in Scripture to the inheritance in heaven and not to any millennial reign of Christ on earth (Phil. 3:20,21).[32]

Altar and pulpit fellowship

On the occasion of the formation of the first Lutheran synod, Muhlenberg correctly noted the importance of unity and fellowship among Christians. The word synod means walking together. Synods are or-

---

[31]Bouman, op. cit., p. 62.

[32]John Theodore Mueller, *My Church and Others* (St. Louis: Rudolph Volkening, 1968), p. 79.

ganized for the purpose of fellowship, namely, the outward expression of unity in faith and doctrine. When altar and pulpit fellowship, which involve joint worship services including holy communion, are practiced without unity in faith and doctrine, participants are guilty of *unionism.* The errors and dangers of unionism are pointed out in the following quotation:

> Unionism, which asks the various denominations to form a union, or at least to maintain church-fellowship among themselves, despite their disagreement in doctrine—that allegedly being a matter of indifference—is a gross violation of the divine command. Furthermore, it does not serve the cause of unity, but perpetuates division, since it demands toleration of the original cause of division, false doctrine. It sins, further, against charity; instead of warning the errorist and the erring Christians, it palliates [conceals] error. It is immoral; it pretends a unity that does not exist and operates with dishonest, ambiguous formulas of union. Finally, it involves a denial of the truth, since he who consciously compromises with errors, compromises and betrays the corresponding truth, Matt. 12:30, and since it springs from indifference and fosters indifference, it tends to bring on the loss of the entire truth (*Popular Symbolics, p. 106*).[33]

The dangers of "open questions"

Leaving important doctrinal matters as "open questions" is the same as saying that the doctrines in question are really not so important after all. However, orthodox Lutheranism holds that *every point of doctrine* is important. Martin Luther stated this clearly when he warned against tolerating even a little false doctrine:

> Doctrine is our only light. It alone enlightens and directs us and shows the way to heaven. If it is shaken in one quarter (*in una parte*), it will necessarily be shaken in its entirety (*in totum*). Where that happens, love cannot help us at all.[34]

Once false doctrine is allowed to slip in through the back door and then tolerated, it quickly becomes entrenched and almost impossible

---

[33]Edward W. A. Koehler, *A Summary of Christian Doctrine* (St. Louis: Concordia Publishing House, 1971), p. 249.

[34]*What Luther Says,* 3 vols., ed. Ewald M. Plass (St. Louis: Concordia Publishing House, 1959), 1:414.

to remove. It weakens and changes the church from within. Sooner or later, it leads to doctrinal compromise, disunity, division, and more false doctrine—all of which will be observed ahead as we continue our examination of the development of Lutheranism in America.

The failure of the General Council to resolve the doctrinal issues raised by the Four Points led the synods in support of confessional Lutheranism to unite and form the Synodical Conference. The formation of the Synodical Conference and the doctrinal controversy that developed within it will be described ahead. But first, because confessional Lutheranism had such an important influence on the later growth of Lutherans in America, it will be helpful to define the term "confessional Lutheranism" and examine its roots and historical development in America.

CONFESSIONAL LUTHERANISM

Confessional Lutheranism is simply a term used to denote the body of believers which holds to the Lutheran Confessions, set down in the *Book of Concord,* as a correct interpretation of the Bible (see Chapter 21). Confessional Lutherans, sometimes referred to as "orthodoxists," remain faithful to the *entire* Lutheran Confessions in *everything* they believe, teach, and confess—both in doctrine and practice.

Orthodoxists and Pietists

The majority of the earliest Lutherans in America were pietists. However, there were some orthodox Lutherans among them who followed the Lutheran Confessions in the strict sense just described. Both the pietists and orthodox Lutherans desired to preserve their Lutheran faith and identity in the new land. Both groups, in formal statements, insisted that all Lutherans should subscribe to the Lutheran faith as set down in the Confessions. However, there were variations between these two groups regarding actual conformity to their formal statements. This is pointed out in *The Lutherans in North America,* a history book edited by Dr. E. Clifford Nelson, professor emeritus of St. Olaf College, American Lutheran Church (ALC), now part of the ELCA.

> *Orthodoxist and Pietists Types of Lutherans.* . . . Insofar as formal statements are concerned . . . all the Lutheran churches and all acknowledged Lutheran ministers subscribed to the Lutheran faith and the official standards [the Lutheran Confessions] which were the historical witnesses to it.
>
> Actually there were some variations within this general conformity. Lutherans in North America inherited from Europe

some tensions between strict and loose interpreters of the confessions. The former were usually called orthodoxists because they were representatives of the tendency to stress correct doctrine which was dominant in the seventeenth century. The latter were usually called pietists because they were representatives of a reaction which emphasized Christian life and piety rather than Christian doctrine and belief and which was dominant in the eighteenth century. Philip Jakob Spener (1635-1705) and August Hermann Francke (1663-1727) were the early leaders of pietism in Germany, and from there the movement spread into the Scandinavian countries. It had the warm support of some rulers and members of the nobility, but it was sternly opposed by others, especially in areas bordering on the North Sea. When pietists met for the cultivation of holiness in assemblies (*collegia pietatis*) outside of churches, these meetings were often suppressed by civil authorities as dangerous conventicles. Pietists did not gain friends among their critics when they denounced the theater, dancing, and other "worldly pleasures." On the other hand orthodoxists were charged with making the Christian faith a matter of knowledge rather than experience and with substituting intellectual assent for heartfelt trust (author's emphasis).

There were echoes of this conflict in North America. Some of the Lutheran colonists came to America with orthodoxist convictions while others came with pietist inclinations. Significantly it was the pietist circles in Europe that responded most quickly and generously to appeals for help from America . . . all were critics of orthodoxism and representatives of pietist emphasis. . . . Men who came to America on their own initiative and became clergymen in America were sometimes pietists . . . and sometimes orthodoxists . . . but the dominant influence among Lutherans in North America was pietistic. The impulse that went out from the Franckean institutions in Halle, Saxony, was especially great both in terms of the number of ministers sent abroad and in terms of the shaping of a style of life.[35]

Further evidence of the conflict between the pietists and orthodox or "confessional" Lutherans can be observed when Muhlenberg and

---

[35]*The Lutherans in North America,* pp. 62-64.

his associates did not invite the confessional Lutherans to the first sessions of the Pennsylvania Ministerium in 1748.[36]

Pietism continued to be the dominant influence among Lutherans in America until almost the middle of the 19th century, when a large number of confessional Lutheran pastors and lay people fled Europe and came to America to escape the doctrinal laxity and the persecution of the previously mentioned *Prussian Union.*

The Prussian Union

As a result of the combined effects of pietism and the onslaughts of the rationalistic Enlightenment (see Chapter 3), people left their churches *en masse.*[37] Religious turmoil along with political upheaval set the stage for the Prussian Union. Kurt E. Marquart, a conservative theologian and seminary professor in the LCMS, describes this significant event in the life of the Lutheran Church:

> The Lutheran territorial churches of Europe have never recovered from the devastation of those years. The dead hand of rationalistic unbelief ruled the theological faculties of the state universities where the clergy were trained, and through them the parishes and church administrations.
>
> Religious turmoil was accompanied and followed by the political upheavals associated with the rise and fall of Napoleon. These crises had their chastening effects. A humbled Prussian king, Frederick William III (1797-1840), ruler of the largest and most powerful of the German states, set about to renew and restore a crumbling Christendom. To this end he deemed it essential to unite the two Protestant churches in his realm, the Lutheran, to which most of the population belonged, and his own Reformed or Calvinistic church, comprising a small minority. Only by combining the spiritual resources of both churches into one united front against unbelief, so it was thought, could the Christian cause be preserved.
>
> Accordingly, the king had already in 1808 merged the Lutheran and Reformed church administrations into one single government department. After 1817 the Minister for Spiritual Affairs was, oddly enough, the unbeliever Baron

---

[36]Ibid., p. 64.

[37]Kurt E. Marquart, *Anatomy of an Explosion* (Grand Rapids: Baker Book House, 1978), p. 19.

von Altenstein, at whose dinner table the subject was sometimes discussed of whether Christianity would endure another twenty or thirty years! For the three-hundredth anniversary of the Reformation (October 31, 1817) the king arranged a combined Lutheran-Reformed communion service in his court chapel; but it was not widely imitated. Then in 1821 the king issued his infamous *Agende,* or liturgy-book, with its compromise form of service. Finally, impatient and irritated by the opposition to his plans, the king simply ordered the introduction of the new union liturgy, including the Reformed custom of breaking the bread, for the three-hundredth anniversary celebration of the Augsburg Confession in 1830.[38]

The king's orders were subsequently enforced and those confessional Lutherans who refused to obey were severely persecuted. Marquart continues:

Distinctively Lutheran services were now simply forbidden and conscientious Lutherans, like Professor Dr. J. G. Scheibel of Breslau, removed from office and persecuted in various incredibly ferocious ways—despite Prussia's claims that it followed an enlightened policy of religion! Noblemen and merchants were fined heavily for allowing Lutheran services on their properties. Lutherans had to meet secretly in forests, cellars, and barns. Judas-money was paid for the betrayal of faithful pastors. Midwives had to report the birth of all Lutheran children. Lutheran baptisms were declared invalid, and babies were sometimes forcibly rebaptized in the official union-church under police compulsion. Faithful pastors were imprisoned. In one village the faithful Lutherans were attacked on Christmas Eve by a military force of five hundred men, who drove the weeping women away from the church with swords and bayonets, forced open the church-doors, and "installed" the union pastor with his union liturgy. The army refused to end the occupation till the protesting parishioners would start attending the union services.[39]

Because of the prevailing indifference to doctrine, many followed the king's edict and worshiped together with the Reformed in the union churches. A minority, however, preferred persecution over de-

---

[38]Ibid., pp. 19, 20.
[39]Ibid., p. 20.

nial of their faith. Some of these faithful confessional Lutherans founded the so-called Breslau Synod of Prussia,[40] remnants of which exist today as German free churches. Of the thousands of others who fled Europe Marquart writes:

> The Confessional Awakening . . . finally led thousands of Lutherans, from many walks of life, to emigrate to the New World, so that they and their children might be free to confess and practice their Biblical, Reformation faith without compromise. This mass migration to Australia and to America laid the foundations of the Lutheran church on the former continent and of the Confessional, Midwestern synods of the latter.
>
> Only after the death of Frederick William III (1840) was the hitherto underground Lutheran church allowed to exist in Prussia as an independent body (1845).[41]

The escapees of the Prussian Union were not alone in their confessional stand. Just before they set sail for America in mid-1839, another group of confessional Lutherans landed in America. Coming into the country largely by way of the Gulf of Mexico and the Mississippi River, they traveled north to Missouri and settled in St. Louis and nearby Perry County in February 1839. These staunchly confessional Lutherans were from Saxony, Germany, where the seminary professors, clergy, and official church had been highly influenced by the prevailing rationalism of the day. In Saxony, as in Prussia, confessional Lutherans rose up in protest and joined with others in the flight to America. Among the six clergymen in this early group of emigrants was the young pastor *Carl Ferdinand Wilhelm Walther.*[42]

C. F. W. Walther

Just as Muhlenberg is referred to as the patriarch of Lutherans in America, Dr. C. F. W. Walther (1811-87) is considered the father of *confessional* Lutheranism in America. An orthodox Lutheran scholar and prolific writer, Walther is regarded by many as one of the finest Lutheran theologians in American history. He was also an outstanding leader. Wentz pays him the following tribute:

> . . . the leadership of the Missouri Lutherans fell to the youthful C. F. W. Walther, one of the six pastors of the first

---

[40]Spitz, op. cit., pp. 102, 103. The Breslau Synod is part of SELK (Selbstandige Evangelisch-Lutherische Kirche).

[41]Marquart, op. cit., p. 21.

[42]Wentz, op. cit., pp. 109, 110.

group of immigrants. From 1839 to his death in 1887 the history of Missouri Lutheranism is closely identified with the story of Walther's life, and he takes his place with Muhlenberg, Schmucker, and Krauth in the quartet of the most outstanding personalities in the history of the Lutheran church in America.[43]

The story of Walther's life is important. This will become clear as we learn of the personal experiences and difficult struggles that led him to discover and deeply appreciate confessional Lutheranism and then staunchly defend it for the remainder of his days. It begins in Saxony in 1811. Of the early years of Walther's life Wentz writes:

> Walther was born in Saxony in 1811 of a long line of ministers. At the University of Leipzig, he belonged to a little band of students who refused to accept the popular rationalism of the day and who cultivated their spiritual lives by studying the Bible and various books of devotion, among them Luther's works, which he read with eagerness. He became pastor at Braeunsdorf, Saxony, in 1837. Here his evangelical position soon involved him in difficulties with his rationalistic superiors. The oath of his office bound him to the Book of Concord, but the entire liturgy, the hymnbook and the catechism that he was compelled to use were rationalistic. So, too, were the textbooks in the schools. His conscience was sorely oppressed by the situation. His efforts to introduce Lutheran doctrine and practice met with determined opposition. The young pastor's position was intolerable. Accordingly he had welcomed most heartily the invitation to help establish an ideal church in America.[44]

Walther's years in America, marked by tireless efforts to establish a strong confessional Lutheran Church, were directly related to his experiences as a student at the University of Leipzig, which had a profound effect on Walther and, subsequently, on confessional Lutheranism in America.

Walther and the small band of students at the University of Leipzig had experienced the emptiness of rationalism. As a result, they had become uncertain of their faith and turned to pietism, avidly reading the classic pietistic writers Arndt, Spener, Francke, Bogatsky,[45]

---

[43]Wentz, op. cit., p. 111.
[44]Ibid.
[45]*The Lutherans in North America*, p. 155.

Fresenius,[46] and others. They became involved in a group, or conventi-cle, at Leipzig under the leadership of an older candidate of theology by the name of Kuhn.[47] It was during one of these gatherings that Walther's conversion took place. In his book *The Proper Distinction Between Law and Gospel,* Walther writes:

> After graduating from college, I entered the university. I was no outspoken unbeliever, for my parents were believers. But I had left my parents home already when I was eight years old, and all my associates were unbelievers; so were all my professors, with the exception of one, in whom there seemed to be a faint trace of faith. When I entered the university I did not know the Ten Commandments by heart and could not recite the list of the books in the Bible. My knowledge of the Bible was pitiful, and I had not an inkling of faith.

> However, I had an older brother, who had entered the university before me. Not long before my arrival he had joined a society of converted people. Upon my arrival he introduced me to this circle of Christian students. I had no premonition of the fate I was approaching, but I had great respect for my brother, who invited me to come with him. At first I was at-tracted merely by the friendly and kind manner in which these students treated me. I was not used to such treatment, for at our college the intercourse of students had been a rather rough affair. I liked the manner of these students ex-ceedingly well. At first, then, it was not the Word of God that attracted me. But I began to like the company of these Christian students so much that I gladly attended even their prayer-meetings—for they conducted such meetings.

> Lo and behold! it was there that God began to work on my soul by means of his Word. In a short time I had really be-come a child of God, a believer, who trusted in His grace. Of course, I was not deeply grounded in Christian knowledge.

[46]C. F. W. Walther, *The Proper Distinction Between Law and Gospel,* repro-duced from the German edition of 1897 by W. H. T. Dau (St. Louis: Concordia Publishing House, 1928), p. 140.

[47]David John Zersen, "C. F. W. Walther and the Heritage of Pietist Conven-ticles" (Chapter III of Dr. Zersen's unpublished Doctor of Ministry Thesis, "The Use of Small Groups in the Mutual Ministry of Christian Priests"), *Con-cordia Theological Institute Quarterly,* Spring 1989, p. 14.

This state of affairs was continued for nearly half a year. Then an old candidate of theology, a genuine Pietist, entered our circle. . . . Now this candidate who came to us said: "You imagine you are converted Christians, don't you? But you are not. You have not yet passed through any real penitential agony."[48]

Having undergone some harrowing spiritual experiences himself, Kuhn believed that anyone who did not undergo similar trials could not truly be converted. He introduced Walther to several books, including one by Fresenius, and Walther soon came to doubt his acceptability before God and his faith in ever-increasing degrees.[49] In later years, after he had turned away from pietism, Walther described many of his negative experiences with pietism in both his lectures and writings. In the following quotation, Walther relates one such experience involving the Reformed error of synergism (see Chapter 24). He writes:

During the first half of the eighteenth century those who were guilty before others of . . . serious confusion of Law and Gospel were the so-called Pietists. . . . These men were guilty of that more refined way of confounding Law and Gospel, namely, of keeping men away from Christ. They did this by making a false distinction between spiritual awakening and conversion; for they declared that, as regards the way of obtaining salvation, all men must be divided into three classes: 1. those still unconverted; 2. those who have been awakened, but are not yet converted; 3. those who have been converted.[50]

Now, it is indeed, true that conversion does not require a day or an hour, but only a moment. For according to the Holy Scriptures it is nothing else than the quickening out of spiritual death unto spiritual life, . . . or the transfer from the kingdom of the devil to the kingdom of Jesus Christ, the Son of God. . . . In other words, a person is either converted or not; there is no intermediary state.[51]

The Pietists claim that faith must be preceded by a long time of penitence; yea, they have warned people not to be-

---

[48]Walther, op. cit., pp. 141, 142.
[49]Zersen, op. cit., pp. 14, 15.
[50]Walther, op. cit., pp. 362, 363.
[51]Walther, op. cit., p. 193.

lieve too soon, telling them that they must allow the Holy
Spirit to work them over thoroughly. A person, they said,
cannot be converted in two weeks; sometimes it takes many
months and years during which God prepares him for conversion. That is an awful doctrine. These preachers do not
consider what a tremendous responsibility they assume
when they warn a person against believing prematurely.
What will become of such a one if he dies before he is ready
to believe? I know the awful effect of this teaching from experience. A Pietistic candidate of theology had instructed
me in the manner which I have described. I did everything
to become truly penitent and finally fell into despair. When
I came to him to tell him my condition, he said: "Now it is
time for you to believe." . . . I said to him: "If you knew my
condition, you would not comfort me. What I want is rules
for my further conduct." He gave me them too; but it was
useless.[52]

The rules Walther mentions above led him and another member of
the conventicle to employ spiritual exercises with such severity that
they suffered both physically and spiritually. Dr. David Zersen, professor at Concordia University Wisconsin (LCMS), writes:

Bunger and C. F. W. Walther employed spiritual exercises
to such a severe degree that they deprived themselves of
nourishment and recreation, considering these things sinful. The eminent philologian and Old Testament critic,
Franz Delitzsch, described Walther's condition at the time
he was forced to leave the university as a result of consump-
tion and asceticism in these words: "During that period of
struggle he was wasted like a skeleton, coughed blood, suffered from insomnia, and experienced the terrors of hell. He
was more dead than alive."[53]

This experience, as well as others, led Walther to realize the dangers of pietism and to reject it completely. During his years in America he not only lectured and wrote against the dangers of pietism, but
also warned against the use of conventicles.[54] His negative experiences with both pietism and conventicles were the impetus behind

---

[52]Walther, op. cit., p. 253.
[53]Zersen, op. cit., p. 15.
[54]Zersen, op. cit., pp. 15, 16.

the writing of his greatest work, *The Proper Distinction Between Law and Gospel.*[55]

Concerning the importance of this book Zersen writes:

> Walther's greatest work, *Law and Gospel,* owes its impetus to his experience in Kuhn's circle. His great emphasis on turning a troubled sinner to the Gospel and its comfort, and not to prescriptions of conduct, became one of the foundation stones for Lutheran preaching in America.[56]

It is important to note that Walther rejected not only pietism but also its counterpart—unionism. Of the faithful confessional Lutherans who rose up in protest against the Prussian Union he later wrote:

> In the year 1818, when this plan [the Prussian Union] was to be executed, *Claus Harms,* in whom there was still some Lutheran blood flowing, wrote ninety-five theses against Rationalism and the union of churches, which he intended as a counterpart to the Ninety-five Theses of Luther. In these theses he said to the advocate church union: You purpose to make the poor handmaid, the Lutheran Church, rich by a marriage. Do not perform the act over Luther's grave. Life will come into his bones, and then—woe to you! This glorious prediction was fulfilled. When the union of churches was actually put into effect in Prussia, multitudes of Lutherans suddenly awoke from their spiritual sleep, remembered that they belonged to the Lutheran Church, and declared that they would never forsake the faith of their fathers. In fact, they chose to see themselves evicted from their homes, imprisoned, and expatriated rather than consent to a union of truth with error, of the Word of God with man's word, of the true Church with a false Church (author's emphasis).[57]

There is a positive factor in Walther's involvement in pietism that must also be mentioned. In addition to introducing Walther to the writings of the classic pietists, Kuhn challenged him to study the Lutheran Confessions. It was through his study of the Confessions

---

[55]*The Proper Distinction Between Law and Gospel* has some excellent passages on pietism, including quotations from Luther, who addressed the same issues. See pietism, p. 142f; feelings, pp. 132, 201, 312; Reformed doctrine, p. 151; trees and fruits, pp. 306, 312.

[56]Zersen, op. cit.

[57]Walther, op. cit., p. 333.

that Walther came to know himself as a Lutheran[58] and to later become a champion of confessional Lutheranism in America.

On the occasion of the commemoration of the 100th anniversary of Walther's death, the following tribute is paid him by Edward Fredrich II, retired pastor and professor emeritus of church history at Wisconsin Lutheran Seminary (WELS):

> Who was this Dr. Carl Ferdinand Wilhelm Walther? He was, in brief, a founder and pillar of his church body, the present Lutheran Church—Missouri Synod. He was at the same time on the larger church scene a tireless champion of his kind of Lutheranism, a Lutheranism that stood firm on Scripture and the Lutheran Confessions. He was also the good neighbor who aided our own church body in its early endeavors more than any other non-member. Walther's death is deserving of century commemoration. His achievements are worthy of a grateful tribute. His cause merits espousal in this present trying hour for Lutheranism in the United States.[59]

The Missouri Synod

The historical roots of the Missouri Synod and its influence on confessional Lutheranism in America is described by Wentz:

> In 1839 there arrived in Missouri a group of Saxon Lutherans imbued with a double portion of the spirit of confessionalism. Their fiery zeal for the whole body of Lutheran doctrine was made even more intense by the ardor of their piety. This union of denominational zeal and religious fervor gave extraordinary power of propagandism, so that the few shiploads of Saxon pilgrims grew into one of the largest of Lutheran bodies, the Missouri Synod, and helped to raise the general standard of confessional loyalty in this country.[60]

The timeliness of their arrival and strategic location also played an important role in Missouri's ability to influence Lutherans in America, both newcomers and those long established in the East. Wentz writes:

---

[58]Zersen, loc. cit.

[59]Edward Fredrich II, "Dr. C. F. W. Walther—American Lutheranism Has Had No Equal," *The Northwestern Lutheran*, May 15, 1987, pp. 187, 188.

[60]Wentz, op. cit., p. 100.

German immigration began to increase about 1840, . . . reaching in 1870 a total of about 400,000, and placing the Lutherans fourth among the Protestant churches.

Fortunately for the church, the advance guard of the army of Lutheran immigrants were stoutly loyal to the Lutheran confessions and able to give reasons for their faith. It was equally fortunate that this advance guard planted its outposts in the heart of the Mississippi Valley where the vast majority of the newcomers were to find their homes. The older Lutheran elements, of the Muhlenberg line, had for the most part solved their problems of rationalism and unionism, had developed their synodical organizations, and were prepared to absorb the new arrivals. But of themselves they would never have met the responsibility imposed by the great immigration. The majority of the incoming multitudes were to belong to an entirely different branch of Lutheranism in America, which was destined to help along the confessional reaction that had already begun within the bodies of Muhlenberg descent.

Of the conservative Lutherans who came to America and found their way into the older congregations and synods of the East, many ignored Wyneken's and Sihler's example [they settled in the midwest] and, remaining where they were, made vigorous contributions to these less conservative bodies. A number of influential Wurttembergers joined the Pennsylvania Ministerium and helped to deepen the current of confessional loyalty. More of the North Germans went into the New York Ministerium, with a similar result. Others, imbued with a lively Lutheran consciousness, came from Germany and took their places in less conspicuous sections of the General Synod.[61]

To the above description of Missouri's influence Jackson adds the following note:

The Missouri Synod, under the leadership of C. F. W. Walther, had a profound impact upon the Pietistic Lutherans. Some of the leaders of the Muhlenberg tradition—such as C. P. Krauth, W. Passavant, T. Schmauk, and the Henkels— led their churches toward a better appreciation for the Lutheran confessions and an awareness of the dangers of

---

[61]Wentz, op. cit., pp. 109, 116.

unionism. The Wisconsin Synod, which started out as a unionistic body, repudiated its past errors and established fellowship with the Missouri Synod.[62]

Just as Muhlenberg recognized that "a twisted cord of many threads will not easily break,"[63] so, too, confessional Lutherans in America sought strength in unity—a unity to be expressed and promoted on the basis of agreement in doctrine and practice. Thus, when the General Council failed to resolve the doctrinal issues raised by the Four Points, confessional Lutherans, under the leadership of Walther, united to form the *Synodical Conference.*

THE SYNODICAL CONFERENCE

Walther is commonly referred to as the father of the Synodical Conference, and his staunchly confessional position was its hallmark from the time of its organization in 1872 until its dissolution in 1966.

The confessional commitment of the six synods that made up the original Synodical Conference was tested soon after the conference was organized when controversy erupted over the doctrine of *election* or *predestination.* Three of the synods "stressed that the individual believer is predestined *unto faith,* solely on the basis of God's grace and the merit of Christ" (what he has done for us). Critics from the remaining synods "insisted that predestination takes place *in view of faith* which God foresees in the individual."[64] The three synods that supported the former view of predestination objected to the latter because it opened the door to the Reformed error of synergism, which teaches "that man is converted and saved partly by his own doing or cooperation."[65] This was the same error that caused Walther to doubt the certainty of his faith while under the influence of pietism (see the Walther quotations).

As a result of this controversy, a split occurred in the Synodical Conference in 1881. Those supporting the synergistic view of the doctrine of election withdrew, and all but a small minority eventually found their way into the larger synodical structures now part of the ELCA. The remaining members, under the leadership of Walther and others, stayed in the conference and continued to further the cause of confessional Lutheranism in America.

[62]Gregory L. Jackson, "Unionism in American Lutheranism," unpublished paper, May 1990, p. 3.

[63]Prange, "Lutherans in America—Henry Melchior Muhlenberg," *The Northwestern Lutheran,* June 15, 1987, p. 227.

[64]Prange, "Lutherans in America—The Synodical Conference," *The Northwestern Lutheran,* October 15, 1987, p. 349.

[65]Marquart, op. cit., p. 34.

THREE CONFESSIONAL POSITIONS

In the middle of the 19th century, Lutherans in America tended to fall into three general categories regarding confessional loyalty—strict interpreters of the Confessions, those who held a more moderate confessional position, and those who had been Americanized.

The most confessional Lutherans possessed the same confessional spirit that characterized Walther and the synods of the Synodical Conference.

The more moderate Lutherans were in agreement with the General Council's decision to leave the Four Points as "open questions" and with those synods that withdrew from the Synodical Conference over the doctrine of election.

The third category was the smaller but very vocal "American Lutherans." The term American Lutherans means "a Lutheranism that has been modified by American Puritanism and American Methodism."[66] Wentz points out some of the characteristics of this group and describes their opposition to the rising tide of confessional Lutheranism in America:

> The rising tide of positive confessional Lutheranism met opposition in some of the older bodies of the Muhlenberg descent. The confessional movement found its antithesis in what was called "American Lutheranism." This was a Lutheranism that was strongly modified by the puritan element of American Christianity and was unable to shake off the denominational indifferentism that had prevailed in the youth of the Republic. Failing to see that the conservative type of Lutheranism would restore to the church something of the ardor and earnestness of Muhlenberg and his colaborers, the "American Lutherans" felt that such a strong infusion of historic Lutheranism would tend to divest the church of spirituality and aggressiveness. They proposed a modification of historic Lutheranism, its confessions and its practices, so as to infuse into it the vigor of Presbyterianism and the warmth of Methodism. In short, they sought to adapt Lutheranism to American soil by divesting it of its distinctive traits and making it conform to the average American type of religion.
>
> The advocates of "American Lutheranism" were a small group, always in the minority both in the district synods and

---

[66]Lars P. Qualben, *A History of the Christian Church* (New York: Thomas Nelson & Sons, 1933, 1958), p. 489 footnote.

in the General synod, but they were exceedingly active and aggressive and their leaders were among the most influential men in the General Synod. They refused to be silenced by the growing strength of conservatives.

One of the leading advocates of "American Lutheranism" was D. S. S. Schmucker, the head of the Gettysburg Seminary [now ELCA]. There were elements in Dr. Schmucker's disposition and training that made it impossible for him to keep ahead of the confessional advance that came in the forties and fifties. In his father's home he had acquired a distinct pietistic strain. Under Dr. Helmuth's [a Lancaster, Pennsylvania pastor educated at Halle] instruction he had imbibed an aversion for sharp theological definitions. . . . [In 1838] he helped to send a circular letter to Germany disparaging the Lutheran view of the Lord's Supper and indicating points of similarity between the General Synod and the Prussian Union [see The General Synod].[67]

The influence of pietism is also evident in the involvement of Schmucker and his associates in the "New Measures." The New Measures were essentially pietistic revival meetings in which specialized techniques were used for bringing individuals through an intense emotional conversion experience. The process reached a climax when the Christians were implored to come forward to the "anxious seat" or the "mourner's bench" and make a commitment to Christ.[68] The whole process was based on Reformed theology, with emphasis placed on adult "born-again" experience rather than the means of grace.[69]

Schmucker and this group were also responsible for the publication of the revised "Americanized" version of the Augsburg Confession—the error that eventually precipitated events causing the split in the General Synod (see the General Synod). In addition, their attitude concerning Reformed doctrine planted the seeds that paved the way for the entrance of the historical-critical method into American Lutheranism.

Nevertheless, despite the efforts of this liberal[70] group of Lutherans to stem the confessional tide brought about by the great wave of German immigration, the church in general continued to move in the direction of a stricter confessional basis.[71]

---

[67]Wentz, op. cit. pp. 131-133.
[68]*The Lutherans in North America,* p. 135.
[69]Jackson, "Unionism in American Lutheranism," p. 3.
[70]Wentz, op. cit., p. 134.
[71]Wentz, op. cit., p. 136.

EARLY BONDS OF UNITY

The movement among Lutherans in America toward increasing loyalty to the Confessions was accompanied by ongoing efforts in the direction of Lutheran unity.

In the early years, as German and Scandinavian emigrants made their way to America, synodical organization was influenced by several factors. Lutheran historians report:

> The influx of so many Lutherans from abroad constituted a gigantic home mission task. Until well into the twentieth century German and Scandinavian immigrants and their offspring were the chief concern of Lutheran home mission effort and the major reservoir upon which the Lutheran churches drew for numerical growth.
>
> The immigration had the effect of establishing and institutionalizing on American soil the Lutheranism of nineteenth-century Europe. Except for those synods in the East . . . whose constituencies still included a number of German-speaking pastors and congregations, the established American synods were linguistically ill-equipped to meet the mission task imposed by the immigration of Germans. For mission work among the Scandinavians they were not at all equipped. The task of churching the immigrants and their offspring, then, fell chiefly to the immigrants themselves. Sharing the common ties of language, heritage, and strangeness in a new land, it was inevitable and necessary that the new Americans organize their own synods and conferences along lines not only of language and nationality but also of theological outlook and religious attitude and custom to which they had adhered in the homeland.
>
> Under the dual pressures of assimilation and self-preservation affecting the immigrants' culture and theology, new church organizations quickly appeared between 1840 and 1875. Almost sixty independent church bodies were organized. . . . [Both] the Scandinavians . . . [and] the Germans gravitated into numerous bodies instead of one general synod. Their theological emphasis and personal tendencies also produced several independent synodical structures.[72]

As the years passed and the various ethnic groups began to blend into the mainstream of American life, language, nationality, and cul-

---

[72]*The Lutherans in North America,* pp. 171, 173, 185.

tural heritage played lesser roles in the struggle for unity. Instead, increased emphasis was placed on doctrinal agreement as a requirement for synodical alignment. Even so, variance in confessional loyalty between Lutherans in America remained, setting the stage for doctrinal controversy, synodical separation, and numerous realignments.[73] Even a short history of the individual synods and the many realignments is beyond the scope of this book.[74] However, the next chapter will briefly examine the formation of some of the larger synodical units and a few realignments.

---

[73]Ibid., pp. 214, 215.

[74]*The Lutherans in North America,* pp. 147-278, provides a detailed account of the formation of the early synodical bodies and their many alignments and realignments.

27.

UNITY AND REALIGNMENT
1875 - 1988

UNITY AND REALIGNMENT 1875 - 1930

In 1875, ten years after the Civil War, the majority of the almost
60 independent synods formed since 1840 belonged to the three major federations described in the preceding chapter: the General Synod, General Council, and Synodical Conference. Regarding doctrine
and practice, these bodies represented the three degrees of confessional loyalty among Lutherans in America. The General Synod
tended to be the most liberal, the General Council more moderate,
and the Synodical Conference solidly confessional. It is important to
note that in American Lutheranism, as well as in other areas of the
Christian church, those holding the moderate view tend to move into
the more liberal position through doctrinal compromise and merger.
This will be observed as we note the major mergers among Lutheran
bodies in America.

At this point, the reader may find it helpful to re-read Chapters 3
and 4, particularly the material and quotations from ELCA historian
Todd Nichol in Chapter 3. Occasional references will be made here
concerning specific issues.

ULCA MERGER—1918

World War I marked the beginning of the development of larger
Lutheran units. One of the most significant events was the organization in 1918 of the United Lutheran Church in America (ULCA). It
was formed by the merger of the General Synod, General Council, and
United Synod South. The last group had come into existence in 1863

when five regional synods of the South withdrew from the General Synod as a result of the Civil War. The ULCA was an organic union of 43 synods that united Muhlenberg Lutheranism.[1] An organic union is one in which merging synods give up their individual synodical identities and become a new body legally bound together by a constitution and bylaws, as opposed to a federation in which each synod maintains its individual identity. The General Synod, General Council, United Synod South, and Synodical Conference were all federations.

The ULCA not only united the Muhlenberg line, it also drew together bodies representing the three categories of confessionalism.[2] The road to union began in the late 1870s when friendly contacts between the three bodies increased. This was soon followed by theological discussions, joint conferences, and cooperative efforts in developing liturgical reform, a common hymnal, and a standard version of the Small Catechism. Later cooperative efforts extended to include practical work in their foreign-mission agencies.[3]

While there was a general return to an appreciation of the Confessions by all three bodies during this period, some questions concerning doctrinal standards remained—those that led to the General Synod split in 1867. There was some concern within the General Council and United Synod South that the General Synod still suffered from the doctrinal heritage of Schmucker and his "American Lutheranism." They wanted the General Synod to modify its 1886 statement, which spoke of the Word of God as *contained* in the Holy Scriptures, and to recognize the entire *Book of Concord* as basic to sound Lutheranism.[4] The General Synod eventually complied but not without protest: "In deference to the General Council and as evidence of a desire for greater unity, but with protestations of the adequacy of its traditional formulations, the General Synod in its conventions of 1909, 1911, and 1913 complied with all of the council's requests."[5] The General Synod affirmed the Bible to be the Word of God and pledged itself to the unaltered Augsburg Confession and *acknowledged* the other confessional writings of the *Book of Concord* in its constitution.[6]

---

[1]Abdel Ross Wentz, *A Basic History of Lutheranism in America* (Philadelphia: Fortress Press, 1964), pp. 293, 142.

[2]*The Lutherans in North America,* ed. E. Clifford Nelson (Philadelphia: Fortress Press, 1975), pp. 305-310.

[3]Wentz, op. cit., pp. 269-271.

[4]*The Lutherans in North America,* op. cit., pp. 374, 375.

[5]Ibid.

[6]Ibid.

The historic freedom of the General Synod concerning communion practices and membership in secret societies and the General Council's stricter stand on these issues, in contrast up to the moment of merger, were never resolved. Concerning these issues Lutheran historians report:

> Other differences between these two bodies remained to the moment of merger but seemed to cause no great difficulties. The General Council's official position barred non-Lutherans from communing or preaching in Lutheran services except in the most unusual circumstances; it officially disapproved of membership by pastors and laymen in secret societies with religious ceremonies; it discouraged participation in general Protestant cooperative ventures. The General Synod allowed freedom to the individual conscience on intercommunion and membership in secret societies, and was more ready to consult and cooperate with non-Lutherans. But the General Council, assured of the General Synod's growing appreciation for the standards of historic Lutheranism did not insist that the synod's position had to be identical with the Council's on these questions. On most counts, the position of the United Synod South was close to that of the General Council.[7]

> No reference was made in the constitution [of the ULCA] to the potentially troublesome matter of secret societies or relationships with non-Lutherans. An invitation in the constitution's preamble for all Lutheran synods in America to unite with the new church on this basis was regarded by its framers as a great contribution to further unity but by the more conservative synods as an arrogant affront.[8]

The merger of the ULCA illustrates doctrinal compromise for the sake of unity and the blending of groups with different degrees of confessional loyalty into one organic body. The ULCA merger efforts were started by conservatives who, as the previous quotation indicates, believed their confessional position would prevail and become dominant once the merger took place. Unfortunately, such was not the case. The ULCA continued to move into a more liberal position and later invited three smaller, like-minded synods to merge into the Lutheran Church in America (LCA) in 1962.

---

[7]Ibid.
[8]Ibid., p. 376.

The mergers that followed the organization of the ULCA were helped along by events of the "roaring 20s." The 1920s were devoted to intense doctrinal discussion. Conferences were held, differences were resolved, and additional organizational unions took place. By 1930 the majority of Lutherans in America were divided into three distinct camps: The *ULCA,* the *American Lutheran Conference,* and the *Synodical Conference.*[9] These three bodies were, once again, representative of the three confessional positions among Lutherans in America.

The organization of the ULCA and its theological heritage has already been described. The constituting membership and theological roots of the latter two groups, both federations, will be identified by their common language backgrounds—the names of the smaller church bodies were often similar and, in many instances, were thus changed several times as realignments occurred. With a few exceptions, the names of the individual synods that united to form some of these larger church bodies will not be used. Readers interested in more detailed study will find ample resources in the footnotes.

THE AMERICAN LUTHERAN
CONFERENCE—1930

The American Lutheran Conference brought together church bodies of various language backgrounds, including Norwegian, Swedish, Danish, and German. The Norwegians were represented by the Evangelical Lutheran Church and the Lutheran Free Church, the Swedish by the Augustana Synod, the Danish by the United Evangelical Lutheran Church, and the Germans by the newly formed American Lutheran Church (ALC). At the time of its organization in 1930, the ALC had a combined membership of 1,334,000, second only in size to the ULCA's 1,520,000 members.[10] The American Lutheran Conference represented the moderate confessional position.

The Norwegian Lutherans

The Norwegian immigrants came to America for better living conditions and a free and independent lifestyle rather than for religious reasons. Their spiritual condition reflected the theological climate of their homeland. During the years of immigration there was a wide range of religious views in Norway, including confessionalism, state-church loyalty, indifference, and elements of rationalism, pietism, and anti-clericalism.[11]

---

[9]Victor H. Prange, "Lutherans in America — The Decade of the 20s," *The Northwestern Lutheran,* December 1987, p. 406.
[10]Ibid.
[11]Wentz, op. cit., pp. 116, 117.

Therefore, from the beginning of their history in America (about 1850), there were disagreements among Norwegian Lutherans over questions of doctrine and church practice. By 1887 they were divided into six synods or groups.[12] Doctrinally, these synods represented the heritage of both European pietism and German orthodoxy, as well as the three degrees of confessional loyalty.

Two groups were the most pietistic, insisting on definite marks of Christian experience and positive proof of conversion, as well as an emphasis on lay leadership in the church.[13] One of these two groups, the Hauge Synod, became part of the large Norwegian merger of 1917, while the Eielsen Synod remains as a tiny independent group into the present day.

The largest of the six groups, the Norwegian Synod, stood for a strict interpretation of Lutheran doctrine. Concerning this confessional group of Lutherans the late Abdel Ross Wentz, historian of the ULCA, reports:

> Formed in 1851 and reorganized in 1853, it was sponsored by a group of men whose names became highly respected among all Norwegians . . . . These men [with one exception] . . . came from the upper classes in Norway, were trained in the university, and were ordained by the state church. In America they stood for a strict interpretation of doctrine and adherence to the ritual and church practices of Norway so far as frontier conditions permitted. . . . They co-operated with the Missouri Synod in the support of the seminary in St. Louis and sent their theological students to Missouri for their training [later they established their own schools for this purpose]. In 1872 the Norwegian Synod joined with the Germans of the Missouri and Wisconsin Synods in forming the Synodical Conference.[14]

As Wentz points out, the Norwegian Synod was an original member of the Synodical Conference. Unfortunately, as noted in the preceding chapter, the Election Controversy caused the synod to withdraw in an effort to preserve its own unity. As a result of the controversy, a split occurred in the Norwegian Synod when one-third of the membership left and formed the Anti-Missourian Brotherhood.[15] This new group held with the synergistic view of the doctrine of election.

---

[12]Ibid., p. 249.
[13]Ibid., pp. 249, 250.
[14]Ibid., p. 250.
[15]Ibid., p. 251.

The middle, or moderate, confessional position was represented by three smaller groups that included a few Danish Lutherans: the Conference of the Norwegian-Danish Evangelical Lutheran Church in America, the Norwegian-Danish Augustana Synod, and the Anti-Missourian Brotherhood. Their position avoided the staunch orthodoxy of the Norwegian Synod and the "emotional pietism" of the Hauge-Eielsen groups.[16] They attracted a large percentage of Norwegians coming into America's Midwest during the last quarter of the 1800s. These three groups holding the middle position became the largest group in 1890 when they united and formed the United Norwegian Lutheran Church (the United Church).[17]

In 1917 the majority of Norwegian Lutherans in America united to form one large body. It was a merger uniting the confessional Norwegian Synod of 1853, the moderate United Church of 1890, and the pietistic Hauge Synod of 1876. The merger exemplified many of the principles and factors that, in varying degrees, have been involved in most Lutheran mergers. Thus, a review of this merger will provide the reader with an example of the process commonly involved in most merger negotiations.

This merger was a victory for the moderate confessional position, with the remaining two-thirds of the once staunchly confessional Norwegian Synod, through negotiation and compromise, becoming one with the moderate position. During the early years of negotiation, the Norwegian Synod held firmly to its confessional position concerning the doctrine of election (see preceding chapter, *The Synodical Conference*), the major stumbling block hindering the merger. But when an impasse was reached in 1910 concerning this doctrine, the synod made a fundamental error common to many Lutheran groups. The late Theodore A. Aaberg, a president and historian of the Evangelical Lutheran Synod (ELS), describes this critical moment in the history of the Norwegian Synod:

> The committees from the three church bodies labored from 1908 to 1910 . . . without agreeing on the doctrine of election. Because of this impasse, the committee from the Synod felt compelled to leave the joint meetings in 1910. . . . The Synod was now at a critical crossroads where two principles, neither of which is contradictory to each other, demanded consideration. The one is the truth that Christians are to seek unity in doctrine where there is disunity, and the other that Chris-

---

[16]Ibid., pp. 250, 251.
[17]Ibid.

tians are to guard their heritage of pure doctrine, loving the truth and both hating and fearing false doctrine. God's people must exercise both principles, and as surely as there are times when Christians who are divided in doctrine will sit down together and earnestly seek to let truth prevail and error be rejected, so surely will there come a time in such instances when truth will prevail, or failing that, the joint efforts to reach agreement will cease. When those in error do not, cannot, or will not, see that error, but rather hold firmly to it, and seek recognition for it, then concern for one's own continued possession of the truth, based on Scripture's warnings and instructions regarding false prophets and false doctrine, will dictate the path to follow. In seeking to rescue others from false doctrine, the Christian has not been told to endanger, much less to sacrifice, the truth of God's Word, of which Moses says, "it is your life" (Deut. 32:47). . . . In spite of that impasse . . . the Norwegian Synod decided not only to continue the meetings, but to elect a new committee as well.[18]

The fundamental error of the Norwegian Synod, as well as other synods that have compromised their doctrinal heritage for the sake of unity, was the failure to keep the second principle even though it would have meant separating from others—including family and friends. Instead of breaking their relationship and separating from the other two bodies, the Norwegian Synod continued negotiations. Factors influencing this decision included cooperative efforts in producing a common hymnal, the election of a more liberal vice-president who felt that the Synod was too strict, the desire to avoid dealing with issues that might be church-divisive, and an eagerness to be "one," which often results in a union of emotions rather than minds.[19]

At any rate, negotiations continued and soon there was only a minority still insisting upon complete doctrinal agreement as a requirement for union. In the end, all but a very small percentage gave in and went along with the merger. Of the minority who finally capitulated to merger pressure, Aaberg has this to say:

The "Austin Settlement" [accepted December, 1916] bears its own special mark of sorrow and tragedy. When the Majority in the Synod cast aside their doctrinal heritage in favor of one united Norwegian Lutheran Church of America,

---

[18]Theodore A. Aaberg, *A City Set on a Hill* (Mankato: Board of Publications, ELS, 1968), pp. 46, 47.

[19]Ibid., pp. 47-52.

they had made it clear in the years from 1912 to 1917 that this is what they wanted to do. The Minority men who went into the Merger of 1917 under the "Austin Settlement," however, had displayed a far different spirit. They too desired a united church, but a church united in the truth. When the true nature of "The Settlement" [the compromise document negotiated in February, 1912 in Madison, WI] was revealed after the 1912 district conventions, they rose up in arms to defend the heritage of truth which God had graciously preserved for them in an earlier generation. There is much evidence in the negotiation of the "Austin Settlement" to show that they not only cherished the truth but also intended that it should sound forth, and eventually prevail over the synergistic error in the new church body. They undoubtedly have proclaimed the truth in their own teaching and preaching in the classroom and in the pulpit where they have served, and have thereby been a blessing to the Merger. Yet the final basis on which they entered the new church body effectively denied to them the opportunity for a true state of confession (*statu confessionis*), and they, by their acceptance of that basis, denied it to themselves (author's emphasis).

It is tragic that so many of the Minority men should choose to devote their time and talents in the service of the Lord in a thoroughly unionistic setting in which their labors would distinctly aid and abet a heterodox church. It is even more tragic that they, by their membership in a unionistic church organization built on false doctrine, should choose to place themselves, their families, and their future descendants in great spiritual temptation which becomes the more acute with the passing of time. This is the great tragedy of that which goes under the name of "Austin Settlement" in Norwegian Lutheran church history in America.[20]

Nevertheless, as tragic as the previous account is, the Lord always preserves a remnant. A small remnant of the minority held fast to their confessional position concerning the doctrine of election and refused to give up their biblical Lutheran heritage. These pastors and their congregations refused to go along with the merger and united

---

[20]Ibid., pp. 69, 70. This history book of the ELS provides a detailed account of the "Settlement" as well as negotiations and compromises preceding the merger. The reader will also find a clear explanation of the doctrine of election and the controversy surrounding it.

to form the Norwegian Synod of the American Evangelical Lutheran Church, renamed in 1957 the ELS. In the following quotation, Aaberg describes the final hours preceding the merger and the courageous commitment of the minority remnant to the truth. The description is representative of many other mergers where spiritual heritage is exchanged for "unity," and is a tribute to all those stalwart souls throughout the ages who have, by God's grace, held fast to the truth of his Word despite seemingly overwhelming odds:

> June 8, 1917, was a memorable day for the Norwegian Synod. What had started in unity in October, 1853, at Luther Valley, Wisconsin, was ending in disunity in June, 1917, at St. Paul, Minnesota. Two groups sat in the closing session of the final convention of the old Norwegian Synod, preparing for the grand march to the St. Paul Auditorium on the morrow for the organization of the Norwegian Lutheran Church in America. There was the Majority group which had freely bargained and sold the spiritual heritage of the 1800's for the gain of one large Norwegian Lutheran Church in America. Tomorrow could hardly come soon enough for the members of this group. Next to them sat the Minority group, or rather, most of it, not wanting to give up its synodical heritage and yet not willing to retain that heritage at all costs. The Minority would henceforth attempt to proclaim the unconditioned Gospel in a conditioned confessional setting. A third group, a remnant of the once strong and determined Minority, while seeking to testify to the synodical brethren to the end, gathered at the Hotel Aberdeen in St. Paul. This remnant had been whittled down to utter insignificance, numerically speaking. God helping them, however, they were determined to hold to the heritage of salvation by grace alone, and, if possible, to unite in an effort to bring it to others.

> The Synodical Conference Committee, having sought since 1912 the same goal as the Minority in regard to "The Settlement," left the Minority remnant that day with the exhortation to testify to the end. They were alone now, and yet, not alone. The Apostle Paul's words were true for them also: "But we have this treasure in earthen vessels, that the excellency of the power may be of God, and not of us. We are troubled on every side, yet not distressed; we are perplexed, but not in despair; persecuted, but not forsaken; cast down, but not destroyed" (II Cor. 4:7-9).

Thus the Evangelical Lutheran Synod came into being in June, 1918. . . . "Hearts of Oak" is the designation given by Dr. Theodore Graebner to the sturdy confessors of the truth who presented the Lutheran Confession to Emperor Charles V at the Diet of Augsburg in 1530. The confessors of the truth who gathered in the Lime Creek congregation, June 14-19, 1918, and there effected the reorganization of the Norwegian Synod deserve no less a title: HEARTS OF OAK. There is, of course, a great difference between Augsburg and Lime Creek in historical scope and significance. The essential ingredients, however, are the same, namely, a bold and determined confession of the truth of God's Word in the face of crushing earthly circumstances.[21]

Committed to furthering the cause of confessional Lutheranism in America and seeking strength through fellowship with others of like mind, the Evangelical Lutheran ("little Norwegian") Synod joined the Synodical Conference in 1920. It continues to exist today as a confessional Lutheran synod with a growth rate 20 times the original membership, again illustrating that the Lord blesses those who remain faithful to his Word.

The merger of 1917 united 92 percent of Norwegian Lutherans in America into one large body later known as the Evangelical Lutheran Church (ELC). Six percent remained in the independent Lutheran Free Church of 1897. Both bodies are listed as members of the American Lutheran Conference and as part of the ALC of 1960.

The two percent remaining outside of these two bodies belonged to the Eielsen Synod and the ELS, previously described, and the Church of the Lutheran Brethren in America. The Church of the Lutheran Brethren, which grew out of a pietistic group of Lutherans influenced by the revivals that swept through the Norwegian settlements in the 1890s, placed emphasis on conscious experience of conversion and a godly life. It continues to exist today as an independent body.[22]

The Swedish Lutherans

While there were some Swedish Lutherans in America as early as 1638,[23] their real history begins in 1845 when five families arrived in southeastern Iowa and established a settlement called New Sweden. Immigration continued, pastors arrived, and by 1860 the Augustana Synod was organized.[24]

---

[21]Ibid., pp. 75, 79.
[22]Wentz, op. cit., pp. 259, 260.
[23]Ibid., p. 187.
[24]Ibid., pp. 122, 125.

Like the Norwegians, the Swedish immigrants brought with them both elements of pietism and Lutheran orthodoxy. Tuve Nilsson Hassequist, described as a pietist and puritan, served as the head of the Augustana college and seminary for 30 years.[25] "By his teaching, preaching, and writing he became the most influential leader the Augustana Synod has had."[26] Confessionally, the Augustana Synod's position was close to that of the General Council, which it joined in 1870. The synod differed with the Council in that it preferred disciplinary action for those holding membership in secret societies rather than the council's "educational" approach. It also favored prohibition and a stricter moral code—reflections of its pietistic roots.[27]

Membership in the General Council continued until 1917, when plans were laid for the merger of the General Council, General Synod, and the United Synod South. When it became clear in the proposed constitution for the ULCA that the new church body would grant broad judicial powers to the general body, the Synod declined membership, withdrew from the General Council, and remained an independent body.[28]

Concerning the confessional position of the Augustana Synod as members of the American Lutheran Conference, and in the years following, Lutheran historians report:

> The Augustana Synod, reflecting a religious heritage that was an amalgam of pietism and theological conservatism, maintained cordial relations with the United Lutheran Church but cast its lot with four other Midwestern Lutheran churches in the recently organized federation called the American Lutheran Conference (1930). It should be noted, however, that Augustana stood on the threshold of a new theological era that was to change the course of the church. From that time on Augustana began to affirm in its own way the theological position articulated by the United Lutheran Church.[29]

As we shall soon see, the Augustana Synod later moved away from the moderate confessional position into the more liberal, becoming a constituting member of the LCA in 1962.

---

[25]Ibid., pp. 124, 126.
[26]Ibid., p. 126.
[27]Ibid., pp. 198, 199.
[28]Ibid., p. 199.
[29]*The Lutherans in North America,* pp. 458, 459.

The Danish Lutherans

Danish Lutherans in America had a late start in organizing a national body. It was 1872 before the first synod came into existence. From the very beginning the members were divided over doctrine. Some held with *Grundtvigianism,* while others followed the emphases of the *Inner Mission* movement.

Grundtvigianism was based on the teaching of Nikolai Grundtvig (1783-1872), who was once a staunch supporter of Lutheran orthodoxy. But, influenced by the rationalism of the Enlightenment and by Nordic mythology, his views changed and he came to doubt the orthodox doctrine of inspiration.[30] Regarding the Bible, Grundtvig made a distinction between what he considered the "dead" word of the Holy Scriptures and the "living" word of the Apostles Creed as confessed at baptism. In his love of the Danish culture, he combined elements of both Christianity and Danish culture to develop a folk or cultural type of religion.[31]

The Inner Mission people traced their roots to the Inner Mission movement, which originated in Denmark through the efforts of laymen of pietistic leanings. They nurtured small-group devotional meetings and advocated lay preaching. This movement emphasized repentance, conversion, and a personal experience of faith, regarded the Bible as the inspired word of God, and objected to the distinctive emphases of Grundtvigianism.[32]

The two groups co-existed within the "roomy folk church" of Denmark, but in the Danish American church there was a polarization of the two views. The Inner Mission people objected to the Grundtvigian view of the Bible and questioned the relationship of the Danish church to various Danish cultural organizations and activities, particularly the nonreligious Danish Folk Society founded by Grundtvig's son, Frederik, in 1887. By 1894 these differences led an Inner Mission minority, consisting of one-third of the synod, to withdraw and form a new body. This body was joined by Danes from a Norwegian-Danish group in 1896 and thus became the larger of the two Danish synods. This synod was later named The United Evangelical Lutheran Church in America and is listed as a member of the American Lutheran Conference[33] and as part of the ALC merger of 1960.

---

[30]Bengt Hagglund, *History of Theology,* trans. Gene J. Lund (St. Louis: Concordia Publishing House), 1968, p. 366.

[31]*The Lutherans in North America,* p. 268.

[32]Ibid., pp. 268, 269.

[33]Ibid., pp. 268-272.

The more liberal Grundtvigian synod became the American Evangelical Lutheran Church and later became one of the synods uniting to form the LCA in 1962.[34]

The German Lutherans

The German Lutherans in the American Lutheran Conference were represented by the ALC (1930), which is commonly referred to as the "old" ALC. It was a merger that united the synods of *Ohio, Iowa,*[35] and *Buffalo.*

The Ohio Synod (1818) was founded by missionaries of the Pennsylvania Ministerium. After a peaceful separation from this body, the Ohio Synod became increasingly conservative and confessional.[36] When the General Council failed to take a strong stand on the Four Points, the synod declined membership in the Council. Later, through colloquy and "free conferences," it found itself in complete doctrinal agreement with the Missouri Synod and in 1872 became co-founder of the Synodical Conference.[37] When the Election controversy erupted in the Synodical Conference, the Ohio Synod took the synergistic view of the doctrine of election and withdrew from the Conference.[38]

The Iowa Synod's (1854) roots went back to Pastor Wilhelm Loehe (1808-72) of Bavaria and the hundreds of missionaries he sent to America's Midwest. Its doctrinal stand was not as solid as other confessional midwestern synods and often came under attack.[39] An indication of weakness can be observed in its relationship with the General Council.

When the General Council failed to take a strong stand on the Four Points, the Iowa Synod also declined membership in the Council but excluded the issue of millennialism from its concerns.[40] This was no doubt due to the influence of Loehe, who had taken a permissive attitude toward this issue.[41] This synod's views concerning fellowship were also more liberal,[42] and it maintained an advisory relationship

---

[34]Ibid., p. 272.

[35]Some historians count the Texas Synod (1851) as a fourth member of the "old" ALC. After 1896 it was a district synod within the Iowa Synod while retaining its legal autonomy and identity. It was a close affiliate of the Iowa Synod but not a merger. See *The Lutherans in North America*, p. 348.

[36]Ibid., p. 174.

[37]Ibid., pp. 248-251.

[38]Ibid., pp. 316-319.

[39]Ibid., pp. 181, 182.

[40]Ibid., p. 236.

[41]Kurt E. Marquart, *Anatomy of an Explosion* (Grand Rapids: Baker Book House, 1978), p. 31.

[42]*The Lutherans in North America*, p. 348.

with the General Council[43] until 1918, when the Council joined in the ULCA merger.[44]

Iowa was an independent synod, but when Ohio withdrew from the Synodical Conference over the doctrine of election, Iowa found itself in agreement with Ohio's position in the controversy, which strengthened the ties between the two synods.[45] Conferences followed where doctrinal issues were debated and minority concerns were voiced, with negotiations continuing over quite a few years. When Iowa severed fellowship with the General Council in 1918, just prior to the ULCA merger, Iowa and Ohio declared fellowship.[46]

The Buffalo Synod (1845) united confessional Lutherans fleeing the *Prussian Union* (see preceding chapter). This synod's early years were marked by conflict with the Missouri Lutherans over the doctrines of church and ministry. By 1866, the majority of the synod found its leader, J. A. A. Grabau, guilty of error and removed him as the synod's head. The synod then reached doctrinal agreement with the Missourians over these issues and joined the Missouri Synod. Two minority synods remained, but by 1877 the larger of the two disbanded and individual members joined the Wisconsin Synod. The smallest, the minority under Grabau, continued to exist as the original Buffalo Synod until it became part of the "old" ALC (less than 3%) in 1930.[47]

The 1930 merger creating the "old" ALC was preceded by a controversy between Iowa and Ohio over the doctrine of inerrancy. Iowa wanted the description of the Bible as inerrant left out of the new constitution, while Ohio made total inerrancy a condition of merger. Compromise was reached by using the word "infallible" in the doctrinal article and "inerrant" in an appendix (see Chapter 3).[48]

More must be said of this compromise. Presented as a benign solution to opposing views, it was in reality a major concession to the liberal position. Up until the onset of the historical-critical method, the words infallible and inerrant were interchangeable—their meanings were the same. With the blossoming of historical-criticism, the theologians began playing games with these words. Infallible came to denote the historical-critical view that the Bible was authoritative

---

[43]Ibid., p. 183.
[44]Ibid., p. 447.
[45]Ibid., p. 325.
[46]Ibid., p. 379.
[47]Ibid., pp. 176, 177.
[48]Todd Nichol, "How Will ELCA View the Bible," *The Lutheran,* October 15, 1986, p. 12.

for the gospel—the saving truth of Jesus Christ—but could not be relied upon in matters of science, history, and geography. Inerrant was used to present the historic Lutheran teaching that the Bible was free of error and the final authority in all matters. In placing infallible in the most important part of the new constitution (the doctrinal statement) and inerrant in an appendix, the conservatives not only allowed for coexistence of two diametrically opposite viewpoints, but they demoted the historic Lutheran teaching to a lesser position.

The theologians all knew the difference. It was the trusting lay people, and perhaps even a few pastors, who did not understand and who were being deceived. It was not a harmless solution to opposing views. It was a major concession to the liberal view that would have catastrophic significance for Lutherans in the years ahead. This concession would not only lead to further compromise on the issue of biblical inerrancy, but it was also the crack that opened the door to the acceptance and use of the historical-critical method.

The ALC, as well as the American Lutheran Conference, regarded itself as a possible mediating force within Lutheranism. It hoped to bring the ULCA to a stricter position on doctrine and inter-church relations and to influence Missouri to establish closer ties with both the ULCA and the bodies of the American Lutheran Conference.[49]

In 1954, when the stage was set for the organic union of most of its members, the American Lutheran Conference was officially dissolved.[50]

THE SYNODICAL CONFERENCE

The Synodical Conference was established in 1872 by those committed to furthering the cause of confessional Lutheranism in America. They wanted to express and promote unity among Lutherans based on agreement in doctrine and practice.

The original membership consisted of the synods of Missouri, Illinois (which merged with Missouri in 1880), Wisconsin, Minnesota, and Ohio, as well as the Norwegian Synod. Unfortunately, the ranks were soon split when the controversy over the doctrine of election (see preceding chapter) led Ohio to withdraw in 1881 followed by the Norwegian Synod in 1883.[51] The confessional commitment of the remaining members continued, and in 1930 the membership consisted of the synods known today as the Lutheran Church—Missouri Synod

---

[49]*The Lutherans in North America*, p. 449.

[50]Ibid., p. 505.

[51]Victor H. Prange, "Lutherans in America—The Synodical Conference," *The Northwestern Lutheran*, October 15, 1987, p. 349.

(LCMS), the Evangelical Lutheran ("little Norwegian") Synod (ELS), the Wisconsin Evangelical Lutheran Synod (WELS), and the Slovak Evangelical Lutheran Church (SELC).

The historical roots of the LCMS (formerly the Missouri Synod) its leader, C. F. W. Walther, and the ELS, the Norwegian remnant of 1917, were previously examined.

The Slovak Synod, formed in 1902, established strong ties with the Missouri Synod and trained its theological students in Missouri's colleges and seminaries. It joined the Synodical Conference in 1908. Throughout the remaining years of the Conference, this synod stood with Missouri on all issues and finally merged with it in 1971.[52]

The history of the WELS is of special significance. Though marked by weakness in its early years, this synod developed strong confessional roots that preserved it as a confessional Lutheran body into the present day.

The Wisconsin Evangelical Lutheran Synod

The WELS is the result of an organic merger in 1917 that united the synods of Wisconsin (1850), Minnesota (1860), Michigan (1860), and Nebraska (1890) into the Evangelical Lutheran Joint Synod of Wisconsin and Other States (renamed the WELS in 1959). These German Lutheran synods had functioned as a federation some years prior to merger and shared a common history and theological development. Many of their leaders were pastors who had been trained by unionistic mission societies in Germany, including Basel, Barmen, Berlin, and Langenberg. Most of them suffered to some degree from the effects of the rationalistic teachings in the German seminaries. The Langenberg Society, an evangelical association in Germany within the *Prussian Union* (see preceding chapter), had been organized for the special purpose of sending pastors to the Protestant German settlers of North America.[53] These societies represented Lutheran, Reformed, and United churches in Europe, and they sought to carry on mission work in America with little regard for doctrinal differences.[54] Congregations in America were allowed to affiliate with the denomination of their choice, and the pastors were expected to tailor their ministry to fit the preference of the congregations, whether it be according to Reformed or Lutheran teaching.[55]

---

[52]*The Lutherans in North America*, pp. 277, 278.

[53]Wentz, op. cit., pp. 262-268.

[54]*The Lutherans in North America*, p. 344.

[55]John Philip Koehler, *The History of the Wisconsin Synod* (Sauk Rapids, MN: Sentinel Printing, 1981), pp. 84, 85.

Despite the weakness inherent in these unionistic practices, the synods all made a gradual but steady move toward a more confessional position. The manner in which this came about can be observed through a look at the early years of the Wisconsin Synod, the largest and most influential of the four synods, and the confessional position of three of its most prominent leaders: John Muehlhaeuser, John Bading, and August Hoenecke.[56]

The Wisconsin Synod membership came by way of scattered German immigration in the late 1830s and 1840s. Among these brave and adventuresome settlers was Muehlhaeuser (1803-67), a clergyman commissioned by the Langenberg Mission Society[57] and the "father" of the Wisconsin Synod. He arrived in Wisconsin in 1848 after serving a congregation in New York and became the leading spirit among the founding pastors of the synod. Soon after his arrival he formed an "evangelical" congregation—one that welcomed Reformed as well as Lutheran members—and was elected the first president of the synod when it was organized two years later.[58] Muehlhaeuser was a much loved, sincere, and caring pastor who desired that all men should come to know the Savior regardless of denominational ties. He wanted to be a Lutheran, but at the same time he failed to recognize the importance of sound doctrine and the vital differences separating Lutherans from the Reformed—a legacy inherited from the German mission societies that gave birth to the Wisconsin Synod.[59] He viewed the Lutheran Confessions as "paper walls of partition" and the "old Lutherans," the Missouri and Buffalo Synods, as extremists for holding to the orthodox confessional position.[60]

It is important to remember, that the "old Lutherans" had fled Europe, at great expense and after much suffering, to escape both the effects of rationalism and unionism (see preceding chapter). We might also add that Muehlhaeuser's prejudicial attitude toward the Confessions and confessional Lutherans bears striking resemblance to those of today's more liberal Lutherans.

Muehlhaeuser's relaxed theological views and unionistic practices, along with friendly relations with unionistic mission societies and

---

[56]*The Lutherans in North America,* pp. 344, 345.

[57]Ibid., p. 183.

[58]*Our Church: Its Life and Mission* (Milwaukee: Northwestern Publishing House, 1990), pp. 20, 23.

[59]John C. Jeske, "Amazing Grace—125 Years of It!", an unpublished manuscript presented to WELS congregations commemorating the 125th anniversary of the founding of the synod, February 13, 1974, p. 2.

[60]*Our Church: Its Life and Mission,* pp. 30, 35.

the Pennsylvania Ministerium, which included financial support, drew sharp criticism from Missouri and other orthodox Lutherans.[61] With the arrival of confessionally-minded pastors, a more conservative spirit began to develop within the synod. When Muehlhaeuser retired from his 20-year presidency in 1860, the role passed to Bading. Under his leadership, Muehlhaeuser's "milder" Lutheranism, as well as that of the synod's, gradually gave way to a firmer stand on the Confessions.[62]

Bading was also a product of the Langenberg Mission Society but with a difference. One of his professors was a foe of German rationalism, and under this professor's influence Bading gained a renewed interest in the Confessions. He arrived in Wisconsin in 1853 and after succeeding Muehlhaeuser as president, took aggressive steps in developing a greater confessional consciousness within the synod. In a short time the synod adopted a new confessional statement of faith, and adherence to this confession was required of all congregations seeking admission to the synod. Thus, a pattern was set for a new theological direction.[63]

Soon after Bading's arrival, Hoenecke (1835-1908) appeared upon the scene. Another emissary of the German-mission societies, he was destined to become the Wisconsin Synod's seminary president, professor of dogmatics, and chief theologian in the 19th century.[64]

Hoenecke had studied at the pietistic University of Halle, which had become a leading exponent of rationalism. He arrived in Wisconsin in 1863 to serve as a parish pastor, but three years later he received a call to the Synod's seminary to be a professor of theology.[65] This was to be the turning point for Hoenecke. The call compelled him to dig deeper into Scripture and into the Lutheran Confessions and, much like Walther, it was here that he came to know himself as a Lutheran. Under the leadership of Hoenecke, as well as Bading and others, the synod turned in the direction of true, Bible-based Lutheranism.[66]

As the synod became more confessional, it became clear that connections with the German mission societies had to be severed.[67] This decision was a difficult one, for it required the struggling young

---

[61]Koehler, op. cit., pp. 79-86.
[62]*Our Church: Its Life and Mission,* p. 30.
[63]*The Lutherans in North America,* p. 184.
[64]Koehler, op. cit., pp. 88, 89, 149, 262.
[65]Ibid., pp. 88, 89, 149.
[66]Jeske, op. cit., p. 4.
[67]Koehler, op. cit., pp. 112-114, 118, 131.

church to sever ties of friendship and love and to appear ungrateful for aid received from the mission societies. In addition, it involved the loss of more than $7,000 of promised funds and of several pastors who were against the move. Despite the hardships this decision created, the synod never regretted having rejected unionism, for the Lord continued to supply for the synod's needs.[68]

Once the ties with the mission societies were gradually loosened and finally officially severed, ties with orthodox Lutherans grew stronger. The Missouri Synod, especially Walther, its founder and leader, were instrumental in helping the Wisconsin Synod develop a more confessional stance.[69] As the Wisconsin Synod fathers began to appreciate the staunch confessionalism of Missouri, relations grew friendlier and doctrinal discussions were soon underway. In 1868 the two synods recognized each other as true Lutheran churches, and full altar and pulpit fellowship was declared. In the following year, they agreed on a plan for cooperation in using the synodical institutions (the Wisconsin Synod's college at Watertown, Wisconsin, and the Missouri Synod's seminary at St. Louis, Missouri) for training pastors and other theological students.[70]

During the same period of time, a closer relationship was developing between Wisconsin and the synods of Minnesota and Michigan. These two synods were also struggling to become more confessional, in much the same manner as the Wisconsin Synod, and were strengthened through closer ties with Wisconsin. As members of the General Council, all three synods objected to the Council's weak stand on the Four Points. This led both Wisconsin and Minnesota to withdraw from the Council and join with Missouri and others to organize the Synodical Conference. Twenty years later Michigan, finally tired of acting as the "conscience" of the Council, severed its connections and also joined the Conference. The Nebraska Synod, formerly a member of the Wisconsin Synod Conference, became a member by way of the merger of 1917 that united the four synods.[71]

Continued fellowship in the Synodical Conference served to strengthen the confessional position of all its members. Concerning the great blessing of the Synodical Conference, Professor John C. Jeske, WELS pastor and chairman of the Old Testament department at Wisconsin Lutheran Seminary, writes:

---

[68]*Our Church: Its Life and Mission*, p. 36.

[69]Edward Fredrich II, "Dr. C. F. W. Walther—American Lutheranism Has Had No Equal," *The Northwestern Lutheran*, May 15, 1987, p. 189.

[70]Jeske, op. cit., pp. 4, 5.

[71]Koehler, op. cit., pp. 177-179.

The year 1872 brought a development which was destined to be of the greatest significance for the cause of true Lutheranism in America. At a convention in St. John's Church, Milwaukee, the Missouri and the Wisconsin Synods, together with four others, established the Evangelical Lutheran Synodical Conference. Only God knows, and only eternity will reveal, the countless blessings that came to American Lutheranism through the Synodical Conference. Standing squarely on the Scripture and the Lutheran Confessions, the Synodical Conference's one mark of distinction was loving, living obedience to the revealed Word and will of her Lord. It was an effective instrument for expressing and propagating true doctrinal unity and the fellowship of faith.[72]

THE DISSOLUTION
OF THE SYNODICAL CONFERENCE

By 1920 the Synodical Conference was the second largest Lutheran body in America, a "seemingly impregnable stronghold" of confessional Lutheranism.[73] Unfortunately, dark clouds loomed on the horizon. Ahead were developments that would strike a severe blow to the cause of confessional Lutheranism in America and ultimately result in the dissolution of the Synodical Conference.

The first sign of the gathering clouds occurred in 1935, when the ULCA and ALC issued invitations to various Lutheran bodies to participate in committee discussions aimed at overcoming obstacles to Lutheran unity. Over the objections of their partners in the Synodical Conference, the Missouri Synod accepted. Their partners also desired unity but declined the invitations because they felt discussions were futile without at least some indication that the ULCA and ALC had moved, or were interested in moving, into a more confessional position.

Nothing in the invitations themselves, nor official publications or convention reports, signaled a change of direction for either body.[74] Therefore, remembering the lessons learned from the 1912-17 old Norwegian Synod negotiations (previously described), the ELS warned of the dangers inherent in the proposed discussions:

> We, who have observed at close range and studied the history of the efforts made to bring the Norwegian Lutherans

---

[72]Jeske, op. cit., p. 5
[73]*Our Church: Its Life and Mission*, p. 57.
[74]Aaberg, op. cit., pp. 135-139.

into agreement by means of committees, are constrained to say, when asked to follow this method again: "*Vestigia terrent*" [the footsteps terrify]. We are afraid of history repeating itself, and therefore consider it a God-given duty to sound a warning to all earnest defenders of the truth against exposing the true welfare of the Church of Christ to the dangers involved in this procedure.[75]

The ELS also pointed out that by the early 1930s church conditions were so well known that there could be little excuse for not knowing the confessional spirit of the various Lutheran Synods. Nor was there an excuse for any Lutheran synod to continue in error through ignorance.[76] Therefore, the ELS issued an even stronger warning:

When we elect a committee to be closeted in confidential negotiations with like committees from errorist bodies who will strive to gain acceptance of their false views, we have every reason to fear that we must reckon with all the wily tactics of the arch-enemy of truth. If I Peter 3:15 is cited to justify such procedure, the passage is misapplied, and though unintentionally, made to nullify Rom. 16:17; Titus 3:10, etc. Let it be noted, too, that the prospects of convincing by our testimony to the truth a committee which represents a body confirmed in error, and through it the body itself, are very, very poor indeed. Be it remembered also that the champions of false doctrine are usually satisfied if they gain for their error equal standing with the truth; hence every manner of compromise is resorted to. The danger is multiplied when, as is common, the errorists shower praises upon their opponents in order to gain their personal good will. When the champions of truth are brought to admire the errorists for their gentlemanly behavior and their fair-mindedness, and begin to think of the many able and good men and women whom they represent, then "the lust of the flesh" is near to victory.

Scripture warns us clearly and emphatically against entanglements with errorists (Roman 16:17; Titus 3:10; 1 Timothy 6:3-5). Any reluctance to heed these warnings and commands of Scripture is unionism already conceived in the heart, which if allowed to develop, will result in full-fledged unionism as history also attests.[77]

---

[75]Ibid., p. 137.
[76]Ibid., p. 139.
[77]Ibid., pp. 139, 140.

Despite the warnings, the LCMS entered into discussions with both the ULCA and ALC. Those with the ULCA were short-lived (1936-39), with the discussions beginning and ending with the issue of biblical authority. It was not long until the LCMS became convinced that the ULCA position was in reality a denial of the Bible as the Word of God. At this point discussions broke off.[78]

Discussions with the ALC began in 1935, but these were to continue for many years. Resolutions and doctrinal statements, drawn up by both the LCMS and ALC, made it appear that all previous doctrinal differences between them had been resolved. However, the ELS and WELS disagreed. Almost every synod convention in the 1940s and 1950s found the ELS and WELS studying these documents and the issues they raised.[79] Both synods urged Missouri to discontinue negotiations with the ALC. When the LCMS repeatedly ignored their requests, the wheels were finally set in motion to break fellowship with Missouri and dissolve the Synodical Conference.[80]

When the pastors and delegates assembled for the 1955 ELS Convention, there was no disagreement among them as to the Scriptural principles regarding termination of church fellowship. After noting that a church body forfeits its orthodox character when it fails to carry out doctrinal discipline and permits error to exist alongside of truth in its pulpits and schools, the president of the synod, C. M. Gullerud, stated:

> Anyone in fellowship with such a body can only remain there as a protesting member and only so long as there is any evidence that his protest is being heard and heeded. When it becomes apparent that all attempts at enforcing doctrinal discipline are in vain, then the word of God demands separation. Here it is not a matter of loyalty to synods but a matter of obedience to God's Word which says to us: "Now I beseech you brethren, mark them which cause divisions and offenses contrary to the doctrine which ye have learned; and avoid them." Rom. 16:17.[81]

Not everyone at the convention was convinced that future attempts at enforcing doctrinal discipline would be in vain. Some felt

---

[78]*The Lutherans in North America,* p. 468.

[79]*Our Church: Its Life and Mission,* loc. cit.

[80]The reader will find a detailed account of the LCMS-ALC merger negotiations and the ELS and WELS response in Aaberg's *A City Set On a Hill,* pp. 134-263.

[81]Aaberg, op. cit., p. 191. Later, President Gullerud left the ELS and joined with others to help form the Church of the Lutheran Confession.

there was still a chance, given more time, that Missouri would turn around. After several days of doctrinal discussion, the ELS suspended fellowship with Missouri but did not officially withdraw from the Synodical Conference until 1961.[82]

A similar situation developed in the WELS. When the 1955 WELS Convention postponed action on a resolution to terminate fellowship with Missouri,[83] a group within the synod insisted on an immediate break. When the convention hesitated to sever the bonds of a 90-year fellowship,[84] the dissenting group separated from both the WELS and Synodical Conference and, along with some pastors and congregations of the ELS,[85] formed the Church of the Lutheran Confession (CLC).[86] In 1961 the WELS voted to suspend fellowship with the LCMS and in 1963 formally withdrew from the Synodical conference. With only two members remaining, the conference became inactive in 1966 and was officially dissolved the following year.[87]

Statistics in 1954 list the Synodical Conference membership as: the LCMS, 1,786,196; the WELS, 311,477; the Slovak Synod, 20,808; and the ELS, 10,663.[88] Considering the ratio between the LCMS and the remaining membership of the conference, the dissolution of the Synodical Conference was a severe blow to confessional Lutheranism in America.

By 1969 the LCMS and ALC had declared fellowship. However, in 1973 the LCMS moved away from developing closer relations with other Lutherans and in 1981 terminated fellowship with the ALC.[89] More must be said of this strange turn of events.

THE LCMS AND THE ENEMY WITHIN

The LCMS preoccupation with Lutheran unity not only destroyed a 90-year confessional Lutheran fellowship, but opened the door to

[82]Ibid., pp. 191-194, 219.

[83]"Mark . . . Avoid . . . Origin of the CLC," a pamphlet authorized by the Coordinating Council of the Church of the Lutheran Confession (Eau Claire, WI: The CLC Book House, reprinted January 1983), p. 7.

[84]*Our Church: Its Life and Mission,* loc. cit.

[85]Aaberg, op. cit., p. 116.

[86]"This is Your Church," a pamphlet authorized by the Board of Education of the Church of the Lutheran Confession, pp. 15-18. This pamphlet provides a detailed account of the formation of the CLC.

[87]*Our Church: Its Life and Mission,* loc. cit.

[88]"Lutheran Bodies in the U.S.A.," a tract issued by the Conference of Presidents, Evangelical Lutheran Joint Synod of Wisconsin and Other States, 1954, No. 1, p. 3.

[89]Victor H. Prange, "Lutherans in America—The Dissolution of the Synodical Conference," *The Northwestern Lutheran,* January 1, 1988, p. 12.

other weakening influences as well. During the years of the unity negotiations, the LCMS had allowed its strong position on the vital importance of sound doctrine to relax, leaving it vulnerable to prevailing theological conditions of the day. During the 1930s, after liberalism had taken over in most mainline denominations and was making
inroads into the more liberal Lutheran bodies in America (see Chapter 3), a "progressive" movement began within the LCMS. It was a
movement designed to change the synod from within. The goal was to
prepare the LCMS for outreach in America by moving it toward a
more open doctrinal stance. This was to be accomplished through the
election of conservative leaders who would listen to suggestions from
seminary presidents, professors, and other officials who held more
progressive views.[90]

By 1964, Dr. John H. Tietjen, future president (1969-73) of the
LCMS Concordia Seminary, St. Louis, Missouri, an outspoken supporter of Lutheran unity, reported that the LCMS was indeed
changing:

> In recent years Concordia Seminary must be given credit for
> its share in the change that has been going on in The
> Lutheran Church—Missouri Synod. There are some who do
> not like to hear it, but the Missouri Synod has changed and
> is changing—in many ways—theologically too. The St. Louis
> seminary has helped produce the change. About the middle
> of the forties the seminary itself experienced a change. With
> the passing of an older generation of professors younger men
> arrived on the scene, men who had studied in institutions
> outside of the Missouri Synod, men who had escaped from
> the cultural isolation. . . . Quietly and unobtrusively the
> seminary faculty prepared the ministry of the future. Slowly
> the synod began to change. The seminary alone is not re-
> sponsible. Yet it has contributed to the change.[91]

Tietjen himself had sought training outside the LCMS having received his Th.D. in 1959 from Union Theological Seminary,[92] a liberal[93]
institution of the Reformed camp. In 1970, as president of Concordia
Seminary, Tietjen clearly revealed his own theological position when
he defended the teaching methods of a professor at the seminary:

---

[90]Marquart, op. cit., pp. 86, 87.

[91]Ibid., pp. 88, 89.

[92]Ibid., p. 88.

[93]Harold Lindsell, *The Battle for the Bible* (Grand Rapids: Zondervan,1976), p. 185.

If the phrase, "higher critical views, refers to the use of historical-critical methodology, then it is not possible for Dr. Ehlen to teach any of his assigned courses at a seminary level of instruction, thus taking the text of the Holy Scriptures with utter seriousness, without using historical-critical methodology. Nor is that possible for any other faculty member who teaches a course in Biblical interpretation, regardless of the department to which he may belong.[94]

Controversy over the use of historical criticism continued at the St. Louis seminary[95] until 1974, when most of the faculty were charged with false doctrine. This event was precipitated by the 1969 election of Dr. J. A. O. Preus, Jr., a conservative, to the presidency of the LCMS. He replaced the more moderate, or progressive, Dr. Oliver Harms who, over the preceding seven years, had been leading the synod into closer relationships with other Lutherans, including membership in the new Lutheran council (described ahead).[96] This signaled a new direction for the LCMS. A historian of the ELCA reports:

. . . the LCMS was convulsed by a quarrel over inspiration, inerrancy, and historical criticism. Controversy swirled around the faculty of its Concordia Seminary in St. Louis. In 1974 most members of the faculty were charged with false doctrine. The chief complaint was that the teachers had embraced the historical-critical approach to the Bible. Eventually, most of the faculty left the seminary and established a new school. Later a number of congregations and clergy left the LCMS to form the Association of Evangelical Lutheran Churches [AELC], one of the partners forming the new Evangelical Lutheran Church in America.[97]

This quotation appeared earlier (see Chapter 3) and at this point needs further explanation. In 1974 a number of students left Concordia Seminary with the exiting faculty and established the Seminary-in-Exile (Seminex),[98] electing Tietjen as president. Later, Seminex graduates were ordained by the LCMS and called to serve in LCMS parishes.[99]

---

[94]Marquart, op. cit., pp. 92, 93.

[95]See *Anatomy of an Explosion* for a detailed account of the controversy and historical events surrounding it.

[96]*The Lutherans in North America*, p. 528.

[97]Todd Nichol, "How Will ELCA View the Bible," *The Lutheran*, October 15, 1986, p. 13. Other historians of the ELCA have also recorded an account of the LCMS controversy. See *The Lutherans in North America*, pp. 527-535, 559, 560.

[98]Later called "Christ Seminary-Seminex."

[99]*The Lutherans in North America*, Supplement, pp. 559, 560.

The AELC was organized in 1976, largely through the efforts of a support group, Evangelical Lutherans in Mission (ELIM), formed in 1973 by members of the LCMS who were supportive of the "moderates" within the synod. However, the exodus of the moderates to the AELC was not as large as anticipated. Many congregations and pastors supportive of Tietjen, the other professors, and Seminex remained in the LCMS and continued to support the moderates through the ELIM.[100] The ELIM continued as a nonprofit corporation in partnership with the AELC until the 1988 ELCA merger, when both the ELIM and its voice, the biweekly *Lutheran Perspective,* ceased to exist.[101]

The AELC has been referred to by an American church historian as the LCMS's "gift" to the ELCA. In conjunction with the preceding information, the following comments are worth noting:

> The Association of Evangelical Lutheran Churches is the Lutheran Church—Missouri Synod's gift to the new church. Although the LCMS did not intend to be a donor, the gift is testimony to its past and to many still within its ranks.

> With Concordia Seminary forging the way, moderating forces peaked in the 1960s when LCMS conventions adopted new mission affirmations, initiated work on an inter-Lutheran hymnal, ratified participation in ecumenical dialogues and the Lutheran Council in the USA, and voted fellowship with the American Lutheran Church. . . . The AELC's 1978 "Call for Lutheran Union" helped push the ALC and the Lutheran Church in America into serious negotiations. Christ Seminary, as Seminex was called in time, deployed its faculty to three LCA and ALC schools.[102]

With the exodus of the dissidents, the LCMS turned away from closer relations with other Lutherans and in 1981 terminated fellowship with the ALC. This turnabout lead others, both inside and outside of Lutheranism, to credit the LCMS as being the first major mainline denomination to successfully defeat the infiltration of liberalism into its church body. One highly respected churchman outside of Lutheranism has documented the liberal takeover of the mainline de-

---

[100]Ibid.

[101]*Lutheran Perspective* (formerly Missouri in Perspective), October 16, 1987, p. 4.

[102]Christa R. Klein, "The AELC: Missouri's Gift," *The Lutheran,* October, 1987, p. 7. This is one of a series of articles designed to educate the laity concerning the historic roots of the ELCA. They were published jointly in *The Lutheran* (LCA) and *The Lutheran Standard* (ALC).

nominations. In his book, *The Battle for the Bible,* Dr. Harold Lindsell describes the LCMS controversy. In conclusion he writes:

> If history has any lesson to teach, it is that defection from inerrancy generally takes place in the educational institutions and then spreads from there. In the case of the Missouri Lutherans it appears to have resulted from postgraduate studies pursued by men trained in Missouri schools who then secured doctorates in secular or liberal institutions. They were enamored of the historical-critical method, and numbers of them left their old moorings with respect to biblical infallibility. More frequently than not, men with this kind of training did not go into the parish ministry, but headed for institutions where the possibility existed to disseminate the newfound learning among younger minds that could easily be influenced away from historic Missouri viewpoints. In addition, this kind of mind enjoyed teaching these new and attractive but irregular doctrines through the literature of the denomination. So they became editors and writers for church school materials. . . . History tells us that in the Fundamentalist-Modernist controversy in the '20s the Fundamentalists lost because the Modernists gained control of the ecclesiastical machinery as well as the theological seminaries. It was a decisive combination.

> Walter A. Maier, an able [LCMS] scholar, put his finger on the pulse of Missouri's problem. He was writing to support his church's stand on an inerrant Scripture [a short article entitled "The Historical-Critical Method of Bible Study"]. He knew that in every large denomination where this battle had been fought, believers in inerrancy had lost. But the battle has not yet been lost in his denomination. Instead of the believers in inerrancy leaving the church, the disbelievers have been doing so. History teaches us that the outcome is by no means assured. But men like Maier know that, at least for the time being, believers in errancy have control of the denomination. Whether they can retain this control and whether they will take the steps necessary to do so, only time will tell.[103]

---

[103]Lindsell, op. cit., pp. 83, 85, 87. This book and its sequel, *The Bible in the Balance,* are excellent resources for detailed study of the mainline denominations' capitulation to liberalism.

Today the LCMS still publicly professes a belief in the inerrancy and authority of Scripture and an adherence to the Lutheran Confessions of the 16th century. However, there are indications that the outcome is still by no means assured. It is not within the scope of this book to document the problems that continue to plague the LCMS, but observers generally conclude that the synod is comprised of three distinct camps: the "conservatives," "the middle-of-the-roaders," and the "liberals" (who call themselves "moderates"). This internal division is clearly illustrated by two contradictory memorials submitted to the 1986 LCMS Convention, one by the faculty of Concordia Theological Seminary in Fort Wayne, Indiana, and the other by the synod's Eastern District (comprising parts of New York and Pennsylvania). The faculty called on the synod to "record its conviction, with deep regret, that the doctrine and practice of the merging churches, the ALC, the LCA, and the AELC [the present-day ELCA], are such that the latter are as such no longer genuine Lutheran churches from a traditional and confessional point of view. . . ." The Eastern District, however, called on the synod to "reconsider its decision of declining to become a part of the new Lutheran church" since "more effective mission and ministry, as well as elimination of duplicate efforts, can be carried out within a united church body. . . ."[104] Neither resolution passed (due no doubt in large measure to the sentiments of the "middle-of-the-roaders" at the convention), but it is enlightening to see the extreme difference between two major entities within the same church body.

Whether the conservatives within the LCMS are willing to join forces and take the steps necessary to preserve their confessional Lutheran heritage remains to be seen. Let it be sufficient to note that the battle does not appear to be over.

THE NATIONAL LUTHERAN COUNCIL

World War I not only marked the development of larger Lutheran units, but it also brought with it a concern among Lutherans to serve members called into America's armed forces. This and other humanitarian needs led to the organization of the National Lutheran Council (NLC) in 1918. The original membership included the ULCA (1918), the Norwegian Church (1917), and the Swedish (Augustana), Ohio, and Iowa Synods. The synods belonging to the Synodical Conference did not join.[105]

---

[104]*The 1986 Lutheran Church — Missouri Synod Convention Workbook*, pp. 134, 113.

[105]Victor H. Prange, "Lutherans in America—World War I and the National Lutheran Council," *The Northwestern Lutheran,* November 1, 1987, p. 368.

The NLC members all recognized the fact that they were not in doctrinal agreement. They also could not agree on the types of projects the NLC should undertake nor the degree of cooperation these should involve. The more liberal ULCA was flexible on this issue and saw no hindrance to full cooperation among Lutherans (or even merger) wherever this seemed advantageous.[106] However, the remaining members were more conservative and cautious about the issue of fellowship among Lutherans not in doctrinal agreement and limited themselves to cooperation in "externals"—activities that were considered purely humanitarian or administrative and did not involve altar and pulpit fellowship. Despite such disagreements, the NLC—which became the Lutheran Council United States of America (LCUSA) in 1966—functioned for many years as an organization for cooperation among Lutherans and was a catalyst for the eventual formation of the ELCA in 1988.[107]

UNITY—A NEW DIRECTION

As previously noted, the year 1930 found Lutherans in America divided into three major groups: the ULCA, American Lutheran Conference, and Synodical Conference. The American Lutheran Conference, like the ALC, regarded itself as a mediator between the ULCA and Synodical Conference, hoping to bring all three bodies into a closer relationship. However, this was not to be. In the years following 1930, doctrinal differences remained and were intensified by what ELCA historians have called "theological reconstruction"— namely the influence of historical-criticism.[108] While the infiltration of historical-criticism into American Lutheran seminaries has already been documented in Chapter 3, its importance is such that it must be noted again.

As early as the 1920s historical criticism had made its way into ULCA seminaries. By 1931 it entered the Swedish (Augustana) Seminary, and in 1947 made its appearance in the Norwegian (now Luther Northwestern) Seminary.[109] The historical-critical method added the issue of inerrancy and biblical authority to the Four Points and election controversies. A polarization took place among members of the American Lutheran Conference and ULCA, and Lutheran unity efforts changed course. The ULCA and the Augustana Synod of the American Lutheran Conference began to establish a closer relation-

---

[106]*The Lutherans in North America,* pp. 403-410.
[107]Prange, loc. cit.
[108]*The Lutherans in North America,* pp. 461-471.
[109]Ibid., p. 497.

ship while the other members of the conference began looking toward the possibility of a future organic merger. Meanwhile, the ALC was also negotiating toward establishing pulpit and altar fellowship with the LCMS. The result was not one united Lutheran church, so long desired by many, but the dissolution of the Synodical Conference and the formation of the ALC and LCA.[110]

THE AMERICAN LUTHERAN CHURCH—1960

The ALC (1960) was an organic union of four of the five members of the American Lutheran Conference: the large Norwegian (ELC, 1917), small Norwegian Lutheran Free Church (LFC, 1897), German (ALC, 1930), and Danish (Inner Mission, 1896) churches. The Swedish (Augustana, 1860) Synod declined the invitation.[111]

The ALC merger was a further blending of varying degrees of confessional loyalty. It was not a victory for the conservative members but a concession to the more liberal elements. As previously noted, historical criticism had entered the Norwegian Synod seminary in 1947. Thus, inerrancy and the authority of Scripture was an important issue both before and after the merger. However, a compromise was reached in much the same manner as in the "old" ALC merger of 1930, and the door was thrown open for the use of the historical-critical method.[112] Interestingly enough, the first president of the new ALC was the late Dr. Fredrik A. Schiotz, president of the merging Norwegian Synod and a strong supporter of historical criticism.[113]

The small Norwegian church (LFC) waited until 1963 to join over the protest of some of its more conservative members. Those who protested refused to join in the merger, withdrew, and formed the Association of Free Lutheran Churches (AFLC).[114] Another group of protesting pastors and congregations withdrew from the ALC in 1965 and organized what is known today as the World Confessional Lutheran Association (WCLA).

THE LUTHERAN CHURCH IN AMERICA—1962

The Lutheran Church in America (1962) was an organic union of the ULCA (the Muhlenberg line, [the General Synod, General Coun-

---

[110]Ibid., pp. 501, 502.

[111]Ibid., pp. 502, 505.

[112]Nichol, op. cit., pp. 12, 13. See also: *The Lutherans in North America,* p. 505.

[113]Fredrik A. Schiotz, *One Man's Story* (Minneapolis: Augsburg Publishing House, 1980), pp. 143-154.

[114]*The Lutherans in North America,* pp. 505, 506.

cil, and United Synod South, 1918]), Swedish (Augustana, 1860), Danish (Grundtvigian, 1872), and Finnish (Suomi, 1890) Synods. This merger created the largest Lutheran body in America: 80% ULCA, 20% Swedish, 1% Danish, and less than 1% Finnish.[115] The ULCA, Swedish, and Danish historical roots have already been described and need no further explanation. A brief history of the Finnish Synod follows.

The Finnish Lutherans

The history of Finnish Lutherans in America begins with the first immigrants in 1865 and the independent congregations formed soon after in the copper mining country of Upper Michigan. Their history is similar to that of the Scandinavian groups, embracing elements of pietism as well as varying degrees of confessional loyalty. They were divided into three groups. Those most concerned about doctrinal uniformity were drawn into the orbit of the Missouri Synod in the early 1920s and eventually became a part of that synod in 1964. The second group formed the Suomi Synod in 1890.[116] By the 1920s, this synod was cooperating in mission work with the ULCA and, as noted previously, became part of the LCA in 1962.[117] The third, and most pietistic, were followers of Lars Laestadius (1800-1861). Commonly called "Laestadians," they began forming independent congregations in 1872 and in 1928 organized as a national church body, the Apostolic Lutheran Church in America (ALCA),[118] which continues to exist today as one of the many smaller Lutheran groups.

The Invitation to Unite

Historical criticism had been making inroads into the ULCA and Swedish (Augustana) Synod since the 1920s and 1930s. Augustana had joined the American Lutheran Conference before the influence of the new theology professors and the break with "old Lutheranism." With the move into the new theological climate, Augustana became increasingly interested in union among all Lutherans—an interest shared by the ULCA. Augustana began to see itself as a possible bridge to union between the ULCA and the American Lutheran Conference. However, doctrinal discussions in the follow-

---

[115]Wentz, op. cit., pp. 379, 380.

[116]*The Lutherans in North America,* pp. 272-274.

[117]*Lutheran Cyclopedia,* ed. Erwin L. Lueker (St. Louis: Concordia Publishing House, 1975), p. 300.

[118]*The Lutherans in North America,* pp. 273, 274.

ing years failed to bring the latter two groups into agreement. When the American Lutheran Conference merger movement made it clear that it was "not open to all Lutheran general bodies and . . . did not include the consideration of the subject of ecumenical relations," Augustana withdrew from the movement and began to move closer to the ULCA. In 1955 the ULCA and the Augustana invited all Lutherans to consider uniting into one body. However, only the Finnish and Danish Synods accepted.[119] The four bodies set up a joint union commission, and at their very first meeting in 1956 they reached a doctrinal agreement. Events moved rapidly, and by early 1960 both an agreement to consolidate and a constitution were presented to the four churches and adopted with almost complete unanimity. In 1962 the merger was completed and the LCA became the largest Lutheran body in America. The constituting convention elected the late Dr. Franklin Clark Fry, president of the ULCA, as its first president.[120] The election of Fry can be regarded as an indication of future unity efforts of the LCA, since Fry was the highly respected chairman of the powerful Central Committee of the World Council of Churches for many years prior to the formation of the LCA, as well as one of the chief architects of the National Council of Churches.[121]

With the forming of the LCA merger, Lutherans in America were still divided into three distinct camps: the liberal LCA, the moderate ALC, and the confessional LCMS, WELS, ELS, CLC, and other smaller Lutheran groups. Lutheran unity efforts would continue in the years ahead. Concerning the doctrinal standards that might be required for future union among Lutherans in America, ELCA historians write:

> The question that had disturbed American Lutheranism since the twenties and thirties—Does confessional unity require theological uniformity?—remained unresolved into the seventies. The United Lutheran Church and, after 1962, the Lutheran Church in America said no; the American Lutheran Church (1960) and the Missouri Synod said yes. There the problem posed by Lutheranism's confessional principle resided until the late sixties and early seventies.[122]

---

[119]Ibid., pp. 460-506.
[120]Wentz, loc. cit.
[121]*Lutherans in North America*, p. 514.
[122]Ibid., p. 471.

THE ROAD TO ELCA—1988

Cooperation in "externals," practical work not involving doctrine, often leads to cooperation in "internals," altar and pulpit fellowship and organic union. The stated purpose of the newly organized NLC (1917) was for pan-Lutheran cooperation in externals. However, by 1954 Lutherans would be voicing their concerns and writing:

> No one had to be a prophet or the son of a prophet to predict the sorry outcome of these ventures in practical cooperation. When Lutherans of various stripes are encouraged to associate with each other and increasingly closer contacts are being cultivated among them, it comes as no surprise if they begin to fellowship on a more intimate spiritual level. To trust that it will be otherwise is to be . . . blissfully unaware of reality.

> In 1917, when the National Lutheran Council was organized by the synods of the present American Lutheran Conference and of the present United Lutheran Church, its purpose was intended to be purely external. They judged that they should be able to work together in "externals" in spite of differences in doctrine and practice. Thirty years later the *Lutheran Outlook* argues: "It is evident from the aggressiveness with which the Council is expanding its cooperative activities in various directions that it is laying the framework for a larger Lutheran unity." First, cooperation with "safeguards"; then the call for complete consolidation, thus bringing the movement to its inevitable climax.[123]

The inevitable climax was the organic union of the bodies of the NLC into the ALC and LCA. Since the NLC was not structured to serve two bodies, it was succeeded in 1966 by the LCUSA. Its membership included the ALC, LCA, LCMS, and the Slovak Synod (SELC—soon to merge with the LCMS). The presence of the LCMS needs further comment.

While the LCMS had declined membership in the NLC, it had cooperated in the NLC's World War II efforts, particularly in the chaplaincy program,[124] the joint operation of service centers,[125] and other war relief efforts. This was seen by some observers as "a minor breach in the wall of Missouri"[126] that "was ultimately to shatter the Synodical Conference and to bring the Missouri Synod into closer relationship with the churches of the National Lutheran Council."[127]

---

[123]"Cooperation in Externals," tract issued by the Conference of Presidents, Evangelical Lutheran Joint Synod of Wisconsin and Other States, 1954, p. 6.

[124]Wentz, op. cit., p. 305.

[125]"Cooperation in Externals," p. 5.

[126]*The Lutherans in North America,* p. 478.

[127]Ibid., pp. 495, 496.

From its very beginning, the LCUSA was looked upon as a sign of the hope that eventually its three major cooperating members might one day unite.[128] Events were clearly moving in that direction. A recorded history of LCUSA, *Golden Visions, Broken Dreams, A Short History of the Lutheran Council in the USA,* reports:

> In 1968 the ALC declared itself to be in "altar and pulpit fellowship" with the LCA, LCMS and SELC. This would permit clergy to preach in congregations of the others and congregational members to participate together in Holy Communion. In 1969 the LCMS declared itself in fellowship with the ALC. The LCA, considering itself to be in fellowship with any denomination subscribing to the Lutheran Confessions, needed no such declaration of its own. So the ALC, as the only Council body in mutually declared fellowship with both its major partners, might be seen as a kind of bridge between the more conservative Missouri Synod and the more liberal LCA, which also began fellowship talks with each other.[129]

At this point it is important to remember that during the 1960s the LCMS was under the influence of those within the Synod promoting historical-criticism. It was during the years of this growing influence that the LCUSA was organized. In fact, the LCUSA chose as its first head of communications the president of the LCMS Concordia Seminary, John Tietjen (see the LCMS section). The LCMS liberals favored cooperative ministry without agreement in doctrine, while the conservatives held to the confessional position and were hesitant about joining the new organization. However, a compromise was reached when the LCMS agreed to join the LCUSA providing that a relatively new area of cooperation, theological studies, would be mandatory for all partners.[130]

In the years following 1969 several important developments occurred that were to affect the "golden visions" of the LCUSA. After the 1974 upheaval in the LCMS, with the exodus from Concordia Seminary and the formation of the AELC, the synod began to cut back financial support of the Council's work and to withdraw from some programs. In 1977 and 1979 the LCMS declared fellowship in protest with the ALC after citing disagreements on the ordination of women,

---

[128]Naomi Frost, *Golden Visions, Broken Dreams: A Short History of the Lutheran Council in the USA* (New York: Lutheran Council in the USA, 1987), p. 1.

[129]Ibid., p. 4

[130]Ibid., pp. 3, 4.

membership in ecumenical bodies, and doctrine. In 1981 the LCMS broke off fellowship with the ALC and began a massive withdrawal from the LCUSA campus ministry programs. It also elected a new president, Dr. Ralph Bohlmann, who called for the formation of a new inter-Lutheran association.[131]

Since 1969 there had been inter-Lutheran negotiations, under the auspices of the LCUSA, exploring the possibility of future Lutheran unity. The LCMS participated in the discussions but since it was officially committed to fellowship based on doctrinal agreement, it was not interested in structural unity.[132]

When the AELC, well known for its eagerness for Lutheran union, joined the LCUSA in 1978 it quickly issued "A Call to Lutheran Union." The proposal called for a commitment to organic union without prior consideration of the process through which this would be accomplished—that could be worked out later. There was no mention of doctrinal discussion. The LCA responded with enthusiasm to the AELC proposal, since this was also their position on union.[133] As Lutheran historians have noted, the LCA was "already committed to inter-Lutheran fellowship and saw no need for doctrinal discussions," holding to the position that "there must be room for theological diversity" among Lutherans within an organic union (the "big umbrella" theory).[134] The ALC response was negative. However, a four-year study plan was agreed upon[135] and the wheels were set in motion for the organic union that would create the Evangelical Lutheran Church in America (ELCA) in 1988. In 1981 another call to merger was issued:

> ALC, LCA, and AELC seminary presidents and deans, convened by the Lutheran Council's Division of Campus Ministry and Educational Services for their annual meeting in January 1981, issued a "Call to Lutheran Union Now." They made the point, "The union of Lutheran churches in the United States at this time is not an option to be considered but an action to be taken."

> By 1982 union was a targeted reality, and the 70-member Commission for a New Lutheran Church succeeded the Committee on Lutheran Unity.[136]

---

[131]Ibid., pp. 7, 8.
[132]*The Lutherans in North America,* Supplement, op. cit., p. 561.
[133]Ibid., p. 562.
[134]Ibid., p. 529.
[135]Ibid., pp. 562, 563.
[136]Frost, op. cit., p. 74.

The Commission for the New Lutheran Church (CNLC) was composed of representatives from the ALC, LCA, and AELC. The LCMS had declined the invitation to union. Negotiations were soon underway, and by 1984 the three churches were committed to forming a new Lutheran church. The major area of concern centered on organizational structure.[137]

Early in the negotiations a decision was made to leave the words inerrant and infallible out of the Statement of Faith in the proposed New Lutheran Church (NLC) constitution.[138] Voices of protest were soon heard from the conservative sector.[139] However, once again a compromise was reached and the statement was worded to allow for the coexistence of both views of Scriptural authority[140] (see Chapter 3). The drafters of the document were Dr. John Tietjen, AELC, president of Christ Seminary—Seminex; Dr. Fred Meuser, ALC, president of Trinity Theological Seminary; and Dr. H. George Anderson, LCA, president of Luther College—all members of the CNLC Task Force on Theology.[141] Thus, the matter was settled once and for all. Later, Michigan Bishop Reginald Holle, ALC, would comment "The key words in the new statement are that Scripture is 'the authority for faith and life' and that's stronger than 'inerrant and infallible.' "[142]

Is it? Members of Lutherans Informed for Truth disagreed with the decision of the CNLC, as well as Holle's evaluation, and their voices were soon numbered among those raised in protest. It was this decision that prompted the research leading to their departure from the ALC and the subsequent publication of this book.

In January 1988, after completion of negotiations and the tally of ALC congregational votes, the ELCA came into existence and began functioning as the largest Lutheran church in American history. It united more than 5 million Lutherans: the 3 million-member LCA, the 2.3 million-member ALC, and the 110,000-member AELC.[143] The bishop of the Minnesota Synod of the LCA, Dr. Herbert W. Chilstrom, was elected to serve as the first president.

---

[137]"A Narrative Description for a New Lutheran Church," CNLC Progress Report #4, *The Lutheran Standard,* December 14, 1984, pp. 39-62.

[138]"Outstanding Document," *The Lutheran Standard,* May 4, 1984, p. 24.

[139]Wilmar Thorkelson, "New US Lutheran Church Commission Acts on Theology, Property, Purpose, Structure," *Lutheran World Information,* October 1984, p. 16.

[140]Nichol, op. cit., p. 13.

[141]Thorkelson, loc. cit.

[142]David Crumm, "Lutheran Merger Virtually Set, But Some Dissent," *Detroit Free Press,* March 21, 1987, Section A, p. 3.

[143]Edgar R. Trexler, "Two Structural Options Proposed for New Church," *The Lutheran,* March 21, 1984, p. 20.

Once again it was a victory for the liberal elements in American Lutheranism. Because of the willingness of the ALC to sacrifice what was left of its doctrinal heritage for the sake of outward unity, the majority of Lutherans were now in the liberal camp.

As with mergers of the past there were pastors, congregations, and individuals who refused to join. In addition, many new congregations were formed by pastors and laity who left congregations that were in agreement with merger efforts. Many joined existing Lutheran bodies. Others remained independent or united with other congregations to form new groups. Of the new groups formed, the largest is the American Association of Lutheran Churches (AALC).

Future Inter-Lutheran Cooperation

During the years of the ELCA negotiations plans were also being made for future inter-Lutheran cooperation through the efforts of a committee established in 1985. Chaired by Dr. Arnold Mickelson, a president of the LCUSA and coordinator of the CNLC, a plan was established that would allow for future ELCA-LCMS cooperation. By late 1987, when the LCUSA disbanded, cooperative efforts focused on four completely separate joint agencies and several other levels of official cooperation, as well as a host of independent organizations clustered around particular concerns, issues, or professions. There is no central coordinating office. However, both the ELCA and LCMS support the legal successor to the LCUSA, the Department of Immigration and Refuge Services, and have representatives on the LIRS board.[144] One cannot help but wonder about the long-term effects of continuing ELCA-LCMS cooperation upon the American Lutheran scene. Only the passage of time will provide the answer.

Theological direction of ELCA

With each merger, the confessional position of the new body has been weakened, not only by compromise, but by the departure of many of the most conservative members and pastors. Thus, the leaven of liberalism is allowed to work unhampered by those voices that might otherwise have continued to be raised in protest. In *Liberalism: Its Cause and Cure—The Poisoning of American Christianity and the Antidote,* the author, Dr. Gregory L. Jackson, a former LCA pastor now serving a WELS congregation, writes:

> When a somewhat more conservative denomination merges with a liberal group, the theology of the liberal group quick-

---

[144]Frost, op. cit., p. 71.

ly dominates the new church body. The degenerative process is actually hastened by merger, since the obvious disparities of faith drive out the more conservative members and pastors, allowing the Left to whoop it up on their own.

When a denomination with property rights merges with another group where the congregation has no property rights [the former LCA], the effect of merger is to take away property rights from the conservatives, not to restore rights to the liberal group. The more liberal the denomination, the more tyrannical the rules concerning the ownership of property. In addition, newer congregations have even fewer rights than the older churches established in more democratic times.[145]

A recent incident reported in the newsletter of Abiding Word Ministries, written by David R. Barnhart, a former LCA pastor now serving an AFLC congregation, supports Jackson's observations:

ELCA CONGREGATION DISCOVERS THAT IT MUST TOE THE LINE WHEN REWRITING ITS CONSTITUTION: Many ELCA congregations are busy rewriting their constitutions to bring them into conformity with that body's model constitution. The congregations are required to have their constitutions rewritten and submitted for approval within the first four years of membership in the new ELCA. One congregation in the state of Washington has discovered that approval of their local desires in a constitution does not come easily.

In a letter to the Washington congregation, a Southwestern Washington Synod (ELCA) official informed the congregation's leadership that their proposed constitution's language would have to be changed to conform with the ELCA. . . . *The congregation was informed that their constitutional language which declared the Bible to be the "inspired, revealed and inerrant Word of God" was unacceptable.* The letter from Synod stated that "such language is not found in either scripture [sic] or any of the Lutheran confessions." That statement by the ELCA is untrue, since both Scripture and

---

[145]Gregory L. Jackson, *Liberalism: Its Cause and Cure: The Poisoning of American Christianity and the Antidote* (Milwaukee: Northwestern Publishing House, 1991), p. 42. The author left LCA over the issues of inerrancy, abortion, and homosexual activism and joined the Wisconsin Synod.

the Lutheran confessions speak of the Word of God as being inspired and without error (author's emphasis).

Regarding the matter of ownership of property, the Washington congregation was told that "you handled the disposition of the assets in a manner similar to the American Lutheran Church constitution." They were instructed to *"use the language of the ELCA model constitution for congregations." This assures that control of church property now rests with the pleasure of the ELCA* (author's emphasis).[146]

At the present time there remain some voices of protest within the ELCA. They are concerned and hope to bring about change that will return the ELCA to a more confessional position.[147] However, judging from past history there seems little likelihood of any real success. The future theological position of the ELCA appears to have already been determined.

In this chapter, as well as the preceding one, we have observed the results of doctrinal compromise for the sake of outward unity. Doctrinal compromise leads to doctrinal indifference and the blurring of denominational lines. This will become clear in the next chapter, which deals with the modern-day Ecumenical Movement.

---

[146]"ELCA Congregation Discovers That it Must 'Toe the Line' when Rewriting its Constitution," *Abiding Word Ministries,* ed. David R. Barnhart, Summer 1991, p. 8.

[147]"Contending for the Lutheran Future," *Forum Letter,* ed. Richard John Neuhaus, July 15, 1991, p.1.

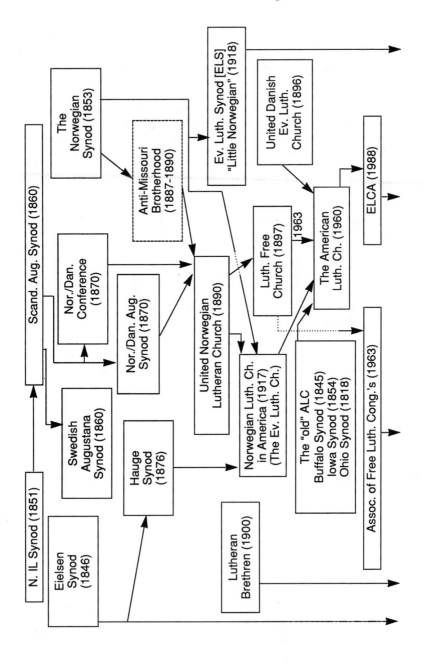

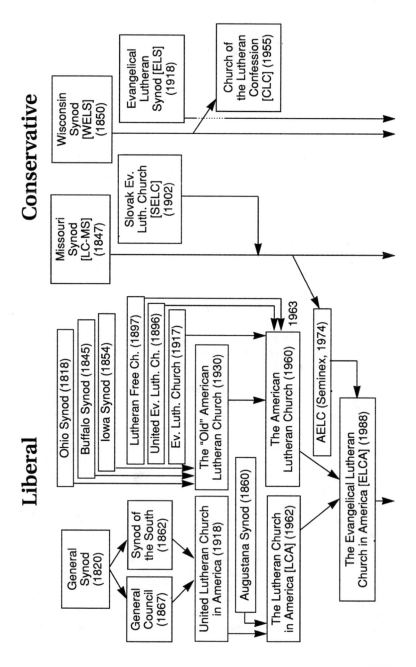

Conservative

Wisconsin Synod [WELS] (1850)

Evangelical Lutheran Synod [ELS] (1918)

Church of the Lutheran Confession [CLC] (1955)

Missouri Synod [LC-MS] (1847)

Slovak Ev. Luth. Church [SELC] (1902)

Liberal

Ohio Synod (1818)

Buffalo Synod (1845)

Iowa Synod (1854)

Lutheran Free Ch. (1897)

United Ev. Luth. Ch. (1896)

Ev. Luth. Church (1917)

The "Old" American Lutheran Church (1930)

1963

The American Lutheran Church (1960)

AELC (Seminex, 1974)

General Synod (1820)

Synod of the South (1862)

General Council (1867)

United Lutheran Church in America (1918)

Augustana Synod (1860)

The Lutheran Church in America [LCA] (1962)

The Evangelical Lutheran Church in America [ELCA] (1988)

28.

ECUMENISM MEANS DOCTRINAL INDIFFERENCE

"For God loved the world so much that He gave His one-and-only Son, so that everyone who believes in Him would not perish but have everlasting life" (John 3:16 NET).[1]

We are saved by grace through faith in Christ. "Salvation is found in no one else, for there is no other name under heaven given to men by which we must be saved" (Acts 4:12). The late Dr. Herman W. Gockel, a conservative Lutheran Church—Missouri Synod (LCMS) pastor and former religious director for the popular TV program "This Is the Life," writes in his book, *What Jesus Means to Me:*

> Christ . . . suffered the punishment of all my sins. He assumed the guilt which was mine. He paid the penalty which I should have paid. He took my place before the bar of God's justice and by His payment of my debt secured my freedom. Because of Christ's atonement I have been acquitted. This atonement theme is the golden thread of assurance which God has woven throughout the pages of the Bible. . . . What does Jesus mean to me?

---

[1]The New Evangelical Translation (NET) of the Bible is a thorough reworking of Lutheran scholar William F. Beck's *An American Translation* (AAT). The NET is a literal translation that is faithful to the oldest original language texts, committed to simplicity and clarity yet conveying every shade of the rich meaning. Perhaps most importantly, the work is being carried out by confessional Lutheran scholars who are committed to the sound Lutheran principles of biblical interpretation. The NET has thus avoided the many, often subtle, mistranslations that flawed such otherwise praiseworthy translations as the NIV and NASV, whose translators were primarily Reformed scholars. We highly recommend the NET to our readers.

Chief of sinners though I be,
Christ is All in all to me;
Died that I might live on high
Lived that I might never die;
As the branch is to the vine,
I am His, and He is mine![2]

What Jesus meant to Gockel is what he has meant to hundreds of millions of other Christians through ages past and what he still means to uncounted multitudes today, including the authors of this book. "What Jesus Means To Us" might very well have been the title of this book, for our faith, and our concern for the faith of others, has been the motivating force behind its authorship.

As we know from the documentation in the preceding chapters, the historic Christian faith is under attack by twin foes—false doctrine and doctrinal indifference. Both are capable of destroying faith and have, in large measure, worked together to create the climate from which the modern ecumenical movement has evolved.

THE IMPORTANCE OF DOCTRINE

The ecumenical movement is the final topic of our comparison column (see Chapter 1). The opening sentence of the historic Lutheran position states: "*All* doctrines of the Bible are important and provide foundation and support for the chief doctrine, the Gospel." This is the key to understanding the error of the ecumenical movement.

Not only are all doctrines important, but they are to be guarded closely. Scripture states:

"Watch your life and doctrine closely. Persevere in them, because if you do, you will save both yourself and your hearers" (1 Timothy 4:16).

Doctrine must be kept "pure, that is, free from man-made errors." The late Dr. C. F. W. Walther (LCMS), patriarch of confessional Lutheranism in America (see Chapter 26), points out the importance of purity of doctrine and refutes those who would label it a "narrow" view:

---

[2]Herman W. Gockel, *What Jesus Means to Me* (St. Louis: Concordia Publishing House, 1948), pp. 17, 135. This small book, although subjective in tone, gives voice only to those Christian experiences and emotions that are common to all believers. The book describes the priceless treasures of the Christian faith in simple, everyday language. We highly recommend it as an example of emotion as a natural outcome of faith based on the objective Word of God.

Christ himself has described the way to heaven as a narrow path. Just so narrow is the path of pure doctrine. For the pure doctrine is nothing else than the doctrine regarding the way to heaven. It is easy to lose your way when it is narrow, rarely traveled, and leads through a dense forest. Without intending to do so and without being aware of it, you may make a wrong turn to the right or left. It is equally easy to lose the narrow way of the pure doctrine, which likewise is traveled by few people and leads through a dense forest of erroneous teachings. You may land either in the bog of fanaticism or in the abyss of rationalism. This is no jest. False doctrine is poison to the soul. An entire banqueting party drinking from cups containing an admixture of arsenic can drink physical death from its cups. So an entire audience can invite spiritual and eternal death by listening to a sermon that contains an admixture of the poison of false doctrine. A person can be deprived of his soul's salvation by a single false comfort or a single false reproof administered to him. This is all the more easy because we are all naturally more accessible to the shining and dazzling light of human reason than to the divine truth. For "the natural man receiveth not the things of the Spirit of God, for they are foolishness unto him; neither can he know them" (1 Cor. 2:14).

From what has been said you can gather how foolish it is, yea, what an awful delusion has taken hold upon so many men's minds who ridicule the pure doctrine and say to us: "Ah, do cease clamoring, Pure doctrine! Pure doctrine! That can only land you in dead orthodoxism. Pay more attention to pure life, and you will raise a growth of genuine Christianity." That is exactly like saying to a farmer: "Do not worry forever about good seed; worry about good fruits." Is not a farmer properly concerned about good fruit when he is solicitous about getting good seed? Just so a concern about pure doctrine is the proper concern about genuine Christianity and a sincere Christian life. False doctrine is noxious seed, sown by the enemy to produce a progeny of wickedness. The pure doctrine is wheat seed; from it spring the children of the Kingdom, who even in the present life belong in the kingdom of Jesus Christ and in the life to come will be received into the Kingdom of Glory. May God even now implant in your hearts a great fear, yea, a real abhorrence, of false doctrine! May He graciously give you a holy desire for the pure, saving truth, revealed by God Himself![3]

False doctrine is, indeed, poison to the soul for it can destroy faith. It must not be allowed to co-exist alongside of pure doctrine. In his commentary on Galatians, Martin Luther observed Paul's reaction to the Galatians, who had taken to following false prophets:

> This whole epistle witnesseth how Paul was grieved with the fall of the Galatians, and how he beat into their heads the exceeding great and horrible enormities that would ensue, unless they repented. This fatherly care moved some of them not at all: for many no longer acknowledged Paul as their teacher, but preferred the false apostles far above him. Moreover, the false apostles, no doubt, slandered Paul, saying that he was an obstinate and contentious fellow, who for a light matter would break the unity of the churches. Through this they made him odious unto many.

> Some others, who had not wholly forsaken his doctrine, thought there was no danger in dissenting a little from him in the doctrine of justification and faith; when therefore they heard that Paul made that matter so heinous, which they thought so light, they marveled, and thought thus: Granted that we have swerved somewhat from his doctrine, and there is some fault in us, yet that being a small matter, he ought to wink thereat, or at least not so greatly amplify it, lest the concord [unity and peace] of the churches be broken.

> Wherefore Paul answereth such an excuse with this sentence: "A little leaven leaveneth the whole lump."

> And this is a caveat, or an admonition which he standeth much upon. And we also ought greatly to observe the same at this day. For our adversaries object against us that we are obstinate in defending our doctrine and even in matters of no importance. But these are the crafty fruits of the devil, whereby he goeth about to overthrow our doctrine. To this we answer with Paul: "A little leaven leaveneth the whole lump."

> In philosophy, a small fault in the beginning, is a great and foul fault in the end. So, in divinity, one little error overthroweth the whole doctrine. The doctrine is not ours, but

---

[3] C. F. W. Walther, *The Proper Distinction Between Law and Gospel,* ed. W. H. T. Dau (St. Louis: Concordia Publishing House, 1928), pp. 20, 21.

God's, whose ministers we are; therefore we may not change, or diminish one tittle thereof. The life is ours: therefore, as touching that, we are ready to do, suffer, forgive, whatsoever our adversaries require of us, so that faith and doctrine remain sound and uncorrupt.[4]

Not only do Paul, Luther, and Walther warn against the leaven of false doctrine—so do others who followed later. The late Dr. Charles Porterfield Krauth, a spiritual ancestor of the Evangelical Lutheran Church in America (ELCA), seminary professor, and leader of the English-speaking branch of the confessional Lutheran awakening in America (which led to the formation of the General Council—see Chapter 26), wrote:

When error is admitted into the Church, it will be found that the stages of its progress are always three. It begins by asking *toleration*. Its friends say to the majority: You need not be afraid of us; we are few, and weak; only let us alone; we shall not disturb the faith of others. The church has her standards of doctrine; of course we shall never interfere with them; we only ask for ourselves to be spared interference with our private opinions. Indulged in this for a time, error goes on to assert *equal rights*. Truth and error are two balancing forces. The Church shall do nothing which looks like deciding between them; that would be partiality. It is bigotry to assert any superior right for the truth. We are to agree to differ, and any favoring of the truth, because it is truth, is partisanship. What the friends of truth and error hold in common is fundamental. Anything on which they differ is *ipso facto* non-essential. Anybody who makes account of such a thing is a disturber of the peace of the church. Truth and error are two co-ordinate powers, and the great secret of church-statesmanship is to preserve the balance between them. From this point error soon goes on to its natural end, which is to assert *supremacy*. Truth started with *tolerating;* it comes to be merely tolerated, and that only for a time. Error claims a preference for its judgments on all disputed points. It puts men into positions, not as at first in spite of their departure from the Church's faith, but in consequence of it. Their recommendation is that they repudiate that faith, and position is given them to teach others to re-

---

[4]Martin Luther, *Commentary on Galatians,* trans. Erasmus Middleton, ed. John Prince Fallowes (Grand Rapids: Kregel Publications, 1979), pp. 317, 318.

pudiate it, and to make them skillful in combating it (author's emphasis).[5]

Luther pictured the articles of faith (doctrines) as a golden chain from which the precious gem, the saving gospel of Christ, is suspended. In the following quotation Luther not only emphasizes the importance of all doctrines of the faith, but he also identifies the enemy and the major instrument of destruction:

> *The Ruinous Virus of Rationalism*—When the devil has persuaded us to surrender one article of faith to him, he has won; in effect he has all of them, and Christ has already lost. He can at will unsettle and take all others, for they are all intertwined and linked together like a golden chain so that if one link is broken, the entire chain is broken and can be pulled apart. There is no article which the devil cannot overthrow once he has succeeded in having reason dabble in doctrine and speculate about it. Reason knows how to turn and twist Scripture in masterly fashion into conformity with its views. This is very agreeable, like sweet poison.[6]

THE RUINOUS VIRUS

Disease can destroy the body—false doctrine can destroy the soul. As we know, the misguided use of reason in the interpretation of Scripture in the Reformed churches became the instrument that divided Protestantism into many branches and planted the seeds for the development, and later acceptance, of the historical-critical method of biblical interpretation. This method substitutes reason for the authority of Scripture (see Chapter 3). Therefore, historical criticism can be seen as the "ruinous virus of Rationalism" described by Luther, for historical criticism is the ultimate imposition of reason upon Scripture. The documentation in preceding chapters clearly illustrates that historical criticism has been the instrument that has broken the "golden chain" of the articles of faith and is, indeed, poison to the soul!

Among the inevitable results of historical criticism is doctrinal indifference. Because historical criticism denies the absolute authority of Scripture, man is placed in judgment over Scripture. As a result,

---

[5]Charles P. Krauth, *The Conservative Reformation and its Theology* (Philadelphia: The United Lutheran Publication House, 1913), first edition, 1871, pp. 195, 196.

[6]*What Luther Says,* 3 vols. ed. Ewald M. Plass, (St. Louis: Concordia Publishing House, 1959), 3:1165.

God's absolutes are replaced by man's opinions, truth becomes relative, certainty gives way to doubt, and confusion reigns. There is no true or false doctrine, only each man's individual interpretation. Doctrine soon becomes a matter of indifference and doctrinal indifference becomes "at once the root of unionism and its fruit."[7]

In answer to the question "What is unionism?" the late Dr. F. Pfotenhauer, a president of the LCMS, wrote:

> Unionism is fellowship between churches without corresponding harmony and unity of confessions and faith. It is toleration of false doctrine, mutual recognition as brethren of the faith by those who push aside and ignore differences in doctrine. This mutual recognition as brethren of the faith is then given expression when members of different confessions band themselves together in one congregation, unite in church federations, or at least practice pulpit, altar, or prayer fellowship, and undertake united efforts in church work. The essential thing in unionism is that differences in doctrine are minimized and ignored and as a matter of principle the sharp distinction between truth and error is removed.[8]

THE ECUMENICAL MOVEMENT

The modern ecumenical movement is simply the promotion of unionism on a grand scale. It cuts across denominational lines and has as its ultimate objective the reuniting of all churches into one. The proponents of the ecumenical movement do not recognize their error because they fail to understand the proper distinction between the invisible church and the visible church—true unity and unionism.

The doctrine of the church

Armin W. Schuetze, theologian and professor emeritus of the Lutheran Confessions at Wisconsin Lutheran Seminary, Wisconsin Evangelical Lutheran Synod (WELS), states the historic Lutheran doctrine of the Church:

> A Christian is not alone. Through faith he is brought into the family of God. St. Paul writes, "You are all sons of God through faith in Christ Jesus" (Galatians 3:26). . . . Whether they are male or female, whether rich or poor, whether

---

[7]J. Michael Reu, *In the Interest of Lutheran Unity, Two Lectures* (Columbus: Lutheran Book Concern, 1940), p. 20.

[8]Herbert O. Lussky, "The Missouri Synod Layman and Lutheran Union," a booklet published by the author (Evanston, IL, 1947), p. 29.

Lutheran or Methodist or Catholic, all who truly believe in Jesus Christ as the Savior from sin, God has brought together into his family, into one body.

Jesus gathers under him all those who have been called out of the mass of unbelieving mankind and have been brought to saving faith. This gathering or congregation of true believers is called the church.

Only true believers are gathered by Christ into his church. . . [and] only someone who can look into man's heart and see the faith that is present there can truly know who is a member of the church. This man cannot do. Man can see no more than "the outward appearance"; only "the LORD looks at the heart" (1 Samuel 16:7). Outward appearance may be deceiving, but he who looks at the heart cannot be deceived. It is therefore only the Lord who "knows those who are his" (2 Timothy 2:19). For this reason the holy Christian church cannot be identified with any outward body or organization. The church has therefore been called invisible.

If the church is invisible, will it not be impossible, or at least difficult to find in this world? Not at all. Although it is invisible in the sense mentioned above, its presence can readily be detected. There are marks by which its presence can be discerned.

Where will the believer, the church, be found? They will be found wherever the means that produce faith are found, and those means are the gospel in word and sacrament. Peter writes, "You have been born again, not of perishable seed, but of imperishable, through the living and enduring word of God" (1 Peter 1:23). In Titus, baptism is called the "washing of rebirth and renewal by the Holy Spirit" (3:5). Wherever, then, the word of God is in use, wherever the regenerating power of baptism is applied, there one can expect believers, that is, the church, to be present. For God says, concerning the regenerating word, "It will not return to me empty, but will accomplish what I desire and achieve the purpose for which I sent it" (Isaiah 55:11). . . . Where the word and sacraments are in use, the assumption is valid that there are those present to whom God has entrusted the use of these means.

Although the church as such remains invisible in that the specific members remain known only to God, the means of

grace are marks whereby the presence of believers is revealed. These means are properly called the marks of the
church.[9]

Unity of faith and doctrine

The historic Lutheran teaching concerning unity of faith and unity of doctrine are stated by the late Dr. Edward Koehler, a noted theologian and scholar of the LCMS:

> The Church is *catholic, universal,* because it is gathered to-
> gether from every nation under the sun. It embraces all true
> Christians that ever lived, are now living, and will live to
> the end of days. Whoever is a true believer in Christ, . . . be-
> longs to this Church. . . . Because Rome usurped this term
> "catholic," and wrongly applied it to its particular denomina-
> tion, which is by no means universal, Luther substituted the
> word "Christian" in the Third Article of the Apostles' Creed.

> Unity of faith exists among all the members of the invisible
> Church as we confess with Luther in the explanation of the
> Third Article of the Apostles' Creed, that the Holy Ghost
> keeps the whole Christian Church on earth with Jesus
> Christ in the one true faith. No matter to which denomina-
> tion a person may belong, or whether or not he is formally a
> member of any denomination, if he trusts for the forgiveness
> of his sins and for his eternal salvation solely in the merits
> of Jesus Christ, then he is in unity of faith with all other
> Christians. He may possibly be ignorant of some other
> teachings of the Bible, or, misunderstanding certain texts,
> he may possibly err in certain doctrines; yet, if his ignorance
> and misunderstanding do not pertain to the central doctrine,
> namely to justification by grace through faith in Christ, then
> he is still in the unity of faith, is a member of the invisible
> Church, and will be saved. The unity of faith is not limited
> by denominational boundaries, but includes all those, wher-
> ever they may be, who trust for grace and salvation in the
> God-man Jesus Christ. On the other hand, such unity of
> faith does not necessarily exist among all the members of
> the same denomination or congregation, for the tares among
> the wheat are certainly not in the unity of faith.

---

[9]Armin W. Schuetze, *Basic Doctrines of the Bible* (Milwaukee: Northwestern Publishing House, 1986), pp. 69-71.

Unity of doctrine consists in this that the members of a church, or a denomination, are united in all the doctrines they teach and confess. There is no unity of doctrine among the various denominations of the visible Church; they are divided because of differences in doctrine. Such division of the visible Church into diverse denominations is a grievous offense both to the world and to the church, especially to weak Christians; it is also most displeasing to God. Responsibility must be placed not on those who strictly adhere to the Word of God and refuse fellowship to those who teach otherwise, but on those "which cause divisions and offenses contrary to the doctrine" we have learned from the apostles (Rom 16:17; Acts 20:29,30; 2 Tim. 2:16-18; 4:3,4).

As the invisible Church is one in faith, so the visible Church should, according to the will of God, be one in the confession of faith and doctrine. "Now I beseech you, brethren, by the name of our Lord Jesus Christ, that ye all speak the same thing, and that there be no divisions" (schism) "among you; but that ye be perfectly joined together in the same mind and in the same judgment" (1 Cor. 1:10); (Eph. 4:3-5; Acts 2:42). For this reason Christians should not perpetuate this offensive division in matters of doctrine, but should labor towards unity in doctrine, which does not consist in an external merger or union, but in this, that they unite in believing, teaching, and confessing the same truths of the Word.[10]

Those who take the ecumenical approach view the church as essentially visible. Their efforts are focused on outward unity regardless of doctrinal differences. Kurt E. Marquart, a conservative Lutheran theologian and LCMS seminary professor, writes:

The Ecumenical Movement, of course, treats the church as essentially visible. Archbishop Temple of Canterbury had put it like this: "I believe in the holy catholic church—and sincerely regret that it does not at present exist." Here the oneness of the church is no longer an article of faith—part and parcel of the very existence of the church, Ephesians 4— but an ideal to be realized (sic) by patient negotiation, ecclesiastical diplomacy, and compromise! Such a view has no use for the old distinction between the church visible and

---

[10]Edward W. A. Koehler, *A Summary of Christian Doctrine* (St. Louis: Concordia Publishing House, 1971), pp. 240, 247-249.

the church invisible. . . . The Ecumenical approach is not content to walk by faith—it must *see* the Body of Christ (author's emphasis)[11]

ELCA IS COMMITTED TO ECUMENISM

The ELCA is committed to ecumenism. This statement is made not only by virtue of the past history of the ELCA's predecessor bodies (see preceding chapter), but also as stated in one of its official organs *The Lutheran*. Shortly after the ELCA began functioning as a new church body the new bishop, Herbert W. Chilstrom, embarked on an unprecedented ten-day ecumenical pilgrimage:

Making the trip during the first month of the ELCA's official life, Chilstrom met in Rome with Pope John Paul II, in Istanbul with Ecumenical Patriarch Demetrios I of the Orthodox Church, in Moscow with Patriarch Pimen of the Russian Orthodox Church and in London with Archbishop of Canterbury Robert Runcie [of the Anglican Church, the mother of the Episcopal Church in America]. At each stop, Chilstrom told the church leaders, "I have come to express visibly the deep commitment of my church and myself personally to the ecumenical movement and to the dialogues between our churches."

Late last year, Chilstrom solidified other ecumenical commitments by visiting the offices in Geneva, Switzerland, of the Word Alliance of Reformed Churches, the Lutheran World Federation and the World Council of Churches.

As Chilstrom completed his ecumenical swing, he reflected on the experiences. . . . "I have the strong feeling that the way for me was prepared by the people who had gone before me, including the leaders of the ELCA's immediate predecessor churches. I am more keenly aware of what I already knew intellectually, that we owe a great debt of gratitude to those who opened the doors to this ecumenical venture. . . . We must move ahead quickly to explore deeper relations with the Reformed churches. As time and energy permit, we must talk with other Christian denominations, both continuing previous dialogues and initiating new ones.[12]

---

[11]Kurt E. Marquart, *Anatomy of An Explosion* (Grand Rapids: Baker Book House, 1978), p. 58.

[12]Edgar R. Trexler, "Warm Reception for Chilstrom, ELCA Bishop Makes Ecumenical Commitment Clear," *The Lutheran*, March 2, 1988, pp. 6, 8.

Chilstrom's reference to leaders of the ELCA's predecessor churches no doubt includes the former American Lutheran Church (ALC) president, the late Dr. Fredrik A. Schiotz, and the former Lutheran Church in America (LCA) president, the late Dr. Franklin C. Fry.

Schiotz assisted in the organization of the Lutheran World Federation (LWF) in 1947, serving for seven years as president and sixteen years as a member of the executive committee. He also served on the World Council of Churches (WCC) Central Committee.[13]

Fry was president of the LWF for six years, served an unprecedented fourteen years as chairperson of the WCC Central Committee,[14] and was one of the architects of the National Council of Churches (NCC), which formed in 1950.[15] Through his leadership, predecessor bodies of the LCA were early members of the NCC.[16] When the WCC was officially constituted in 1948, predecessor bodies of both the ALC and LCA were included in its membership.[17]

Dialogue continues between the ELCA and the Roman Catholic Church[18] and various churches of the Reformed tradition, including the Episcopal,[19] Methodist,[20] Presbyterian, Reformed Church in America, and the United Church of Christ.[21]

Full communion

As this chapter is being written, the ELCA congregations and seminaries are studying a 30-page statement on ecumenism which is scheduled for a vote at the ELCA 1991 Churchwide Assembly.[22]

---

[13]"Schiotz, Former ALC Leader, Dies," *The Lutheran,* March 22, 1989, p. 23.

[14]E. Theodore Bachmann, "ULCA: Building Blocks for Unity," *The Lutheran,* November, 1987, p. 9.

[15]*The Lutherans in North America,* ed. E. Clifford Nelson (Philadelphia: Fortress Press, 1975), p. 514.

[16]E. Theodore Bachmann, *The Ecumenical Involvement of the LCA Predecessor Bodies: A Brief History 1900-1962* (New York: Division for World Mission and Ecumenism, Lutheran Church in America, 1982), pp. 89-101.

[17]Dorris A. Flesner, *American Lutherans Help Shape World Council: The Role of the Lutheran Churches of America in the Formation of the World Council of Churches* (Dubuque, IA: Wm. C. Brown Co. Publishers, 1981), p. 1.

[18]"Visions for ELCA's Direction," *The Lutheran,* April 20, 1988, p. 25.

[19]Sura Rubenstein, "Lutheran-Episcopal Accord Issued," *The Lutheran,* May 11, 1988, p. 28.

[20]"Closer Lutheran-Methodist Ties Urged," *The Lutheran,* January 6, 1988, p. 26.

[21]Jean Caffey Lyles, "ELCA, Reformed Efforts Get Back on Track," *The Lutheran,* March 22, 1989, p. 29.

[22]Darrell Turner, "ELCA's Proposed Statement on Ecumenism Still Drawing Dissent," *Religious News Service,* January 9, 1991, reprinted in *Christian News,* January 21, 1991, p. 16.

According to the executive director of the ELCA's Office of Ecumenical Affairs, Dr. William Rusch, the goal is "full communion" with other Christian bodies. Full communion between churches is defined by Dr. David L. Tiede, president of Luther Northwestern Theological Seminary, St. Paul, Minnesota, as commonly meaning "that churches recognize each other as holding the essentials of Christian faith, that members of each church may receive sacraments in the other church, and that clergy of one body may exercise liturgical functions in a congregation of the other body."[23]

There is some dissent over the proposed statement, primarily from the seminaries. Concerns seem to be focused on "full communion" as a goal. The argument is that reaching full communion with some churches may drive the ELCA further from other churches. Rusch points out that "full communion is a goal, not a model. As full communion would get lived out, it would clearly take on different characteristics." Tiede added that "the specific content of 'full communion' varies depending upon whether you're talking with Catholics or Protestants." He pointed out that full communion for Catholics "involves a recognition of the primacy of the pope," while this would not be a requirement for Protestant bodies. However, Tiede remains optimistic. "I don't think this is an insurmountable difficulty. I think this takes some respectful conversation between people of differing views, including those within the ELCA."[24]

The following observations, as expressed by Paul Fleischer, a pastor in the conservative Church of the Lutheran Confession (CLC), mirror those of the authors of this book as regarding the future ecumenical commitment of the ELCA:

> Church history has shown that, when churches or entire church bodies become guilty of error in doctrine and practice, the fault most often lies with the leaders. The leaders of the various Lutheran synods which united to form the ELCA have for years been actively promoting an ecumenism which encourages organizational union without doctrinal unity. The current ELCA Bishop is leading his new synod down the same path. We are not surprised, therefore, that mainstream Lutheranism is continuing on the unionistic path it has been traveling. Nor should we be surprised that, before long, it will claim union with Rome itself. We are alive to witness some of the saddest days in the history of Lutheranism.[25]

---

[23]Ibid.

[24]Ibid.

[25]Paul Fleischer, "On Unity and Union or the ELCA and Bankrupt Lutheranism," *The Lutheran Spokesman,* July 1989, p. 11.

Sad days indeed. The ELCA's statement on ecumenism was over-whelmingly approved (919-67) by the delegates to the Churchwide Assembly.[26] In its rush to embrace the error of ecumenism, the LCA has added one more error to the long list of errors already recorded in this book. Instead of upholding the historic Lutheran position that true unity must be based upon agreement on *all* doctrines of the Bible, the ELCA has reduced the requirement for unity to *one*.

Gospel reductionism

The position of the ELCA concerning requirements for unity is sometimes referred to as "Gospel reductionism"—reducing the gospel to the lowest common denominator. It consists of making belief in the saving gospel of Jesus Christ the only requirement for "full commu-nion" between churches. Belief in the supporting doctrines is left as optional—subject to negotiation and compromise. Position B of our comparison column states it this way:

> Joining with non-Lutherans, both in worship and eventually even merging with them, is desirable as long as we agree with them, in a sense, that "Jesus Christ is Lord." Our differ-ences can be worked out through dialogue and compromise.

This position is supported by Dr. David Preus, the president of the former ALC, in a major address presented at an annual pastoral con-vocation held at Luther Northwestern Theological Seminary in 1986. The following quotation is taken from an article in the ALC's official organ, *The Lutheran Standard:*

> The time has come, Dr. David Preus believes, "for Lutherans to make a course correction in relations with other Christian churches." Preus, presiding bishop of the American Luther-an Church and an internationally respected Lutheran leader . . . urged that Lutherans acknowledge altar and pulpit fel-lowship with other churches as long as there is agreement on the gospel, even though differences may remain on other questions such as church organization.

> Preus pointed to "unity in reconciled diversity" as the direc-tion in which churches should move. "Lutherans are unique-ly equipped to affirm the practice of unity in reconciled di-versity," he said. "We are in position to take doctrinal differ-

---

[26]Gustav Spohn, "Lutherans Embrace Ecumenism at Assembly in Orlan-do," *Religious News Service,* September 3, 1991, reprinted in *Christian News,* September, 16, 1991, p. 6.

ences seriously without always making them church divisive and fellowship prohibitive." He explained that this is because Lutherans see agreement in the gospel as sufficient for expressing unity, even when disagreement persists on other matters of the Christian faith.

Preus recalled that interim eucharistic fellowship [joint communion services] has been practiced between Lutherans and Episcopalians in the United States since 1982, but he noted that "some Episcopalians continue to have trouble in fully accepting ministries that do not share in the catholic tradition of apostolic succession." In instances where Lutheran pastors are not recognized [by Episcopalians] as having a valid ministry, he said Lutherans are advised to withhold the sharing of communion until a time when the occasion can be fully mutual.

"Lutherans need not insist on complete doctrinal agreement before welcoming altar and pulpit fellowship with other Christians. Agreement in the gospel and sacraments does not require total doctrinal agreement."[27]

Nowhere in the article did Preus mention the critical difference between the Lutherans and the Reformed concerning the Lutheran doctrine of the Real Presence and the Reformed denial of communion as a means of grace (see Chapter 24). Instead, his only concern appears to be disagreement with the Episcopalian form of church government. It is important for the reader to understand the source of Preus's concern. Dr. Lewis W. Spitz, LCMS, a professor emeritus of systematic theology, offers the following explanation:

For the Anglican Church and its American daughter, the Protestant Episcopal Church, the form of church government is of greater importance than doctrine. The bishop (Greek: *episkopos*, hence Episcopalian) is considered supreme. As long as they recognize the bishops' authority, churchmen of all kinds are welcome in his church (author's emphasis).

Episcopalians attach great importance to the theory of the apostolic succession. They insist that the apostles ordained bishops, these in turn ordained their successors, and so down through the centuries, so that the present-day bishops are the

---

[27]"Preus Urges Ecumenical Change," *The Lutheran Standard,* January 24, 1986, p. 22.

successors of the apostles through an unbroken chain. Scripture knows nothing of such a theory. Episcopalians hold that only bishops who have received their authority in this way can properly ordain ministers and that without such episcopal ordination a minister cannot validly perform the sacraments.[28]

Preus's concern is a far cry from the spirit of Dr. Theodore Schmauk, another spiritual forefather of the ELCA and president of the conservative General Council (1903-18), who wrote:

> Is the Lord's Supper the place to display my toleration, my Christian sympathy, or my fellowship with another Christian, when that is the very point in which most of all we differ; and in which the difference means for me everything—means for me, the reception of my Savior's atonement? Is this the point to be selected for the display of Christian union, when in fact it is the very point in which Christian union does not exist?"[29]

Agreeing to disagree

The essence of religious unionism has been defined as "an agreement to disagree."[30] This basic concept, the hallmark of the ecumenical movement, reflects the influence of historical criticism. David Preus himself has stated that historical criticism is a "legitimate intellectual tool" to be used in "the study of the biblical text" (see Chapter 3). Preus says that churches should move in the direction of "unity in reconciled diversity" and that Lutherans are "uniquely equipped" for this endeavor. He could have more accurately said: Lutherans, along with those in other denominations, who have embraced historical criticism are uniquely equipped to affirm the practice of unity in reconciled diversity. Since those who accept historical criticism can no longer answer with any real certainty the question "What is truth?" they are, in a real sense, already united. Their unity, the unity of the mainline churches, is expressed most clearly by

---

[28]Lewis W. Spitz, *Our Church and Others* (St. Louis: Concordia Publishing House, 1960), pp. 76, 77.

[29]Theodore E. Schmauk and C. Theodore Benze, *The Confessional Principle and the Confessions, as Embodying the Evangelical Confession of the Christian Church* (Philadelphia: General Council Publication Board, 1911), p. 905f. Schmauk's book is considered a companion volume to Charles P. Krauth's, *The Conservative Reformation and its Theology*. All conservative Lutheran pastors value both books.

[30]*The Concordia Cyclopedia* (St. Louis, 1927), p. 774. Cited in: *Lutheran Cyclopedia* (St. Louis: Concordia Publishing House, 1975), p. 784.

Braaten and Jenson's *Christian Dogmatics* which is a rejection of all the basic doctrines of the Christian faith. If they are unwilling to refute the heresy of historical criticism, one might conclude that they may as well strive for organic union and learn to live with their doctrinal confusion by "agreeing to disagree." However, this is contrary to the will of God, and those who indulge in this practice are guilty of religious unionism. It is far better that they remain separate. Krauth says it most succinctly:

> Truthful separation is far better than dishonest union, and two churches are happier, and more kindly in their mutual relations, when their differences are frankly confessed, than when they are clouding with ambiguities and double meanings the real divergences."[31]

Doctrinal compromise

However, like-minded people tend to join together, "error loves ambiguities,"[32] and ambiguities are the product of dialogue.

We must keep in mind that historic critics believe that there are no absolute truths, no definite standards of right and wrong, and therefore, no certain answers (see Chapter 19). Thus they see nothing wrong with doctrinal compromise using formulas which can be understood in more than one sense. Even the deliberate manipulation of the less informed laity is not wrong in their system—it is simply one of many methods employed to keep moving them along in preparation for the moment they will be ready to be "enlightened" and accept the new thinking.

For some historic critics, agreement on the gospel, at least in some sense, still remains a requirement for union. For others, dialogue has opened the door to the possibility that even that requirement represents too narrow a view. "Mature" Christians are called upon to give up their "one-wayism" concerning the gospel and consider the possibility that non-Christian religions may be equally as valid as Christianity (see Chapter 18).

The process of doctrinal compromise for the sake of union is described by the late Dr. J. Michael Reu, theologian and seminary professor of the old ALC, who defended the inerrancy of Scripture.[33] He wrote:

---

[31]Krauth, op. cit., p. 326.

[32]Ibid., p. 215.

[33]Reu was an early critic of inerrancy and sought to show that this concept was foreign to Luther's understanding of Scripture. However, after studying Luther he reversed his former position; see his *Luther and the Scriptures,* published posthumously in 1944.

Here we discover the *first mark* of unionism: A difference in doctrine which hitherto has been regarded as divisive, is suddenly made to lose its divisive significance. The *second mark* of unionism, therefore, is this: Differences in doctrine are made to lose their divisive significance with a view to uniting hitherto separate churches. The *third mark* of unionism, therefore, is this: A formula of unification is found which each of two hitherto separate churches may accept but which each of them interprets differently. An external bond is found for internally divided groups. We find this attitude of tolerance quite frequently among unionists. It is often used to assuage a troubled conscience, one's own as well as that of others; for the unionist declares that every one may continue to hold his own private convictions and merely needs to respect and tolerate those of another. This attitude is totally wrong, for it disregards two important factors: (a) In tolerating divergent doctrines one either denies the perspicuity and clarity of the Scriptures, or one grants to error the right to exist alongside of truth, or one evidences indifference over against Biblical truth by surrendering its absolute validity; and (b) in allowing two opposite views concerning one doctrine to exist side by side, one has entered upon an inclined plane which of necessity leads ever further into complete doctrinal indifference, as may plainly be seen from the most calamitous case on record, viz., the Prussian Union. *Doctrinal indifference is at once the root of unionism and its fruit.* Whoever accepts, in theory as well as in practice, the absolute authority of the Scriptures and their unambiguousness with reference to all fundamental doctrines, must be opposed to every form of unionism.[34]

OTHER INFLUENCES

The following illustration of the combined attitudes of doctrinal indifference and tolerance will no doubt strike a familiar note:

If Americans believed in saints, Benjamin Franklin would be among them. He exemplified so many virtues Americans have come to admire. People found him practical, earthy, affable, witty and, above all, tolerant.

---

[34]Reu, op. cit., pp. 19, 20.

A few weeks before he died Ben responded to an inquiry by President Ezra Stiles of Yale concerning his religious faith. Said Franklin: As to Jesus of Nazareth, . . . I have . . . some doubts as to his Divinity, tho' it is a question I do not dogmatize upon, having never studied it, and think it needless to busy myself with it now, when I expect soon an opportunity of knowing the truth with less trouble. I see no harm, however, in its being believed, if that belief has the good consequence . . . of making his doctrines more respected and better observed."

Something of the American spirit is there. It is the spirit of Franklin's time, the Age of Reason (1648-1789). Questions of dogma seemed unimportant, hardly worth fretting about. What was immensely more important was behavior. Do our beliefs make us more tolerant, more respectful of those who differ with us, more responsive to the true spirit of Jesus?

If that hatred of religious bigotry, coupled with a devotion to tolerance of all religious opinions, has a familiar ring, it is because the attitudes of the Age of Reason are not a thing of the past. They live on today in the values of the Western world.[35]

And so they do. They are a part of the American culture, making their appearance during the formative years in America's history.

For millions of Europeans, America became a symbol of freedom and opportunity, a land that offered the hope of building a new and better life.[36] As America went through the pangs of birth, freedom became the great watchword—freedom from oppressive government and state control of religion: freedom of speech, press, peaceable assembly, and religion—all stated in a Bill of Rights that guarantees the rights and liberties of the individual: "Congress shall make no law respecting the establishment of religion." For many, this topped the list in importance. Americans were free to choose church membership or reject it, affiliate with the body of their choice or none at all, without fear of government interference or reprisal.[37]

The emphasis on freedom combined with the baggage of European rationalism and pietism had predictable results:

---

[35]Bruce L. Shelley, *Church History in Plain Language* (Waco: Word Books, 1982), p. 329.

[36]*The Lutherans in North America,* op. cit., p. 147.

[37]Herbert J. A. Bouman, *A Look at Today's Churches: A Comparative Guide* (St. Louis: Concordia Publishing House, 1980), pp. 9, 10.

It is hardly extraordinary that America should be the land which has brought forth the most churches. Unlike the European nations, the United States has no state church supported by the government. Anyone is free to start a new church. In this new nation with its emphasis on liberty and individual rights, there was a certain contempt for tradition and authority. Private reason and individual experience in religious matters were considered more important than seeking guidance from a confessional writing like the Lutheran *Book of Concord.* Just as this nation was created by the consent of the people, so the prevailing theory is that churches are created by the voluntary consent and decision of human beings.[38]

The hardships of life on the American frontier further diverted people from the importance of doctrinal differences between church bodies and increased the attitude of tolerance:

Around 1800 the frontier was in western Pennsylvania, eastern Ohio, Kentucky, and Tennessee. People of many diverse cultural, educational, political, economic and religious backgrounds populated the frontier and devoted themselves to the difficult task of wresting a living from the wilderness and protecting their families from hostile attacks by Indians and from other hardships. In such a setting the preservation and promotion of separate denominational groups seemed to many people a luxury they could no longer afford. Having made common cause with their neighbors in all phases of the work and worry on the frontier, they were ready to do their worshiping together also.[39]

The isolation of the American frontier has long since been broken. The American landscape has changed from a predominantly rural America to an industrialized nation. With this change came increased mobility, instant communication, and social changes that included a great increase in the number of interdenominational marriages. No longer is it possible to live out one's life isolated from people of differing religious views. Add to these the influence of historical criticism, which has moved much of American society away from the absolutes of Scripture, and one can see why tolerance can be called the second watchword of American culture.

---

[38]Victor H. Prange, *Why So Many Churches?* (Milwaukee: Northwestern Publishing House, 1960), pp. 56, 57.

[39]Bouman, op. cit., p. 49.

THE CHARISMATIC MOVEMENT

Another influence that has greatly increased levels of doctrinal indifference and tolerance in America's religious scene is the development and growth of the charismatic movement or Neo-Pentecostalism. While a thorough documentation of this movement is not within the scope of this book, its doctrinal emphasis and ecumenical influence must be noted. The reader is encouraged to make a more detailed study through the resources in the footnotes.[40]

The charismatic movement, or charismatic renewal as it is often called, is a more recent development on America's religious scene, coming out openly in the early 1960s. It can be seen as an example of the on-going influence of Reformed theology and a result of the use of historical criticism.

The charismatic movement has been defined as a penetration of the mainline denominations, as well as many smaller church bodies, by the Pentecostal movement. Charismatics have adopted the chief doctrine of the Pentecostals, tongues speaking, while retaining membership in mainline denominations including the Roman Catholic Church, the Lutheran churches, and the churches of the Reformed tradition. Charismatic renewal is Pentecostalism. However, the two groups remain separate with the Pentecostal movement maintaining its own church bodies, the largest of which is the Assemblies of God. Like the original Pentecostal movement, the effects of this movement are world-wide [41]

Its onset and spread

The onset and spread of the charismatic movement is described by Arthur J. Clement, a WELS pastor, in his book *Pentecost or Pretense? An Examination of the Pentecostal and Charismatic Movements.* He writes:

> The presence of charismatics in main-line churches seems to be (at least in the beginning) the result of an *active recruitment from without by Pentecostals.* So in effect, a charismatic Christian is a Pentecostal who holds membership in a non-Pentecostal church (author's emphasis).

---

[40]The following books provide a history and biblical analysis of the charismatic movement. *Pentecost or Pretense? An Examination of the Pentecostal and Charismatic Movements,* by Arthur J. Clement (Milwaukee: Northwestern Publishing House, 1981), and *Liberalism: Its Cause and Cure: The Poisoning of American Christianity and the Antidote,* by Gregory L. Jackson (Milwaukee: Northwestern Publishing House, 1991).

[41]Clement, op. cit.

An example of this is the experience of Harold Bredesen, a Dutch Reformed minister, who traced his tongues experience to a Pentecostal camp meeting. It was Bredesen who later brought the movement to Yale University. Lawrence Christenson, a Lutheran pastor in San Pedro, California, spoke in tongues after having attended a Four Square Pentecostal Church service. He is now a recognized leader in the Lutheran charismatic renewal.

It is not unreasonable to tie the beginnings of the charismatic movement to the work of the Full Gospel Business Men's Fellowship International, founded in 1953 by the wealthy Los Angeles dairyman Demos Shakarian [a Pentecostal]. The FGBMFI began to attract other Christians to its gatherings, which first took the form of prayer breakfasts. Soon they added other meetings, conferences, and programs. Through their efforts the word about Pentecostalism traveled across America. Given this respectable impetus, testimonials began to surface among other Protestants, and sometimes even non-Christians and Jews, and still later by Roman Catholics.

At the time of this writing, FGBMFI meetings are held all over the world. They feature Pentecostal-type worship, charismatic speeches, and tongues. This "full-gospel" group (salvation plus the gifts of the Spirit), teaches that every Christian can have the gift of tongues. At their meetings, the businessmen and women carry on with tongue-speaking, clapping, singing, and testimonies. Guests are invited from the historic churches, and not a few bow to the Pentecostal spirit. Edward D. O'Connor of the University of Notre Dame, and a leading charismatic Catholic, observes that most charismatic Catholics had their Pentecost through the influence of a non-Catholic Pentecostal. He cites especially the influence of a book, *The Cross and the Switchblade,* and of the FGBMFI. He also gives credit to non-Catholic neighbors and prayer groups.[42]

Shakarian was aided in starting the FGBMFI by Oral Roberts.[43] Other well-known religious media personalities have also helped fur-

---

[42]Ibid., pp. 65, 66.

[43]Gregory L. Jackson, *Liberalism: Its Cause and Cure: The Poisoning of American Christianity and the Antidote* (Milwaukee: Northwestern Publishing House, 1991), Notes, 5, p. 113.

ther the phenomenal growth of the charismatic movement. These include Rev. J. Bakker and Rev. Jimmie Swaggert, formerly of the Assemblies of God, and Pat Robertson, a charismatic Southern Baptist and founder of the Christian Broadcasting Network.[44] Also of immeasurable influence is the vast amount of religious reading material available today, a large majority of which has been produced by authors in the Reformed camp, the original source of the charismatic movement.

Doctrinal emphasis

Neo-Pentecostalism or charismatic renewal is a legacy of both Reformed theology and historical criticism. Since it is very important that this relationship be understood, it will be helpful at this point to re-read chapters 24 and 25.

The error of Reformed theology that gave birth to Pentecostalism and charismatic renewal is directly connected to the Reformation, when Huldreich Zwingli and John Calvin broke with Luther on the sacraments of Baptism and Holy Communion.

Zwingli and Calvin taught that the sacraments were only symbols, outward ceremonies commanded by God whereby man would show, or give witness, that he had faith. In contrast Luther, based on the clear words of Scripture, taught that the sacraments were the means of grace whereby the Holy Spirit imparts, or works, faith and preserves it. For the Reformed the sacrament became something *man* does *for* God, while for Lutherans,.they are the source of God's power, something *God* does *in* man.

The fundamental error on the part of the Reformed undermined certainty of salvation. Thus they tended to seek certainty through various means, including reason, obedience to God's laws, experience, emotions, and, for some, visible proof.

Pentecostalism emerged from the roots of Methodism and the teaching of John Wesley. Wesley adopted Zwingli and Calvin's error and searched for certainty of salvation through a striving after perfection and a "born again" experience. In turn, his followers in the Wesleyan holiness movement added the doctrine of "entire sanctification." Dr. Herbert J. A. Bouman, LCMS, a professor emeritus of systematic theology, writes:

> According to the Scriptures it is the Holy Spirit who creates faith and produces the holy life. Therefore the Holy Spirit is very prominent in Holiness teaching. The "baptism with the

---

[44]Ibid., pp. 80, 81.

Holy Spirit" produces "born again" Christians, who are transformed instantly into a state where they no longer commit a willful sin and are therefore entirely sanctified. Such imperfections as remain, it is claimed, do not come from inner prompting of the heart but are stimulations coming from outside. Justification is said to provide forgiveness for sins actually committed, while sanctification is alleged to remove original, or "inbred," sin, a condition involving no guilt. Remembering the Arminian emphasis on free will and man's less than total depravity after the Fall, it is only consistent for Holiness people to believe that since God demands holiness, it must be in man's power to achieve it even in this life.[45]

The Pentecostals broke from the Holiness groups and added another doctrine. Bouman continues:

Another group of churches within the Methodist family quite closely related to the Holiness churches are the Pentecostals. As the name implies, the outpouring of the Holy Spirit at the first Pentecost is in the center of their teaching. But while the Holiness groups emphasize the work of the Holy Spirit in entire sanctification, the Pentecostals lay stress on the miraculous, the charismatic gifts of the Holy Spirit. The Constitution of the Pentecostal Fellowship of North America affirms, in addition to basic beliefs as summarized in the ancient Christian creeds:

(5) that the full gospel includes holiness of heart and life, *healing for the body and the baptism in the Holy Spirit with the initial evidence of speaking in other tongues as the Spirit gives utterance* (emphasis added; cited in Mayer, p. 310).

Pentecostals regard "baptism in the Holy Spirit" as far more important and effective than the water Baptism instituted by Christ. Baptism in the Spirit is said to endow those Christians fortunate enough to receive it with extra gifts not experienced by "ordinary" Christians.[46]

This is contrary to Scripture and historic Lutheran doctrine. Scripture teaches only one baptism:

---

[45]Bouman, op. cit., pp. 42, 43.
[46]Ibid., p. 43.

> There is one body and one Spirit—just as you were called to one hope when you were called—one Lord, one faith, one baptism; one God and Father of all, who is over all and through all and in all (Ephesians 4:4-6).

Despite the fact that God's Word teaches only one baptism, the Pentecostals and charismatics seek "something more." Dr. Gregory L. Jackson, WELS pastor and author of *Liberalism: Its Cause and Cure, The Poisoning of American Christianity and the Antidote,* writes:

> Wesley's unfortunate misunderstanding about the Christian life led him to set the stage for his followers to teach two baptisms, water and Spirit. Much of Wesley's terminology was taken over by the Pentecostals, since he taught there was something beyond justification by faith, a deeper experience, which he called entire sanctification. Since he taught a waiting and a wrestling for this higher, deeper experience, Pentecostals converted the same into tarrying, yielding, and struggling for the "gift of tongues."

> Pentecostals teach that the Holy Spirit is a reward bestowed by God upon those who earn it, through sacrifice, yielding, tarrying, and praying. That is the rabbinical understanding of the Holy Spirit, not the teaching of the Bible, which tells us that the Spirit is received as a gift through the sacrament of baptism. Teaching tongues-speaking as a reward from God only serves to widen the gulf between Pentecostals and historic Christianity.

> The distortions of Scripture are bad enough, but no one can calculate the damage these egregious errors cause to the spiritual well-being of believers. Although they deny it at first, Pentecostals believe they are the only true Christians. They cast doubt on genuine scriptural doctrine and steal from people the assurance of their salvation.[47]

Historical criticism

Pentecostalism might very well have remained confined to the various Pentecostal churches were it not for the onset and growth of historical criticism. The charismatic movement originated out of the historical context of undermining the Scriptures as the Word of God.

Reformed theology undermined certainty of salvation by denying the means of grace in the sacraments. Historical criticism under-

---

[47]Jackson, op. cit., pp. 91-94.

mined certainty of salvation by denying the certainty of the Word (also the means of grace). This can be more easily understood if we remember that God is a "hidden" God. He is found only in the Scriptures, not in experiences, emotions, yielding, tarrying, or prayer. Since historical criticism undermines the authority of Scripture, it undermines the certainty of God's Word, and thus tends to create uncertainty of salvation. We must remember that John Wesley's theology and Methodism resulted not only from the Reformed error concerning the sacraments, but also from the rationalism that had infiltrated the theology of the Anglican Church of his day—rationalism that had robbed the Christian message of much of its basic content. We see the same situation today. Jackson writes:

> As Methodism (as it was called) became more respectable and academic, liberalism drove away elements loyal to the Wesleyan spirit, making Methodism even more liberal. Since the trend in all mainline churches was toward liberalism, from 1900 on, the growth of Pentecostalism owes some debt of gratitude to liberals for making the choice so obvious for people.

> Some view the growth of Pentecostalism and the charismatic movement as signs of God's blessing. A more realistic view is that the apostasy of the mainline denominations has become so obvious to members that they are driven from their congregations to those organizations which offer an alternative. Mainline ministers, too, have found comfort and support in their charismatic affiliations. The mainline churches teach against the Bible, while the Pentecostals and charismatics seem to view the Scriptures as authoritative.

> It is worth noting that charismatic flare-ups have been strongest in the most liberal denominations, those which had long abandoned the authority of Scripture. In many cases, the clergy trained in destructive criticism of the Bible, the historical-critical method, find joy and meaning in their ministry for the first time in decades through Pentecostalism. No one should be surprised that a minister or layman feels exhilarated after hearing that the miracles really happened, that Jesus is the Son of God, that prayer is something more than relaxation therapy.

> The entire mainline seminary system produces ministers who cannot preach the gospel because their faith has been undermined by the historical-critical method and a new reli-

gion of social and political activism has been substituted for the gospel. The Roman Catholic Church has joined this self-destructive crusade and found ways to outdo the liberal Protestants. Results:

1. Some Assemblies of God churches report half of their members to be former Catholics. A large proportion are former Lutherans.

2. Many mainline charismatics stay in their home congregations while floating over to the Assemblies of God for "spiritual enrichment."

Charismatics have properly diagnosed the ills of corpse-cold liberalism: lifeless worship, political harangues disguised as sermons, unbelieving ministers and officials, attacks on the Bible in the name of scholarship, and a lack of genuine Christian nurture.[48]

However, despite the fact that the charismatics have correctly diagnosed the ills of liberalism, charismatic renewal is not a return to orthodox Christianity. Jackson continues:

The American religious scene has long labored under the myth that charismatics are conservatives. One reason may be that some of them have publicly identified with conservative political causes. This should not be confused with a conservative or strict approach to the Scriptures. Many charismatics reject the inerrancy of Scripture and use the historical-critical method to justify their compromise. The characteristics of liberal theology match almost exactly the dominant themes of charismatics and Pentecostals.

Larry Christenson, an American Lutheran Church pastor in California, was distressed already in seminary with the demythologizing methods of the infidel Rudolph Bultmann. A member of the Foursquare Gospel Church in San Pedro, California, invited Christenson to a revival where a woman preached about the gifts of the Spirit. Later that night he began tongues-speaking and started influencing others. This happened about 1963. Christenson has remained a leader among Lutheran charismatics. His opposition to the inerrancy of Scripture was echoed by other Lutheran charismatic leaders during the formation of the Evangelical Lutheran

---

[48]Ibid., pp. 82, 84, 86.

Church in America and gave great comfort to opponents of inerrancy. Christenson wrote in *Welcome Holy Spirit:* "Charismatics would insist on the classic understanding and use of the historical-critical method of biblical interpretation, that is, the attempt to interpret Scripture according to the way it was meant by those who wrote it, and the way it was understood by those to whom it was addressed. . . . "[49]

Ecumenical influence

The influence of the charismatic movement can be compared to that of pietism. In fact, the charismatic movement *is* the modern manifestation of 17th century pietism. Its importance is two-fold.

For Lutherans its importance lies in the fact that, once again, it is the vehicle through which Reformed theology is being introduced on a wide scale to Lutheran pastors and laity.

On the ecumenical scene its importance lies in the manner in which it crosses denominational lines and bases fellowship on subjective experience. It is another example of "gospel reductionism," for it reduces requirements for unity to the least common denominator—salvation plus the subjective experience of the so-called second baptism of the Holy Spirit. It ignores doctrinal differences, tends to set aside the law, and seeks to make the invisible church visible through the physical manifestation of speaking in tongues. Its ecumenical impact cannot be overstated. Jackson writes:

> *Ecumenism, Unionism by Another Name*—Tongues-speaking spread in liberal Protestant bodies because the members were sacrament-starved. Thomas Merton, the Trappist monk who grew up a liberal Protestant, wrote in *The Seven Storey Mountain* about the arid intellectuals who served as liberal Protestant ministers. One minister could speak glibly about novels of D. H. Lawrence, but could not talk about Christ.
>
> As mainline members, Protestant and Catholic, became distressed over the clergy's assault on the Bible and support of political activism, they found a common solution in this new movement. The new sacrament of tongues-speaking created by Pentecostals has united all church bodies, many of them already used to ecumenical services, whether sponsored by liberal groups associated with the National Council of Churches or more conservative leaders like Billy Graham. The confession of faith is usually not, "I am a Catholic (or

---

[49]Ibid., pp. 81, 87.

Lutheran or Baptist) charismatic," but "I am a charismatic." There is instant identification and fellowship among all charismatics and Pentecostals, with certain key words used to signal a common identity: Spirit-filled, on fire, praise, prayer group, and healing service. If charismatics were genuinely conservative, they would have qualms about the varying doctrinal standards of other groups. However, the common saying among charismatics is: "Doctrine divides." Indeed. Doctrine divides the sheep from the goats.[50]

False doctrine and doctrinal indifference are poison to the soul. The effects of either can lead to loss of faith. The most dangerous aspect of the charismatic movement is the false doctrine and doctrinal indifference upon which it has been built. When the emotional high of subjective experience wears off and the on-going difficulties of life seem overwhelming, many become disillusioned, certainty of faith is lost and many fall away.

A BIBLICAL MANDATE

The ecumenical movement seeks to unite all churches on the basis of "reconciled diversity"—the compromise of truth and error. This violates the biblical doctrine of fellowship and places upon every Christian a responsibility mandated by Scripture:

> I urge you, brothers, to watch out for those who cause divisions and put obstacles in your way that are contrary to the teaching you have learned. Keep away from them. For such people are not serving our Lord Christ, but their own appetites. By smooth talk and flattery they deceive the minds of naive people (Romans 16:17,18).

It is the responsibility of every Christian to distinguish between orthodox and heterodox churches. This is to be determined on the basis of doctrine. The late Dr. Francis Pieper, an outstanding LCMS orthodox theologian, makes this very clear in an essay titled "The Difference Between Orthodox and Heterodox Churches." Delivered over a century ago (1889) to the Southern District Convention of the Missouri Synod, Pieper's message is timeless. He writes:

> Christians have the duty *on the basis of doctrine* to distinguish between orthodox and heterodox churches. But *can* they do this? Certainly! For Christ the Lord tells them to do this, and this at the same time implies that by God's grace

---

[50]Ibid., p. 101.

they can do it. Many suppose that only pastors are in a position to distinguish between orthodox and heterodox churches. But this is altogether wrong. Precisely all Christians, and not only the pastor, are exhorted by Christ the Lord, in Matt. 7:15: "Beware of false prophets." And John says: "Beloved, believe not every spirit, but try the spirits whether they are of God: because many false prophets are gone out into the world" (1 John 4:1); this passage is likewise addressed to all Christians alike. Christ the Lord has so arranged it, that all His dear Christians, the unlearned as well as the learned, can distinguish between truth and falsehood in spiritual things. He has revealed all doctrines in perfectly clear passages, in passages which can be understood by the unlearned as well as the learned. The Holy Scriptures are such a testimony, that makes wise also the *simple* (Psalm 19:7). When, therefore, a Christian simply holds to the Word of Scripture, then he can very well distinguish between truth and error (author's emphasis).

That the Christians sometimes are confused and imagine that they do not know which is the true doctrine, is due to the fact, that *they lose sight of the Word of Scripture,* that they want to judge this matter with their blind reason, and not with God's Word, which refutes all errors as soon as it is brought into the discussion. Thus, for example, there once was a dispute in a Methodistic gathering concerning perfect sanctification of a Christian already in this life. Most of them claimed that a Christian, already here on earth, can be entirely without sin. Then, one man arose and said that he had committed no sin for years! Another arose and, instead of making a long reply, simply quoted 1 John 1:8: "If we say we have no sin, we deceive ourselves, and the truth is not in us." By this one passage all were silenced. Before the eyes of all, the error was condemned by the clear Word of God. And so it is with respect to every doctrine (author's emphasis).

The Christian who knows his Small Lutheran Catechism can defend himself with this knowledge against all errors, for the fundamental articles of Christian doctrine are the very ones against which the errorists offend.[51]

---

[51]Francis Pieper, *The Difference Between Orthodox and Heterodox Churches,* and Supplement, ed. Pastor E. L. Mehlberg, Coos Bay, Oregon, 1981, pp. 24, 25. Pieper is the author of the 3 vol. set of *Christian Dogmatics,* the main dogmatics textbooks used in the seminaries of the ELS and the LCMS.

The Scriptures

The importance of every Christian having a thorough knowledge of the Scriptures and the fundamental articles of the faith cannot be over-emphasized. And, although God is the one who creates faith in us through the Word, he allows us to handle the logistics for the battle.[52] Thus every Christian, by God's grace, is expected to faithfully study the Word and to prayerfully guard against growing weary of the Word.[53] Hear what Luther says:

> *Christians Should Be Firmly Grounded in the Bible and Be Able to Defend Their Faith*—Christendom must have men who are able to floor their adversaries and take armor and equipment from the devil, putting him to shame. But this calls for strong warriors who have complete control of Scripture, can refute a false interpretation, know how to wrest the sword they wield, that is, their Bible passages, from the hands of the adversaries and beat them back with them. Not all people can be so adept at defending doctrine and the articles of faith. Therefore we must have preachers and teachers who daily study and search Scriptures and can fight on behalf of all the others. Yet every Christian should certainly be so well armed that for himself he is sure of his faith and doctrine, and he should be so firmly grounded on passages from God's Word that he is able to hold his own against the devil and to defend himself when people want to convert him to some other view. In this way he helps to uphold and defend the doctrine.

> *Tired of the Word? Ah, No!*—But, say flesh and blood, it is disgusting to hear you always harping on the same string. Give us something new; otherwise we tire of the same old message. Not so, says Christ, but think of Me. For the others, who are so overcurious and want to hear something new, have never correctly understood the first message . . . because the Word of God does not make a man satiated or disgusted when it really takes possession of his heart. The very opposite is true. The longer a man hears it, the more he wants to hear it. Therefore when people become weary of the word, all is not well; for it certainly is a message which one cannot hear often enough or learn well enough. There-

---

[52]Gregory L. Jackson, *Shepherd of Peace Lutheran Church Newsletter,* Winter, 1991, p. 1.

[53]*What Luther Says,* op. cit., 3:1487.

fore the first psalm praises God's Word so highly and says that those are blessed who constantly use the Word and find their delight in it (author's emphasis).[54]

The Confessions

It is vitally important that we do not allow ourselves to become complacent in our faith and about what we really believe. It has been said that if you put a frog in a pan of boiling water, he will immediately jump out. But if you put that same frog in a pan of cold water and steadily increase the temperature, he will adjust to the temperature changes and eventually boil to death! So it can be for those Christians who fail to faithfully study God's Word. For Lutherans this must include maintaining a working knowledge of the Lutheran Confessions (see Chapter 21). "A confessional church must not only have confessions but must study them. This is true not only of the clergy and teachers, but also of its laity."[55] Lutherans must be Lutherans by conviction. Spitz explains:

> A study of the churches and religious cults should lead a Lutheran to a deeper appreciation of his own confessions. The more faithfully he compares the Lutheran confessions with the Word of God, the more deeply will he appreciate in humble gratitude the mercy of God, who has preserved for him the truth of His Word in its purity.

> A Lutheran must be a Lutheran by conviction. Having examined the Lutheran Confessions in light of God's Word and found them in accord with it, he will join his fellow Lutherans of nearly four centuries ago in declaring: "Therefore we also have determined not to depart even a finger's breadth either from the subjects themselves or from the phrases which are found in them [the confessions] but, the Spirit of the Lord aiding us, to persevere constantly, with the greatest harmony, in this godly agreement, and we intend to examine all controversies according to this true norm and declaration of the pure doctrine." ("Preface" to the Book of Concord, 1580).[56]

---

[54]Ibid., 1:1486, 1487.

[55]A book review by Armin W. Schuetze of the *I Believe* series, *Wisconsin Lutheran Quarterly*, vol. 73, October 1976, p. 325. The *I Believe* series is an excellent introduction to the *Book of Concord*. By Dr. Bjarne W. Teigen, this series contains a history and doctrinal summary of the Confessions and is intended for both lay people and pastors.

[56]Spitz, op. cit., pp. 153, 154.

Orthodox or heterodox?

Armed with knowledge of the Scripture and the Lutheran confessions, how does one determine whether a church is orthodox or heterodox? The "Brief Statement," a document adopted by the LCMS in 1932 as a correct expression of biblical doctrine, provides the answer to this question:

> 29. The orthodox character of a church is established not by its mere name nor by its outward acceptance of, and subscription to, an orthodox creed, but by the doctrine which is *actually* taught in its pulpits, in its theological seminaries, and in its publications. On the other hand, a church does not forfeit its orthodox character through the casual intrusion of errors, provided these are combated and eventually removed by means of doctrinal discipline, Acts 20:30; 1 Tim. 1:3 (author's emphasis).[57]

Pieper, one of the authors of the "Brief Statement,"[58] had addressed this question 42 years earlier:

> We Missourians consider a church body to be an orthodox fellowship only then when the true doctrine sounds forth from all its pulpits, professors' chairs, and in all writings which publicly appear within the fellowship, and when every error, just as soon as it makes its appearance, *is removed* in the manner prescribed by God. According to this standard we judge others; according to this rule we will also permit ourselves to be judged (author's emphasis).

> We Missourians must and will permit ourselves to be judged according to that doctrine which is taught by our individual pastors, whether it be in San Francisco or New York, St. Paul or New Orleans, or what is taught in our pe-

---

[57]*Brief Statement of the Doctrinal Position of the Missouri Synod* (St. Louis: Concordia Publishing House, 1932), p. 13.

[58]"In order to give clear biblical answers to a number of doctrinal questions in regard to which many Lutheran churches were becoming uncertain, Dr. Franz [Francis] Pieper and Dr. Theo. Engelder, two outstanding LCMS orthodox theologians at the beginning of the 20th century, worked out a little document which is called 'Brief Statement.' This excellent document was in 1932 accepted as a correct expression of the biblical doctrine by the LCMS, which at that time was still a church teaching the pure doctrine." Seth Erlandsson, *Church Fellowship, What Does the Bible Say?*, translated by S. W. Becker (Milwaukee: Northwestern Publishing House, 1979), p. 28.

riodicals, whether they be published officially or unofficially. If any one shows us that even only *one* pastor preached false doctrine, or that even only *one* periodical is in the service of false doctrine, and we did not remove this false doctrine, we thereby would have ceased to be an orthodox Synod, and we would have become a unionistic fellowship (author's emphasis).

Briefly, *the characteristic mark of an orthodox fellowship (church body) is that everywhere in it the pure doctrine alone not only has official standing but also actually is in effect and prevails* (author's emphasis).[59]

It is important to note that in determining the orthodox or heterodox character of a church one must be careful not to confuse liberal practice with "adiaphora," a Greek word meaning "indifferent things." The Lutheran confessions speak of adiaphora as "church rites which are neither commanded nor forbidden in the Word of God."[60] Not all change is liberal nor does it always originate from a liberal view of Scripture. Modification and changes from time to time are not only permissible but helpful as long as they do not depart from sound Lutheran doctrine.

A time to act

If, after careful research and questioning (see Appendix II), a pastor or layman determines that he is, indeed, a member of a heterodox church body or congregation, then he is commanded by God's Word to act according to this knowledge and *depart* (Romans 16:17, 18; Matthew 7:15; 2 John 10, 11; Acts 20:30, 31). Pieper writes:

Therefore a Christian can and should distinguish between orthodox and heterodox churches. He should then also act according to this knowledge. While avoiding all fellowship with the heterodox, he should adhere only to the orthodox church. This [avoiding such fellowship] God's Word declares in all passages which admonish the Christian not to *listen* to false prophets, but to *flee* from them. For by belonging to heterodox *congregations* you listen to their preachers, the false prophets, and thus do the very opposite of that which Christ has commanded regarding false teachers (author's emphasis).

---

[59]Pieper, op. cit., p. 55.
[60]*The Concordia Cyclopedia,* op. cit., p. 4.

The objection is raised: "You yourselves admit that also in heterodox bodies there are still dear children of God, and yet by separating from these churches, you separated yourselves from these children of God; yes, you condemn them by avoiding these heterodox churches. In that case, isn't it better to practice fellowship with the heterodox?" First of all, we answer: No! It cannot be better, because God expressly forbids us to do this. Moreover, we do not even separate ourselves *from the children of God* among the sects, but *from the sects as such*. Rather, the sects separate these dear children of God from us. They hold those who belong to us— for children of God are determined to accept the whole Word of God—captive among themselves. So these believers must outwardly support the wicked cause of the sects while in their hearts they belong to us. These children of God would at once come over to an orthodox congregation if they were better informed. It is also for the benefit of the children of God among the heterodox that we refuse church fellowship to these churches. Thereby we are constantly reminding them that they are in the wrong camp. According to God's Word, Christians do not belong in the company of those who openly contradict some doctrines of Christ. Many a person for this reason also steps out of the wrong camp into the right one (author's emphasis).

It must also by all means be held, that *we* do not cause any divisions in the Church when we avoid fellowship with the heterodox. According to Rom. 16:17, they cause divisions and offenses in the Church who teach doctrines besides the revealed truth. According to the word of God, the situation is this: Whoever adheres to false teachers, and thereby strengthens their cause, cooperates in the division of the Church. But he that avoids false teachers and their followers, and practices no fellowship with them, is engaged in the holy work of preventing divisions within Christendom. But, sad to say, the devil has been successful here in falsifying the concepts and the language. The destroyers of unity are called the promoters thereof, and, on the other hand, the promoters of unity are called the destroyers thereof (author's emphasis).[61]

There are, of course, many reasons given for joining or remaining in heterodox church bodies. Pieper lists some of those most commonly expressed:

---

[61]Pieper, op. cit., pp. 26, 28, 29.

The reasons which should be named here were already partly covered in the discussion on the first five theses. Let us briefly refer only to a few of them. The reasons partly sound very pious, but considered in the light of God's Word, they are altogether invalid. At times their origin, namely, that they come from the flesh, is written plainly on their face. So, for example, when it is argued that a man out of *consideration for his business* must belong to a heterodox church. To this we simply say: That is turning one's faith into a business. In other words, we subordinate the question: "What must I do to be saved?" to that other one: "What shall we eat? What shall we drink? Wherewithal shall we be clothed?" Others say: *Faith* does not matter at all, the most important things, finally, are the *deeds*. That is an altogether heathenish statement. Faith matters so much, that, "He that believeth on Him (Christ) is not condemned: but he that believeth not is condemned already, because he hath not believed in the name of the only begotten Son of God" John 3:18. And as for works which are well-pleasing to God, and through which faith should manifest itself, the chief work among them is this, that you firmly cling to the whole Word of God and confess it, and thus adhere to the orthodox Church (author's emphasis).

This reason, however, sounds more honorable: "*My relatives, yes, members of my family* belong to a heterodox church, so I do not want to cause disturbance and disorder in my family by my lone membership in the orthodox Lutheran Church. I love my own too much for that." If you earnestly love your relatives, then in all love and patience bring the testimony of Bible truth to them, that they may in all things give honor to the Word of God, and depart from error. You should not go over to them but they should come over to you—that is God's will. If you do not succeed, then you must forego the good fortune of being united with your loved ones in one and the same Church. True it is: it hurts, not to be able to have church fellowship with those near and dear to you. But, Christ the Lord has already taken such a case into consideration, and has definitely settled it. He says, Matt. 10:37, 38: "He that loveth father or mother more than Me is not worthy of Me: and he that loveth son or daughter more than Me is not worthy of Me. And he that taketh not his cross, and followeth after Me is not worthy of Me." And Matt. 19:29:

"And everyone that hath forsaken houses, or brethren, or sisters, or father, or mother, or wife, or children, or lands, for my name's sake, shall receive an hundred fold, and shall inherit everlasting life." Therefore, at such a time, and in such a situation, consider this: the Lord, your God, is testing you whether you love Him, whether you love Him more than all others, who is the Savior of your soul and who shed His blood for you (author's emphasis).

You may say: "I want to remain in the heterodox church in order to accomplish good in it, namely, to prevent it from losing the truth altogether." If you happen to be in a heterodox church, then first of all, bear witness to the truth clearly and definitely. If they listen to you, good. Under certain circumstances, you can *wait* a little, to see whether the truth is accepted. But as soon as it is *clear* that they will not accept the truth, you must separate yourself from that group which holds to the error. If you, nevertheless, remain in it, then you are no longer reinforcing the *truth*, but rather, the *error*. It is blindness if you suppose that you are still a witness-bearer for the truth when you continue in fellowship with openly known errorists. It is an absolute contradiction to be both a witness-bearer for the truth, and an associate of false teachers. As *Luther* says: You "cannot remain in the stall with others who propagate false doctrine or are attached to it or always speak good words to the devil and his crowd." (XVII, 1477) (author's emphasis).[62]

To the last reason cited by Pieper we must add an additional consideration. While the Lord holds both pastors and laymen accountable for witnessing to the truth, the greater responsibility is vested in the pastor. In Hebrews 13:17 (NET) we read: "Obey your leaders and submit to them, for they must give an account of how they watch over your souls. Obey them so that they may be happy in their work and do not have to complain about you, for that would not be to your advantage." It is, of course, assumed in the above text that these "leaders" are faithful to God's Word. Luther says:

It is not enough that we preach correctly, which the hireling can also do; but we must watch over the sheep, that the wolves, false teachers, may not break in, and we must contend for the sheep against the wolves, with the Word of God,

---

[62]Ibid., pp. 48, 49.

even to the sacrifice of our lives. Such are good shepherds, of whom few are found.[63]

The role of the pastor in guarding the flock in his care includes seeing to it that his congregation has fellowship only with other orthodox congregations. This cannot be overemphasized. A congregation's relationship to a given synod will set the mold for the congregation's future regardless of the doctrinal soundness of its present pastor. Future pastors will more and more fit the mold of the synod that trains them. When the Holy Spirit has given a pastor charge over one of his flocks, it is that pastor's responsibility to safeguard that flock through training and guidance. Nothing is more important to this end than being part of a thoroughly sound confessional synod. In the following quotation Pieper lists one more common excuse for joining or remaining in a heterodox church body and then concludes his essay:

Another says; "I can very well take care of my soul, also in those church bodies which proclaim error in addition to the truth. Whatever is said there against God's Word, I will not accept." So speaks the *presumptuous* flesh. He who is really concerned about his soul will not speak that way. Do not trust yourself too much! Error is not such a harmless thing. Your heart is a breeding ground for all sins, also for every doctrinal error. This is proved already by your objection. The objection itself already reveals that you no longer have the right *abhorrence* for false doctrine. You are already half *gone astray.* Besides, you absolutely cannot take care of your own soul. That *God* must do. He wants to do it, and He will do it. He will protect you, so that you will not "dash your foot against a stone," also in spiritual matters. That He has promised. But this He has promised to do, and He does this, *when you walk in God's Ways.* That is, when you abide in God's Word, when you avoid the fellowship of errorists, as God has commanded (author's emphasis).

If, therefore, we judge on the basis of God's Word, and not according to our own thoughts, then it is certain, that by avoiding all church fellowship with errorists, we walk according to God's will and thereby serve the best interests of the Church in general, and also of our own soul in particular. May God always give us enlightened, spiritual eyes of our understanding, that we may at all times actively recog-

---

[63]Martin Luther, *The Sermons of Martin Luther,* 8 vols. (Grand Rapids: Baker Book House, 1983), III, p. 34.

nize the difference between orthodox and heterodox churches, and give us the right, holy love for the truth, that we
may at all times act in accordance with this knowledge.[64]

By way of conclusion, the authors of this book cannot improve
upon the words of Dr. Pieper. We simply add the fifth stanza[65] of a familiar hymn:

> God's Word is our great heritage
> And shall be ours forever;
> To spread its light from age to age
> Shall be our chief endeavor.
> Through life it guides our way,
> In death it is our stay.
> Lord, grant, while worlds endure,
> We keep its teachings pure
> Throughout all generations. Amen.[66]

Therefore, we join with Jude in urging you, the reader of this
book, to "contend for the faith that was once for all entrusted to the
saints" (Jude 3).

---

[64]Pieper, op. cit., pp. 49, 50.

[65]The fifth stanza of Nikolai F. S. Grundtvig's Danish version of Martin
Luther's "A Mighty Fortress" was first published in *Salmer ved Jubelfesten,*
1817. It later appeared separately in Danish and Norwegian hymnals and is
used on festival occasions and as a closing stanza. W. G. Polack, *The Handbook to the Lutheran Hymnal* (St. Louis: Concordia Publishing House, 1942),
Rep. Northwestern Publishing House, 1975, #206.

[66]Nikolai B. S. Grundtvig, "God's Word Is Our Great Heritage," *The Lutheran Hymnal (TLH)* (St. Louis: Concordia Publishing House, 1941), #283. This
was the joint hymnal of the synods of the old Synodical Conference. The phrase
"Lord, grant, while worlds endure, We keep its teachings pure" was changed by
the ELCA's predecessor bodies to read "Lord, grant while time shall last, Thy
Church may hold it fast." See *The Service Book and Hymnal (SBH)* (Minneapolis: Augsburg Publishing House and Philadelphia: Board of Publication,
Lutheran Church in America, 1958), #257. Hymn changes sometimes reflect a
changing theological stance of a church body and are often made without the
members' awareness. Other examples are "I Love Thy Kingdom Lord" (*TLH,*
#462—*SBH*, #158) and "The Church's One Foundation" (*TLH*, #473—*SBH*,
#149). In both hymns the *SBH* deleted stanzas referring to the presence of
false prophets and the division they cause, respectively. The former deleted
phrase reads "Should I with scoffers join, Her altars to abuse? No! Better far
my tongue were dumb, My hand its skill should lose." The latter phrase reads
"Tho' there be those that hate her, false sons within her pale, Against both foe
and traitor She ever shall prevail. Though with a scornful wonder, Men see her
sore oppressed, By schisms rent asunder, By heresies distressed."

APPENDIX I

QUESTIONS FOR DISCUSSION

SECTION I

The Historic Lutheran Faith or the New Thinking

Chapter 1

1. The 1987 formation of the Evangelical Lutheran Church in America created considerable controversy about Christian doctrine and the Scriptures. What are the two positions that distinguish liberal Lutherans from traditional Lutherans? (p. 16)

2. Which view of the Bible do you remember from your childhood Christian education? Is the Bible the very Word of God or does the Bible contain factual errors and contradictions? (p. 16)

3. Today we usually hear about evolution rather than creation. Does the plain language of the Bible teach evolution or creation? Were Adam and Eve real people or merely symbolic of grunting, hairy cave men? (p. 17)

4. The claim that events must be reproduced in the lab to prove their historical reliability is called logical positivism. Did God create the universe, speak through prophets about the coming Messiah, become God in the flesh in Jesus, perform miracles, and rise from the dead? Which position, the liberal or traditional one, teaches the plain doctrine of the Bible? (pp. 16-19)

5. Every verse in the Bible relates in some way to the coming of Christ, his atoning death on the cross, and that faith which comes through the Means of Grace. Did Jesus die for our sins (traditional view) or does the cross portray an unjust heavenly Father (liberal view)? The message of religious liberals has been defined as a God without wrath sending Christ without a cross into a world without sin. (p. 19)

6. Does the Bible teach moral absolutes of the Creator, or are the commandments of the Bible the result of primitive and superstitious men who used God's name to oppress women, homosexuals, and advocates of free love? (p. 20)
7. Should Lutherans belong to the social activist National Council of Churches and the related World Council of Churches? Are the WCC and NCC traditional or liberal in their view of the Bible? Are they the last organizations left that still believe in Marxism? (p. 21)
8. Where can the doctrinal decline of the mainline churches be documented? (*Christian News Encyclopedia,* Herman Otten's *Baal or God*, Gregory L. Jackson's *Liberalism: Its Cause and Cure,* pp. 22-24)

Chapter 2

1. What are the sources of the quotations in this book? (p. 28)
2. When the Braaten/Jensen *Christian Dogmatics* volumes were published by the LCA's Fortress Press, what were the positions of the authors of the work? (p. 28)
3. What does *Search,* the official Bible-study program of the ELCA, teach: the traditional or liberal view of the Scriptures? (p. 29)

Chapter 3

1. What does Professor Kurt Marquart write about the use of human reason to attack Christian doctrines? (p. 31)
2. Did the liberal historical-critical view of the Bible originate with Luther or Jesus, according to Dr. Robert Preus? (p. 32)
3. How would you compare the liberal historical-critical view of the Bible to the traditional historical-grammatical view? (pp. 32-34)
4. Is the liberal historical-critical method of interpreting the Scriptures neutral, according to Dr. Siegbert Becker? (p. 37)
5. Which view of the Bible was adopted by Albert Schweitzer, Rudolph Bultmann, Karl Barth, Paul Tillich, and other highly publicized modern theologians? (p. 39f.)
6. What did Dr. J. Kincaid Smith, a pastor now in the conservative Evangelical Lutheran Synod, believe when he graduated from a Lutheran Church in America seminary? (pp. 42, 58f.)
7. What does the ELCA professor Todd Nichol write about the ELCA's view of scripture and how it changed? (p. 44)
8. What did Craig Stanford write about the ELCA's *Search* Bible-study program and its impact upon conservatives still left in the denomination? (p. 50)

Chapter 4

1. Is the traditional view of scripture supported by the writings of Luther? Which Biblical verses are the foundation for Luther's teaching? (pp. 53-55)
2. What does the ELCA *Christian Dogmatics* claim about the truth of the Bible and the ELCA's break with Luther? (p. 55f.)

3. What did ELCA presiding bishop Herbert Chilstrom write about teaching inerrancy? (p. 57)
4. Is it good to lose your faith in seminary, according to the ELCA seminary professor Jay C. Rochelle? (p. 59f.)

Chapter 5

What happens, according to Dr. J. Kincaid Smith, when the thread of creation is pulled from the seamless garment of God's inerrant Word? (p. 63)

Chapter 6

1. Does the New Testament view the Old Testament as full of myths and legends? Which NT passages assume the truth of OT passages about Adam, Eve, and Jonah? (p. 65f.)
2. What is the proper place of reason for the Christian, according to Dr. Siegbert Becker? (p. 66)

Chapter 7

1. Did Jesus indicate in his question to the Sadducees that he believed Moses wrote the first five books of the Bible? (p. 70)
2. What does the ELCA teach about the author of Genesis, Exodus, Leviticus, Numbers, and Deuteronomy? (p. 70f.)

Chapter 8

1. How would you describe the difference between the traditional and the liberal view of Old Testament Messianic prophecies? (pp. 74, 75)
2. Is Genesis 3:15 (the Proto-Evangelism, or First Gospel) a prophecy about Christ, according to retired seminary professor William A. Poovey? (p. 75f.)

Chapter 9

1. Does the Bible correctly quote Jesus, or did the biblical authors invent sayings that gained credibility by having them come from Christ? (p. 78)
2. What does the ELCA *Search* Bible-study program say about "generous portions of imagination" in the gospels? (p. 79)
3. What did the ecumenical Jesus Seminar say about the reliability of the sayings of Christ in the Bible? (p. 81)

Chapter 10

1. Did Luther support the traditional view of God working through miracles to accomplish his will? (p. 84)
2. What does the ELCA's *Christian Dogmatics* state about the miraculous element of the Bible? (p. 84f.)

3. Would most ELCA members agree with ELCA seminary professor Terence Fretheim about the "legendary" elements of the Elisha narrative? (p. 86)

Chapter 11

1. Is the Virgin Birth of Christ taught in the Bible? Does the Book of Concord also teach this doctrine? Is the Virgin Birth an important doctrine? (p. 88)
2. Does the ELCA's *Christian Dogmatics* teach the Virgin Birth of Christ as a myth? (p. 90)
3. What did ELCA seminary professor Michael Root write about the importance and truth of the Virgin Birth of Christ? (pp. 92, 93)

Chapter 12

1. Does the Bible teach the deity of Christ, as we always believed before, or did the early Church invent the doctrines of the Christian creeds without biblical evidence, as claimed by the ELCA's *Christian Dogmatics?* (p. 97, 98)
2. What has Lutheranism always taught about the two natures of Christ, based upon the Scriptures and the creeds of the Church? (p. 100)

Chapter 13

1. Those who deny the doctrine of the Trinity are "idolaters and blasphemers," according to the *Book of Concord,* Apology of the Augsburg Confession. Does this apply to what the ELCA's *Christian Dogmatics* authors (p. 102) and seminary professor Paul Jersild (p. 102f.) have written?
2. Liberal theologians deny the Trinity along with which anti-Christian cults? (p. 103)

Chapter 14

1. Where would one find biblical support for the atonement, Jesus dying for the sins of the world? (p. 106)
2. Why would the ELCA's *Christian Dogmatics* call the traditional, biblical doctrine of the atonement "crass"? (p. 107)
3. What does a confessional Lutheran really believe? (p. 111)

Chapter 15

1. Do Christians have any doubt about whether Jesus rose from the dead after being crucified? (pp. 113, 114)
2. How many passages from the ELCA can be listed that clearly deny the bodily resurrection of Christ? (pp. 114-119)
3. Should we avoid the term "physical resurrection" according to ELCA seminary professor Michael Root? (p. 119)
4. What happens to Christian faith and preaching if Christ is not resurrected, according to St. Paul? (1 Corinthians 15:12-19) (p. 121)

Chapter 16

1. ELCA seminary professor Stanley Olson has written in the *Search* Bible-study program that it is "inappropriate" to speak of the immortality of the soul. Why is it "unhelpful" or "ambiguous" to speak of this at a funeral, according to Dr. Olson? (p. 124)
2. How many other ELCA leaders have denied the immortality of the soul? (pp. 123-125)

Chapter 17

1. What is the relationship between immorality and falling away from the Christian faith, according to Wisconsin Synod Pastor Richard Starr? (p. 129)
2. ELCA Bishop Herbert Chilstrom, who opposes inerrancy, has reinterpreted the biblical passages about homosexuality and has come to what conclusions? (pp. 130-132)
3. What did Bishop Chilstrom suggest about unrepentant homosexuals actively involved in leadership positions in the Church? (p. 131)
4. Should homosexuals be ordained, according to Bishop Chilstrom? (p. 134) What does an ELCA adjunct seminary professor write about homosexuality and the Bible? (p. 135)
5. How has the ELCA's view of the Bible allowed for a divided denomination with regard to the ordination of openly homosexual men and women? (p. 135f.)
6. Where does Bishop Chilstrom admit that ELCA predecessor bodies ordained known homosexuals? (p. 137f.)
7. At which homosexual advocacy gatherings did Dr. John Tietjen and Pastor Barbara Lundblad preach? (p. 148)
8. What does Reconciled in Christ mean for a congregation, district, or denomination? (p. 142)
9. Lutheran Social Services of Minnesota, an inter-Lutheran agency, uses X-rated films for the treatment of sex offenders. Which church body called these "erotically explicit" films "edifying"? (p. 154)

Chapter 18

Is it possible to reconcile Christ's statement, "I am the way, the truth, and the life. No one comes to the Father except through Me" (John 14:6), with calling non-Christian religions "valid expressions of God's power and grace"? (p. 164)

Chapter 19

1. How have Edmund and Julia Robb explained the frantic political lobbying of the liberal, mainline denominations? (p. 174f.)
2. How many social activist groups work within the ELCA? (p. 175) How many are homosexual lobbies?

3. What did ELCA leader Paul Jersild say about what we can learn from Marxism, a system of thought that now has few defenders where it was long practiced? (p. 184)

Chapter 20

1. What kinds of activities characterize the National Council of Churches? (p. 192)
2. Where has a Yale Ph.D. documented the work of the World Council of Churches in defending the Soviet Union and attacking Western democracies? (p. 192, 193)
3. Which recent book deals with homosexual activity at the NCC headquarters and the NCC's reaction to *Reader's Digest* and *Sixty Minute's* coverage of their radical activism? (p. 196)
4. Is the ELCA a member of the National Council of Churches and the World Council of Churches? (p. 197)

SECTION II

The Great Strengths of Lutheranism

Chapter 21

1. Why is it important to be in fellowship with those who cling to the truths of the Scriptures? (p. 201f.)
2. Why should we avoid those teachers who mock the Bible, pervert Christian truth, and persuade others to adopt the new thinking that opposes God's Word? How many biblical passages deal with these issues of fellowship? (pp. 202-204)

Chapter 22

What are the major divisions within the Christian faith? (p. 214)

Chapter 23

1. In which papal bull was the claim made that the pope has supreme power over the Church? (p. 216)
2. How has tradition supplanted the Scriptures in the Roman Catholic Church? (p. 93)

Chapter 24

1. Why do the Reformed denominations fail to find agreement among themselves, according to Evangelical Lutheran Synod Pastor David Jay Webber? (p. 226)
2. How has the misuse of reason among the Reformed led to a denial of the Real Presence of Christ in the sacrament of communion? (p. 228)
3. How do our feelings oppose faith rather than confirm it, according to Luther? (p. 235)
4. How did the Pentecostal and charismatic movements grow out of the Reformed tenets of Methodism? (pp. 246-249)

Chapter 25

1. What led Lutherans into pietism, according to Wisconsin Lutheran Seminary professor John Brenner? (p. 253)
2. What problems were created by Spener's use of lay-led cell groups or affinity groups? (p. 257)
3. How did the "born-again" experience enter Lutheranism, even though it opposed the biblical doctrine of the Means of Grace? (p. 258)
4. How did pietism war against the historic Lutheran liturgy? (p. 260f.)
5. How did pietism promote doctrinal indifference in the name of love and sanctification? (p. 261f.)
6. How did pietism influence John Wesley? (pp. 266, 267)
7. How did pietism influence Lutheranism in America? (p. 272, next chapter)

SECTION III

American Lutheranism's Drift into the New Thinking

Chapter 26

1. How was the oldest Lutheran church body in America (the General Synod, later part of the LCA, then the ELCA) born in pietism? (p. 272)
2. How did the General Synod express its approval of the Prussian Church Union, a union that ultimately led to the formation of the Lutheran Church-Missouri Synod? (p. 275f.)
3. How did a weak position on the Masonic lodge movement blunt the teaching of the General Council? (p. 276)
4. How did millennialism influence American Lutheranism? (p. 281)
5. The unionists (now called ecumenists) advocated and practiced altar and pulpit fellowship with the Reformed denominations. Why is this wrong? (p. 282f.)
6. Why is it dangerous to leave doctrinal questions open and unresolved? (p. 283)
7. How did the Prussian Church Union, forced by the king, lead to the formation of the Lutheran Church-Missouri Synod by C. F. W. Walther and others? (pp. 286-288)
8. How did Walther's agonizing experience with pietism lead to his masterpiece, *Law and Gospel?* (p. 291)
9. What are the three confessional positions of Lutherans? (pp. 291, 292)

Chapter 27

1. What doctrinal issues were left unresolved during the 1918 ULCA merger of the General Synod, the more conservative General Council, and the United Synod of the South? (p. 303)

2. How did the Midwestern pietistic Lutheran groups work through the American Lutheran Conference? (pp. 304-312)

Chapter 28

1. What is the purpose of this book? John 3:16 (p. 342)
2. What are the twin foes of the historic Christian faith? (p. 343)
3. What did Martin Luther write about small errors in doctrine? (p . 345f.)
4. What are the three stages of doctrinal error, according to ELCA pioneer Charles P. Krauth? (p. 346f.)
5. How did Missouri Synod President F. Pfotenhauer define unionism? (p. 348)
6. How do ecumenists confuse the visible and invisible Church, according to Professor Kurt Marquart? (p. 351f.)
7. Is the ELCA committed to unionism, according to *The Lutheran* and Bishop Herb Chilstrom? (p. 352)
8. What did ALC Bishop David Preus fail to mention when he encouraged his denomination to celebrate communion with the Reformed? Note the Schmauk quotation about toleration and the Lord's Supper. (p. 356, 357)
9. What is better than dishonest union, according to Charles P. Krauth? (p. 358)
10. What are the marks of unionism, according to ALC pioneer Professor M. Reu? (p. 359)
11. How has the charismatic movement promoted unionism? (p. 369f.)
12. Is the charismatic movement the answer to Lutheranism's problems with liberal doctrine? Note Larry Christensen's approach to the Bible. (p. 368)
13. What determines the orthodoxy of a Lutheran body according to Francis Pieper, one of the Missouri Synod's great authors and leaders? (p. 374)
14. Why is it wrong to stay in a heterodox church body because of our relatives? (p. 377)
15. According to Luther, what happens when one doctrine is lost? (p. 379)

APPENDIX II

ASK YOUR PASTOR

The following questions are provided to assist our readers in determining the theological position of their pastors.

These questions should be asked exactly as worded. Your pastor should be able to answer them with a simple yes or no.

Questions

1. *Inspiration and Inerrancy*

   Do *you* personally believe that the writers of the Bible were so controlled by the Holy Spirit that they wrote exactly what God wanted them to write?

   Do *you* personally believe that the Bible contains no errors or contradictions?

2. *Creation*

   Do *you* personally believe that God created everything in six 24-hour days as recorded in Scripture?

3. *Adam and Eve*

   Do *you* believe that Adam and Eve were real, historical people? What about Jonah, Noah, and Job?

4. *The Words of Jesus*

   Do *you* personally believe that the Words of Jesus, as recorded in the New Testament, were *all* actually spoken by him?

5. *Miracles*

   Do *you* personally believe that *every* miracle recorded in the Bible was a real, historical event?

6. *The Virgin Birth*

   Do *you* truly believe that Jesus did not have a human father?

   Do *you* believe that the Bible and therefore the Apostles Creed contains myth?

7. *Deity of Christ*

   Do *you* personally believe that Jesus is 100% *God* and 100% *man?*

8. *The Trinity*

   Do *you* believe that the Bible teaches of God the Father, God the Son and God the Holy Spirit—three Persons in one God?

   Do *you* personally believe in God the Father, God the Son, and God the Holy Spirit—three in One—as is stated in the Athanasian Creed, one of the three great ecumenical creeds of the Christian church?

9. *Atonement*

   Do *you* personally believe that God took his anger for our sins out on Christ—that he was the final blood sacrifice that *appeased* God's *wrath* and bought the forgiveness of our sins?

10. *Resurrection*

    Do *you* personally believe that Christ was *physically* raised from the dead. . . . that these *our* physical bodies will be raised from the dead?

11. *Immortality of the Soul*

    Do *you* personally believe that man has a soul that survives the death of the physical body?

12. *Homosexuality*

    Do *you* personally believe that the Bible condemns the practice of homosexuality?

    If he (the ALC official) says it is no worse than any other sin, say you agree but then *add:* Homosexuality, like all sin requires *repentance* (sorrow over sins) and the faithful resolve that, with God's help, a person can give it up and sin no more. Do *you* agree with that statement?

    Do *you* personally believe that homosexuality is an acceptable alternate lifestyle ordained by God—a gift from God to be celebrated and enjoyed?

BIBLIOGRAPHY

Aaberg, Theodore A. *A City Set on a Hill*. Mankato: Board of Publications, Evangelical Lutheran Synod, 1968.

Abbott, S. J., Walter, ed. *Documents of Vatican II*. New York: Herder and Herder, 1966.

ALC. "The Victims of Pornography." Office of Church in Society, The American Lutheran Church, 1985.

Anderson, Phyllis. *The Bible As Liberating Word: An Introduction to Liberation Theology*. Minneapolis: Augsburg Publishing House, 1986.

Arndt, William. *Bible Difficulties and Seeming Contradictions*. eds. Robert G. Hoerber and Walter Roehrs, St. Louis: Concordia Publishing House, 1987.

Bachmann, E. Theodore. *The Ecumenical Involvement of the LCA Predecessor Bodies: A Brief History, 1900-1962*. New York: Division for World Mission and Ecumenism, Lutheran Church in America, 1982.

_____ . "ULCA: Building Blocks for Unity." *The Lutheran*, November, November 1987, p. 9.

Balge, Richard D. "Pietism's Teaching on Church and Ministry." *Wisconsin Lutheran Quarterly*, Fall, 1985, p. 248.

Barkenquast, James L., John Stevens Kerr, Frank W. Klos, and Donald R. Pichaske. *Word and Witness*. LCA Adult Bible Study Program, Philadelphia: Fortress Press, 1977.

Barnhart, David R. *The Church's Desperate Need for Revival*. Eagan, MN: Abiding Word Publications, 1986.

_____ , ed. "ELCA Congregation Discovers That it Must 'Toe the Line' when Rewriting its Constitution." *Abiding Word Ministries*, Summer 1991.

Beck, Norman. "A New Future for Jews, Christians, and Muslims." *Dialogue*, Spring, 1984, reprinted in *Christian News Encyclopedia*, 4 vols. ed. Herman Otten, Washington: Missourian Publishing Company, 3:2171.

Beck, Roy Howard. *On Thin Ice: A Religion Reporter's Memoir*. Wilmore, Kentucky: Bristol Books, 1988.

Becker, David. "ELCA Still Promoting Homosexuality." *Christian News*, April 3, 1989, p. 17.

Becker, Siegbert W. "The Historical-Critical Method of Bible Interpretation." *Wisconsin Lutheran Quarterly,* vol. 74, 1977, pp. 13-24, 133-148.

_____ . *The Foolishness of God: The Place of Reason in the Theology of Martin Luther.* Milwaukee: Northwestern Publishing House, 1982.

Bodensieck, Julius, ed. *The Encyclopedia of the Lutheran Church.* 3 vols., Minneapolis: Augsburg Publishing House, 1965.

Bouman, Herbert J. A. *A Look at Today's Churches: A Comparative Guide.* St. Louis: Concordia Publishing House, 1980.

Braaten, Carl E., and Robert W. Jenson. *Christian Dogmatics.* 2 vols., Philadelphia: Fortress Press, 1987.

Braun, Marcus. *What is the Nature of Truth?* Kansas City: Marcus Braun, 1970.

Brenner, John. "Pietism, Past and Present." unpublished paper, January 23, 1989.

Bright, Bill. *Have You Heard of the Four Spiritual Laws?* San Bernadino: Campus Crusade for Christ, 1965.

Brokoff, John R. "Morning Has Broken." *The Lutheran,* April 18, 1984, p. 4.

Brown, Dale. *Understanding Pietism.* Grand Rapids: Wm. B. Eerdmans Publishing Company, 1978.

Bucke, Emory Stevens, ed. *The Interpreter's Dictionary of the Bible.* 4 vols., Nashville: Abingdon Press, 1962.

CBS. "The Gospel According to Whom?" January 23, 1983, CBS "Sixty Minutes" Transcript.

Chicago Tribune. "Support Porno Films." October 2, 1976.

Chilstrom, Herbert. "A Pastoral Letter." March 20, 1988.

_____ . "A Pastoral Letter: The Church and the Homosexual Person." 1979.

Christian News. "Martin Luther King, Jr.—A Dream Lives On—Local Congregation Risks . . ." February 8, 1988, p. 24.

_____ . "Playboy Foundation and ALC Funding Same Anti-Christian Sex Program." October 11, 1976, p. 7. Cf. Chicago Tribune's "Support Porno Films," supra.

Clement, Arthur J. *Pentecost or Pretense? An Examination of the Pentecostal And Charismatic Movements,* Milwaukee: Northwestern Publishing House, 1981.

Clouse, Robert G. *The Church in the Age of Orthodoxy and the Enlightenment.* St. Louis: Concordia Publishing House, 1980.

Concord. newsletters of Lutherans Concerned/North America—A Christian Ministry for Lesbian and Gay Understanding, 1987-1990.

"Cooperation in Externals." the Conference of Presidents, Evangelical Lutheran Joint Synod of Wisconsin and Other States, 1954.

Crumm, David. "Lutheran Merger Virtually Set, But Some Dissent." *Detroit Free Press,* March 21, 1987, Section A, p. 3.

Curnock, Nehemiah, ed. *The Journal of the Rev. John Wesley.* A. M., Vol 1, London: Epworth Press, 1912, pp. 475, 476.

Denef, Lawrence W., trans. *Evangelical Catechism.* Minneapolis: Augsburg Publishing House, 1982.

Dowley, Tim, ed. *Eerdmans' Handbook to the History of Christianity.* Grand Rapids: Wm. B. Eerdmans Publishing House, 1977.

Ehlke, Roland C. *Faith on Trial*. Milwaukee: Northwestern Publishing House, 1980.

_____ . *Understanding the Bible*. Milwaukee: Northwestern Publishing House, 1977.

ELCA. *Working For Justice: A 1988 Directory of Lutheran Ministries*. Chicago: Justice Network of the Lutheran Church, 1988.

Erlandsson, Seth. *Church Fellowship: What Does the Bible Say?*, trans. S. W. Becker, Milwaukee: Northwestern Publishing House, 1979.

Fleischer, Paul. "On Unity and Union or The ELCA and Bankrupt Lutheranism." *The Lutheran Spokesman*, July 1989, p. 11.

Flesner, Dorris A. *American Lutherans Help Shape World Council: The Role of the Lutheran Churches of America in the Formation of the World Council of Churches*. Dubuque, IA: Wm. C. Brown Company, 1981.

Franzmann, Werner H. *Bible History Commentary*. 3 vols., Milwaukee: Northwestern Publishing House, 1980, 1989.

Fredrich, Edward, Sr. "C. F. W. Walther—American Lutheranism Has Had No Equal." *The Northwestern Lutheran*, May 15, 1987, pp. 187, 188.

Fretheim, Terence E. *Search, Unit 9, Deuteronomy, Joshua, Judges*. Leaders Guide, Minneapolis: Augsburg Publishing House, 1985.

_____ . *Search, Unit 10, Ruth, 1 & 2 Samuel, 1 & 2 Kings*. Leaders Guide, Minneapolis: Augsburg Publishing House, 1985.

Frost, Naomi. *Golden Visions, Broken Dreams: A Short History of the Lutheran Council in the USA*. New York: Lutheran Council in the USA, 1987.

Fuerbringer, L., Th. Engelder, and P. E. Kretzmann, eds. *The Concordia Cyclopedia*. St. Louis: Concordia Publishing House, 1927.

Funk, Robert W., Bernard Brandon Scott, and James R. Butts. *The Parables of Jesus: A Report of the Jesus Seminar*. Sonoma: Polebridge Press, 1988.

Gockel, Herman W. *What Jesus Means to Me*. St. Louis: Concordia Publishing House, 1948.

Graham, Billy. *How to be Born Again*. New York: Warner Books, 1977.

Hagglund, Bengt. *History of Theology*. trans. Gene J. Lund, St. Louis: Concordia Publishing House, 1968.

Hall, George. "A Religion of Grace." *Augsburg Adult Bible Studies*, July, 1987, p. 9.

Hanson, Richard Simon. *The Comings of God*. Minneapolis: Augsburg Publishing House, 1981.

Heick, Otto W. *The History of Christian Thought*. 2 vols. Philadelphia: Fortress Press, 1966.

Heinecken, Martin J. *We Believe and Teach*. Philadelphia: Fortress Press, 1980.

Highley, Joanne. "Prancing White Horse." *Words of L.I.F.E.* December, 1987, p. 3.

Institute for Religion and Democracy. "A Time For Candor, Mainline Churches and Radical Social Witness." Washington: IRD, 1983.

Isaac, Rael Jean. "Do You Know Where Your Church Offerings Go?" *Readers Digest*, January, 1983.

Jackson, Gregory L. "The Impact of A. D. Mattson Upon the Social Consciousness of the Synod." U. of Notre Dame, Ph. D. diss., published as *Prophetic Voice for the Kingdom*, Rock Island: Augustana Historical Society, 1986.

Bibliography

_____. *Liberalism Its Cause and Cure: The Poisoning of American Christianity And the Antidote*. Milwaukee: Northwestern Publishing House, 1991.

_____. "Pietism in America." unpublished paper, May, 1990.

_____. "Questions and Answers about Pietism." *Christian News,* October 16, 1989, p. 6.

_____., *Shepherd of Peace Lutheran Church* newsletter. Winter, 1991, p. 1.

_____. "Unionism in American Lutheranism." Unpublished paper, May, 1990.

Jackson, Samuel M. and Lefferts A. Loetscher. *The New Schaff-Herzog Encyclopedia of Religious Knowledge*. Grand Rapids: Baker Book House, 1957.

Jersild, Paul. *Invitation to Faith*. Minneapolis: Augsburg Publishing House, 1978.

Jeske, John C. "Amazing Grace—125 Years of It!" unpublished paper, February 13, 1974.

Johlas, Michell Sanden. "Search Program Remains Popular; Sparks Renewal." September 5, 1986, *The Lutheran Standard.*

Johnson, Arthur L. *Faith Misguided: Exposing the Dangers of Mysticism*. Chicago: Moody Bible Institute, 1988.

Johnson, Marshall. *Affirm Series: The Apostles Creed*. Teacher's Guide, eds. Irene Getz, Susan Niemi Tetlie, and Gretchen L. Weidenbach, Minneapolis: Augsburg Publishing House, 1984.

Jones, E. Michael. *Is Notre Dame Still Catholic?* South Bend: Fidelity Press, 1989.

Juel, Donald H. *Search, Unit 5, Matthew 1-16*. Leaders Guide, Minneapolis: Augsburg Publishing House, 1984.

_____. *Search, Unit 6, Matthew 17-28*. Leaders Guide, Minneapolis: Augsburg Publishing House, 1984.

Kaplan, David B. *Search, Unit 8, Exodus 19-40, Leviticus, Numbers*. Leader Guide, Minneapolis: Augsburg Publishing House, 1985.

Kennedy, D. James. *Evangelism Explosion*. Wheaton: Tyndale Publishers, 1970.

Klein, Christa R. "The AELC: Missouri's Gift." *The Lutheran*, October, 1987, p. 7.

Koehler, Edward W. A. *A Summary of Christian Doctrine*. St. Louis: Concordia Publishing House, 1971.

Koehler, John Philip. *The History of the Wisconsin Synod*. Sauk Rapids, MN: Sentinel Printing, 1981.

Kovaciny, Roger. "Twenty Questions." *Christian News Encyclopedia*, 4 vols., ed. Herman Otten, Washington: Missourian Publishing Company, 1988, 4:2636.

Krauth, Charles P. *The Conservative Reformation and its Theology*. Philadelphia: The United Lutheran Publication House, 1913.

Kretzmann, Paul S. *Popular Commentary of the Bible*. St. Louis: Concordia Publishing House, 1923.

Lefever, Ernest W. *Amsterdam to Nairobi: The World Council of Churches and and the Third World, 1975-1987*. Washington: Ethics and Public Policy Center, 1987.

Lekmann, Daniel J. "ELCA Lutherans Vote to Remain in National World Council of Churches." *Christian News,* September 11, 1989, p. 6.

Leppien, Patsy A. "An Open Letter to the Laity of the ALC." *Christian News Encyclopedia*, 4 vols., ed. Herman Otten, Washington: Missourian Publishing Company, 1988, 3:2166.

LeRoy, William R. "Liberation Theology." *Christian News Encyclopedia,* 4 vols., ed. Herman Otten, Washington: Missourian Publishing Company, 1988, 2:1133.

Limburg, James. *Search, Unit 3, Genesis 1-17.* Leaders Guide, Minneapolis: Augsburg Publishing House, 1983.

Lindsell, Harold. *The Battle for the Bible.* Grand Rapids: Zondervan, 1976.

_____ . *The Bible in the Balance.* Grand Rapids: Zondervan, 1979.

Lueker, Erwin L., ed. *Lutheran Cyclopedia.* St. Louis: Concordia Publishing House, 1975.

Lull, Timothy. "A Church Called Lutheran." *The Lutheran,* December, 1987, p. 13.

Lussky, Herbert O. *The Missouri Synod Layman and Lutheran Union.* Evanston: 1947.

Luther, Martin. *What Luther Says, An Anthology.* 3 vols., ed. Ewald M. Plass, St. Louis: Concordia Publishing House, 1959.

_____ . *Commentary on Galatians.* trans. Erasmus Middleton, Grand Rapids: Kregel Publications, 1979.

_____ . *Commentary on Romans.* trans. J. Theodore Mueller, Grand Rapids: Kregel Publications, 1976.

_____ . *The Sermons of Martin Luther.* 8 vols., Grand Rapids: Baker Book House, 1983.

The Lutheran. "Faces." June 1, 1988. p. 42.

_____ . "Closer Lutheran-Methodist Ties Urged." January 6, 1986, p. 26.

_____ . "Marty Has Bishops Support." April 2, 1986, p. 21.

_____ . "Schiotz, Former ALC Leader, Dies." March 22, 1989, p. 23.

_____ . "Scholars Vote on the Sayings of Jesus." January 15, 1986, p. 17.

_____ . "Visions for ELCA's Direction." April 20, 1988, p. 25.

"Lutheran Bodies in the U.S.A." Conference of Presidents, Evangelical Lutheran Joint Synod of Wisconsin and Other States, 1954, No. 1.

The Lutheran Church—Missouri Synod Convention Workbook. 1986.

The Lutheran Hymnal (TLH). St. Louis: Concordia Publishing House, 1941.

Lutheran Perspective. (formerly *Missouri in Perspective*), October 16, 1987.

The Lutheran Standard. "A Narrative Description for a New Lutheran Church." CNLC Progress Report #4, December 14, 1984, pp. 39-62.

_____ . "Outstanding Document." May 4, 1984, p. 24.

_____ . "Preus Urges Ecumenical Change." January 24, 1986, p. 22.

Lyles, Jean Caffey. "ELCA, Reformed Efforts Get Back on Track." *The Lutheran,* March 22, 1989, p. 29.

_____ . "Guidelines for Sexual Conduct OK'd." *The Lutheran,* October 12, 1988, p. 23.

_____ . "Reumann to Chair Ministry Task Force." *The Lutheran,* August 10, 1988, p. 20.

_____ . "Western Bishops Back Action on Gays." *The Lutheran,* March 16, 1988, p. 23.

"Mark . . . Avoid . . . Origin of the CLC." Coordinating Council of the Church of the Lutheran Confession, Eau Claire, WI: The CLC Book House, 1983.

Marquart, Kurt E. *Anatomy of an Explosion.* Grand Rapids: Baker Book House, 1978.

Marty, Martin E. "What Ever Happened to Hell?" *The Lutheran,* April 2, 1986, pp. 15-17.

McCurley, Foster R., and John Reumann. *Word and Witness.* LCA Adult Bible Study Program, Philadelphia: Fortress Press, 1977.

Meyer, F. S. *The Religious Bodies of America.* St. Louis: Concordia Publishing House, 1954.

Morphew, Clark. "Did Jesus Actually Say That?" *St. Paul Pioneer Press Dispatch,* October 17, 1987; reprinted in *Christian News,* November 1, 1987, p. 22.

Morris, Henry N. and Gary E. Parker. *What Is Creation Science?* El Cajon: Master Books, 1987.

Mueller, J. T. *My Church and Others.* St. Louis: Volkening, 1968.

Nelson, E. Clifford, ed. *The Lutherans in North America.* Philadelphia: Fortress Press, 1975.

Nelson, James B. *Embodiment.* Minneapolis: Augsburg Publishing House, 1978.

Neuhaus, Richard John, ed. "Contending for the Lutheran Future." *Forum Letter,* July 15, 1991, p. 1.

Nichol, Todd W. "How Will ELCA View the Bible?" *The Lutheran,* October 15, 1986, p. 11, id. "Pure Power," *The Lutheran Standard,* October 24, 1986, pp. 4-8.

Nichols, James Hastings. *History of Christianity, 1650-1950: Secularization of the West.* New York: The Ronald Press Company, 1956.

Niebuhr, Gustav. "Liberal Scholars Assert That Jesus Did Not Compose the Lord's Prayer." *Christian News,* October 24, 1988, p. 1.

_____ . "Watch Out, Martin Scorcese! 'Christ the Man' Being Planned." *Christian News,* November 21, 1988, p. 1.

Ochsenford, S. E. *Documentary History of the General Council of the Evangelical Lutheran Church in North America.* Philadelphia: General Council Publication House, 1912.

Olson, Stanley N. *Search, Unit 11, 1 Corinthians.* Leaders Guide, Minneapolis: Augsburg Publishing House, 1985.

Otten, Herman. *Baal or God.* Washington: Missourian Publishing Company, 1988.

_____ . "Pastor-Scholar Leaves The Lutheran Church in America." *Christian News Encyclopedia,* 4 vols., Washington: Missourian Publishing Company, 1988, 3:2195.

_____ . "Voices of Jesus Seminar Scholars Adopted at Roman Catholic and Protestant Seminaries." *Christian News,* January 2, 1989, p. 1.

_____ . "What Is Going On? Going into Exile." *Christian News Encyclopedia,* 4 vols., Washington: Missourian Publishing Company, 1983, 1:632.

_____ , ed., transcript of "Here's Life." November 27, 1976. *Christian News Encyclopedia,* 4 vols., Washington: Missourian Publishing Co., 1983, 1:297.

Our Church: Its Life and Mission. Milwaukee: Northwestern Publishing House, 1990.

Petersen, Wilhem W. "Pastor, I Have A Question." *The Lutheran Sentinel,* February 1985, p. 4.

Pieper, Francis, and Theodore Engelder. *Brief Statement of the Doctrinal Position of the Missouri Synod.* St. Louis: Concordia Publishing House, 1932.

Pieper, Francis. *Christian Dogmatics.* 3 vols., St. Louis: Concordia Publishing House, 1953.

_____ . *The Difference Between Orthodox and Heterodox Churches.* and Supplement, ed. Pastor E. L. Mehlberg, Coos Bay, Oregon, 1981.

Polack, W. G. *The Handbook to the Lutheran Hymnal.* St. Louis: Concordia Publishing House, 1942.

Poovey, William A. "Question Box." *The Lutheran Standard,* March 2, 1984, p. 28.

Prange, Victor H. "Lutherans in America." series of articles, *Northwestern Lutheran,* June 15, 1987—January 1, 1988.

_____ . *Why So Many Churches?* Milwaukee: Northwestern Publishing House, 1985.

Presbyterian Layman. "The World Council of Churches." September, 1987, p. 7.

Preus, David W. "From the Presiding Bishop—Creation and Evolution." *ACTS,* The American Lutheran Church, April, 1987.

_____ . "God's Word—Our Great Heritage." *The Lutheran Standard,* May 18, 1984, p. 29.

Preus, Robert D. *Getting Into the Theology of Concord.* St. Louis: Concordia Publishing House, 1977.

_____ . "May the Lutheran Theologian Legitimately Use the HCM?" *Affirm,* Spring, 1973.

Qualben, Lars P. *A History of the Christian Church.* New York: Thomas Nelson and Sons, 1933.

Reid, J. K. S., trans. and ed. *Calvin: Theological Treatise.* Westminister Press, 1954.

Reu, J. Michael. *In the Interest of Lutheran Unity: Two Lectures.* Columbus: Lutheran Book Concern, 1940

_____ . *Luther and the Scriptures.* Columbus: The Wartburg Press, 1944.

Reumann, John. *Jesus in the Church's Gospels.* Philadelphia: Fortress Press, 1968.

Richardson, Alan, ed. *A Theological Word Book of the Bible.* New York: MacMillan and Company, 1950.

Ringo, Stephen. *Affirm Series: Old Testament.* Teachers Guide, eds. Susan Niemi Tetlie and Lori L. J. Rosenkvist, Minneapolis: Augsburg Publishing House, 1984.

Robb, Edmund W., and Julia Robb. *The Betrayal of the Church: Apostasy and Renewal in the Mainline Denominations.* Westchester: Crossway Books, 1986.

Rochelle, Jay C. "On Spiritual Life and the Sayings and Finding Thereof." *Lutheran Partners* (ELCA), p. 13.

Rongstad, L. James. *How to Respond to the Lodge.* St. Louis: Concordia Publishing House, 1977.

Root, Michael. "FACES." *The Lutheran,* June 1, 1988, p. 42.

_____ . Letter to Gregory L. Jackson. December 17, 1986, LIFT file.

Rubenstein, Sura. "Lutheran-Episcopal Accord Issued." *The Lutheran,* May 11, 1988, p. 28.

Saarnivaara, Uuras. *Can the Bible Be Trusted?* Minneapolis: Osterhus Publishing House, 1983.

Sasse, Herman. *Here We Stand.* trans. Theodore G. Tappert, Adelaide, South Australia: Lutheran Publishing House, 1979.

Schaeffer, Francis A. *The Great Evangelical Disaster.* Westchester: Crossway Books, 1984.

Schaller, John. *Book of Book: A Brief Introduction to the Bible.* Milwaukee: Northwestern Publishing House, 1990.

Schiotz, Fredrik A. *One Man's Story.* Minneapolis: Augsburg Publishing House, 1980.

Schmauk, Theodore E., and C. Theodore Benze. *The Confessional Principle and the Confessions, as Embodying the Principle and the Confession of the Christian Church.* Philadelphia: General Council Publication Board, 1911 .

Schmid, Heinrich. *The Doctrinal Theology of the Evangelical Lutheran Church.* Philadelphia: Lutheran Publication Society, 1889.

Schruhl, Joe E. "Historical-Critical Method of Biblical Interpretation," *Christian News Encyclopedia,* 4 vols., ed. Herman Otten, Washington: Missourian Publishing Company, 1983, 1:237.

Schuetze, Armin W. *Basic Doctrines of the Bible.* Milwaukee: Northwestern Publishing House, 1986.

_____ . "Book Review." *Wisconsin Lutheran Quarterly,* vol. 23, October 1976, p. 325.

Schwarz, Hans. *What Christians Believe.* Philadelphia: Fortress Press, 1987.

_____ . *Beyond the Gates of Death: A Biblical Examination of Evidence For Life After Death.* Minneapolis: Augsburg Publishing House, 1981.

Scroggs, Robin. *Homosexuality in the New Testament.* Philadelphia: Fortress Press, 1983.

Senkbeil, Harold. *Sanctification: Christ in Action.* Milwaukee: Northwestern Publishing House. 1989.

The Service Book and Hymnal (SBH). Minneapolis: Augsburg Publishing House and Philadelphia: Board of Publication, Lutheran Church in America, 1958.

Shelley, Bruce. *Church History in Plain Language.* Waco: Word Books, 1982.

Skov, Oswald. *What Is Truth.* Northridge: Oswald Skov n.d.

Smith, J. Kincaid. "The 'Dismantling' of the Christian Faith or the HCM." *Christian News,* April 29, 1985, p. 11.

_____ . "The Confession of a Former Liberal LCA Pastor." *Christian News Encyclopedia,* 4 vols., ed. Herman Otten, Washington: Missourian Publishing Company, 1988, 3:2165.

_____ . *Interpreting the Scriptures: Twelve Guiding Principles.* unpublished manuscript.

_____ . "Reflections." unpublished paper, October, 1989.

_____ . "The Real Virgin Birth of Our Lord Jesus Christ." *The Lutheran Sentinel,* December, 1987, p. 4.

_____ . "A Progression of Error: The Unraveling of the Christian Faith." unpublished paper.

Smith, Verlyn O. "Gay and Lesbian Ministry in the ELCA." *Entree,* October, 1988, p. 4.

_____ . "Gay and Lesbian Ministry in the ELCA." *Ministries with Young Adults* (ELCA periodical), Spring, 1989, pp. 1-4.

Sohn, Otto E. "What's the Answer?" *Lutheran Witness,* April 9, 1957.

Spener, Philip Jacob. *Pia Desideria.* trans. Theodore G. Tappert, Philadelphia: Fortress Press, 1964.

Spitz, Lewis W. *Our Church and Others.* St. Louis: Concordia Publishing House, 1960.

Spohn, Gustav. "Lutherans Embrace Ecumenism at Assembly in Orlando." *Christian News,* September 16, 1991, p. 6.

_____ . "New ELCA Grapples With Question of Identity, Authority and Teaching." *Christian News,* May 2, 1988, p. 1.

Stanford, Craig. *The Death of the Lutheran Reformation.* Ft. Wayne: Stanford Publishing, 1988.

Starr, Richard. *Speaking the Unspeakable! Homosexuality—A Biblical and Modern Perspective.* Milwaukee: Northwestern Publishing House, 1987.

Stumme, Wayne, ed. *Christians and the Many Faces of Marxism.* Minneapolis: Augsburg Publishing House, 1984.

Stump, Joseph. *Luther's Catechism with an Explanation.* Philadelphia: United Lutheran Publishing, 1907.

Tappert, Theodore, E., ed. *The Book of Concord.* Philadelphia: Fortress Press, 1959.

Teigen, Bjarne W. *I Believe.* 5 vols., Mankato: Lutheran Synod Book Company, 1976-1980.

Teskey, Frank. "Belli Denounces Liberation Theology in Nicaragua." *Christian News Encyclopedia,* 4 vols., ed. Herman Otten, Washington: Missourian Publishing Company, 1988, 4:2554.

"This is Your Church." Board of Education of the Church of the Lutheran Confession.

This We Believe. A statement of belief of the Wisconsin Ev. Lutheran Synod, Milwaukee: Northwestern Publishing House, 1980.

Thorkelson, W. L. "Pastor Agrees to End Homosexual Blessings." *The Lutheran,* April 4, 1984, p. 22.

Thorkelson, Wilmar. "New US Lutheran Church Commission Acts on Theology, Property, Purpose, Structure." *Lutheran World Information,* October 1984.

_____ . "Scholars Debating Jesus' Sayings Spell Trouble for Lutheran Seminary." *Christian News,* November 2, 1987, p. 22.

Tiede, David. *Search, Unit 1 Acts 1-8.* Leaders Guide, Minneapolis: Augsburg Publishing House, 1983.

Tillich, Paul. *Systematic Theology.* 3 vols., Chicago: University of Chicago Press, 1957.

Trexler, Edgar. "Editorial." *The Lutheran,* March 16, 1988, p. 50

_____ . "Two Structural Options Proposed for New Church." *The Lutheran,* March 21, 1984, p. 20.

_____ . "Warm Reception for Chilstrom, ELCA Bishop Makes Ecumenical Commitment Clear." *The Lutheran,* March 2, 1988, pp. 6, 8.

Turner, Darrell. "ELCA's Proposed Statement of Ecumenism Still Drawing Dissent." *The Lutheran,* January 21, 1991, p. 16.

Vanguard. "Lutherans Concerned Issues 'A Call for Dialogue.'" May, 1986, pp. 4-6.

Walther, C. F. W. *Die Evangelische-Lutherische Kirche auf Erden.* St. Louis: Concordia Publishing House, 1981.

_____ . *The Proper Distinction Between Law and Gospel.* trans. W. K. T. Dau, St. Louis: Concordia Publishing House, 1897.

Webber, David Jay. "Catholic Doctrine and the Authority of Scripture." *Lutheran Synod Quarterly,* December, 1988.

_____ . "Luther and Calvin on the Interpretation of Scripture." *Lutheran Synod Quarterly,* December, 1988, p. 77.

Wendland, Ernst. "Present-Day Pietism." *Wisconsin Lutheran Quarterly,* January, 1953.

Wentz, Abdel Ross. *A Basic History of Lutheranism in America.* Philadelphia: Fortress Press, 1964.

Wilson, Howard A. *The Invasion from the East.* Minneapolis: Augsburg Publishing House, 1978.

Wold, Margaret. "Women of Spirit." *Scope,* August, 1985, p. 7.

Zersen, David John. "C. F. W. Walther and the Heritage of Pietist Conventicles." *Concordia Historical Institute Quarterly,* Spring, 1989.

ADDRESSES FOR RESOURCES

Publishing Houses:

Augsburg Fortress Press (ELCA), 426 South Fifth Street, Box 1209, Minneapolis, MN 55440, Phone: 800-447-6129.

Concordia Publishing House (LCMS), 3558 South Jefferson Avenue, St. Louis, MO 63118-3968, Phone: 800-325-3040.

Lutheran Synod Book Company (ELS), 734 Marsh Street, Mankato, MN 56001, Phone: 507-388-3674.

Northwestern Publishing House (WELS), 1250 North 113th Street, Milwaukee, WI 53226-3284, Phone: 800-662-6022.

Periodicals:

Christian News, RR1, Box 309A, New Haven, MO 63068. An independent, conservative weekly. Editor: Rev. Herman Otten.

Faith-Life, PO Box 2141, LaCrosse, WI 54602-2141. The official magazine of the Protes'tant Conference.

The Lutheran, Augsburg Fortress, 426 South Fifth Street, Box 1209, Minneapolis, MN 55440, Phone: 612-330-3300. The official magazine of the Evangelical Lutheran Church in America.

The Lutheran Sentinel, 204 North Second Avenue West, Lake Mills, IA 50450. The official magazine of the Evangelical Lutheran Synod.

The Lutheran Spokesman, 2750 Oxford Street North, Roseville, MN 55113. The official magazine of the Church of the Lutheran Confession.

Lutheran Synod Quarterly, 447 North Division Street, Mankato, MN 56001. The theology journal of the Evangelical Lutheran Synod.

The Lutheran Witness, Concordia Publishing House, 3558 South Jefferson Avenue, St. Louis, MO 63118-3968, Phone: 800-325-3381. The official magazine of the Lutheran Church Missouri Synod.

The Northwestern Lutheran, Northwestern Publishing House, 1250 North 113th Street, Milwaukee, WI 53226-3284, Phone: 414-475-6600, ext. 5. The official magazine of Wisconsin Evangelical Lutheran Synod.

For additional information write to:

Lutherans Informed for the Truth (L.I.F.T.), P.O. Box 6475, Saginaw, MI 48608.

Lincoln Out-Of-Print Book Search, 33 Mount Hygeia Road, Fostor, RI 02825, Phone/FAX: 401-647-2825.

NAME INDEX

Aaberg, Theodore A., 307, 322
Anderson, Phyllis, 179
Arndt, John, 254
Arndt, William, 83, 116

Bachmann, E. Theodore, 353
Barnhart, David R., 56, 151-154, 338
Barth, Karl, 40
Beck, Norman,160ff., 166
Beck, Roy Howard, 195, 196
Becker, David, 42, 65f., 150
Becker, Siegbert W., 32, 37, 39, 42, 65f.
Book of Concord, 88, 96, 101, 105, 113f., 204, 220, 230, 233
Bouman, Herbert J. A., 210, 229, 238, 245f., 280
Braaten, Carl E., 28
Braun, Marcus R., 38
Brenner, John M., 2f., 25, 256-260
Bright, Bill, 232
Brokoff, John R., 117, 124
Brown, Dale, 264
Bultmann, Rudolph, 40
Burgess, Faith, 183, 229, 236-239

Calvin, John, 223, 226, 229, 236-239
Chilstrom, Herbert W., 56, 130-135, 137f., 352

Christenson , Larry, 368
Clement, Arthur J., 362f.
Clouse, Robert G., 255
Conference of Presidents, Wisconsin Synod, 333

Documents of Vatican II, 217

Ehlke, Roland C., 215, 241
ELCA, 22
Engelder, Theodore, 374
Ewing, Wayne, 168f.

Flesner, Dorris A., 353
Forde, Gerhard O., 28, 107
Francke, August Hermann, 263, 285
Franklin, Ben, 360
Franzmann, Werner H., 33
Fredrich, Edward, 294
Fretheim, Terence E., 71, 85, 91
Friberg, H. Daniel, 56
Frost, Naomi, 334
Fry, Franklin C., 353

Gockel, Herman W., 342f.
Graham, Billy, 231
Grundvig, Nikolai F. S., 380

Hagglund, Bengt, 218, 223

Hanson, Richard Simon, 86
Harms, Claus, 293
Hefner, Philip J., 28, 76
Heick, Otto W., 262, 273, 281
Heinecken, Martin J., 118, 125
Herzfeld, Will L., (Bishop), 183

Jackson, Gregory, 9, 92f., 118, 262,
    265, 296, 298, 338, 362-364,
    366-370, 372
Jacobson, Arland, 82

Jenson, Robert T., 56
Jenson, Robert W., 28
Jersild, Paul, 68, 92, 99 102f., 160ff.,
    167, 183f.
Jeske, John C., 317
Jeske, Richard L., 82
Johnson, Arthur L., 254
Johnson, Marshall D., 109
Juel, Donald H., 79, 115

Kaplan, David B., 71, 85
Keller, Arnold, 150
Kennedy, D. James, 232f.
Klein, Christa, 326
Koehler, Edward W. A., 207f., 283,
    351
Koehler, John Philip, 316
Kovaciny, Roger, 23
Krauth, Charles P., 295, 347
Kretzmann, Paul E., 203
Kysar, Robert D., 82

Lefever, Ernest W., 192-195
Lehmann, Daniel J., 197
Leppien, Patsy A., 116
LeRoy, William R., 178
LIFT, 9, 22
Limburg, James, 62
Lindsell, Harold, 324, 327f.
Lull, Timothy F., 13, 118, 125, 183
Lundblad, Barbara, 151
Lussky, Herbert O., 348
Luther, Martin, 54, 66, 84, 106, 114,
    122, 127f., 160, 208f., 213, 221,
    223, 226, 229, 235, 242, 244,
    283, 346f., 372, 378f.

Lyles, Jean Caffey, 353

Marquart, Kurt A., 31, 251, 286, 296,
    324f., 351f.
Martensen, Daniel F., 112
Marty, Martin, 161, 166
Mau, Carl, 150
McCurley, Foster R., Jr., 62
Meyer, F. E., 227
Miller, Lyle, (Bishop), 151
Morris, Henry M., 63
Muehlhaeuser, John, 317
Mueller, John Theodore, 219, 265,
    282
Muhlenberg, Henry Melchior, 272

Nelson, E. Clifford, 284, 299f., 302
Nelson, James B., 143f.
Neuhaus, Richard, 339
Nichol, Todd W., 43ff., 325
Nichols, James Hastings, 263

Ochsenford, S. E., 276
Olsen, Stanley, (Bishop), 136
Olson, Stanley N., 124
Otten, Herman, 22, 24

Passavant, W., 295
Petersen, Wilhelm W., 205
Pfotenhauer, F., 348
Pia Desideria, 253f.
Pieper, Francis, 28, 371, 374-378,
    379f.
Playboy Foundation, 152
Poovey, William A., 75
Prange, Victor H., 223, 271, 276, 323,
    328f., 361
Preus, David W., 43, 62, 355
Preus, Robert D., 31, 105, 201, 203,
    206, 241, 267

Qualben, Lars P., 297
Quanbeck, Warren, 49

Reu, J. Michael, 348, 358f.
Reumann, John, 51, 62, 80, 98f.
Robb, Edmund W., 174, 190

Rochelle, Jay C., 59
Rongstad, L. James, 277
Root, Michael, 92, 118

Saarnivaara, Uuras, 35
Sasse, Herman, 255
Schaeffer, Francis A., 30
Schaller, John, 72
Schiotz, Fredrik A., 49, 353
Schmauk, Theodore E., 295, 357
Schruhl, Joe E., 34, 348-350, 373
Schuetze, Armin W., 173, 260, 348-
     350, 373
Schwarz, Hans, 79f., 93, 124
Schweitzer, Albert, 39
Scroggs, Robin, 135
Skov, Oswald, 172
Smith, J. Kincaid, 42, 51, 52, 58, 63,
     94, 109f., 119, 166, 183, 185-
     187
Smith, Verlyn O., 139ff.
Sohn, Otto E., 89
Spener, Philip Jacob, 253-256, 285
Spitz, Lewis W., 211-214, 216, 219-
     221, 224, 225, 230f., 276f., 356,
     373

Stanford, Craig, 49
Starr, Richard, 128f.
Strauss, David Frederick, 39
Stumme, Wayne, 183
Stump, Joseph, 122f.

Teigen, Bjarne W., 373
Tidemann, Paul, 145f.
Tiede, David, 85
Treadway, Leo, 145, 146
Trexler, Edgar R., 137, 352

Utziz, Mario, 183

Walther, C. F. W., 54, 243, 288-294,
     343, 345
Webber, David Jay, 9, 217, 226-228
Wendland, Ernst, 256
Wentz, Abdel Ross, 272, 302
Wesley, John, 225, 266-268
Wilson, Howard A., 164f.

Zersen, David John, 290-294
Zinzendorf, Nicholas, Count, 265f.,
     272
Zwingli, Ulrich, 223, 229

TOPIC INDEX

Adam and Eve, 17, 65-69
Affirm Series (ALC), 67
ALC, 43
Allegorical method, 66
American Lutheran Church, 330
American Lutheran Conference, 304-310
Anti-Missourian Brotherhood, 305
Atonement, 19
Augustana Synod, 310-312

Bethany Lutheran Seminary, 205
Blessing gay couples, 141, 146

Calvinist denominations, 224
Cell groups, 292
Chart of Lutheran Synods, 340f.
Christian Dogmatics (Braaten/Jenson), 28, 40f., 55, 76, 78, 84, 90, 97, 102, 107, 114f., 119, 123, 358
Church of the Lutheran Confession, 323
CNLC (ELCA Merger Commission), 336
Concord (Lutherans Concerned), 147
Confessional Lutheranism, 284-298
Conservative Lutheran position A, 15
Cooperation in Externals, 333

Creation, 17, 61-64

Danish Lutherans, 312, 313
Deity of Christ, 18, 96-100

Ecumenical Creeds, 97
Ecumenical Movement, 21
ELCA, 26
Enlightenment, 30f., 45
Evangelical Catechism (ALC), 67
Evangelical Lutheran Synod, 307-310, 320f.
Faith and Feelings, 234-236

Gay ordination, 141
General Council, 276-284
General Synod, 273-276
German Lutherans, 313-315

Hamma School of Theology (LCA), 58
Historical-critical method, 31, 33ff., 52, 120
Historical-grammatical method, 32
Immortality of the soul, 20, 122-125
Inerrancy, 16, 53-60
Inspiration, 16, 53-60

Jesus Seminar, 80f.

Langenberg Mission Society, 316f.

Law and Gospel, 241-242
LCA, 43
Liberal Lutheran position B, 15
Liberation theology, 178-185
Luther Northwestern Seminary, 81
Lutheran Church in America 331, 332
Lutheran Confessions, 26, 373
Lutheran mergers, 301-341
Lutheran orthodoxy, 251, 253, 284f.
Lutherans Concerned about Gays and Lesbians, 147-151
Lutherans in America, 271-300

Masonic Lodge, 276-279
Means of Grace, 157, 258
Millennialism, 279-282
Miracles, 35, 83-87
Missions, 21, 170-188
Mosaic authorship, 17, 70-77

National Council of Churches, 189-198, 21, 353
National Lutheran Council, 328f.
NET, 342
New Morality, 20, 126-158
Norwegian Synod, 305

Old Testament Prophecy, 17, 74-77

Pennsylvania Ministerium, 273
Pentecostal/Holiness, 246-249
Pietism, 250-268
Pietism/influence, 260f., 284, 289-292, 295
Pope, 212
Pornography, 152-154
Position B (see Liberal Lutheran position B)
Postion A (see Conservative Lutheran position A)
Problem of losing faith, 59
Prussian Union, 286-288

Real Presence, 228f.
Reconciled in Christ, 148f.
Reformed and Scripture, 222-249
Reformed and the Law, 236-239
Reformed tradition, 215
Resurrection, 19, 113-121
Roman Catholic Church, 215
Roman Catholics and Scripture, 216-221

Sanctification, 242-244
Search (ALC), 29, 49ff., 61ff., 67, 70ff., 76, 79, 85, 90, 104, 123f.
Seeds for the Parish (ELCA), 175
Seminex (AELC), 22, 324-328
Sixty Minutes, 197
Social activism in ELCA, 175ff.
Synergism, 231-234
Synodical Conference, 296, 315-316
Synodical Conference Dissolution, 320-323

This We Believe (WELS), 54f., 173
Trinity, 19, 101-104

ULCA, 301-304
United Testimony on Faith and Life (ALC), 47
University of Halle, 263f., 272

Virgin Birth, 18, 88-95

Way to heaven, 20, 159-169
Wesleyan tradition, 238-241
Wingspan, 145
Wisconsin Synod, 316-320
Word and Witness (LCA), 49, 51, 62ff., 76, 86, 91
Words of Jesus, 18, 78-82
Working For Justice (ELCA), 175
World Council of Churches, 21, 189-198, 353